T0225771

More iPhone Development with Objective-C

David Mark
Jayant Varma
Jeff LaMarche
Alex Horovitz
Kevin Kim

Apress®

More iPhone Development with Objective-C

ISBN-13 (pbk): 978-1-4302-6037-0

ISBN-13 (electronic): 978-1-4302-6038-7

Managing Director: Welmoed Spahr
Lead Editor: Michelle Lowman
Technical Reviewer: Ron Natalie
Technical Reviewer: Jim Graham
Editorial Board: Steve Anglin, Mark Beckner, Gary Cornell, Louise Corrigan, James DeWolf,
    Jonathan Gennick, Robert Hutchinson, Michelle Lowman, James Markham, Matthew Moodie,
    Jeffrey Pepper, Douglas Pundick, Ben Renow-Clarke, Gwenan Spearing, Matt Wade, Steve Weiss
Coordinating Editor: Kevin Walter
Copy Editor: Kim Wimpsett
Compositor: SPi Global
Indexer: SPi Global
Artist: SPi Global
Cover Photo: Michelle Lowman

Distributed to the book trade worldwide by Springer Science+Business Media New York, 233 Spring Street, 6th Floor, New York, NY 10013. Phone 1-800-SPRINGER, fax (201) 348-4505, e-mail orders-ny@springer-sbm.com, or visit www.springeronline.com. Apress Media, LLC is a California LLC and the sole member (owner) is Springer Science + Business Media Finance Inc (SSBM Finance Inc). SSBM Finance Inc is a Delaware corporation.

For information on translations, please e-mail rights@apress.com, or visit www.apress.com.

Apress and friends of ED books may be purchased in bulk for academic, corporate, or promotional use. eBook versions and licenses are also available for most titles. For more information, reference our Special Bulk Sales–eBook Licensing web page at www.apress.com/bulk-sales.

Any source code or other supplementary material referenced by the author in this text is available to readers at www.apress.com/9781430266013. For detailed information about how to locate your book's source code, go to www.apress.com/source-code/.

To my loving parents and family.

—Jayant Varma

Contents at a Glance

Contents

About the Authors

David Mark is a longtime Mac developer and author who has written a number of books on Mac and iOS development, including *Beginning iPhone 4 Development* (Apress, 2010), *More iPhone 3 Development* (Apress, 2010), *Learn C on the Mac* (Apress, 2008), *The Macintosh Programming Primer series* (Addison-Wesley, 1992), and *Ultimate Mac Programming* (Wiley, 1995). Dave loves the water and spends as much time as possible on it, in it, or near it. He lives with his wife and three children in Virginia.

Jayant Varma is the founder of OZ Apps (www.oz-apps.com), a consulting and development company providing IT solutions with specialization in mobile technology. He is an experienced developer with more than 20 years of industry experience spread across several countries. He is the author of a number of books on iOS development, including *Learn Lua for iOS Game Development* (Apress, 2012), *Xcode 6 Essentials* (Packt, 2015), and *More iPhone Development with Swift* (Apress, 2015).
He has also been a university lecturer in Australia where he currently resides. He loves traveling and finds Europe to be his favorite destination.

Jeff LaMarche is a Mac and iOS developer with more than 20 years of programming experience. Jeff has written a number of iOS and Mac development books, including *Beginning iPhone 3 Development* (Apress, 2009), *More iPhone 3 Development* (Apress, 2010), and *Learn Cocoa on the Mac* (Apress, 2010). Jeff is a principal at MartianCraft, an iOS and Android development house. He has written about Cocoa and Objective-C for *MacTech Magazine*, as well as for Apple's developer web site. Jeff also writes about iOS development for his widely read blog at http://iphonedevelopment.blogspot.com.

Alex Horovitz was a cofounder of AppOrchard and is currently the managing partner at Applied Intelligence Group in Acton, Massachusetts, where he develops enterprise iOS applications and large back-end systems leveraging the Model-View-Controller design pattern and reusable frameworks. During the 1990s he worked at both NeXT Computer and Apple.

Kevin Kim is a founder and partner of AppOrchard LLC, a Tipping Point Partners company focused on sustainable iOS development. A graduate of Carnegie Mellon University, he was first exposed to the NeXTStep computer (the ancestor of today's iPhone) while a programmer at the Pittsburgh Supercomputing Center and has been hooked ever since. His career has spanned finance, government, biotech, and technology, including Apple where he managed the Apple Enterprise Services team for the New York metro area. He resides in the Alphabet City section of New York City with his wife and a clowder of rescued cats.

About the Technical Reviewer

Ron Natalie has 35 years of experience developing large-scale applications in C, Objective-C, and C++ on Unix, OS X, and Windows.

He has a degree in electrical engineering from Johns Hopkins University and has taught professional courses in programming, network design, and computer security.

He splits his time between Virginia and North Carolina with his wife Margy.

Acknowledgments

I would like to acknowledge and appreciate the efforts of David Mark and Jeff LeMarche, who laid the foundation for the first *More* book. It was a pleasure and a lot of hard work to build and expand on their work. I am thankful to the staff of Apress, the technical reviewer, and my family who supported and made even the challenging stages easy to achieve.

Specifically, I would like to mention Michelle Lowman, James Markham, Kevin Walter, and Kim Wimpsett from Apress for their generous support and professionalism through this process. I would like to also thank Ron Natalie for his attention to detail as a technical reviewer.

I would like to thank my family who supported me while I worked on the book. It would not have been possible without their understanding and support.

Lastly, I'd like to thank you, the reader—the most integral part of this equation—for believing in this book and reading it. I hope it helps you in your iOS development journey.

I would like to thank everyone else who has been part of this book in some way, and I hope that I have been able to do that. Thank you all.

—Jayant Varma

Introduction

In 2008, interest in iPhone app development exploded. At the time, Apress signed on Dave Mark and Jeff LaMarche to publish what in 2009 became Apress' most successful edition of a book ever and the resulting book, Beginning iPhone Development, "taught the world to program the iPhone". It was both well done and comprehensive. The book, in its Swift edition, is currently still the number one iPhone development book on the market today (having gone through seven editions) and it remains one of the great computer programming books.

In 2009, realizing that a single book could not do justice to both beginners and advanced users, Dave and Jeff were asked to create an advanced book that would stand alone, but also follow up on the Beginning iPhone book. They created another masterpiece taking in many of the advanced features, (notably the best discussion of Core Data in any book), that programmers doing first class apps would want in their code. The book succeeded in being both a sequel to the beginning book and a great book for any programmer who had been tinkering or had created some apps but needed to add features fast to keep up with the competition.

Over the following years, we added authors whose expertise was both in teaching and programming to revise the book, changing the book based on the needs of the hundreds of thousands of programmers who were pretty good, but often were self-taught and needed to take it up a notch. The book has always succeeded in delivering to that audience through clear instruction and excellent choice of code examples. The focus was changed to iOS and the book remains a tool for iOS development today.

In this edition, we added Jayant Varma to the team with the goal of completely recasting all the examples in the book to meet today's coding style standards. The book has always excelled at clearly teach programmers at a variety of levels to program like professionals using many of the most important SDKs for iOS. So, whether you're a self-taught iPhone development genius or have just made your way through the pages of *Beginning iPhone Development* in one of its many editions, this is the choice that continues to work.

More iPhone Development with Objective-C digs deeper into Apple's latest SDK, covering topics like Core Data, peer-to-peer over Bluetooth using Multipeer Connectivity, network streams, using reverse geocoding with MapKit, in-application e-mail and text messages, sending to Twitter or Facebook, audio and video players, programming for the cameras, using Interface Builder, unit testing, debugging and more. All the concepts and APIs are clearly presented with code snippets you can customize and use, as you like, in your own apps. All the code for the book is available free on Apress.com on this book's page (apress. com/9781430260370). As a huge bonus, all of the code from the Swift version of this book *More iPhone Development with Swift* is also free on Apress.com, so if you are interested, many of the programs in this book are translated into Swift in the other book's free code download (apress.com/9781484204498).

Whether you are a relative newcomer to iPhone development or an old hand looking to expand your horizons, there's something for everyone in *More iPhone Development with Objective-C*.

What you'll learn

- All about Core Data: key concepts and techniques for writing larger application

- How to utilize a variety of networking mechanisms, including peer-to-peer connections over Bluetooth

- How to embed maps with MapKit and use in-application email

- Essentials of concurrent programming and advanced debugging techniques

We hope you will agree with the tens of thousands of users who have used this book that this is a great aid in adding features to your program that will enhance your understanding of the options available to you in the SDK and as a programmer in general.

—Jeffrey M. Pepper
Associate Publisher

Here We Go Round Again

So, you're still creating iPhone applications, huh? Great! iOS and the App Store have enjoyed tremendous success, fundamentally changing the way mobile applications are delivered and completely changing what people expect from their mobile devices. Since the first release of the iOS Software Development Kit (SDK) in March 2008, Apple has been busily adding new functionality and improving what was already there. It's no less exciting a platform than it was back when it was first introduced. In fact, in many ways, it's more exciting, because Apple keeps expanding the amount of functionality available to third-party developers like us.

Since the last release of this book, *More iOS 6 Development* (Apress, 2012), Apple has released a number of frameworks, tools, and services. These include, but aren't limited to, the following:

- *Core frameworks*: Core Motion, Core Telephony, Core Media, Core View, Core MIDI, Core Image, and Core Bluetooth

- *Utility frameworks*: Event Kit, Quick Look Framework, Assets Library, Image I/O, Printing, AirPlay, Accounts and Social Frameworks, Pass Kit

- *Services and their frameworks*: iAds, Game Center, iCloud, Newsstand

- *Developer-centric enhancements*: Blocks, Grand Central Dispatch (GCD), Weak Linking Support, Automatic Reference Counting (ARC), Storyboards, Collection Views, UI State Preservation, Auto Layout, UIAutomation

Obviously, there are too many changes to cover completely in a single book. But we'll try our best to make you comfortable with the ones that you'll most likely need to know.

What This Book Is

This book is a guide to help you continue down the path to creating better iOS applications. In *Beginning iPhone Development*, the goal was to get you past the initial learning curve and help you get your arms around the fundamentals of building your first iOS applications. In this book, we're assuming you already know the basics. So, in addition to showing you how to use several of the new iOS APIs, we're going to weave in some more advanced techniques that you'll need as your iOS development efforts grow in size and complexity.

In *Beginning iPhone Development*, every chapter was self-contained, each presenting its own unique project or set of projects. We'll be using a similar approach in the second half of this book, but in Chapters 2 through 8, we'll focus on a single, evolving Core Data application. Each chapter will cover a specific area of Core Data functionality as we expand the application. We'll also be strongly emphasizing techniques that will keep your application from becoming unwieldy and hard to manage as it gets larger.

What You Need to Know

This book assumes you already have some programming knowledge and that you have a basic understanding of the iOS SDK, either because you've worked through *Beginning iPhone Development* or because you've gained a similar foundation from other sources. We assume that you have experimented a little with the SDK, perhaps have written a small program or two on your own, and have a general feel for Xcode. You might want to quickly review *Beginning iPhone Development*.

What You Need Before You Can Begin

Before you can write software for iOS devices, you need a few things. For starters, you need an Intel-based Macintosh running Mavericks (Mac OS X 10.9 or newer). Any Macintosh computer—laptop or desktop—that has been released since 2009 should work just fine, but make sure your machine is Intel-based and is capable of running Mavericks.

This may seem obvious, but you'll also need an iPhone (5S/5C or newer), iPod touch (5th generation or newer), or iPad (iPad 2 or newer). While much of your code can be tested using the iPhone/iPad simulator, not all programs will run in the simulator. And you'll want to thoroughly test any application you create on an actual device before you ever consider releasing it to the public.

Finally, you'll need to sign up to become a Registered iOS Developer. If you're already a Registered iOS Developer, download the latest and greatest iPhone development tools and skip ahead to the next section.

If you're new to Apple's Registered iOS Developer programs, navigate to http://developer. apple.com/ios/, which will bring you to a page similar to that shown in Figure 1-1. Just below the iOS Dev Center banner, on the right side of the page, you'll find links labeled Log in and Register. Click the Register link. On the page that appears, click the Continue button. Follow the sequence of instructions to use your existing Apple ID or create a new one.

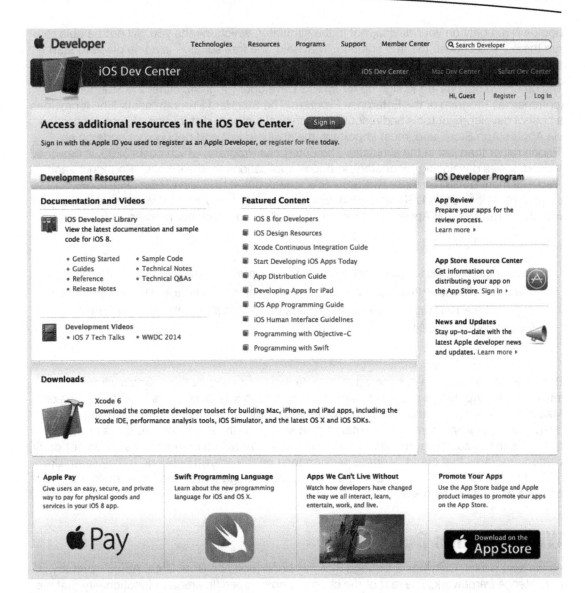

Figure 1-1. Apple's iOS Dev Center web site

At some point, as you register, you'll be given a choice of several paths, all of which will lead you to the SDK download page. The three choices are free, commercial, and enterprise. All three options give you access to the iOS SDK and Xcode, Apple's integrated development environment (IDE). Xcode includes tools for creating and debugging source code, compiling applications, and performance-tuning the applications you've written. Please note that although you get at Xcode through the developer site, your Xcode distribution will be made available to you via the App Store.

The free option is, as its name implies, free. It lets you develop iOS apps that run on a software-only simulator but does not allow you to download those apps to your iPhone, iPod touch, or iPad, nor sell your apps on Apple's App Store. In addition, some programs in this book will run only on your device, not in the simulator, which means you will not be able to run them if you choose the free solution. That said, the free solution is a fine place to start if you don't mind learning without doing for those programs that won't run in the simulator.

The other two options are to sign up for an iOS Developer Program, either the Standard (commercial) Program or the Enterprise Program. The Standard Program costs $99. It provides a host of development tools and resources, technical support, distribution of your application via Apple's App Store, and, most important, the ability to test and debug your code on an iPhone rather than just in the simulator. The Enterprise Program, which costs $299, is designed for companies developing proprietary, in-house applications for the iPhone, iPod touch, and iPad. For more details on these two programs, check out `http://developer.apple.com/ programs/`. (Prices are in USD, and might vary based on the country that you reside in along with the formalities that Apple might require to enroll in the developer program).

> **Note**   If you are going to sign up for the Standard or Enterprise Program, you should go do it right now. It can take a while to get approved, and you'll need that approval to be able to run applications on your iPhone. Don't worry, though—the projects in the early chapters of this book will run just fine on the iPhone simulator.

Because iOS devices are connected mobile devices that utilize a third party's wireless infrastructure, Apple has placed far more restrictions on iOS developers than it ever has on Macintosh developers, who are able to write and distribute programs with absolutely no oversight or approval from Apple except when selling on the App Store. Apple is not doing this to be mean but rather to minimize the chances of people distributing malicious or poorly written programs that could degrade performance on the shared network. It may seem like a lot of hoops to jump through, but Apple has gone through quite an effort to make the process as painless as possible.

What's In this Book

As we said earlier, Chapters 2 through 7 of this book focus on Core Data, Apple's primary persistence framework. The rest of the chapters cover specific areas of functionality that are either new with the iOS SDK or were simply too advanced to include in *Beginning iPhone Development*.

Here is a brief overview of the chapters that follow:

- *Chapter 2, "Core Data: What, Why, and How"*: In this chapter, we'll introduce you to Core Data. You'll learn why Core Data is a vital part of your iPhone development arsenal. We'll dissect a simple Core Data application and show you how all the individual parts of a Core Data–backed application fit together.

- *Chapter 3, "A Super Start: Adding, Displaying, and Deleting Data"*: Once you have a firm grasp on Core Data's terminology and architecture, you'll learn how to do some basic tasks, including inserting, searching for, and retrieving data.

- *Chapter 4, "The Devil in the Detail View"*: In this chapter, you'll learn how to let your users edit and change the data stored by Core Data. We'll explore techniques for building generic, reusable views so you can leverage the same code to present different types of data.

- *Chapter 5, "Preparing for Change: Migrations and Versioning"*: Here, we'll look at Apple tools that you can use to change your application's data model, while still allowing your users to continue using their data from previous versions of your application.

- *Chapter 6, "Custom Managed Objects"*: To really unlock the power of Core Data, you can subclass the class used to represent specific instances of data. In this chapter, you'll learn how to use custom managed objects and see some benefits of doing so.

- *Chapter 7, "Relationships, Fetched Properties, and Expressions"*: In this final chapter on Core Data, you'll learn about some mechanisms that allow you to expand your applications in powerful ways. You'll refactor the application you built in the previous chapters so that you don't need to add new classes as you expand your data model.

- *Chapter 8, "Behind Every iCloud"*: The iCloud Storage APIs are among the coolest features of iOS. The iCloud APIs will let your apps store documents and key-value data in iCloud. iCloud will wirelessly push documents to a user's device automatically and update the documents when changed on any device—automatically. You'll enhance your Core Data application to store information on iCloud.

- *Chapter 9, "Peer-to-Peer Over Bluetooth Using Multipeer Connectivity"*: The Multipeer Connectivity framework makes it easy to create programs that communicate over Bluetooth and WiFi, such as multiplayer games for the iPhone and iPad. You'll explore Multipeer Connectivity by building a simple two-player game.

- *Chapter 10, "MapKit"*: This chapter explores another great new piece of functionality added to the iOS SDK: an enhanced CoreLocation. This framework now includes support for both forward and reverse geocoding location data. You will be able to convert back and forth between a set of map coordinates and information about the street, city, and country (and so on) at that coordinate. Plus, you'll explore how all this interoperates with enhanced MapKit.

- *Chapter 11, "Messaging: Mail, Social, and iMessage"*: Your ability to get your message out has gone beyond e-mail. In this chapter, we'll take you through the core options of Mail, the Social Framework, and iMessage, and you'll see how to leverage each appropriately.

- *Chapter 12, "Media Library Access and Playback"*: It's now possible to programmatically get access to your users' complete library of audio tracks stored on their iPhone or iPod touch. In this chapter, you'll look at the various techniques used to find, retrieve, and play music and other audio tracks.

- *Chapter 13, "Lights, Camera and Action"*: In this chapter, you'll be taking a detailed look into the AVFoundation framework, which provides a standard set of APIs and classes for iOS applications to play audio and video and even capture the same. In addition to the basic interfaces of this framework, you will utilize some additions for managing capturing, saving images, and audio.

- *Chapter 14, "Interface Builder and Storyboards"*: The new additions to Interface Builder allow you to have live previews and create custom controls to use in your projects. You will create custom transitions between your views and view controllers.

- *Chapter 15, "Unit Testing, Debugging, and Instruments"*: No program is ever perfect. Bugs and defects are a natural part of the programming process. In this chapter, you'll learn various techniques for preventing, finding, and fixing bugs in iOS SDK programs.

- *Chapter 16, "The Road Goes Ever On…"*: Sadly, every journey must come to an end. We'll wrap up this book with fond farewells and some resources we hope you'll find useful.

iOS is an incredible computing platform, an ever-expanding frontier for your development pleasure. In this book, we're going to take you further down the iPhone development road, digging deeper into the SDK and touching on new and, in some cases, more advanced topics.

Read the book and be sure to build the projects yourself—don't just copy them from the archive and run them once or twice. You'll learn most by doing. Make sure you understand what you did, and why, before moving on to the next project. Don't be afraid to make changes to the code. Experiment, tweak the code, and observe the results. Rinse and repeat.

Got your iOS SDK installed? Turn the page, put on some iTunes, and let's go. Your continuing journey awaits.

Chapter 2

Core Data: What, Why, and How

Core Data is a framework and set of tools that allow you to save (or *persist*) your application's data to an iOS device's file system automatically. Core Data is an implementation of something called *object-relational mapping* (ORM). This is just a fancy way of saying that Core Data allows you to interact with your Objective-C objects without having to worry about how the data from those objects is stored in and retrieved from persistent data stores such as relational databases (such as SQLite) or flat files.

Core Data can seem like magic when you first start using it. Core Data objects are, for the most part, handled just like plain old objects, and they seem to know how to retrieve and save themselves "automagically." You won't create SQL strings or make file management calls, ever. Core Data insulates you from some complex and difficult programming tasks, which is great for you. By using Core Data, you can develop applications with complex data models much faster than you could using straight SQLite, object archiving, or flat files.

Technologies that hide complexity the way Core Data does can encourage "voodoo programming," that most dangerous of programming practices where you include code in your application that you don't necessarily understand. Sometimes that mystery code arrives in the form of a project template. Or, perhaps you download a utilities library that does a task for you that you just don't have the time or expertise to do for yourself. That voodoo code does what you need it to do, and you don't have the time or inclination to step through it and figure it out, so it just sits there, working its magic…until it breaks. As a general rule, if you find yourself with code in your own application that you don't fully understand, it's a sign you should go do a little research, or at least find a more experienced peer to help you get a handle on your mystery code.

The point is that Core Data is one of those complex technologies that can easily turn into a source of mystery code that will make its way into many of your projects. Although you don't need to know exactly how Core Data accomplishes everything it does, you should invest some time and effort into understanding the overall Core Data architecture.

This chapter starts with a brief history of Core Data, and then it dives into a Core Data application. By building a Core Data application with Xcode, you'll find it much easier to understand the more complex Core Data projects you'll see in the following chapters.

A Brief History of Core Data

Core Data has been around for quite some time, but it became available on iOS with the release of iPhone SDK 3.0. Core Data was originally introduced with Mac OS X 10.4 (Tiger), but some of the DNA in Core Data actually goes back about 15 years to a NeXT framework called Enterprise Objects Framework (EOF), which was part of the toolset that shipped with NeXT's WebObjects web application server.

EOF was designed to work with remote data sources, and it was a pretty revolutionary tool when it first came out. Although there are now many good ORM tools for almost every language, when WebObjects was in its infancy, most web applications were written to use handcrafted SQL or file system calls to persist their data. Back then, writing web applications was incredibly time- and labor-intensive. WebObjects, in part because of EOF, cut the development time needed to create complex web applications by an order of magnitude.

In addition to being part of WebObjects, EOF was also used by NeXTSTEP, which was the predecessor to Cocoa. When Apple bought NeXT, the Apple developers used many of the concepts from EOF to develop Core Data. Core Data does for desktop applications what EOF had previously done for web applications: it dramatically increases developer productivity by removing the need to write file system code or interact with an embedded database.

Let's start building your Core Data application.

Creating a Core Data Application

Fire up Xcode and create a new Xcode project. There are many ways to do this. When you start Xcode, you may get the Xcode startup window (Figure 2-1). You can click "Create a new Xcode project," you can select File ➤ New ➤ Project, or you can use the keyboard shortcut ⇧⌘N—whatever floats your boat. Going forward, we're going to mention the options available in the Xcode window or the menu options, but we won't use the keyboard shortcut. If you know and prefer the keyboard shortcuts, feel free to use them. Let's get back to building your app.

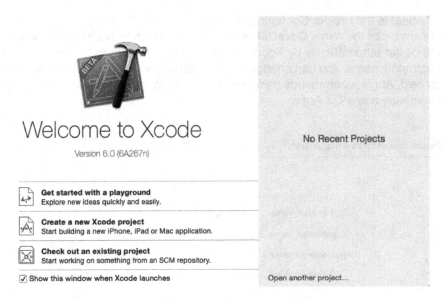

Figure 2-1. *Xcode startup window*

Xcode will open a project workspace and display the Project Template sheet (Figure 2-2). On the left are the possible template headings: iOS and OS X. Each heading has a bunch of template groups. Select the Application template group under the iOS heading, and then select Master-Detail Application on the right. On the bottom right, there's a short description of the template. Click the Next button to move to the next sheet.

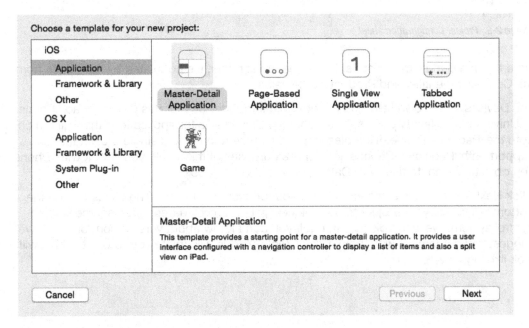

Figure 2-2. *Project Template sheet*

The next sheet is the Project Configuration sheet (Figure 2-3). You'll be asked to provide a product name; use the name **CoreDataApp**. The Organization Name and Company Identifier fields will be set automatically by Xcode; by default these will read MyCompanyName and com.mycompanyname. You can change these to whatever you like, but for the Company Identifier field, Apple recommends using the reverse domain name style (such as com.oz-apps for the company name OZ Apps).

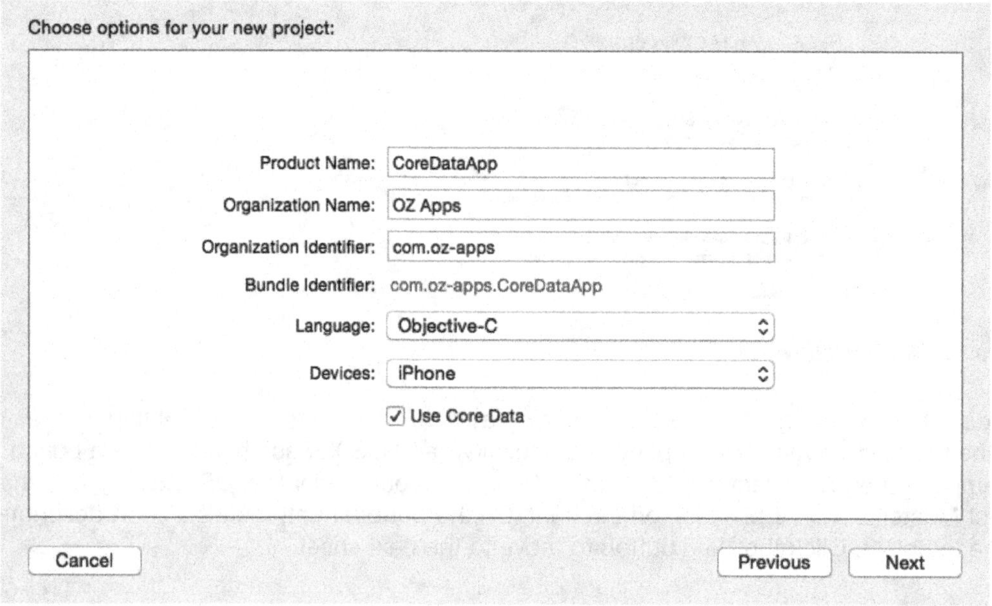

Figure 2-3. Project Configuration sheet

Note that the Bundle Identifier field is not editable; rather, it's populated by the values from the Company Identifier and Product Name fields.

The Devices drop-down field lists the possible target devices for this project: iPad, iPhone, or Universal. The first two are self-explanatory. Universal is for applications that will run on both the iPad and iPhone. It's a blessing and a curse to have to a single project that can support both iPads and iPhones. But for the purposes of this book, you'll stick with iPhone. You obviously want to use Core Data, so select its check box.

Click Next and choose a location to save your project (Figure 2-4). The check box on the bottom will set up your project to use Git (www.git-scm.com), a free, open source version control system. We won't discuss it, but if you don't know about version control or Git, we suggest you get familiar with them. Click Create. Xcode will create your project, which will look like Figure 2-5.

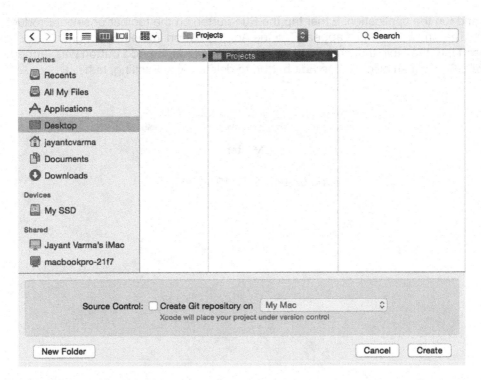

Figure 2-4. Choosing a location to put your project

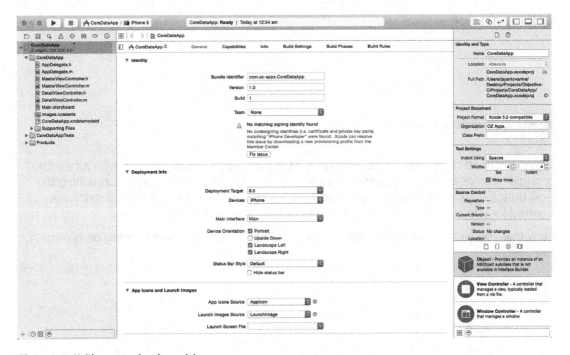

Figure 2-5. Voilà, your project is ready!

Build and run the application. Either tap the Run button on the toolbar or select Product ➤ Run. The simulator should appear. Tap the Add (+) button in the upper right. A new row will insert into the table that shows the exact date and time the Add button was tapped (Figure 2-6). You can also use the Edit button to delete rows. Exciting, huh?

Figure 2-6. CoreDataApp in action

Under the hood of this simple application a lot is happening. Think about it: without adding a single class or any code to persist data to a file or interact with a database, touching the Add button created an object, populated it with data, and saved it to a SQLite database created for you automatically. There's plenty of free functionality here.

Now that you've seen an application in action, let's take a look at what's going on behind the scenes.

Core Data Concepts and Terminology

Like most complex technologies, Core Data has its own terminology that can be a bit confusing to newcomers. Let's break down the mystery and get your arms around Core Data's nomenclature.

Figure 2-7 shows a simplified, high-level diagram of the Core Data architecture. Don't expect it all to make sense now, but as you look at different pieces, you might want to refer to this diagram to cement your understanding of how they fit together.

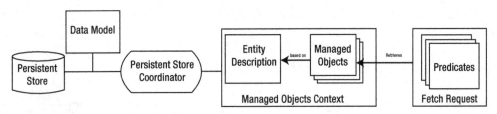

Figure 2-7. The Core Data architecture

There are five key concepts to focus on here. As you proceed through this chapter, make sure you understand each of the following:

- Data model
- Persistent store
- Persistent store coordinator
- Managed object and managed object context
- Fetch request

Once again, don't let the names throw you. Follow along and you'll see how all these pieces fit together.

The Data Model

What is a data model? In an abstract sense, it's an attempt to define the organization of data and the relationship between the organized data components. In Core Data, the data model defines the data structure of objects, the organization of those objects, the relationships between those objects, and the behavior of those objects. Xcode allows you, via the model editor and Inspector, to specify your data model for use in your application.

If you expand the CoreDataApp group in the Navigator content pane, you'll see a file called CoreDataApp.xcdatamodel. This file is the default data model for your project. Xcode created this file for you because you selected the Use Core Data check box in the Project Configuration sheet. Single-click CoreDataApp.xcdatamodel to bring up Xcode's model editor. Make sure the Utility pane is visible (it should be the third button on the View bar), and select the Inspector. Your Xcode window should look like Figure 2-8.

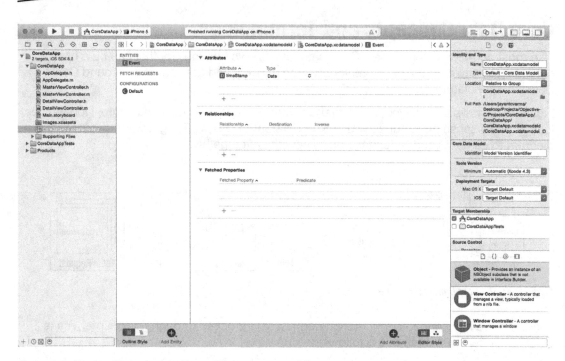

Figure 2-8. Xcode with the model editor and inspector

When you selected the data model file, `CoreDataApp.xcdatamodel`, the Editor pane changed to present the Core Data model editor (Figure 2-9). Along the top, the jump bar remains unchanged. Along the left, the gutter has been replaced by a wider pane, the Top-Level Components pane. The Top-Level Components pane outlines the entities, fetch requests, and configurations defined in the data model (we'll cover these in detail in a little bit). You can add a new entity by clicking the Add Entity button at the bottom of the Top-Level Components pane. Alternately, you can use the Editor ➤ Add Entity menu option. If you click and hold the Add Entity button, you will be presented with a pop-up menu of choices: Add Entity, Add Fetch Request, and Add Configuration. Whatever option you choose, the single-click behavior of the button will change to that component, and the label of the button will change to reflect this behavior. You can find the menu equivalents for adding fetch requests and configurations below the Editor ➤ Add Entity menu item.

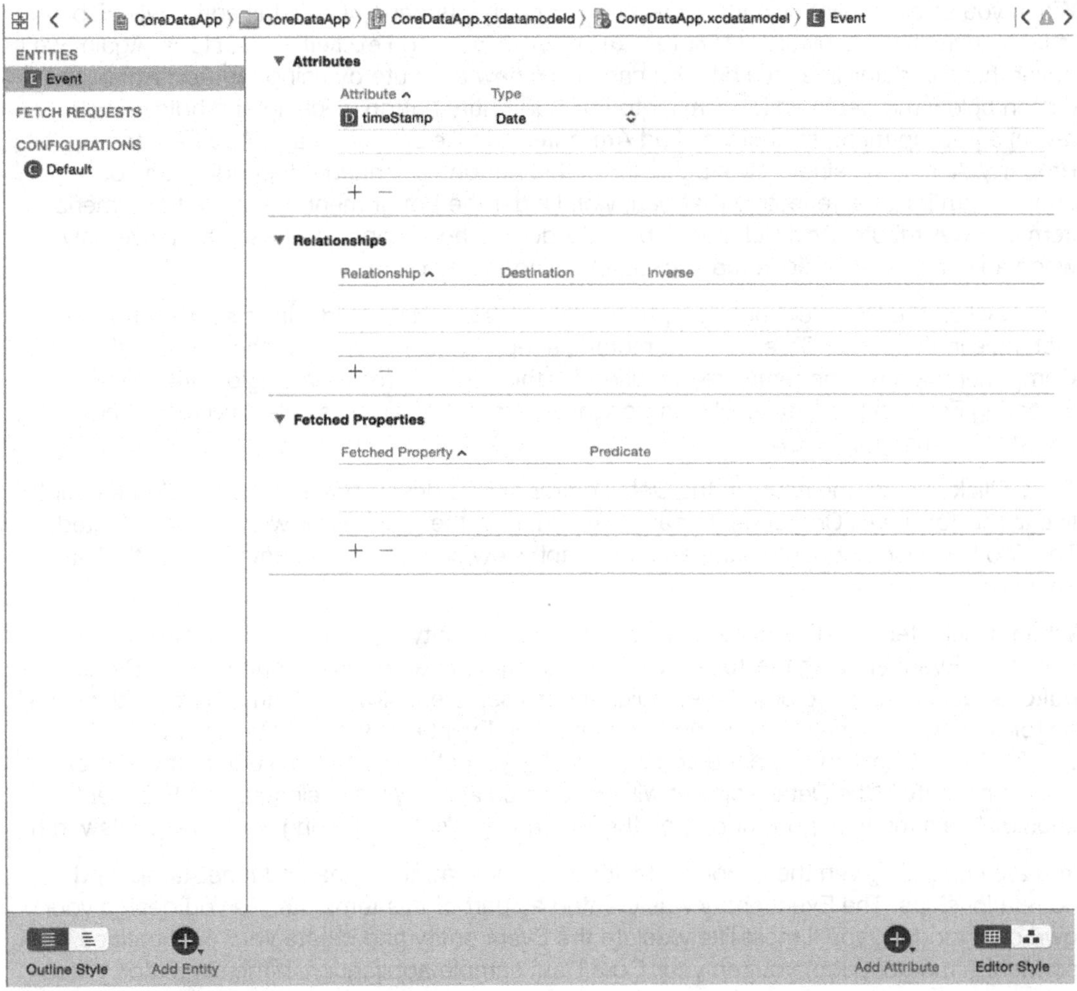

Figure 2-9. A close look at the model editor

The Top-Level Components pane has two styles: list and hierarchical. You can toggle between these two styles by using the Outline Style selector group found at the bottom of the Top-Level Components pane. Switching styles with the CoreDataApp data model won't change anything in the Top-Level Components pane because there's only one entity and one configuration, so there's no hierarchy to be shown. If you had a component that depended on another component, you'd see the hierarchical relationship between the two with the hierarchical outline style.

The bulk of the Editor pane is taken up by the Detail editor. The Detail editor has two editor styles: table and graph. By default (and pictured in Figure 2-9), the Detail editor is in table style. You can toggle between these styles by using the Editor Style selector group on the bottom right of the Editor pane. Try it. You can see the difference in the two styles.

When you select an entity in the Top-Level Components pane, the Detail editor will display, in table style, three tables: Attributes, Relationships, and Fetched Properties. Again, we'll cover these in detail in a little bit. You can add a new attribute by using the Add Attribute button below the Detail editor. Similar to the Add Entity button, clicking and holding will reveal a pop-up menu of choices: Add Attribute, Add Relationship, and Add Fetched Property. Again, the single-click behavior of this button will change depending on your choice, with its label reflecting that behavior. Under the Editor menu there are three menu items: Add Attribute, Add Relationship, and Add Fetched Property. These are active only when an entity is selected in the Top-Level Components pane.

If you switch the Detail editor to graph style, you'll see a large grid with a single rounded rectangle in the center. This rounded rectangle represents the entity in the Top-Level Components pane. The template you used for this project creates a single entity, Event. Selecting Event in the Top Level Components pane is the same as selecting the rounded rectangle in the graph view.

Try it. Click outside the entity in the Detail editor grid to deselect it and then click the Event line in the Top-Level Components pane. The entity in the graph view will also be selected. The Top Level Components pane and the graph view show two different views of the same entity list.

When unselected, the title bar and lines of the Event entity square should be pink. If you select the Event entity in the Top-Level Components pane, the Event entity in the Detail editor should change color to blue, indicating it's selected. Now click anywhere on the Detail editor grid, outside the Event rounded square. The Event entity should be deselected in the Top Level Components pane and should change color in the Detail editor. If you click the Event entity in the Detail editor, it will be selected again. When selected, the Event entity should have a resize handle (or dot) on the left and right sides, allowing you to resize its width.

You are currently given the Event entity. It has a single attribute, named timeStamp, and no relationships. The Event entity was created as part of this template. As you design your own data models, you'll most likely delete the Event entity and create your own entities from scratch. A moment ago, you ran your Core Data sample application in the simulator. When you clicked the + icon, a new instance of Event was created. Entities, which we'll look at more closely in a few pages, replace the Objective-C data model class you would otherwise use to hold your data. We'll get back to the model editor in just a minute to see how it works. For now, just remember that the persistent store is where Core Data stores its data, and the data model defines the form of that data. Also remember that every persistent store has one, and only one, data model.

The inspector provides greater detail for the items selected in the model editor. Since each item could have a different view in the inspector, we'll discuss the details as we discuss the components and their properties. That being said, let's discuss the three top-level components: entities, fetch requests, and configurations.

Entities

An entity can be thought of as the Core Data analog to an Objective-C class declaration. In fact, when using an entity in your application, you essentially treat it like an Objective-C class with some Core Data–specific implementation. You use the model editor to define the properties that define your entity. Each entity is given a name (in this case, Event), which must begin with a capital letter. When you ran CoreDataApp earlier, every time you clicked the Add (+) button, a new instance of Event was instantiated and stored in the application's persistent store.

Make sure the Utility pane is exposed and select the Event entity. Now look at the inspector in the Utility pane (make sure the Inspector is showing by selecting the Inspector button in the Inspector selector bar). Note that the Inspector pane now allows you to edit or change aspects of the entity (Figure 2-10). We'll get to the details of the inspector later.

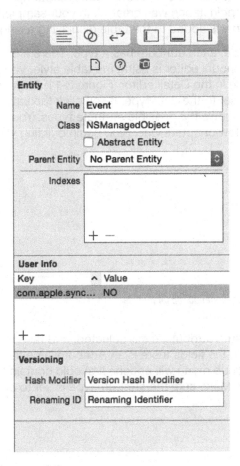

Figure 2-10. The inspector for the Event entity

Properties

While the Editor pane lists all the data model's entities, the Inspector pane allows you to "inspect" the properties that belong to the selected entity. An entity can consist of any number of properties. There are three different types of properties: attributes, relationships, and fetched properties. When you select an entity's property in the model editor, the property's details are displayed in the Inspector pane.

Attributes

The property that you'll use the most when creating entities is the attribute, which serves the same function in a Core Data entity as an instance variable does in an Objective-C class: they both hold data. If you look at your model editor (or at Figure 2-10), you'll see that the Event entity has one attribute named timeStamp. The timeStamp attribute holds the date and time when a given Event instance was created. In your sample application, when you click the + button, a new row is added to the table displaying a single Event's timeStamp.

Just like an instance variable, each attribute has a type. There are two ways to set an attribute's type. When the model editor is using the table style, you can change an attribute's type in the Attributes table in the Detail editor (Figure 2-11). In your current application, the timeStamp attribute is set to the date type. If you click the Date cell, you'll see a pop-up menu. That pop-up menu shows the possible attribute types. You'll look at the different attribute types in the next few chapters when you begin building your own data models.

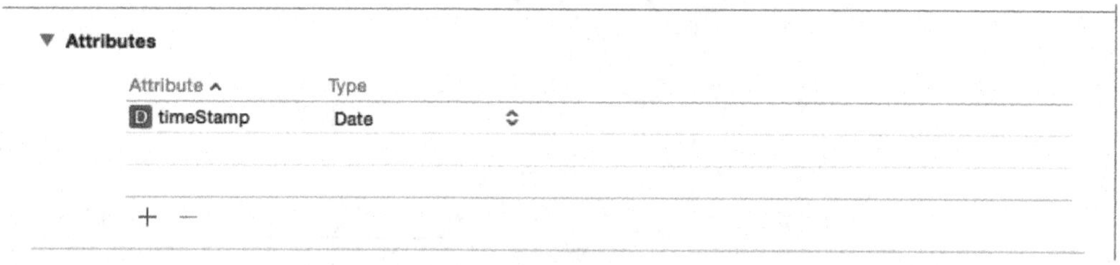

▼ Attributes		
Attribute ∧	Type	
Ⓓ timeStamp	Date	⇕

| + − | | |

Figure 2-11. Attributes table in the model editor, table style

Make sure that the timeStamp attribute is still selected, and take a look at the inspector (Figure 2-12). Notice among the fields there is an Attribute Type field with a pop-up button. Click the button, and a pop-up menu will appear. It should contain the attribute's types you saw in the Attribute table. Make sure the attribute type is set to date.

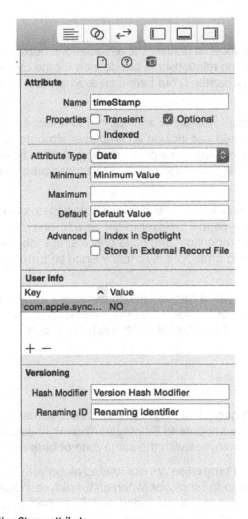

Figure 2-12. *Inspector for the timeStamp attribute*

A date attribute, such as timeStamp, corresponds to an instance of NSDate. If you want to set a new value for a date attribute, you need to provide an instance of NSDate to do so. A string attribute corresponds to an instance of NSString, and most of the numeric types correspond to an instance of NSNumber.

> **Tip** Don't worry too much about all the other buttons, text fields, and check boxes in the model editor. As you make your way through the next few chapters, you'll get a sense of what each does.

Relationships

As the name implies, a relationship defines the associations between two different entities. In the template application, no relationships are defined for the Event entity. We'll begin discussing relationships in Chapter 7, but here's an example just to give you a sense of how they work.

Suppose you created an Employee entity and wanted to reflect each Employee's employer in the data structure. You could just include an employer attribute, perhaps an NSString, in the Employee entity, but that would be pretty limiting. A more flexible approach would be to create an Employer entity and then create a relationship between the Employee and Employer entities.

Relationships can be to one or to many, and they are designed to link specific objects. The relationship from Employee to Employer might be a to-one relationship, if you assume that your Employees do not moonlight and have only a single job. On the other hand, the relationship from Employer to Employee is to many since an Employer might employ many Employees.

To put this in Objective-C terms, a to-one relationship is like using an instance variable to hold a pointer to an instance of another Objective-C class. A to-many relationship is more like using a pointer to a collection class like NSMutableArray or NSSet, which can contain multiple objects.

Fetched Properties

A fetched property is like a query that originates with a single managed object. For example, suppose you add a birthdate attribute to Employee. You might add a fetched property called sameBirthdate to find all Employees with the same date of birth as the current Employee.

Unlike relationships, fetched properties are not loaded along with the object. For example, if Employee has a relationship to Employer, when an Employee instance is loaded, the corresponding Employer instance will be loaded, too. But when an Employee is loaded, sameBirthdate is not evaluated. This is a form of lazy loading. You'll learn more about fetched properties in Chapter 7.

Fetch Requests

While a fetched property is like a query that originates with a single managed object, a fetch request is more like a class method that implements a canned query. For example, you might build a fetch request named canChangeLightBulb that returns a list of Employees who are taller than 80 inches (about 2 meters). You can run the fetch request any time you need a lightbulb changed. When you run it, Core Data searches the persistent store to find the current list of potential lightbulb-changing Employees.

You will create many fetch requests programmatically in the next few chapters, and you'll be looking at a simple one a little later in this chapter in the "Creating a Fetched Results Controller" section.

Configurations

A configuration is a set of entities. Different configurations may contain the same entity. Configurations are used to define which entities are stored in which persistent store. Most of the time, you won't need anything other than the default configuration. We won't cover using multiple configurations in this book. If you want to learn more, check the Apple Developer site.

The Data Model Class: NSManagedObjectModel

Although you won't typically access your application's data model directly, you should be aware of the fact that there is an Objective-C class that represents the data model in memory. This class is called NSManagedObjectModel, and the template automatically creates an instance of NSManagedObjectModel based on the data model file in your project. Let's take a look at the code that creates it now.

In the Navigation pane, open the CoreDataApp group and AppDelegate.m. In the Editor jump bar, click the last menu (it should read No Selection) to bring up a list of the methods in this class (see Figure 2-13). Select -managedObjectModel in the Core Data Stack section, which will take you to the method that creates the object model based on the CoreDataApp.xcdatamodel file.

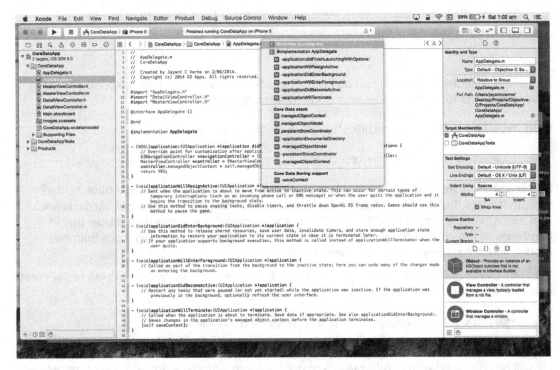

Figure 2-13. Setting the Editor pane to show counterparts will allow you to see the declaration and implementation

The method should look like this:

```
- (NSManagedObjectModel *)managedObjectModel {
    // The managed object model for the application. It is a fatal error for the application
    not to be able to find and load its model.
    if (_managedObjectModel != nil) {
        return _managedObjectModel;
    }
    NSURL *modelURL = [[NSBundle mainBundle] URLForResource:@"CoreDataApp"
    withExtension:@"momd"];
    _managedObjectModel = [[NSManagedObjectModel alloc] initWithContentsOfURL:modelURL];
    return _managedObjectModel;
}
```

This first checks the instance variable _managedObjectModel to see whether it's nil. This accessor method uses a form of lazy loading. The underlying instance variable doesn't actually get instantiated until the first time the accessor method is called. For this reason, you should never access _managedObjectModel directly (except within the accessor method itself, of course). Always make sure to use the accessor methods. Otherwise, you could end up trying to make calls on an object that hasn't been created yet.

> **Tip**   The data model class is called NSManagedObjectModel because, as you'll see a little later in the chapter, instances of data in Core Data are called *managed objects*.

If _managedObjectModel is nil, you can go get your data model. By default Xcode should have written the following two lines of code to accomplish this for you:

```
NSURL *modelURL = [[NSBundle mainBundle] URLForResource:@"CoreDataApp"
                                         withExtension:@"momd"];
_managedObjectModel = [[NSManagedObjectModel alloc] initWithContentsOfURL:modelURL];
```

Remember how we said that a persistent store was associated with a single data model? Well, that's true, but it doesn't tell the whole story. You can combine multiple .xcdatamodel files into a single instance of NSManagedObjectModel, creating a single data model that combines all the entities from multiple files. If you are planning on having more than one model, you can change those two lines of code to one.

This one line of code will take any .xcdatamodel files that might be in your Xcode project and combine them into a single instance of NSManagedObjectModel:

```
_managedObjectModel = [NSManagedObjectModel mergedModelFromBundles:nil];
```

So, for example, if you create a second data model file and add it to your project, that new file will be combined with CoreDataApp.xcdatamodel into a single managed object model that contains the contents of both files. This allows you to split up your application's data model into multiple smaller and more manageable files.

The vast majority of iOS applications that use Core Data have a single persistent store and a single data model, so the default template code will work beautifully most of the time. That said, Core Data does support the use of multiple persistent stores. You could, for example, design your application to store some of its data in a SQLite persistent store and some of it in a binary flat file. If you find that you need to use multiple data models, remember to change the template code here to load the managed object models individually using mergedModelFromBundles:.

The Persistent Store and Persistent Store Coordinator

The persistent store, which is sometimes referred to as a *backing store*, is where Core Data stores its data. By default, on iOS devices Core Data uses a SQLite database contained in your application's Documents folder as its persistent store. But this can be changed without impacting any of the other code you write by tweaking a single line of code. We'll show you the actual line of code to change in a few moments.

> **Caution**   Do not change the type of persistent store once you have posted your application to the App Store. If you must change it for any reason, you will need to write code to migrate data from the old persistent store to the new one, or else your users will lose all of their data—something that will almost always make them quite unhappy.

Every persistent store is associated with a single data model, which defines the types of data that the persistent store can store.

The persistent store isn't actually represented by an Objective-C class. Instead, a class called NSPersistentStoreCoordinator controls access to the persistent store. In essence, it takes all the calls coming from different classes that trigger reads or writes to the persistent store and serializes them so that multiple calls against the same file are not being made at the same time, which could result in problems because of file or database locking.

As is the case with the managed object model, the template provides you with a method in the application delegate that creates and returns an instance of a persistent store coordinator. Other than creating the store and associating it with a data model and a location on disk (which is done for you in the template), you will rarely need to interact with the persistent store coordinator directly. You'll use high-level Core Data calls, and Core Data will interact with the persistent store coordinator to retrieve or save the data.

Let's take a look at the method that returns the persistent store coordinator. In AppDelegate.m, select -persistentStoreCoordinator from the function pop-up menu. Here's the method:

```
- (NSPersistentStoreCoordinator *)persistentStoreCoordinator {
    // The persistent store coordinator for the application. This implementation creates and
    return a coordinator, having added the store for the application to it.
    if (_persistentStoreCoordinator != nil) {
        return _persistentStoreCoordinator;
    }
```

```
// Create the coordinator and store

_persistentStoreCoordinator = [[NSPersistentStoreCoordinator alloc]
initWithManagedObjectModel:[self managedObjectModel]];
NSURL *storeURL = [[self applicationDocumentsDirectory]
                URLByAppendingPathComponent:@"CoreDataApp.sqlite"];
NSError *error = nil;
NSString *failureReason = @"There was an error creating or loading the application's
saved data.";
if (![_persistentStoreCoordinator
        addPersistentStoreWithType:NSSQLiteStoreType
                    configuration:nil
                              URL:storeURL
                          options:nil
                            error:&error]) {
    // Report any error we got.
    NSMutableDictionary *dict = [NSMutableDictionary dictionary];
    dict[NSLocalizedDescriptionKey] = @"Failed to initialize the application's saved data";
    dict[NSLocalizedFailureReasonErrorKey] = failureReason;
    dict[NSUnderlyingErrorKey] = error;
    error = [NSError errorWithDomain:@"YOUR_ERROR_DOMAIN" code:9999 userInfo:dict];
    // Replace this with code to handle the error appropriately.
    // abort() causes the application to generate a crash log and terminate. You should
    not use this function in a shipping application, although it may be useful during
    development.
    NSLog(@"Unresolved error %@, %@", error, [error userInfo]);
    abort();
}

return _persistentStoreCoordinator;
}
```

As with the managed object model, this persistentStoreCoordinator accessor method
uses lazy loading and doesn't instantiate the persistent store coordinator until the first time
it is accessed. Then it creates a path to a file called CoreDataApp.sqlite in the Documents
directory in your application's sandbox. The template will always create a filename based on
your project's name. If you want to use a different name, you can change it here, though it
generally doesn't matter what you call the file since the user will never see it.

Caution   If you do decide to change the filename, make sure you don't change it after you've
posted your application to the App Store, or else future updates will cause your users to lose all of
their data.

Take a look at this line of code:

```
if (![_persistentStoreCoordinator
        addPersistentStoreWithType:NSSQLiteStoreType
                    configuration:nil
                              URL:storeURL
                          options:nil
                            error:&error]) {
```

The first parameter to this method, `NSSQLiteStoreType`, determines the type of the persistent store. `NSSQLiteStoreType` is a constant that tells Core Data to use a SQLite database for its persistent store. If you want your application to use a single, binary flat file instead of a SQLite database, you could specify the constant `NSBinaryStoreType` instead of `NSSQLiteStoreType`. The vast majority of the time, the default setting is the best choice, so unless you have a compelling reason to change it, leave it alone.

> **Note**   A third type of persistent store supported by Core Data on iOS devices is called an
> *in-memory store*. The primary use of this option is to create a caching mechanism, storing the data
> in memory instead of in a database or binary file. To use an in-memory store, specify a store type of
> `NSInMemoryStoreType`.

Reviewing the Data Model

Before you move on to other parts of Core Data, let's quickly review how the pieces you've looked at so far fit together. You might want to refer to Figure 2-7.

The persistent store (or backing store) is a file on an iOS device's file system that can be either a SQLite database or a binary flat file. A data model file, contained in one or more files with an extension of `.xcdatamodel`, describes the structure of your application's data. This file can be edited in Xcode. The data model tells the persistent store coordinator the format of all data stored in that persistent store. The persistent store coordinator is used by other Core Data classes that need to save, retrieve, or search for data. Easy enough, right? Let's move on.

Managed Objects

Entities define the structure of your data, but they do not actually hold any data themselves. The instances of data are called *managed objects*. Every instance of an entity that you work with in Core Data will be an instance of the class `NSManagedObject` or a subclass of `NSManagedObject`.

Key-Value Coding

The NSDictionary class allows you to store objects in a data structure and retrieve an object using a unique key. Like the NSDictionary class, NSManagedObject supports the key-value methods valueForKey: and setValue:forKey: for setting and retrieving attribute values. It also has additional methods for working with relationships. You can, for example, retrieve an instance of NSMutableSet representing a specific relationship. Adding managed objects to this mutable set or removing them will add or remove objects from the relationship it represents.

If the NSDictionary class is new to you, take a few minutes to fire up Xcode and read about NSDictionary in the documentation viewer. The important concept to get your head around is key-value coding (KVC). Core Data uses KVC to store and retrieve data from its managed objects.

In your template application, consider an instance of NSManagedObject that represents a single event. You could retrieve the value stored in its timeStamp attribute by calling valueForKey:, like so:

```
NSDate *timeStamp = [managedObject valueForKey:@"timeStamp"];
```

Since timeStamp is an attribute of type date, you know the object returned by valueForKey: will be an instance of NSDate. Similarly, you could set the value using setValue:forKey:. The following code would set the timeStamp attribute of managedObject to the current date and time:

```
[managedObject setValue:[NSDate date] forKey:@"timeStamp"];
```

KVC also includes the concept of a keypath. Keypaths allow you iterate through object hierarchies using a single string. So, for example, if you had a relationship on your Employee entity called whereIWork, which pointed to an entity named Employer, and the Employer entity had an attribute called name, then you could get to the value stored in name from an instance of Employee using a keypath like so:

```
NSString *employerName = [managedObject valueForKeyPath:@"whereIWork.name"];
```

Notice that you use valueForKeyPath: instead of valueForKey:, and you provide a dot-separated value for the keypath. KVC parses that string using the dots, so in this case, it would parse it into two separate values: whereIWork and name. It uses the first one (whereIWork) on itself and retrieves the object that corresponds to that key. It then takes the next value in the keypath (name) and retrieves the object stored under that key from the object returned by the previous call. Since Employer is a to-one relationship, the first part of the keypath would return a managed object instance that represented the Employee's employer. The second part of the keypath would then be used to retrieve the name from the managed object that represents the Employer.

> **Note** If you've used bindings in Cocoa, you're probably already familiar with KVC and keypaths. If not, don't worry—they will become second nature to you before long. Keypaths are really quite intuitive.

Managed Object Context

Core Data maintains an object that acts as a gateway between your entities and the rest of Core Data. That gateway is called a *managed object context* (often just referred to as a *context*). The context maintains state for all the managed objects that you've loaded or created. The context keeps track of changes that have been made since the last time a managed object was saved or loaded. When you want to load or search for objects, for example, you do it against a context. When you want to commit your changes to the persistent store, you save the context. If you want to undo changes to a managed object, you just ask the managed object context to undo. (Yes, it even handles all the work needed to implement undo and redo for your data model.)

When building iOS applications, you will have only a single context the vast majority of the time. However, iOS makes having more than one context easy. You can create nested managed object contexts, in which the parent object store of a context is another managed object context rather than the persistent store coordinator.

In this case, fetch and save operations are mediated by the parent context instead of by a coordinator. You can imagine a number of usage scenarios, including things like performing background operations on a second thread or queue and managing discardable edits from an inspector window or view. A word of caution: nested contexts make it more important than ever that you adopt the "pass the baton" approach of accessing a context (by passing a context from one view controller to the next) rather than retrieving it directly from the application delegate.

Because every application needs at least one managed object context to function, the template has very kindly provided you with one. Click AppDelegate.m again, and select -managedObjectContext from the Function menu in the Editor jump bar. You will see a method that looks like this:

```objc
// Returns the managed object context for the application.
// If the context doesn't already exist, it is created and bound to the persistent store
coordinator for the application.
- (NSManagedObjectContext *)managedObjectContext
{
    if (_managedObjectContext != nil) {
        return _managedObjectContext;
    }

    NSPersistentStoreCoordinator *coordinator = [self persistentStoreCoordinator];
    if (!coordinator) {
        return nil;
    }
```

```
_managedObjectContext = [[NSManagedObjectContext alloc] init];
[_managedObjectContext setPersistentStoreCoordinator:coordinator];

    return _managedObjectContext;
}
```

This method is pretty straightforward. Using lazy loading, _managedObjectContext is checked for nil. If it is not nil, its value is returned. If managedObjectContext is nil, you check to see whether your NSPersistentStoreCoordinator exists. If so, you create a new _managedObjectContext and then use setPersistentStoreCoordinator: to tie the current coordinator to your managedObjectContext. When you're finished, you return _managedObjectContext.

> **Note** Managed object contexts do not work directly against a persistent store; they go through a persistent store coordinator. As a result, every managed object context needs to be provided with a pointer to a persistent store coordinator in order to function. Multiple managed object contexts can work against the same persistent store coordinator, however.

Saves On Terminate

While you're in the application delegate, scroll up to another method called applicationWillTerminate:, which saves changes to the context if any have been made. The changes are saved to the persistent store. As its name implies, this method is called just before the application exits.

```
- (void)applicationWillTerminate:(UIApplication *)application
{
    // Saves changes in the application's managed object context before the application
    // terminates.
    [self saveContext];
}
```

This is a nice bit of functionality, but there may be times when you don't want the data to be saved. For example, what if the user quits after creating a new entity but before entering any data for that entity? In that case, do you really want to save that empty managed object into the persistent store? Probably not. You'll look at dealing with situations like that in the next few chapters.

Load Data from the Persistent Store

Run the Core Data application you built earlier and press the plus button a few times (see Figure 2-6). Quit the simulator and then run the application again. Note that the timestamps from your previous runs were saved into the persistent store and loaded back in for this run.

Click MasterViewController.m so you can see how this happens. As you can probably guess from the filename, MasterViewController is the view controller class that acts as your application's, well, master view controller. This is the view controller for the view you can see in Figure 2-6.

Once you've clicked the filename, you can use the Editor jump bar's Function menu to find the viewDidLoad: method, although it will probably be on your screen already since it's the first method in the class. The default implementation of the method looks like this:

```
- (void)viewDidLoad
{
    [super viewDidLoad];
    // Do any additional setup after loading the view, typically from a nib.
    self.navigationItem.leftBarButtonItem = self.editButtonItem;

    UIBarButtonItem *addButton =
        [[UIBarButtonItem alloc] initWithBarButtonSystemItem:UIBarButtonSystemItemAdd
                                                      target:self
                                                      action:@selector(insertNewObject:)];
    self.navigationItem.rightBarButtonItem = addButton;
}
```

The first thing the method does is call super. Next, it sets up the Edit and Add buttons. Note that MasterViewController inherits from UITableViewController, which in turn inherits from UIViewController. UIViewController provides a property named editButtonItem, which returns an Edit button. Using dot notation, you retrieve editButtonItem and pass it to the leftBarButtonItem property of the navigationItem property. Now the Edit button is the left button in the navigation bar.

Now let's focus on the Add button. Since UIViewController does not provide an Add button, use alloc to create one from scratch and then add it as the right button in the navigation bar. The code is fairly straightforward.

```
UIBarButtonItem *addButton =
    [[UIBarButtonItem alloc] initWithBarButtonSystemItem:UIBarButtonSystemItemAdd
                                                  target:self
                                                  action:@selector(insertNewObject:)];
self.navigationItem.rightBarButtonItem = addButton;
```

So, with the basic user interface set up, it's time to look at how the fetched results controller works.

The Fetched Results Controller

Conceptually speaking, the fetched results controller isn't quite like the other generic controllers you've seen in the iOS SDK. If you've used Cocoa bindings and the generic controller classes available on the Mac, such as NSArrayController, then you're already familiar with the basic idea. If you're not familiar with those generic controller classes, a little explanation is probably in order.

Most of the generic controller classes in the iOS SDK (such as UINavigationController, UITableViewController, and UIViewController) are designed to act as the controller for a specific type of view. View controllers, however, are not the only types of controller classes that Cocoa Touch provides, although they are the most common. NSFetchedResultsController is an example of a controller class that is not a view controller.

NSFetchedResultsController is designed to handle one specific job, which is to manage the objects returned from a Core Data fetch request. NSFetchedResultsController makes displaying data from Core Data easier than it would otherwise be because it handles a bunch of tasks for you. It will, for example, purge any unneeded objects from memory when it receives a low-memory warning and reload them when it needs them again. If you specify a delegate for the fetched results controller, your delegate will be notified when certain changes are made to its underlying data.

Creating a Fetched Results Controller

You start by creating a fetch request and then use that fetch request to create a fetched results controller. In your template, this is done in MasterViewController.m, in the fetchedResultsController method. fetchedResultsController starts with a lazy load to see whether there is already an active instantiated _fetchedResultsController. If that is not there (resolves to nil), it sets out to create a new fetch request. A fetch request is basically a specification that lays out the details of the data to be fetched. You need to tell the fetch request which entity to fetch. In addition, you want to add a sort descriptor to the fetch request. The sort descriptor determines the order in which the data is organized.

Once the fetch request is defined appropriately, the fetched results controller is created. The fetched results controller is an instance of the class NSFetchedResultsController. Remember that the fetched results controller's job is to use the fetch request to keep its associated data as fresh as possible.

Once the fetched results controller is created, you do your initial fetch. You do this in MasterViewController.m at the end of fetchedResultsController by sending your fetched results controller the PerformFetch message.

Now that you have your data, you're ready to be a data source and a delegate to your table view. When your table view wants the number of sections for its table, it will call numberOfSectionsInTableView:. In your version, you get the section information by passing the appropriate message to fetchResultsController. Here's the version from MasterViewController.m:

```
- (NSInteger)numberOfSectionsInTableView:(UITableView *)tableView
{
    return [[self.fetchedResultsController sections] count];
}
```

The same strategy applies in tableView:numberOfRowsInSection:.

```
- (NSInteger)tableView:(UITableView *)tableView numberOfRowsInSection:(NSInteger)section
{
    id <NSFetchedResultsSectionInfo> sectionInfo =
        [self.fetchedResultsController sections] objectAtIndex:section];
    return [sectionInfo numberOfObjects];
}
```

You get the idea. You used to need to do all this work yourself. Now you can ask your fetched results controller to do all the data management for you. It's an amazing time-saver!

Let's take a closer look at the creation of the fetched results controller. In `MasterViewController.m`, use the function menu to go to the method `-fetchedResultsController`. It should look like this:

```objc
- (NSFetchedResultsController *)fetchedResultsController
{
    if (_fetchedResultsController != nil) {
        return _fetchedResultsController;
    }

    NSFetchRequest *fetchRequest = [[NSFetchRequest alloc] init];
    // Edit the entity name as appropriate.
    NSEntityDescription *entity = [NSEntityDescription entityForName:@"Event"
                        inManagedObjectContext:self.managedObjectContext];
    [fetchRequest setEntity:entity];

    // Set the batch size to a suitable number.
    [fetchRequest setFetchBatchSize:20];

    // Edit the sort key as appropriate.
    NSSortDescriptor *sortDescriptor = [[NSSortDescriptor alloc] initWithKey:@"timeStamp"
                                                        ascending:NO];
    NSArray *sortDescriptors = @[sortDescriptor];

    [fetchRequest setSortDescriptors:sortDescriptors];

    // Edit the section name key path and cache name if appropriate.
    // nil for section name key path means "no sections".
    NSFetchedResultsController *aFetchedResultsController = [[NSFetchedResultsController alloc]
                        initWithFetchRequest:fetchRequest
                        managedObjectContext:self.managedObjectContext
                        sectionNameKeyPath:nil cacheName:@"Master"];
    aFetchedResultsController.delegate = self;
    self.fetchedResultsController = aFetchedResultsController;

        NSError *error = nil;
        if (![self.fetchedResultsController performFetch:&error]) {
            // Replace this implementation with code to handle the error appropriately.
            // abort() causes the application to generate a crash log and terminate. You should
            // not use this function in a shipping application, although it may be useful during
            // development.
            NSLog(@"Unresolved error %@, %@", error, [error userInfo]);
            abort();
        }

    return _fetchedResultsController;
}
```

As discussed earlier, this method uses lazy loading. The first thing it does is check _fetchedResultsController for nil. If _fetchedResultsController already exists, it is returned; otherwise, the process of creating a new fetchedResultsController is started.

As the first step, you need to create an NSFetchRequest and NSEntityDescription and then attach the NSEntityDescription to the NSFetchRequest.

```
NSFetchRequest *fetchRequest = [[NSFetchRequest alloc] init];
// Edit the entity name as appropriate.
NSEntityDescription *entity = [NSEntityDescription entityForName:@"Event"
                                        inManagedObjectContext:self.managedObjectContext];
[fetchRequest setEntity:entity];
```

Remember, you're building a fetched results controller, and the fetch request is part of that. Next, set the batch size to 20. This tells Core Data that this fetch request should retrieve its results 20 at a time.

```
// Set the batch size to a suitable number.
[fetchRequest setFetchBatchSize:20];
```

Next, build an NSSortDescriptor and specify that it use timeStamp as a key, sorting the timestamps in descending order (earlier dates last).

```
// Edit the sort key as appropriate.
NSSortDescriptor *sortDescriptor = [[NSSortDescriptor alloc] initWithKey:@"timeStamp"
ascending:NO];
```

Now you create an array of sort descriptors. Since you'll be using only one, you pass in sortDescriptor.

```
NSArray *sortDescriptors = @[sortDescriptor];
[fetchRequest setSortDescriptors:sortDescriptors];
```

Try this experiment: change ascending:NO to ascending:YES and run the application again. What do you think will happen? Don't forget to change it back when you are finished.

Tip   If you need to restrict a fetch request to a subset of the managed objects stored in the persistent store, use a predicate. The default template does not use predicates, but you'll be working with them in the next several chapters.

Now you create an NSFetchedResultsController using your fetch request and context. You'll learn about the third and fourth parameters, sectionNameKeyPath and cacheName, in Chapter 3.

```
// Edit the section name key path and cache name if appropriate.
// nil for section name key path means "no sections".
NSFetchedResultsController *aFetchedResultsController =
    [[NSFetchedResultsController alloc] initWithFetchRequest:fetchRequest
                                managedObjectContext:self.managedObjectContext
                                  sectionNameKeyPath:nil
                                           cacheName:@"Master"];
```

Next, you set self as the delegate and set fetchedResultsController to the fetched results controller you just created.

```
aFetchedResultsController.delegate = self;
self.fetchedResultsController = aFetchedResultsController;
```

Finally, you perform the fetch; if there are no errors, you assign the results to your private instance variable _fetchedResultsController and return the results.

```
NSError *error = nil;
if (![self.fetchedResultsController performFetch:&error]) {
    // Replace this implementation with code to handle the error appropriately.
    // abort() causes the application to generate a crash log and terminate. You should not
    use this
    // function in a shipping application, although it may be useful during development.
    NSLog(@"Unresolved error %@, %@", error, [error userInfo]);
    abort();
}

return _fetchedResultsController;
```

Don't worry too much about the details here. Try to get your head around the big picture. As you make your way through the next few chapters, the details will come into focus.

The Fetched Results Controller Delegate Methods

The fetched results controller must have a delegate, and that delegate must provide four methods, which we will describe in the pages that follow. These four methods are defined in the protocol NSFetchedResultsControllerDelegate. The fetched results controller monitors its managed object context and calls its delegates as changes are made to its context.

Will Change Content Delegate Method

When the fetched results controller observes a change that affects it—such as an object it manages being deleted or changed or when a new object is inserted that meets the criteria of the fetched results controller's fetch request—the fetched results controller will notify its delegate before it makes any changes, using the method controllerWillChangeContent:.

The vast majority of the time a fetched results controller will be used along with a table view, and all you need to do in that delegate method is to inform the table view that updates about to be made might impact what it is displaying. This is the method that ensures it gets done:

```
- (void)controllerWillChangeContent:(NSFetchedResultsController *)controller
{
    [self.tableView beginUpdates];
}
```

Did Change Contents Delegate Method

After the fetched results controller makes its changes, it will then notify its delegate using the method controllerDidChangeContent. At that time, if you're using a table view (and you almost certainly will be), you need to tell the table view that the updates you told it were coming in controllerWillChangeContent: are now complete. This is handled for you like so:

```
- (void)controllerDidChangeContent:(NSFetchedResultsController *)controller
{
    [self.tableView endUpdates];
}
```

Did Change Object Delegate Method

When the fetched results controller notices a change to a specific object, it will notify its delegate using the method controller:didChangeObject:atIndexPath:forChangeType:newIndexPath:. This method is where you need to handle updating, inserting, deleting, or moving rows in your table view to reflect whatever change was made to the objects managed by the fetched results controller. Here is the template implementation of the delegate method that will take care of updating the table view for you:

```
- (void)controller:(NSFetchedResultsController *)controller didChangeObject:(id)anObject
        atIndexPath:(NSIndexPath *)indexPath forChangeType:(NSFetchedResultsChangeType)type
      newIndexPath:(NSIndexPath *)newIndexPath
{
    UITableView *tableView = self.tableView;

    switch(type) {
        case NSFetchedResultsChangeInsert:
            [tableView insertRowsAtIndexPaths:@[newIndexPath]
                            withRowAnimation:UITableViewRowAnimationFade];
            break;

        case NSFetchedResultsChangeDelete:
            [tableView deleteRowsAtIndexPaths:@[indexPath]
                            withRowAnimation:UITableViewRowAnimationFade];
            break;
```

```
        case NSFetchedResultsChangeUpdate:
            [self configureCell:[tableView
                                cellForRowAtIndexPath:indexPath]
                                    atIndexPath:indexPath];
            break;

        case NSFetchedResultsChangeMove:
            [tableView deleteRowsAtIndexPaths:@[indexPath]
                        withRowAnimation:UITableViewRowAnimationFade];
            [tableView insertRowsAtIndexPaths:@[newIndexPath]
                        withRowAnimation:UITableViewRowAnimationFade];
            break;
    }
}
```

Most of this code is fairly straightforward. If a row has been inserted, you receive a type of NSFetchedResultsChangeInsert, and you insert a new row into the table. If a row was deleted, you receive a type of NSFetchedResultsChangeDelete, and you delete the corresponding row in the table. When you get a type of NSFetchedResultsChangeUpdate, it means that an object was changed, and the code calls configureCell to ensure that you are looking at the right data. If a type of NSFetchedResultsChangeMove was received, you know that a row was moved, so you delete it from the old location and insert it at the location specified by newIndexPath.

Did Change Section Delegate Method

Lastly, if a change to an object affects the number of sections in the table, the fetched results controller will call the delegate method controller:didChangeSection:atIndex:forChangeType:. If you specify a sectionNameKeyPath when you create your fetched results controller, you need to implement this delegate method to take care of adding and deleting sections from the table as needed. If you don't, you will get runtime errors when the number of sections in the table doesn't match the number of sections in the fetched results controller. Here is the template's standard implementation of that delegate method that should work for most situations:

```
- (void)controller:(NSFetchedResultsController *)controller
        didChangeSection:(id <NSFetchedResultsSectionInfo>)sectionInfo
        atIndex:(NSUInteger)sectionIndex
        forChangeType:(NSFetchedResultsChangeType)type
{
    switch(type) {
        case NSFetchedResultsChangeInsert:
            [self.tableView insertSections:[NSIndexSet indexSetWithIndex:sectionIndex]
                    withRowAnimation:UITableViewRowAnimationFade];
            break;

        case NSFetchedResultsChangeDelete:
            [self.tableView deleteSections:[NSIndexSet indexSetWithIndex:sectionIndex]
                    withRowAnimation:UITableViewRowAnimationFade];
            break;
    }
}
```

Using these four delegate methods, when you add a new managed object, the fetched results controller will detect that, and your table will be updated automatically. If you delete or change an object, the controller will detect that, too. Any change that affects the fetched results controller will automatically trigger an appropriate update to the table view, including properly animating the process. This means that you don't need to litter your code with calls to reloadData every time you make a change that might impact your dataset. Very nice!

Retrieving a Managed Object from the Fetched Results Controller

Your table view delegate methods have become much shorter and more straightforward since your fetched results controller does much of the work that you previously did in those methods. For example, to retrieve the object that corresponds to a particular cell, which you often need to do in tableView:cellForRowAtIndexPath: and tableView:didSelectRowAtInd exPath:, you can just call objectAtIndexPath: on the fetched results controller and pass in the indexPath parameter, and it will return the correct object.

```
NSManagedObject *object = [[self fetchedResultsController] objectAtIndexPath:indexPath];
```

Creating and Inserting a New Managed Object

From the function menu in the Editor pane, select insertNewObject, which is the method that is called when the + button is pressed in the sample application. It's a nice, simple example of how to create a new managed object, insert it into a managed object context, and then save it to the persistent store.

```
- (void)insertNewObject:(id)sender
{
    NSManagedObjectContext *context = [self.fetchedResultsController managedObjectContext];
    NSEntityDescription *entity = [[self.fetchedResultsController fetchRequest] entity];
    NSManagedObject *newManagedObject =
        [NSEntityDescription insertNewObjectForEntityForName:[entity name]
                                    inManagedObjectContext:context];

    // If appropriate, configure the new managed object.
    // Normally you should use accessor methods, but using KVC here avoids the need to add a
    custom class to the template.
    [newManagedObject setValue:[NSDate date] forKey:@"timeStamp"];

    // Save the context.
    NSError *error = nil;
    if (![context save:&error]) {
        // Replace this implementation with code to handle the error appropriately.
        // abort() causes the application to generate a crash log and terminate.
        // You should not use this function in a shipping application,
        // although it may be useful during development.
        NSLog(@"Unresolved error %@, %@", error, [error userInfo]);
        abort();
    }
}
```

Notice that the first thing the code does is to retrieve a managed object context from the fetched results controller. In this simple example where there's only one context, you could also have retrieved the same context from the application delegate. There are a few reasons why the default code uses the context from the fetched results controller. First, you already have a method that returns the fetched results controller, so you can get to the context in just one line of code.

```
NSManagedObjectContext *context = [self.fetchedResultsController managedObjectContext];
```

More importantly, though, a fetched results controller always knows which context its managed objects are contained by, so even if you decide to create an application with multiple contexts, you'll be sure that you're using the correct context if you pull it from the fetched results controller.

Just as you did when you created a fetch request, when inserting a new object, you need to create an entity description to tell Core Data which kind of entity you want to create an instance of. The fetched results controller also knows what entity the objects it manages are, so you can just ask it for that information.

```
NSEntityDescription *entity = [[self.fetchedResultsController fetchRequest] entity];
```

Then it's simply a matter of using a class method on NSEntityDescription to create the new object and insert it into a context.

```
NSManagedObject *newManagedObject =
    [NSEntityDescription insertNewObjectForEntityForName:[entity name]
                            inManagedObjectContext:context];
```

It does seem a little odd that you use a class method on NSEntityDescription, rather than an instance method on the context you want to insert the new object into, but that's the way it's done.

Though this managed object has now been inserted into the context, it still exists in the persistent store. To insert it from the persistent store, you must save the context, which is what happens next in this method:

```
// Save the context.
NSError *error = nil;
if (![context save:&error]) {
    // Replace this implementation with code to handle the error appropriately.
    // abort() causes the application to generate a crash log and terminate.
    // You should not use this function in a shipping application,
    // although it may be useful during development.
    NSLog(@"Unresolved error %@, %@", error, [error userInfo]);
    abort();
}
```

As the comment says, you need to handle the error more appropriately than calling abort. We'll cover this more in the ensuing chapters. Also, notice that you don't call reloadData on your table view. The fetched results controller will realize that you've inserted a new object that meets its criteria and will call the delegate method, which will automatically reload the table.

Deleting Managed Objects

Deleting managed objects is pretty easy when using a fetched results controller. Use the function menu to navigate to the method called tableView:commitEditingStyle:forRowAtIndexPath:. That method should look like this:

```
-(void)tableView:(UITableView *)tableView
     commitEditingStyle:(UITableViewCellEditingStyle)editingStyle
     forRowAtIndexPath:(NSIndexPath *)indexPath
{
    if (editingStyle == UITableViewCellEditingStyleDelete) {
        NSManagedObjectContext *context = [self.fetchedResultsController
        managedObjectContext];
        [context deleteObject:[self.fetchedResultsController objectAtIndexPath:indexPath]];

        NSError *error = nil;
        if (![context save:&error]) {
            // Replace this implementation with code to handle the error appropriately.
            // abort() causes the application to generate a crash log and terminate.
            // You should not use this function in a shipping application,
            // although it may be useful during development.
            NSLog(@"Unresolved error %@, %@", error, [error userInfo]);
            abort();
        }
    }
}
```

The method first makes sure that you're in a delete transaction (remember that this same method is used for deletes and inserts).

```
if (editingStyle == UITableViewCellEditingStyleDelete) {
```

Next, you retrieve the context.

```
NSManagedObjectContext *context = [self.fetchedResultsController managedObjectContext];
```

Then the context is asked to delete that object.

```
[context deleteObject:[self.fetchedResultsController objectAtIndexPath:indexPath]];
```

Next, the managed object context's save: method is called to cause that change to be committed to the persistent store.

```
NSError *error = nil;
if (![context save:&error]) {
    // Replace this implementation with code to handle the error appropriately.
    // abort() causes the application to generate a crash log and terminate. You should not use this
    // function in a shipping application, although it may be useful during development.
    NSLog(@"Unresolved error %@, %@", error, [error userInfo]);
    abort();
}
```

No need to admonish you again about the call to abort, as we discussed this previously.

And that's all there is to deleting managed objects.

Putting Everything in Context

At this point, you should have a pretty good handle on the basics of using Core Data. You've learned about the architecture of a Core Data application and the process of using entities and properties. You've seen how the persistent store, managed object model, and managed object context are created by your application delegate. You learned how to use the data model editor to build entities that can be used in your program to create managed objects. You also learned how to retrieve, insert, and delete data from the persistent store.

Enough with the theory! Let's move on and build some Core Data applications, shall we?

Chapter 3

A Super Start: Adding, Displaying, and Deleting Data

Well, if that previous chapter didn't scare you off, then you're ready to dive in and move beyond the basic template you explored in Chapter 2.

In this chapter, you'll create an application designed to track some superhero data. Your application will start with the Master-Detail Application template, though you'll be making lots of changes right from the beginning. You'll use the model editor to design your superhero entity. Then you'll create a new controller class derived from `UIViewController` that will allow you to add, display, and delete superheroes. In Chapter 4, you'll extend your application further and add code to allow the user to edit her superhero data.

Take a look at Figure 3-1 to get a sense of what your app will look like when it runs. It looks a lot like the template app. The major differences lie in the entity at the heart of the application and in the addition of a tab bar at the bottom of the screen. Let's get to work.

Figure 3-1. The SuperDB application as it will look once you've finished this chapter

Setting Up the Xcode Project

It's time to get your hands dirty. Launch Xcode if it's not open and bring up your old friend, the new project assistant (Figure 3-2).

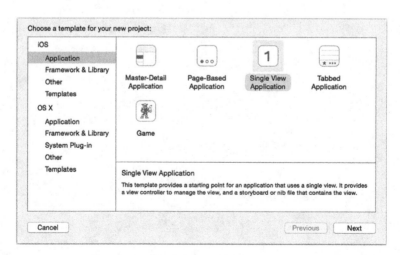

Figure 3-2. Your dear old friend, Xcode's new project assistant

In the previous chapter, you started with the Master-Detail Application template. When you're creating your own navigation applications, it's a good template to use because it gives you a lot of the code you're likely to need in your application. However, to make it easier to explain where to add or modify code and also to reinforce your understanding of how applications are constructed, you'll build the SuperDB application from scratch, just as you did throughout most of *Beginning iPhone Development*.

Select Single View Application and click Next. When prompted for a product name (Figure 3-3), enter **SuperDB**. Select iPhone for the device family, and make sure that the Use Core Data check box is selected. After clicking Next again, use the default location to save the project and click Create.

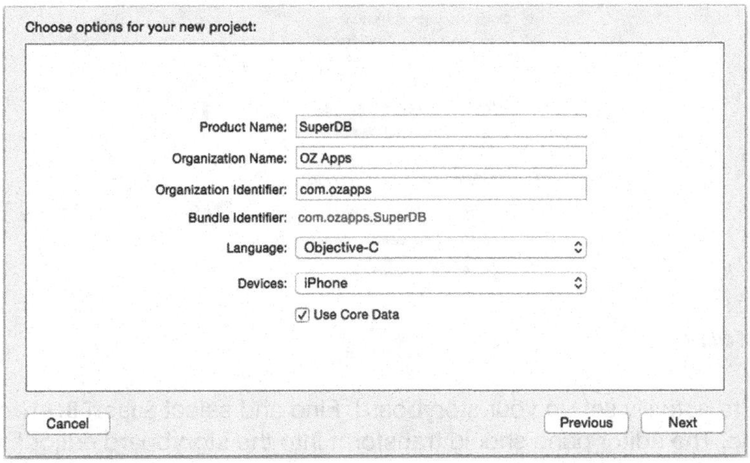

Figure 3-3. Entering project details

First, click the Main.storyboard file; it should appear in the Navigator pane. Click the filename, rename this Main.storyboard file to SuperDB.storyboard, and save it.

Finally, you need to tell Xcode that you want to use the new SuperDB.storyboard file. Select the SuperDB project at the top of the Navigator pane. When the project editor appears, select the SuperDB target and go to the project summary editor (Figure 3-4). In the section Deployment Info, select the name SuperDB for the Main Interface field.

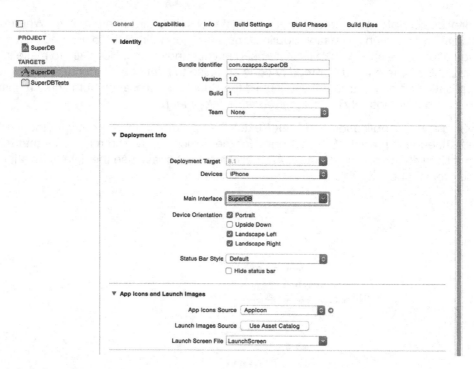

Figure 3-4. Project editor

Now you need to actually set up your storyboard. Find and select SuperDB.storyboard in the Navigation pane. The editor pane should transform into the storyboard editor (Figure 3-5). There is a button on the bottom left; click it.

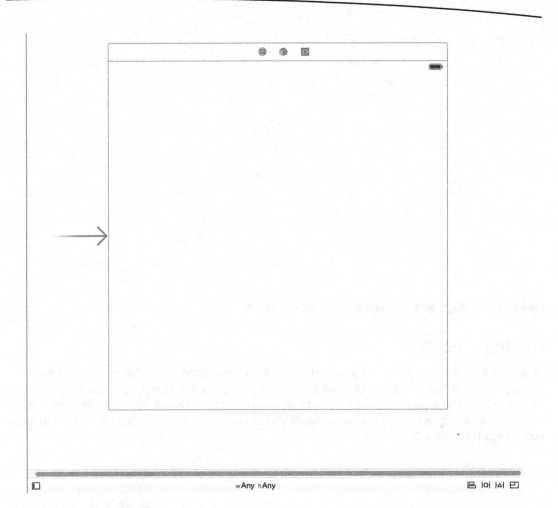

Figure 3-5. The storyboard editor

The storyboard document outline (Figure 3-6) should appear on the left of the storyboard editor. Right now this view is empty with no scenes (I'll define *scenes* in a little bit). Normally, the storyboard document outline provides a hierarchical view of the scenes and their view controllers, views, and UI components.

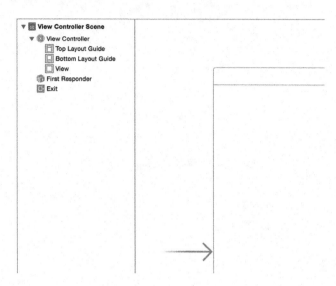

Figure 3-6. The storyboard document outline and Disclosure button

Adding a Scene

You want the scene to support navigation, so drag a navigation controller from the Object Library (which should be at the bottom of the Utility pane) to the storyboard editor and then delete this default view controller by selecting it and pressing Delete. You can click the view controller scene (provided to you by default) and delete it. Your storyboard editor should look something like Figure 3-7.

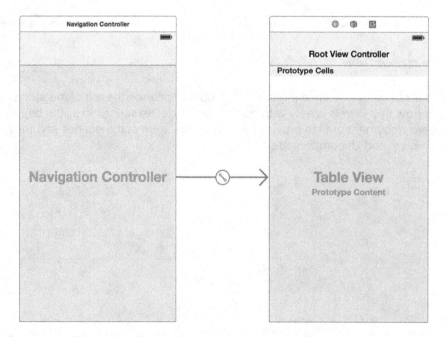

Figure 3-7. Storyboard editor with a navigation controller

Note   In case you find that you have slightly larger and squarer scenes than those that resemble an iPhone, press Cmd+Opt+1; then under Interface Builder Document, deselect the use Auto Layout check box. A dialog will appear; make sure that the drop-down displays iPhone and then click the Disable Size Classes button.

Scenes and Segues

Interestingly, Xcode decided that along with the navigation controller, you wanted a table view controller and set it up. What you see now are two scenes, labeled Navigation Controller Scene and Root View Controller Scene. Between the two scenes is a segue. It's the arrow pointing from the navigation controller to the root view controller. It has an icon in the middle of it that tells you this is a manual segue.

A scene is basically a view controller. The leftmost scene is labeled Navigation Controller; the rightmost is labeled Root View Controller. The navigation controller is used to manage the other view controllers. In Chapter 2, the navigation controller managed the master and detail view controllers. The navigation controller also provided the navigation bar that allowed you to edit and add events in the master view controller and provided the Back button in the detail view controller.

A segue defines the transition from a scene to the next scene. In the application from Chapter 2, when you selected an event in the master view controller, you triggered the segue to transition to the detail view controller.

One more thing to note: if you were to simply run the project now, it would display a black screen because it would fail to instantiate the default view controller. Each storyboard requires a starting point, which is the view controller that is displayed first. The arrow to the left specifies this, and since there is no view controller that is set at the initial view controller, it would display nothing. You select the navigation controller, and in the Attributes Inspector (Cmd+Opt+4), you can select the check box "is Initial View Controller." This will display the arrow to the left of the view controller.

Storyboard Document Outline

Now that you have something in your storyboard editor, let's take a look at the storyboard document outline. Open it (if it is not showing). Now you can see the hierarchical view of the scenes described earlier (Figure 3-8), with their view controllers, views, and UI components.

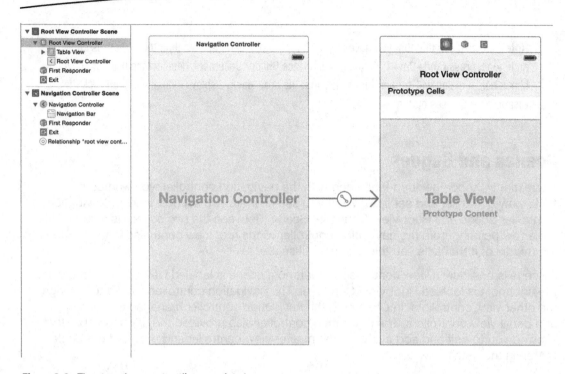

Figure 3-8. The story document outline, populated

Let's take a look at your work so far. Build and run the SuperDB app. You should see something like Figure 3-9.

Figure 3-9. The SuperDB app so far

Application Architecture

There's no single right architecture for every application. One obvious approach would be to make the application a tabbed application and then add a separate navigation controller for each tab. In a situation where each tab corresponds to a completely different view showing different types of data, this approach would make perfect sense. In *Beginning iPhone Development*, you used that exact approach because every single tab corresponded to a different view controller with different outlets and different actions.

In this case, however, you'll implement two tabs (with more to be added in later chapters), but each tab will show the same data, just ordered differently. When one tab is selected, the table will be ordered by the superhero's name. If the other tab is selected, the same data will be shown but ordered by the superhero's secret identity.

Regardless of which tab is selected, tapping a row on the table will do the same thing; it will drill down to a new view where you can edit the information about the superhero you selected (which you will add in the next chapter). Regardless of which tab is selected, tapping the Add button will add a new instance of the same entity. When you drill down to another view or edit a hero, the tabs are no longer relevant.

For your application, the tab bar is just modifying the way the data in a single table is presented. There's no need for it to actually swap in and out other view controllers. Why have multiple navigation controller instances all managing identical sets of data and responding the same way to touches? Why not just use one table controller and have it change the way it presents the data based on which tab is selected? This is the approach you'll take in this application. As a result, your application won't be a true tabbed application.

Your root view controller will be a navigation controller, and you'll use a tab bar purely to receive input from the user. The end result that is shown to the user will be identical to what they'd see if you created separate navigation controllers and table view controllers for each tab. Behind the scenes you'll be using less memory and won't have to worry about keeping the different navigation controllers in sync with each other.

Your application's root view controller will be an instance of UINavigationController. You'll create your own custom view controller class, HeroListController, to act as the root view controller for this.

UINavigationController. HeroListController will display the list of superheroes along with the tabs that control how the heroes are displayed and ordered.

Here's how the app will work. When the application starts, an instance of HeroListController is loaded from the storyboard file. Then an instance of UINavigationController is created with the HeroListController instance as its root view controller. Finally, the UINavigationController is set as the application's root view controller. The view associated with the HeroListController contains your tab bar and your superhero table view.

In Chapter 4, you'll add a table view controller into the mix to implement a detail superhero view. When the user taps a superhero in the superhero list, this detail controller will be pushed onto the navigation stack, and its view will temporarily replace the HeroListController's view in the UINavigationController's content view. There's no need to worry about the detail view now; we just wanted you to see what's coming.

Designing the View Controller Interface

Your application's root view controller is now a stock UINavigationController. You didn't need to write any code for it; you just dropped a navigation controller object into your storyboard. Xcode also gave you a UITableViewController as the root of the navigation controller's stack. Even though you will be using a table to display the list of heroes, you're not going to subclass UITableViewController. Because you also need to add a tab bar to your interface, you'll create a subclass of UIViewController and create your interface in the storyboard editor. The table that will display the list of heroes will be a subview of your view controller's content pane.

If not already selected, select the SuperDB.storyboard file in the Navigation pane. Also make sure the Utility pane is exposed. The storyboard should have two scenes: the navigation controller and the root view controller. Select the root view controller. Only the root view controller scene and label should be highlighted blue. Delete the table view controller by hitting the Delete key or by selecting Edit ➤ Delete. You should now have only the navigation controller.

From the bottom of the Utility pane, select a view controller from the Object Library and drag it to the storyboard editor. A view controller should appear; place it to the right of the navigation controller (Figure 3-10).

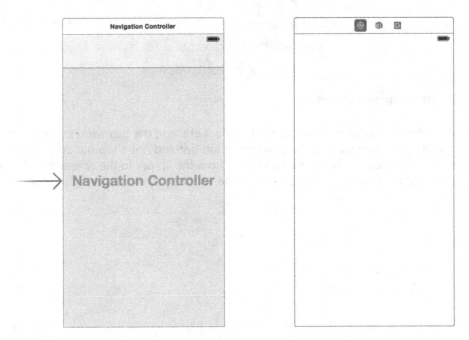

Figure 3-10. The storyboard with a new view controller scene

Before you lay out the new view controller, let's connect it to the navigation controller. Select the navigation controller. Hover the pointer over the leftmost icon (Figure 3-11). A pop-up window should appear with the words *navigation controller*. Control-drag from the navigation controller icon to the view of the view controller. When you release the pointer, you should see a pop-up menu of possible segue assignments (Figure 3-12). Select root view controller in the Relationship Segue section. You should see a segue appear between the navigation controller and the view controller. Also, the view controller should now have a navigation bar along the top.

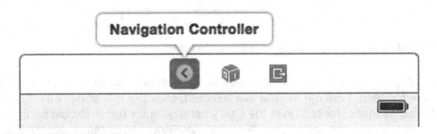

Figure 3-11. Navigation controller label icons

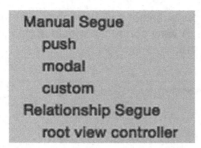

Figure 3-12. *Possible segue assignments*

Now you can design the view controller's interface. Let's add the tab bar first. Look in the library for a tab bar. Make sure you're grabbing a tab bar and not a tab bar controller. You only want the user interface item. Drag a tab bar from the library to the scene called View Controller, and place it snugly in the bottom of the window, as shown in Figure 3-13.

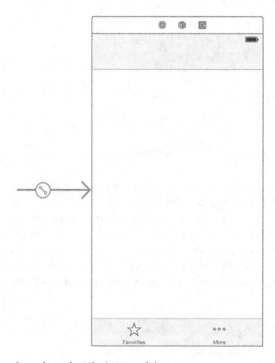

Figure 3-13. *The tab bar placed snugly against the bottom of the scene*

The default tab bar has two tabs, which is exactly the number you want. Let's change the icon and label for each. With the tab bar still selected, click the star above Favorites. Then click the Attributes Inspector button in the Utility pane selector bar (it should be the fourth button). Alternately, you can select View ➤ Utilities ➤ Show Attributes Inspector. The menu shortcut is ⌥⌘4.

If you've correctly selected the tab bar item, the Attributes Inspector pane should say Tab Bar Item, and the Identifier pop-up should say Favorites. In the Attributes Inspector, give this tab a title of **By Name** and an image of name_icon.png (Figure 3-14). Now click the three dots above the word *More* on the tab bar to select the right tab. Using the inspector, give this tab a title of **By Secret Identity** and an image of secret_icon.png.

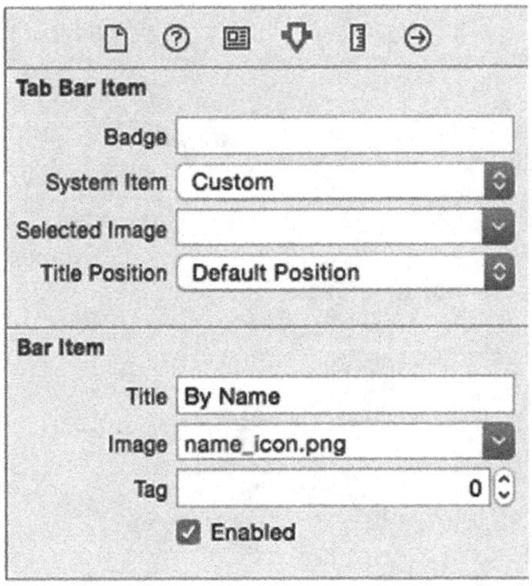

Figure 3-14. Setting the attributes of the left tab

> **Note**   You can find the files name_icon.png and secret_icon.png in the download archive for this book.

Back in the Object Library, look for a table view. Again, make sure you're getting the user interface element, not a table view controller. Drag this to the space above the tab bar. It should resize automatically to fit the space available. After you drop it, it should look like Figure 3-15.

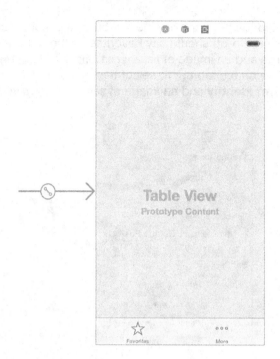

Figure 3-15. *The table view in the scene*

Finally, grab a table view cell and drag it on top of the table view. Xcode should automatically align it to the top of the table view (Figure 3-16).

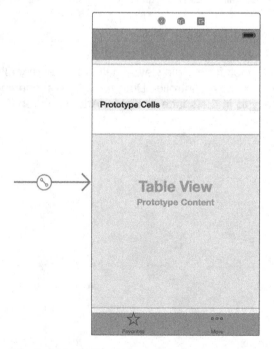

Figure 3-16. *The table view cell on the table view*

Select the table view cell and expose the Attributes Inspector in the Utility pane. You need to change some of the attributes to get the behavior you want. First, set the style to Subtitle; your Attributes Inspector should look like Figure 3-17. This gives you a table view cell with a large title and a smaller subtitle below the title. Next, give it an identifier value of HeroListCell. This value will be used later when creating table view cells. Finally, change the selection from Default to None. This means when you tap a table view cell, it won't highlight.

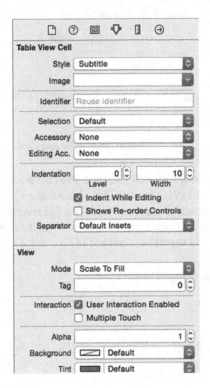

Figure 3-17. The table view cell attributes

Your interface is complete. Now you need to define your view controller interface to make the outlet, delegate, and data source connections.

Creating HeroListController

Single-click the SuperDB group in the Navigator pane. Now create a new file (⌘N or File ➤ New ➤ File). When the New File Assistant appears (Figure 3-18), select Cocoa Touch Class from under the iOS heading in the left pane, and click the Next button.

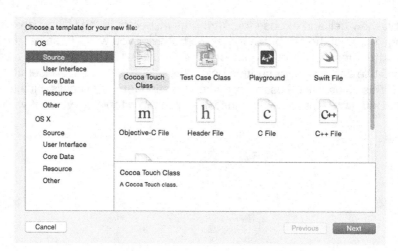

Figure 3-18. Selecting the Cocoa Touch Class template in the new file assistant

In the second file assistant pane (Figure 3-19), give the class a name of HeroListController and make it a subclass of UITableViewController. Make sure "Also create XIB file" is unchecked. With that done, click the Next button. The file dialog should be set to the SuperDB project folder, so just click Create. Two files should have been added to the project view: HeroListController.h and HeroListController.m.

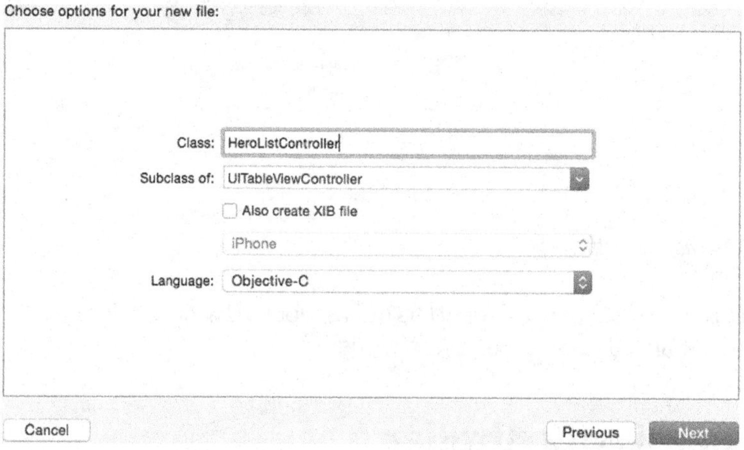

Figure 3-19. Selecting the UITableViewController in the file assistant

Wait a minute. When you made the interface in MainStoryboard.storyboard, you used a plain UIViewController, not a UITableViewController. And we said earlier that you didn't want to use a UITableViewController. So, why did you have to make HeroListController a subclass of UITableViewController?

If you look back at Figure 3-1, you can see that your application displays a list of heroes in a table view. That table view will need a data source and a delegate. The HeroListController will be that data source and delegate. By asking the New File Assistant to make a subclass of UITableViewController, Xcode will use a file template that will predefine a bunch of table view data source and delegate methods. Select HeroListController.m in the Navigator pane and take a look at the file in the Editor pane. You should see the methods Xcode gave you for free. These methods are mostly commented out, and they are a good starting point to use as a stub rather than figuring out what functions to implement.

However, you do need to make the HeroListController a subclass of UIViewController. Single-click HeroListController.h in the Navigator pane. Find the @interface declaration, and change it from this:

```
@interface HeroListController : UITableViewController
```

to this:

```
@interface HeroListController : UIViewController <UITableViewDataSource,
UITableViewDelegate>
```

Now you need to connect the table view data source and delegate to the HeroListController. While you're at it, create the outlets needed for the tab bar and table view. You could add them manually, but you already know how to do that. Let's try using an alternate method.

Select SuperDB.storyboard in the Navigator pane and expose the storyboard editor. Scroll the view controller such that the three icons above are visible. Hover the pointer over the leftmost icon, which is a yellow circle with a white square. Xcode should pop up a label that reads *View Controller*. Single-click to select it. In the Utility pane, select the Identity Inspector (⌥⌘3 or Cmd+Opt+3), as shown in Figure 3-20. Change the Class field (under the Custom Class header) to HeroListController.

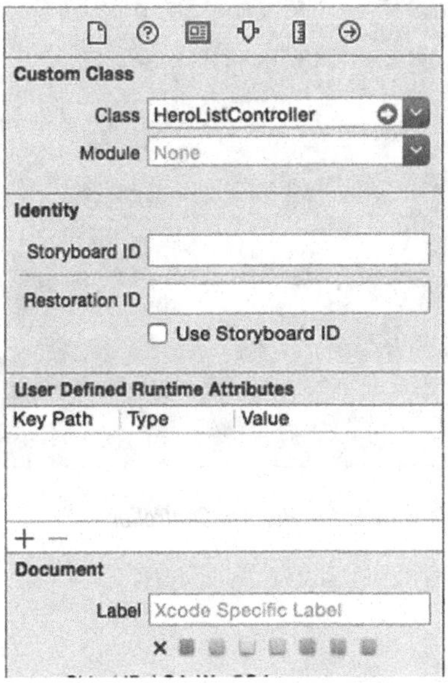

Figure 3-20. View controller's Identity Inspector

What have you done here? You've told Xcode that your view controller is not a plain old UIViewController but now a HeroListController. If you hover the pointer over the view controller icon, the pop-up will read Hero List Controller now.

Making the Connections and Outlets

First, make the HeroListController the table view data source and delegate. Control-drag from the table view area to the HeroListController (Figure 3-21). When you release, an Outlets pop-up window should appear (Figure 3-22). Select dataSource. Control-drag again, this time selecting delegate.

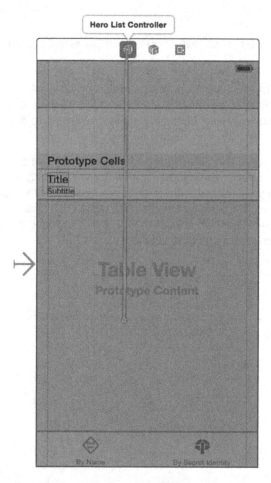

Figure 3-21. Control-drag from the table view to the HeroListController

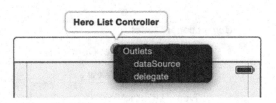

Figure 3-22. Table view Outlets pop-up window

Now you'll add the outlets for the tab bar and the table view. On the toolbar, change the editor from the Standard editor to the Assistant editor. The Editor pane should split into two views (Figure 3-23). The left view will have the storyboard editor; the right view will have a code editor showing the interface file of HeroListController.

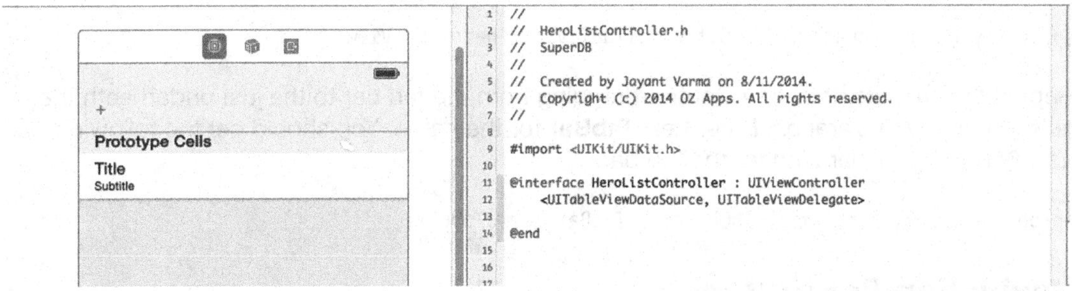

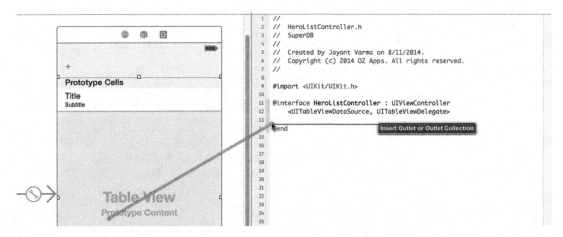

Figure 3-23. The Assistant editor

Again, Control-drag from the table view area, but this time go to the code editor, just between the @interface and @end declarations (Figure 3-24). Once you release, a Connection pop-up window will appear (Figure 3-25). Enter **heroTableView** in the Name field and leave the rest of the fields at their default settings. Click the Connect button.

Figure 3-24. Control-drag from the table view to the HeroListController interface file

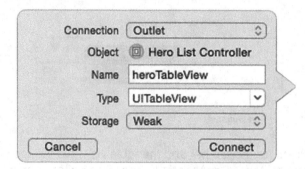

Figure 3-25. The Connection pop-up window

The following line should be added after the @interface declaration:

@property (weak, nonatomic) IBOutlet UITableView *heroTableView;

Repeat the process, this time Control-dragging from the tab bar to the just underneath the new @property declaration. Enter **heroTabBar** for the name. You should get the following new @property declaration for the tab bar:

@property (weak, nonatomic) IBOutlet UITabBar *heroTabBar;

Navigation Bar Buttons

If you build and run the SuperDB app, you should get something like Figure 3-26.

Figure 3-26. SuperDB so far. Looking good!

Let's add the Edit and Add (+) buttons. Make sure the Standard Editor toggle is selected in the toolbar and then select HeroListController.m in the Navigator pane. In the Editor pane, find the following method:

```
- (void)viewDidLoad
```

At the bottom of the method, you should see the following lines:

```
// Uncomment the following line to display an Edit button in the navigation bar for this
view controller.
// self.navigationItem.rightBarButtonItem = self.editButtonItem;
```

Uncomment the second line, like so:

```
// Uncomment the following line to display an Edit button in the navigation bar for this
view controller.
self.navigationItem.rightBarButtonItem = self.editButtonItem;
```

To add the Add (+) button, you need to go back to the storyboard editor. Select
SuperDB.storyboard in the Navigator pane. Drag a bar button item from the Object
Library to the left side of the navigation bar in the Hero view controller. In the Utility pane,
select the Attributes Inspector. You should see the Attributes Inspector for a bar button item
(Figure 3-27). If not, make sure the bar button item you just added is selected. Change the
Identifier field to Add. The bar button item's label should change from Item to +.

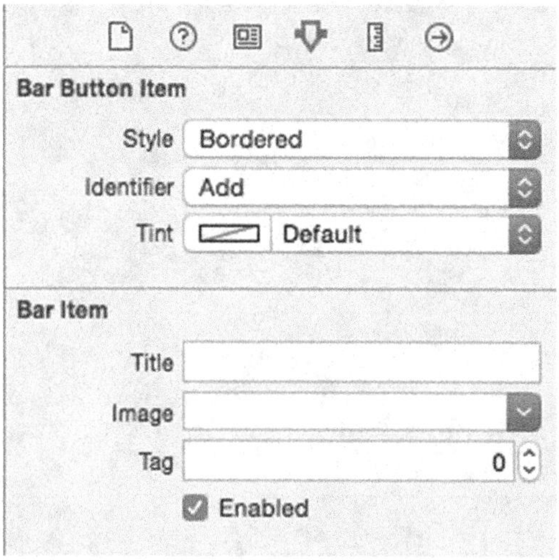

Figure 3-27. *Bar button item's Attributes Inspector*

Toggle back to the Assistant editor. Control-drag from the bar button item to just below
the last @property in the HeroListController interface file. When the connection pop-up
window appears, add a connection named **addButton**. Control-drag from the bar button
item again to just above the @end. This time, when the connection pop-up appears, change
the Connection value to Action, and set the name to **addHero** (Figure 3-28). Click Connect.
You should see a new method declaration, like so:

```
- (IBAction)addHero:(id)sender;
```

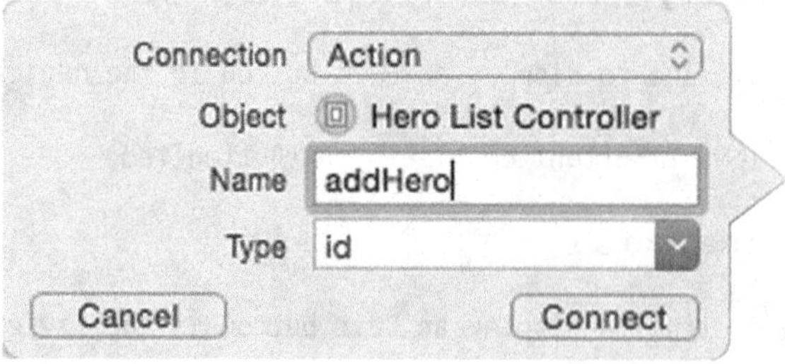

Figure 3-28. *Adding the addHero: action*

If you go to the HeroListController implementation file, you'll see the (empty) method implementation.

```
- (IBAction)addHero:(id)sender {
}
```

Build and run the app. Everything looks in place (Figure 3-29). Tap the Edit button. It should turn into a Done button. Tap the Done button, and it should go back to Edit. Tap the Add (+) button. Nothing happens. That's because you haven't written the -addHero: method to do anything. You'll get to that soon.

Figure 3-29. Everything is in the right place

However, right now the tab bar does not have either tab button selected. When you start the app, both buttons are off. You can select one and then toggle between the two. But shouldn't one of the buttons be selected at launch? You'll implement that next.

Tab Bar and User Defaults

You want the application to start with one of the tab bar buttons selected. You can do that pretty easily by adding something like this to the viewDidLoad: method of the HeroListController:

```
// Select the Tab Bar Button
UITabBarItem *item = [self.heroTabBar.items objectAtIndex:0];
[self.heroTabBar setSelectedItem:item];
```

Try it. The application starts, and the By Name tab is selected. Now, select the By Secret Identity tab and stop the app in Xcode. Restart the app. The By Name tab is selected. Wouldn't it be nice if the application remembered your last selection? You can use user defaults to do that remembering for you.

In the HeroListController.h interface, add the following lines before the @interface declaration:

```
#define kSelectedTabDefaultsKey @"Selected Tab"

enum {
    kByName,
    kBySecretIdentity,
};
```

kSelectedTabDefaultsKey is the key you'll use to store and retrieve the selected tab bar button index from the user defaults. The enumeration is just a convenience for the values 0 and 1.

Switch to the HeroListController.m implementation file, and add the following to the end of the viewDidLoad: method:

```
// Select the Tab Bar button
NSUserDefaults *defaults = [NSUserDefaults standardUserDefaults];
NSInteger selectedTab = [defaults integerForKey:kSelectedTabDefaultsKey];
UITabBarItem *item = [self.heroTabBar.items objectAtIndex:selectedTab];
[self.heroTabBar setSelectedItem:item];
```

(If you entered the earlier tab bar selection code, make sure you make the changes correctly.)

Build and run the app. Toggle the tab bar. Quit the app, and make sure the By Secret Identity button is selected. Quit the app, and start it again. It should remember the selection, right? Not yet. You haven't written code to write the user default when the tab bar selection changes. You're only reading it at launch. Let's write the default when it changes.

Select the SuperDB.storyboard file and Control-drag from the tab bar to the Hero view controller. When the Outlets pop-up appears, select delegate (it should be your only choice). Next, select HeroListController.h and change the @interface declaration from this:

```
@interface HeroListController : UIViewController <UITableViewDataSource,
UITableViewDelegate>
```

to this:

```
@interface HeroListController : UIViewController <UITableViewDataSource,
UITableViewDelegate, UITabBarDelegate>
```

Now UITabBarDelegate has a required method: -tabBar:didSelectItem:. Select
HeroListController.m and navigate the editor to just above the -addHero: method. Add
these lines:

```
#pragma mark - UITabBarDelegate Methods

- (void)tabBar:(UITabBar *)tabBar didSelectItem:(UITabBarItem *)item
{
    NSUserDefaults *defaults = [NSUserDefaults standardUserDefaults];
    NSUInteger tabIndex = [tabBar.items indexOfObject:item];
    [defaults setInteger:tabIndex forKey:kSelectedTabDefaultsKey];
}
```

Now when you quit and launch the application, it remembers your last tab bar selection.

Designing the Data Model

Now you need define the application's data model. As discussed in Chapter 2, the Xcode
model editor is where you design your application's data model. In the Navigator pane, click
SuperDB.xcdatamodel. This should bring up the model editor (Figure 3-30).

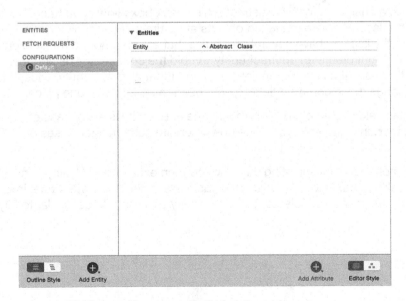

Figure 3-30. The empty model editor awaiting your application's data model

Unlike the data model from Chapter 2, you should be starting with a completely empty data model. So, let's dive right in and start building. The first thing you need to add to your data model is an entity. Remember, entities are like class definitions. Although they don't store any data themselves, without at least one entity in your data model, your application won't be able to store any data.

Adding an Entity

Since the purpose of your application is to track information about superheroes, it seems logical that you're going to need an entity to represent a hero. You'll start off simple in this chapter and track only a few pieces of data about each hero: name, secret identity, date of birth, and sex. You'll add more data elements in future chapters, but this will give you a basic foundation upon which to build.

Add a new entity to the data model. A new entity, named Entity, should appear in the Top-Level Components pane. This entity should be selected, and the text *Entity* should be highlighted. Enter **Hero** to name this entity.

Editing the New Entity

Let's verify that your new Hero entity has been added to the default configuration. Select Default Configuration in the Top-Level Configuration pane. The Data Editor Detail pane to the right should have changed with a single table named Entities. There should be one entry in this table, the entity you just named Hero.

Next to Hero is a check box called Abstract. This check box allows you to create an entity that cannot be used to create managed objects at runtime. The reason why you might create an abstract entity is if you have several properties that are common to multiple entities. In that case, you might create an abstract entity to hold the common fields and then make every entity that uses those common fields a child of that abstract entity. Thus, if you needed to change those common fields, you'd need to do it in only one place.

Next, the Class field should blank. This means the Hero entity is a subclass of NSManagedObject. In Chapter 6, you'll see how to create custom subclasses of NSManagedObject to add functionality.

You can see more detail by selecting this row and then exposing the Utility pane. Let's expose the Utility pane. Once the Utility pane appears, select the Data Model Inspector (the third button on the inspector selector bar). The Utility pane should be similar to Figure 3-31.

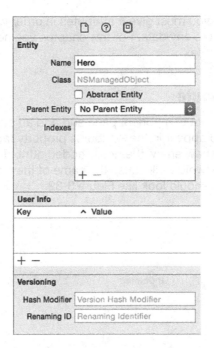

Figure 3-31. The Utilities pane for the new entity

The first three fields (Name, Class, and Abstract Entity) mirror what you saw in the Data Detail pane. Below the Abstract Entity check box is a Parent Entity pop-up menu. Within a data model, you have the ability to specify a parent entity, which is similar to subclassing in Objective-C. When you specify another entity as your parent, the new entity receives all the properties of the parent entity along with any additional ones you specify. Leave the Parent Entity set to No Parent Entity.

> **Note** You may be wondering about the additional areas in the Data Model Inspector, titled User Info, Versioning, and Entity Sync. These settings give you access to more advanced configuration parameters that are only rarely used. You won't be changing any of the configurations.
>
> If you're interested in finding out more about these advanced options, you can read more about them in *Pro Core Data for iOS*. Apple has the following guides online as well: the Core Data Programming Guide at http://developer.apple.com/library/ios/#documentation/Cocoa/Conceptual/CoreData/cdProgrammingGuide.html and the Core Data Model Versioning and Data Migration Guide at http://developer.apple.com/library/ios/#documentation/Cocoa/Conceptual/CoreDataVersioning/Articles/Introduction.html. Adding Attributes to the Hero Entity.

Now that you have an entity, you must give it attributes in order for managed objects based on this entity to be able to store any data. For this chapter, you need four attributes: name, secret identity, birthDate, and sex.

Adding the Name Attribute

Select the Hero entity in the data component pane and add an attribute. Once added, an entry named Attribute should appear in the Attributes property table in the detail pane. Just like when you created a new entity, the newly added attribute has been automatically selected for you. Type **name**, which will cause the name of the new attribute to be updated. The Attributes property pane should look like Figure 3-32.

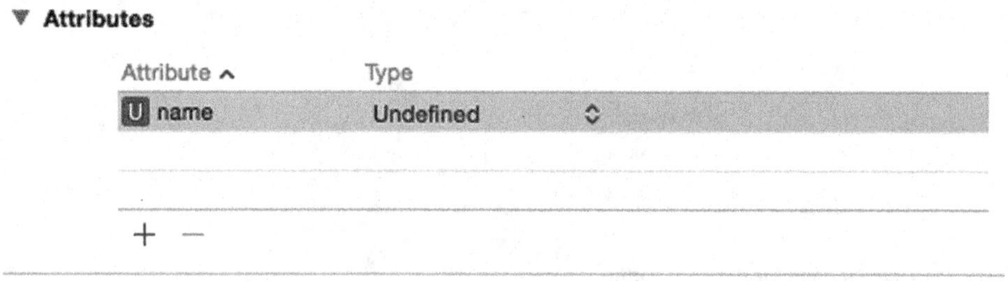

▼ **Attributes**

Attribute ⌃	Type	
Ⓤ name	Undefined	⬍

+ −

Figure 3-32. Attributes detail

> **Tip**   It's not an accident that you chose to start your entity Hero with a capital *H* but your attribute name with a lowercase *n*. This is the accepted naming convention for entities and properties. Entities begin with a capital letter; properties begin with a lowercase letter. In both cases, if the name of the entity or property consists of more than one word, the first letter of each new word is capitalized.

The Type column of the table specifies the data type of the attribute. By default, the data type is set to Undefined.

Now, let's expose the Utilities pane again (if it's not already open). Make sure the name attribute is selected in the detail pane, and choose the Data Model Inspector (Figure 3-33). The first field should be titled Name, and it should have the value of name.

Figure 3-33. The Data Model Inspector for the new name attribute

Below the Name field are three check boxes: Transient, Optional, and Indexed. If Optional is checked, then this entity can be saved even if this attribute has no value assigned to it. If you uncheck it, then any attempt to save a managed object based on this entity when the name attribute is `nil` will result in a validation error that will prevent the save. In this particular case, name is the main attribute that you will use to identify a given hero, so you probably want to require this attribute. Single-click the Optional check box to uncheck it, making this field required.

The Transient check box allows you to create attributes that are not saved in the persistent store. They can also be used to create custom attributes that store nonstandard data. For now, don't worry too much about Transient. Just leave it unchecked; you'll revisit this check box in Chapter 6.

The final check box, Indexed, tells the underlying data store to add an index on this attribute. Not all persistent stores support indices, but the default store (SQLite) does. The database uses an index to improve search speeds when searching or ordering based on that field. You will be ordering your superheroes by name, so check the Indexed check box to tell SQLite to create an index on the column that will be used to store this attribute's data.

> **Caution**   Properly used, indices can greatly improve performance in a SQLite persistent store. Adding indices where they are not needed, however, can actually degrade performance. If you don't have a reason for selecting Indexed, leave it unchecked.

Attribute Types

Every attribute has a type, which identifies the kind of data that the attribute is capable of storing. If you single-click the Attribute Type drop-down (which should currently be set to Undefined), you can see the various data types that Core Data supports out of the box (Figure 3-34). These are all the types of data that you can store without having to implement a custom attribute, like you'll do in Chapter 6. Each of the data types corresponds to an Objective-C class that is used to set or retrieve values, and you must make sure to use the correct object when setting values on managed objects.

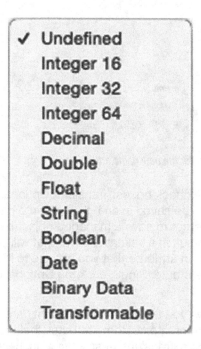

Figure 3-34. The data types supported by Core Data

The Integer Data Types

Integer 16, Integer 32, and Integer 64 all hold signed integers (whole numbers). The only difference between these three number types is the minimum and maximum sizes of the values they are capable of storing. In general, you should pick the smallest-size integer that you are certain will work for your purposes. For example, if you know your attribute will never hold a number larger than 1,000, make sure to select Integer 16 rather than Integer 32 or Integer 64. Table 3-1 lists the minimum and maximum values that these three data types are capable of storing.

Table 3-1. *Integer Type Minimums and Maximums*

Data Type	Minimum	Maximum
Integer 16	−32,768	32, 767
Integer 32	−2,147,483,648	2,147,483,647
Integer 64	−9,223,372,036,854,775,808	9,223,372,036,854,775,807

At runtime, you set integer attributes of a managed object using instances of NSNumber created using a factory method such as numberWithInt: or numberWithLong:

The Decimal, Double, and Float Data Types

The decimal, double, and float data types all hold decimal numbers. Double and float hold floating-point representations of decimal numbers similar to the C data types of double and float, respectively. Floating-point representations of decimal numbers are always an approximation because they use a fixed number of bytes to represent data. The larger the number to the left of the decimal point, the less bytes there are available to hold the fractional part of the number. The double data type uses 64 bits to store a single number, while the float data type uses 32 bits of data to store a single number. For many purposes, these two data types will work just fine. However, when you have data, such as currency, where small rounding errors would be a problem, Core Data provides the decimal data type, which is not subject to rounding errors. The decimal type can hold numbers with up to 38 significant digits stored internally using fixed-point numbers so that the stored value is not subject to the rounding errors that can happen with floating-point numbers.

At runtime, you set double and float attributes using instances of NSNumber created using the NSNumber factory method numberWithFloat: or numberWithDouble:. Decimal attributes, on the other hand, must be set using an instance of the class NSDecimalNumber.

The String Data Type

The string data type is one of the most common attribute types you will use. String attributes are capable of holding text in nearly any language or script since they are stored internally using Unicode. String attributes are set at runtime using instances of NSString.

The Boolean Data Type

Boolean values (YES or NO) can be stored using the Boolean data type. Boolean attributes are set at runtime using instances of NSNumber created using numberWithBOOL:.

The Date Data Type

Dates and timestamps can be stored in Core Data using the date data type. At runtime, date attributes are set using instances of NSDate.

The Binary Data Type

The binary data type is used to store any kind of binary data. Binary attributes are set at runtime using NSData instances. Anything that can be put into an NSData instance can be stored in a binary attribute. However, you generally can't search or sort on binary data types.

The Transformable Data Type

The transformable data type is a special data type that works along with something called a value transformer to let you create attributes based on any Objective-C class, even those for which there is no corresponding Core Data data type. You would use transformable data types to store a UIImage instance, for example, or to store a UIColor instance. You'll see how transformable attributes work in Chapter 6.

Setting the name Attribute Type

A name, obviously, is text, so the obvious type for this attribute is string. Select string from the Attribute Type drop-down. After selecting it, a few new fields will appear in the Detail pane (Figure 3-35). Just like Interface Builder's inspector, the Detail pane in the model editor is context-sensitive. Some attribute types, such as the string type, have additional configuration options.

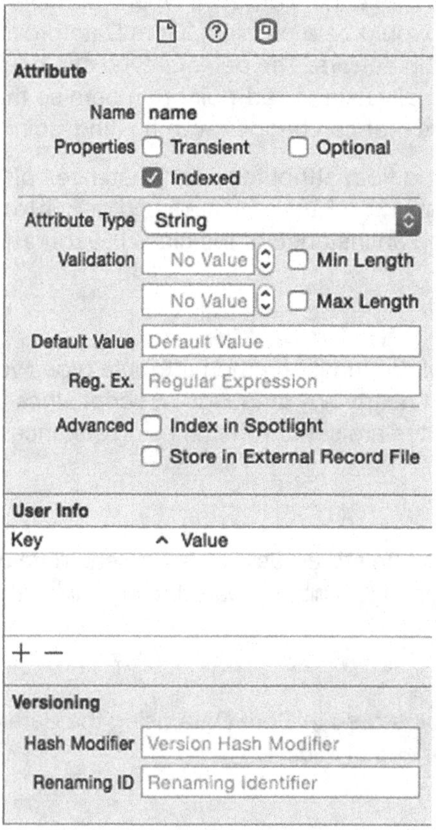

Figure 3-35. *The Detail pane after selecting the string type*

The Min Length and Max Length fields allow you to set a minimum and maximum number of characters for this field. If you enter a number into either field, any attempt to save a managed object that has fewer characters than the Min Length or more characters than Max Length stored in this attribute will result in a validation error at save time.

Note that this enforcement happens in the data model, not in the user interface. Unless you specifically enforce limitations through your user interface, these validations won't happen until you actually save the data model. In most instances, if you enforce a minimum or maximum length, you should also take some steps to enforce that in your user interface. Otherwise, the user won't be informed of the error until they try to save, which could be quite a while after they've entered data into this field. You'll see an example of enforcing this in Chapter 6.

The next field is Default Value. You can use this to, well, set a default value for this property. If you type a value into this field, any managed object based on this entity will automatically have its corresponding property set to whatever value you type in here. So, in this case, if you were to type Untitled Hero into this field, any time you created a new Hero managed object, the name property would automatically get set to Untitled Hero. Heck, that sounds like a good idea, so type **Untitled Hero** into this field.

The last field is labeled Reg. Ex., which stands for regular expression. This field allows you to do further validation on the entered text using regular expressions, which are special text strings that you can use to express patterns. You could, for example, use an attribute to store an Internet Protocol (IP) address in text and then ensure that only valid numerical IP addresses are entered by entering the regular expression \b\d{1,3}\.\d{1,3}\.\d{1,3}\.\d{1,3}\b. You're not going to use regular expressions for this attribute, so leave the Reg. Ex. field blank.

> **Note**   Regular expressions are a complex topic on which many full books have been written. Teaching regular expressions is way beyond the scope of this book, but if you're interested in using regular expressions to do data model–level validation, a good starting point is the Wikipedia page on regular expressions at http://en.wikipedia.org/wiki/Regular_expression, which covers the basic syntax and contains links to many related resources.

Finally, for good measure, save.

Adding the Rest of the Attributes

Your Hero entity needs three more attributes, so let's add them now. Click the Add Attribute button again. Give this one a name of **secretIdentity** and a type of string. Since, according to Mr. Incredible, every superhero has a secret identity, you'd better uncheck the Optional check box. You will be sorting and searching on secret identity, so select the Indexed box.

For Default Value, enter **Unknown**. Because you've made the field mandatory by unchecking the Optional check box, it's a good idea to provide a default value. Leave the rest of the fields as is.

> **Caution**   Be sure to enter default values for the name and secretIdentity attributes. If you don't, the program will behave badly. If your program crashes, check to make sure you've saved your source code files and your storyboard files.

Click the plus button a third time to add yet another attribute, giving it a name of **birthDate** and a type of date. Leave the rest of the fields at their default values for this attribute. You may not know the date of birth for all of your superheroes, so you want to leave this attribute as optional. As far as you know now, you won't be doing a lot of searching or ordering on birthdate, so there's no need to make this attribute indexed. You could do some additional validation here by setting a minimum, maximum, or default date, but there really isn't much need. There's no default value that would make sense, and setting a minimum or maximum date would preclude the possibility of an immortal superhero or a time-traveling one, which you certainly don't want to do!

This leaves you with one more attribute for this first iteration of your application: sex. There are a number of ways that you could choose to store this particular piece of information. For simplicity's sake (and because it will help you see a few helpful techniques in Chapter 6), you're just going to store a character string of either Male or Female. Add another attribute and select a type of string. Let's leave this as an optional setting; there might just be an androgynous masked avenger or two out there. You could use the regular expression field to limit inputs to either Male or Female, but, instead, you'll enforce that in the user interface by presenting a selection list rather than enforcing it here in the data model.

Guess what? You've now completed the data model for the first iteration of the SuperDB application. Save it and let's move on.

Declaring the Fetched Results Controller

To populate the table view, you need to fetch all the Hero entities stored in your persistent store. The best way to accomplish this is to use a fetched results controller inside the HeroListController.h file. To use a fetched results controller, you need to define its delegate to be notified when the fetched results change. To make things easy, you'll make the HeroListController the fetched results controller delegate.

Select HeroListController.h and change the @interface declaration to this:

```
@interface HeroListController : UIViewController <UITableViewDataSource,
UITableViewDelegate, UITabBarDelegate, NSFetchedResultsControllerDelegate>
```

Note   At this point, you might find that Xcode does not highlight the NSFetchedResultsControllerDelegate and might flag it as unknown or missing. This is because there has to be a reference to CoreData.h; you can either add the #import <CoreData/CoreData.h> or, as we have, add the #import AppDelegate.h, which imports the CoreData.h file.

Now that you've declared the NSFetchedResultsControllerDelegate, you need the controller. You could declare the property in HeroListController.h, but you don't actually need this property to be public. You're going use it only within the HeroListController. So, you'll make this a private property.

Select HeroListController.m, and scroll the editor to the top of the file, if necessary. Right above the @implementation declaration, you should find these lines:

```
#import "HeroListController.h"
#import "AppDelegate.h"

@interface HeroListController ()

@end
```

The @interface declaration is actually a category declaration. Note the empty parentheses at the end of the line. This is just a convention for declaring a category inside the implementation file. So, you'll change it to read as follows:

```
#import "HeroListController.h"
#import "AppDelegate.h"

@interface HeroListController ()
@property (nonatomic, strong, readonly) NSFetchedResultsController
*fetchedResultsController;
@end
```

You added the #import because you'll need it later. Add the appropriate @synthesize declaration after the @implementation, like so:

```
@synthesize fetchedResultsController = _fetchedResultsController;
```

Note   You may hear developers claim that using the underscore prefix is reserved by Apple and that you shouldn't use it. This is a misconception. Apple does, indeed, reserve the underscore prefix for the names of methods. It does not make any similar reservation when it comes to the names of instance variables. You can read Apple's naming convention for instance variables, which makes no restriction on the use of the underscore, at http://developer.apple.com/library/ios/#documentation/Cocoa/Conceptual/CodingGuidelines/Articles/NamingIvarsAndTypes.html.

Notice that the fetchedResultsController property is declared with the readonly keyword. You will be lazily loading the fetched results controller in the accessor method. You do not want other classes to be able to set fetchedResultsController, so you declare it readonly to prevent that from happening.

Implementing the Fetched Results Controller

Somewhere in the @implemention of HeroListController you need your managedObjectContext and fetchedResultsController methods. Let's add it just above the addHero: method.

```
#pragma mark - NSFetchedResultsControllerDelegate Property

- (NSFetchedResultsController *)fetchedResultsController
{
}
```

Like they used to say, where's the beef? Well, we wanted to step you through this line by line and explain the code. The full listing is available at the end of the chapter if you want to look ahead.

First, we said the fetched results controller was going to be lazily loaded, so here's the code to handle that:

```
if (_fetchedResultsController != nil) {
    return _fetchedResultsController;
}
```

If you get past this point, it means that the _fetchResultsController instance variable (or ivar) is nil, so you'll have to create one. First, you need to instantiate a fetch request.

```
NSFetchRequest *fetchRequest = [[NSFetchRequest alloc] init];
```

Now you get the entity description for your Hero entity and set the fetch request entity. While you're at it, set the fetch batch size, which breaks up the fetch into batches for performance reasons.

```
AppDelegate *appDelegate = (AppDelegate *)[[UIApplication sharedApplication] delegate];
NSManagedObjectContext *managedObjectContext = [appDelegate managedObjectContext];
NSEntityDescription *entity = [NSEntityDescription entityForName:@"Hero"
                                    inManagedObjectContext:managedObjectContext];
[fetchRequest setEntity:entity];
[fetchRequest setFetchBatchSize:20];
```

The order of the fetch results is going to depend on which tab you've selected, so you'll get that value. As a sanity check, read the user defaults if no tab is selected.

```
NSUInteger tabIndex = [self.heroTabBar.items indexOfObject:self.heroTabBar.selectedItem];
if (tabIndex == NSNotFound) {
    NSUserDefaults *defaults = [NSUserDefaults standardUserDefaults];
    tabIndex = [defaults integerForKey:kSelectedTabDefaultsKey];
}
```

Now you set the fetch request's sort descriptors. A sort descriptor is a simple object that tells the fetch request what property (attribute) should be used to compare instances of entities and whether it should be ascending or descending. A fetch request expects an array of sort descriptors, and the order of sort descriptors determines the order of priority when comparing.

```
NSString *sectionKey = nil;
switch (tabIndex) {
    // Notice that the kByName and kBySecretIdentity Code are nearly identical.
    // A refactoring opportunity?
    case kByName: {
        NSSortDescriptor *sortDescriptor1 = [[NSSortDescriptor alloc]
                                             initWithKey:@"name"
                                             ascending:YES];
        NSSortDescriptor *sortDescriptor2 = [[NSSortDescriptor alloc]
                                             initWithKey:@"secretIdentity"
                                             ascending:YES];
        NSArray *sortDescriptors =
            [[NSArray alloc] initWithObjects:sortDescriptor1, sortDescriptor2, nil];
        [fetchRequest setSortDescriptors:sortDescriptors];
        sectionKey = @"name";
        break;
    }
    case kBySecretIdentity:{
        NSSortDescriptor *sortDescriptor1 = [[NSSortDescriptor alloc]
                                             initWithKey:@"secretIdentity"
                                             ascending:YES];
        NSSortDescriptor *sortDescriptor2 = [[NSSortDescriptor alloc]
                                             initWithKey:@"name"
                                             ascending:YES];
        NSArray *sortDescriptors =
            [[NSArray alloc] initWithObjects:sortDescriptor1, sortDescriptor2, nil];
        [fetchRequest setSortDescriptors:sortDescriptors];
        sectionKey = @"secretIdentity";
        break;

    }
}
```

If the By Name tab is selected, you ask the fetch request to sort by the name attribute and then the secretIdentity. For the By Secret Identity tab, you reverse the sort descriptors. You set a sectionKey string, which you'll use next.

Now you finally instantiate the fetched results controller. Here's where you use the sectionKey and assign it a cache name of Hero. You assign the fetched results controller delegate to the HeroListController.

```
_fetchedResultsController =
    [[NSFetchedResultsController alloc] initWithFetchRequest:fetchRequest
                                 managedObjectContext:managedObjectContext
                                 sectionNameKeyPath:sectionKey
                                         cacheName:@"Hero"];
_fetchedResultsController.delegate = self;

return _fetchedResultsController;
```

Finally, you return the fetched results controller.

Fetched Results Controller Delegate Methods

Since you assigned the fetched results controller delegate to the HeroListController, you need to implement those methods. Add the following after the fetchedResultsController method you just created:

```
#pragma mark - NSFetchedResultsControllerDelegate Methods

- (void)controllerWillChangeContent:(NSFetchedResultsController *)controller
{
    [self.heroTableView beginUpdates];
}

- (void)controllerDidChangeContent:(NSFetchedResultsController *)controller
{
    [self.heroTableView endUpdates];
}

- (void)controller:(NSFetchedResultsController *)controller
  didChangeSection:(id <NSFetchedResultsSectionInfo>)sectionInfo
           atIndex:(NSUInteger)sectionIndex
     forChangeType:(NSFetchedResultsChangeType)type
{
    switch(type) {
        case NSFetchedResultsChangeInsert:
            [self.heroTableView insertSections:[NSIndexSet indexSetWithIndex:sectionIndex]
                              withRowAnimation:UITableViewRowAnimationFade];
            break;

        case NSFetchedResultsChangeDelete:
            [self.heroTableView deleteSections:[NSIndexSet indexSetWithIndex:sectionIndex]
                              withRowAnimation:UITableViewRowAnimationFade];
            break;
    }
}
```

```
- (void)controller:(NSFetchedResultsController *)controller
    didChangeObject:(id)anObject
        atIndexPath:(NSIndexPath *)indexPath
      forChangeType:(NSFetchedResultsChangeType)type
       newIndexPath:(NSIndexPath *)newIndexPath
{
    switch(type) {
        case NSFetchedResultsChangeInsert:
            [self.heroTableView insertRowsAtIndexPaths:@[newIndexPath]
                                    withRowAnimation:UITableViewRowAnimationFade];
            break;

        case NSFetchedResultsChangeDelete:
            [self.heroTableView deleteRowsAtIndexPaths:@[indexPath]
                                    withRowAnimation:UITableViewRowAnimationFade];
            break;

        case NSFetchedResultsChangeUpdate:
        case NSFetchedResultsChangeMove:
            break;

    }
}
```

For an explanation of these methods, refer to the "The Fetched Results Controller Delegate Methods" section of Chapter 2.

Making It All Work

You're almost done. You still need to do the following:

- Implement the Edit and Add (+) buttons
- Code the table view data source and delegate methods correctly
- Make the tab bar selector sort the table view
- Run the fetch request at launch
- Handle errors

It seems like a lot, but it's not. Let's start with the error handling first.

Error Handling

You'll make things simple by using a simple alert view to display errors. In the earlier versions of the iOS SDK, you would use the UIAlertView, but it also required you to set a delegate to handle the UIAlertViewDelegate methods. Now you can use the UIAlertController and pass it a block as the standard handler.

In HeroListController.m, you'll add a simple alert view handler method.

```
#pragma mark - UIAlertController Handler Method

-(void) dismissButtonOnAlertController:(UIAlertAction *)action {
    exit(-1);
}
```

All this method does is cause your application quit. And you can call it from a block while setting up the action buttons for the UIAlertController.

You also need a generic showAlert function that you can call to display an alert box on the screen.

```
-(void) showAlert:(NSString *) title
        message:(NSString*) message
     buttonText:(NSString *) buttonText
        handler:(void (^)(UIAlertAction *alert)) handler {
    UIAlertController *alert = [UIAlertController
            alertControllerWithTitle:title
                             message:message
                      preferredStyle:UIAlertControllerStyleAlert];
    UIAlertAction *OKButton = [UIAlertAction
            actionWithTitle:buttonText
                      style:UIAlertActionStyleDefault
                    handler:handler];
    [alert addAction:OKButton];
    [self presentViewController:alert animated:YES completion:nil];
}
```

Implementing Edit and Add

When the user taps the Add (+) button, the application does more than just add a row to the table view. It adds a new Hero entity to the managed object context. In the HeroListController.m file, modify the addHero method to read as follows:

```
- (IBAction)addHero:(id)sender
{
    NSManagedObjectContext *managedObjectContext =
        [self.fetchedResultsController managedObjectContext];

    NSEntityDescription *entity = [[self.fetchedResultsController fetchRequest] entity];
    [NSEntityDescription insertNewObjectForEntityForName:[entity name]
                                  inManagedObjectContext:managedObjectContext];

    NSError *error = nil;
    if (![managedObjectContext save:&error]) {
        NSString *message = [NSString
                stringWithFormat:@"Error was %@: quitting",[error localizedDescription]];
        [self showAlert:NSLocalizedString(@"Error saving entity", @"Error saving entity")
            message:NSLocalizedString(message, message);
```

```
                      buttonText:NSLocalizedString(@"Aw, nuts", @"Aw, nuts")
                      handler:^(UIAlertAction *alert) {
                        [self dismissButtonOnAlertController:alert];
                      }];
        }
}
```

When the Edit button is tapped, the setEditing:animated: method is automatically called.
So, you just need to add that method to your HeroListController.m without having declare
it in the interface file.

```
- (void)setEditing:(BOOL)editing animated:(BOOL)animated
{
    [super setEditing:editing animated:animated];
    self.addButton.enabled = !editing;
    [self.heroTableView setEditing:editing animated:animated];
}
```

All you do here is call the super method, disable the Add (+) button (you don't want to be
adding heroes while editing!), and call setEditing:animated on the table view.

Coding the Table View Data Source and Delegate

Using the CoreDataApp from Chapter 2 as an example, you need to change the following
table view data source methods:

```
- (NSInteger)numberOfSectionsInTableView:(UITableView *)tableView
{
    return [[self.fetchedResultsController sections] count];
}

- (NSInteger)tableView:(UITableView *)tableView numberOfRowsInSection:(NSInteger)section
{
    id <NSFetchedResultsSectionInfo> sectionInfo =
    [[self.fetchedResultsController sections] objectAtIndex:section];
    return [sectionInfo numberOfObjects];
}
```

Next, you handle the table view cell creation, like so:

```
- (UITableViewCell *)tableView:(UITableView *)tableView
        cellForRowAtIndexPath:(NSIndexPath *)indexPath
{
    static NSString *CellIdentifier = @"HeroListCell";
    UITableViewCell *cell = [tableView dequeueReusableCellWithIdentifier:CellIdentifier];

    // Configure the cell...
    NSManagedObject *aHero = [self.fetchedResultsController objectAtIndexPath:indexPath];
    NSInteger tab = [self.heroTabBar.items indexOfObject:self.heroTabBar.selectedItem];
```

```
    switch (tab) {
        case kByName:
            cell.textLabel.text = [aHero valueForKey:@"name"];
            cell.detailTextLabel.text = [aHero valueForKey:@"secretIdentity"];
            break;
        case kBySecretIdentity:
            cell.textLabel.text = [aHero valueForKey:@"secretIdentity"];
            cell.detailTextLabel.text = [aHero valueForKey:@"name"];
            break;
    }

    return cell;
}
```

Finally, you uncomment tableView:commitEditingStyle:forRowAtIndexPath: to handle
deleting rows.

```
// Override to support editing the table view.
- (void)tableView:(UITableView *)tableView
        commitEditingStyle:(UITableViewCellEditingStyle)editingStyle
        forRowAtIndexPath:(NSIndexPath *)indexPath
{
    NSManagedObjectContext *managedObjectContext = [self.fetchedResultsController
                                                    managedObjectContext];

    if (editingStyle == UITableViewCellEditingStyleDelete) {
        // Delete the row from the data source
        [managedObjectContext deleteObject:[self.fetchedResultsController
                                            objectAtIndexPath:indexPath]];

        NSError *error = nil;
        if (![managedObjectContext save:&error]) {
            NSString *message = [NSString
                    stringWithFormat:@"Error was %@: quitting",[error localizedDescription]];
            [self showAlert:NSLocalizedString(@"Error saving entity", @"Error saving entity")
                message: NSLocalizedString(message, message);
              buttonText:NSLocalizedString(@"Aw, nuts", @"Aw, nuts")
              handler:^(UIAlertAction *alert) {
                [self dismissButtonOnAlertController:alert];
                }];
        }
    }
}
```

Sorting the Table View

You need to make the table view order change when you toggle the tab bar. You need to add the following code to the tabBar:didSelectItem: delegate method:

```
- (void)tabBar:(UITabBar *)tabBar didSelectItem:(UITabBarItem *)item
{
    NSUserDefaults *defaults = [NSUserDefaults standardUserDefaults];
    NSUInteger tabIndex = [tabBar.items indexOfObject:item];
    [defaults setInteger:tabIndex forKey:kSelectedTabDefaultsKey];

    [NSFetchedResultsController deleteCacheWithName:@"Hero"];
    _fetchedResultsController.delegate = nil;
    _fetchedResultsController = nil;

    NSError *error;
    if (![self.fetchedResultsController performFetch:&error]) {
        NSLog(@"Error performing fetch: %@", [error localizedDescription]);
    }

    [self.heroTableView reloadData];
}
```

Loading the Fetch Request at Launch

Add the following to the HeroListController.m viewDidLoad method:

```
// Fetch any existing entities
NSError *error = nil;
if (![[self fetchedResultsController] performFetch:&error]) {
        NSString *message = [NSString
                stringWithFormat:@"Error was %@: quitting",[error localizedDescription]];
        [self showAlert:NSLocalizedString(@"Error fetching entity", @"Error fetching entity")
            message: NSLocalizedString(message, message)
          buttonText:NSLocalizedString(@"Aw, nuts", @"Aw, nuts")
            handler:^(UIAlertAction *alert) {
              [self dismissButtonOnAlertController:alert];
            }];
}
```

And that's pretty much everything.

Let 'Er Rip

Well, what are you waiting for? That was a lot of work; you deserve to try it. Make sure everything is saved and then build and run the app.

If everything went OK, when the application first launches, you should be presented with an empty table with a navigation bar at the top and a tab bar at the bottom (Figure 3-36). Pressing the right button in the navigation bar will add a new unnamed superhero to the database. Pressing the Edit button will allow you to delete heroes.

Figure 3-36. The SuperDB application at launch time

> **Note**   If your app crashed when you ran it, there's a couple of things to look for. First, make sure you saved all your source code before you ran your project. Also, make sure you have defaults specified for your hero's name and secret identity in your data model editor. If you did that and your app still crashes, try resetting your simulator. Here's how: bring up the simulator, and from the iPhone Simulator menu, select Reset Contents and Settings. That should do it. In Chapter 5, you'll see how to ensure that changes to your data model don't cause such problems.

Add a few unnamed superheroes to your application and try the two tabs to make sure that the display changes when you select a new tab. When you select the By Name tab, it should look like Figure 3-1, but when you select the By Secret Identity tab, it should look like Figure 3-37.

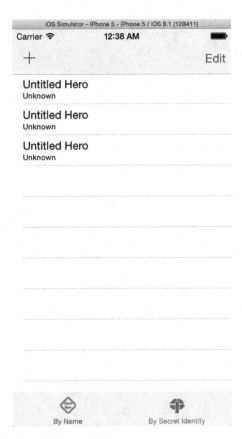

Figure 3-37. Selecting the By Secret Identity tab doesn't change the order of the rows yet, but it does change which value is displayed first

Done, but Not Done

In this chapter, you did a lot of work. You saw how to set up a navigation-based application that uses a tab bar, and you learned how to design a basic Core Data data model by creating an entity and giving it several attributes.

This application isn't done, but you've now laid a solid foundation upon which to move forward. When you're ready, turn the page and start creating a detail editing page to allow users to edit their superheroes.

Chapter 4

The Devil in the Detail View

In Chapter 3, you built your application's main view controller. You set it up to display heroes ordered by their name or their secret identity, and you put in place the infrastructure needed to save, delete, and add new heroes. What you didn't do was give the user a way to edit the information about a particular hero, which means you're limited to creating and deleting superheroes named Untitled Hero. Guess you can't ship your application yet.

That's OK. Application development is an iterative process, and the first several iterations of any application likely won't have enough functionality to stand on its own. In this chapter, you'll create an editable detail view to let the user edit the data for a specific superhero.

The controller you'll write will be a subclass of `UITableViewController`, and you'll use an approach that is somewhat conceptually complex but one that will be easy to maintain and expand. This is important because you're going to be adding new attributes to the `Hero` managed object, as well as expanding it in other ways, so you'll need to keep changing the user interface to accommodate those changes.

After you've written your new detail view controller, you will then add functionality to allow the user to edit each attribute, *in place.*

View Implementation Choices

In *Beginning iPhone Development* you learned how to build a user interface using Interface Builder. Building your editable detail views in Interface Builder is definitely one way to go. But another common approach is to implement your detail view as a grouped table. Take a look at your iPhone's Contacts application or the Contacts tab of the Phone application (Figure 4-1). The detail editing view in Apple's navigation applications is often implemented using a grouped table rather than using an interface designed in Interface Builder.

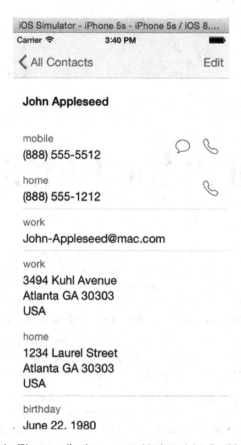

Figure 4-1. *The Contacts tab of the iPhone application uses a table-based detail editing view*

The iOS Human Interface Guidelines (http://developer.apple.com/library/ios/ documentation/UserExperience/Conceptual/MobileHIG) do not give any real guidance as to when you should use a table-based detail view as opposed to a detail view designed in Interface Builder, so it comes down to a question of which feels right. Here's our take: if you're building a navigation-based application and the data can reasonably and efficiently be presented in a grouped table, it probably should be. Since your superhero data is structured much like the data displayed in the Contacts application, a table-based detail view seems the obvious choice.

The table view shown in Figure 4-2 displays data from a single hero, which means that everything in that table comes from a single managed object. Each row corresponds to a different attribute of the managed object. The first section's only row displays the hero's name, for example. When in editing mode, tapping a specific row will display the appropriate subview to modify that attribute. For a string, it will present a keyboard; for a date, it will present a date picker.

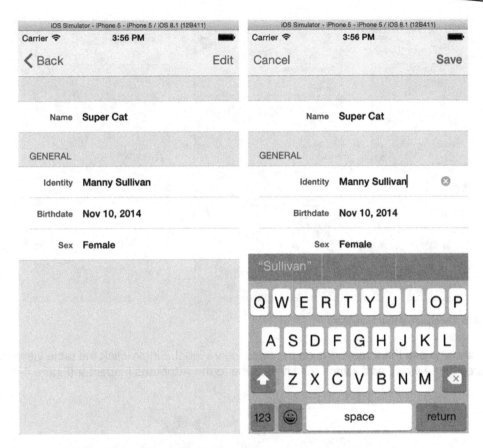

Figure 4-2. The detail view that you'll be building in this application, in view and editing mode

The organization of the table view into sections and rows is not determined by the managed object. Instead, it is the result of design decisions you, as the developer, must make by trying to anticipate what will make sense to your users. You could, for example, put the attributes in alphabetical order, which would put birthDate first. That wouldn't have been very intuitive because birthdate is not the most important or defining attribute of a hero. In our minds, the hero's name and secret identity are the most important attributes and thus should be the first two elements presented in your table view.

Creating the Detail View Controller

Find your SuperDB project folder from Chapter 3 and make a copy of it. This way, if things go south when you add your new code for this chapter, you won't have to start at the beginning. Open this new copy of your project in Xcode.

Next, create the detail view controller. Remember that you're creating a table-based editing view, so you want to subclass UITableViewController. Select SuperDB.storyboard and open the storyboard editor. Open the Utility pane, if it's not already open, and find the table view controller in the Object Library. Drag it onto the storyboard editor, to the right of the HeroListController (Figure 4-3).

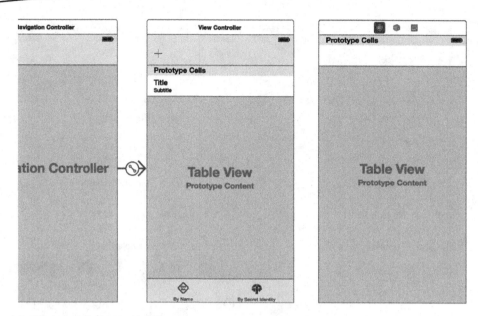

Figure 4-3. *The layout of your storyboard*

Make sure you see the three icons on the table view's label. Single-click the table view (the grey area of the view), and switch the Utility pane to the Attributes Inspector (Figure 4-4).

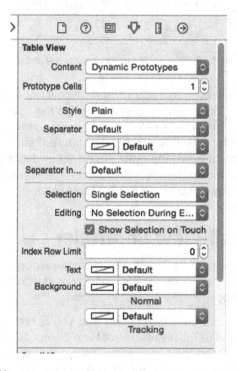

Figure 4-4. *Table view's attributes*

Let's look at Figure 4-2 again. Your detail view has two sections, so let's configure the table view that way. Change the Style field from Plain to Grouped. Once that's done, the Separator field should have changed itself to Default. Next, you know the number of rows in each section: one and three, respectively. Since that number is fixed, you can change the Content field from Dynamic Prototypes to Static Cells. Again, the field right below the Content field automatically changed from Prototype Cells to Sections. You know the number of sections is two, so enter 2 in that field. Finally, you don't want to have the cells highlight on selection, so change the Selection field to No Selection. The Attributes Inspector for the table view should look like Figure 4-5.

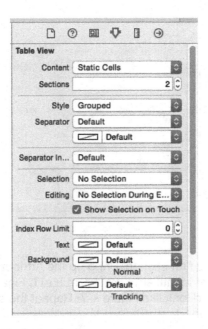

Figure 4-5. The final state of your table view attributes

Your table view should have two sections of three cells each (Figure 4-6). Section 1 has too many cells. You need only one cell. Select the second cell in section 1. It should highlight. Delete the cell (press the Delete key, or Edit ➤ Delete). Section 1 should now have two cells, with the bottom cell highlighted. Delete that cell, too.

Figure 4-6. Table view

Select the table view cell in the first section. Bring up the Attributes Inspector. Change Style from Custom to Left Detail. Set Identifier to HeroDetailCell. Finally, set Selection to None. The Attributes Inspector should look like Figure 4-7. Repeat the settings for the three table view cells in the second section.

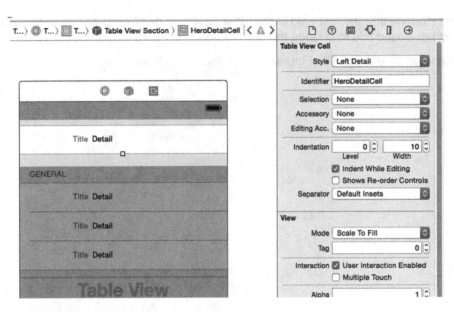

Figure 4-7. Table view cell's attributes

The second section needs a header label, General. Select the area right above or right below the three cells in the second section. The Attributes Inspector should change to Table View Section (Figure 4-8). In the Header field, enter **General**. Now the second section should have the correct header label.

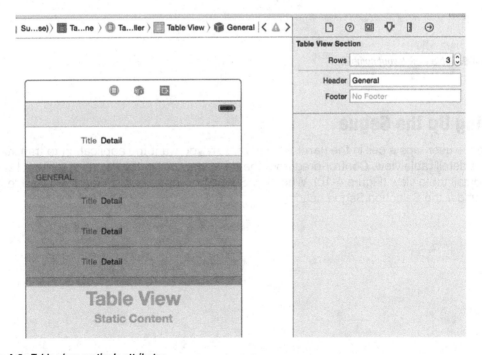

Figure 4-8. Table view section's attributes

By the way, notice that the first field in the table view section's Attributes Inspector is Rows. You could have used this to change the first section's row count from three to one.

Your table view should look like Figure 4-9. The layout is all set.

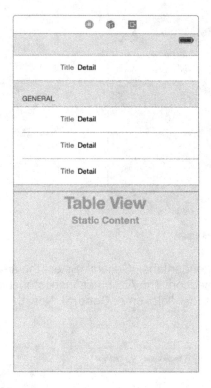

Figure 4-9. *Table view layout complete*

Wiring Up the Segue

When the user taps a cell in the HeroListController, you want the application to transition to your detail table view. Control-drag from the table view cell in the HeroListController to your detail table view (Figure 4-10). When the Segue pop-up appears (Figure 4-11), select push under the Selection Segue header.

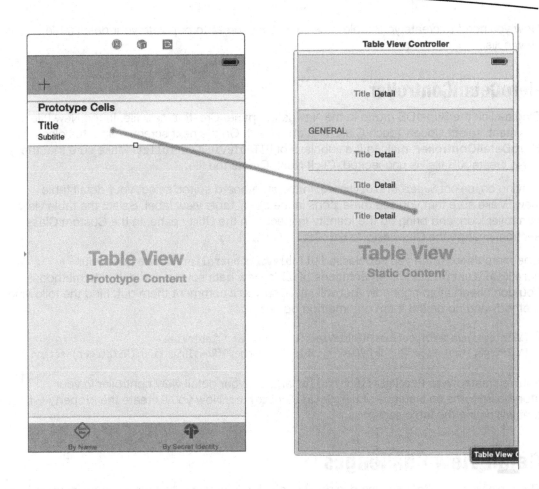

Figure 4-10. Control-drag to create the segue

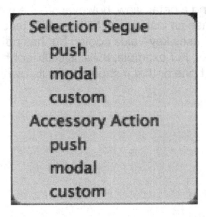

Figure 4-11. Segue pop-up selector

Now you need to create your table view subclass in order to populate your detail table view cells.

HeroDetailController

Single-click the SuperDB group in the Navigation pane. Create a new file. In the New File Assistant, select Cocoa Touch Class and click Next. On the next screen, name the class **HeroDetailController**, making it a subclass of UITableViewController. Make sure that the "Also create XIB file" is unchecked. Click Next. Create the file.

Moving on, select SuperDB.storyboard. In the storyboard editor, select your detail table view. Make sure that you see three icons in the detail table view label. Select the table view controller icon, and bring up the Identity Inspector in the Utility pane. In the Custom Class section, change the Class field to HeroDetailController.

One more thing: when you subclassed UITableViewController, Xcode gave your HeroDetailController implementations of table view data source and delegate methods. You don't need them right now (but will later), so you'll comment them out. Find the following methods and comment them out (method bodies, too):

```
- (NSInteger)numberOfSectionsInTableView:(UITableView *)tableView
- (NSInteger)tableView:(UITableView *)tableView numberOfRowsInSection:(NSInteger)section
```

You've created your HeroDetailController and set your detail view controller in your storyboard to be an instance of HeroDetailController. Now you'll create the property list that will define the table sections.

Detail View Challenges

The table view architecture was designed to efficiently present data stored in collections. For example, you might use a table view to display data in an NSArray or in a fetched results controller. When you're creating a detail view, however, you're typically presenting data from a single object, in this case an instance of NSManagedObject that represents a single superhero. A managed object uses key-value coding but has no mechanism to present its attributes in a meaningful order. For example, NSManagedObject has no idea that the name attribute is the most important one or that it should be in its own section the way it is in Figure 4-2.

Coming up with a good, maintainable way to specify the sections and rows in a detail editing view is a nontrivial task. The most obvious solution, and one you'll frequently see in online sample code, uses an enum to list the table sections, followed by additional enums for each section, containing constants and a count of rows for each section, like so:

```
enum HeroEditControllerSections {
    HeroEditControllerSectionName = 0,
    HeroEditControllerSectionGeneral,
    HeroEditControllerSectionCount
};

enum HeroEditControllerNameSection {
    HeroEditControllerNameRow = 0,
    HeroEditControllerNameSectionCount
};

enum HeroEditControllerGeneralSection {
    HeroEditControllerGeneralSectionSecretIdentityRow,
    HeroEditControllerGeneralSectionBirthdateRow,
    HeroEditControllerGeneralSectionSexRow,
    HeroEditControllerGeneralSectionCount
};
```

Then, in every method where you are provided with an index path, you can take the appropriate action based on the row and section represented by the index path, using switch statements, like this:

```
- (void)tableView:(UITableView *)tableView didSelectRowAtIndexPath:(NSIndexPath *)indexPath
{
    NSUInteger section = [indexPath section];
    NSUInteger row = [indexPath row];

    switch (section) {
        case HeroEditControllerSectionName:
            switch (row)
        {
            case HeroEditControllerNameRow :
                // Create a controller to edit name
                // and push it on the stack
                ...
                break;
            default:
                break;
        }
            break;
```

```
    case HeroEditControllerSectionGeneral:
        switch (row) {
            case HeroEditControllerGeneralSectionSecretIdentityRow:
                // Create a controller to edit secret identity
                // and push it on the stack
                ...
                break;
            case HeroEditControllerGeneralSectionBirthdateRow:
                // Create a controller to edit birthdate and
                // push it on the stack
                ...
                break;
            case HeroEditControllerGeneralSectionSexRow:
                // Create a controller to edit sex and push it
                // on the stack
                ...
                break;
            default:
                break;
        }
        break;
    default:
        break;
    }
}
```

The problem with this approach is that it doesn't scale well at all. A nested set of switch statements like this will need to appear in almost every table view delegate or data source method that takes an index path, which means that adding or deleting rows or sections involves updating your code in multiple places.

Additionally, the code under each of the case statements is going to be relatively similar. In this particular case, you will have to create a new instance of a controller or use a pointer to an existing controller, set some properties to indicate which values need to get edited, and then push the controller onto the navigation stack. If you discover a problem in your logic anywhere in these switch statements, chances are you're going to have to change that logic in several places, possibly even dozens.

Controlling the Table Structure with Property Lists

As you can see, the most obvious solution isn't always the best one. You don't want to have similar chunks of code scattered throughout your controller class, and you don't want to have to maintain multiple copies of a complex decision tree. There's a better way to do this.

You can use property lists to mirror the structure of your table. As the user navigates down the app, you can use the data stored in a property list to construct the appropriate table. Property lists are a simple but powerful way to store information.

Let's quickly review property lists here.

Property Lists Explained

Property lists are a simple way to represent, store, and retrieve data. Both Mac OS X and iOS make extensive use of property lists. Within property lists, two kinds of data types can be used: primitive and collections. The primitive types available are strings, numbers, binary data, dates, and Boolean values. The available collection types are arrays and dictionaries. The collections types can contain both primitive types and additional collections. Property lists can be stored in two file types: XML and binary data. Xcode provides a property list editor to make the management of property lists easier for you. We'll discuss that in a little bit.

Property lists start with a *root node*. Technically, the root node can be of any type, primitive or collection. However, a property list of a primitive type has limited usefulness because it would be a "list" of one value. More common is a root node of a collection type: an array or a dictionary. When you create a property list with the Xcode property list editor, the root node will be a dictionary.

> **Note**   To learn more detail about property lists, read Apple's documentation at
> `http://developer.apple.com/library/ios/documentation/Cocoa/Conceptual/`
> `PropertyLists/Introduction/Introduction.html`.

Modeling Table Structure with a Property List

So, how can you use a property list to describe your table? Refer to Figure 4-2. Looking at the table, you can see two sections. The first section has no header, but the second section has a header of General. Each section has a certain number of rows (one and three, respectively) where each row represents a specific attribute of your managed object. Additionally, each row also has a label, which tells you what value is being displayed.

To start, you represent the table as an array, with each item in the array representing a section of the table. Each section, in turn, will be represented by a dictionary. You have a header key in the section dictionary, which stores the string value of the header. Note that the first section of the table does not have a header; you just use an empty string to represent it.

> **Note**   If you recall, there are only five primitive data types in a property list: string, numbers, binary data, dates, and Booleans. That doesn't leave you with a way to represent `nil` values. So you must rely on an empty string to represent `nil`.

The second key of the section dictionary will be rows. The value for this key will be another array, where each item of the rows array will represent the data to render the row. To represent a row, you'll use another dictionary. This row dictionary will have a key of label, referencing a string that will be used as the row label plus a key of attribute, which will be a string of the managed object's attribute to render in the row.

Confused? Don't worry, it's difficult to model things descriptively. Figure 4-12 explains it graphically.

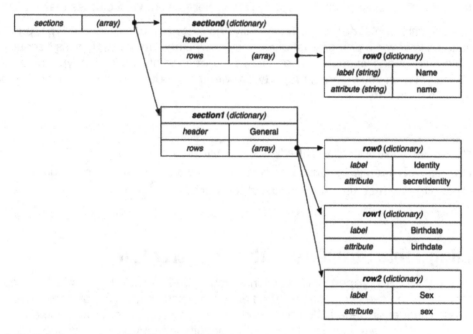

Figure 4-12. *Graphical representation of your property list*

That should be all the data structures you need to represent the table's structure to start. Fortunately, if you discover that you need additional information for each row, you can always add data later without impacting your existing design.

Let's begin building your detail view.

Defining the Table View via Property List

In the Navigator pane, select the Supporting Files group so that it is highlighted. Now, create a new file. Once the new file template appears, select Resource under the iOS heading. Choose the Property List template (Figure 4-13) and click Next. Name the file HeroDetailConfiguration.plist and click Create. A new file, named HeroDetailConfiguration.plist, should appear in the Supporting Files group. The file should be selected, and the editor should switch to the property list editor (Figure 4-14).

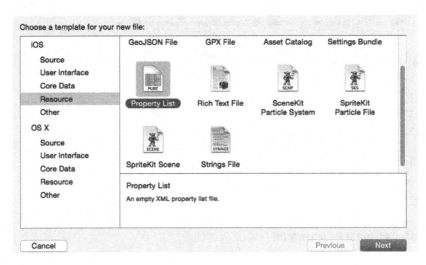

Figure 4-13. Resource file templates

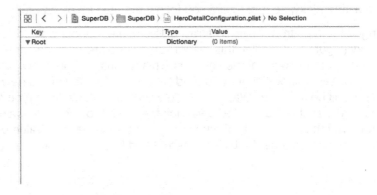

Figure 4-14. Xcode property list editor mode

Earlier we stated that the root node of a property list is a dictionary. That means each node will be a key/value pair. You can treat the key as a string, and the value can be of any of the primitive (string, number, binary data, date, or Boolean) or collection (array or dictionary) data types.

You're going to start by creating the sections array, as we discussed earlier. To do so, you need to add a new item to the property list. There are two ways to do this. Both methods require you select the row with the name Root in the Key column. Using the first method, Control-click in the blank area of the property list editor. When the pop-up menu appears, choose Add Row. Alternately, you can use the regular menu Editor ➤ Add Item option. Either way, a new row should appear in the property list editor (Figure 4-15). The item should have a key of New item, which will be selected and highlighted. Type **sections** and press Return to change the key name.

Figure 4-15. Adding an item to the property list

Next, click the arrows next to string under the Type column to expose the possible data types. Select array. The Value column should change to read (0 items). Adding items to the sections array is a little tricky, so make sure you follow the next steps carefully.

When you changed the type from string to array, a disclosure triangle was added to the left of the sections key (Figure 4-16). Click this triangle so it is pointed downward (Figure 4-17). Now click the + button to the right of the sections. This will insert a new row. Additionally, the Value column for sections will change to read "(1 item)." The key of the new row will be Item 0; the type will be string; the Value column will be selected. Don't type anything; select the sections row so it is highlighted and click the + next to sections again. This will insert another row with the key Item 1, of type string, with no value. The Value cell should be selected with a cursor. Change the type for Item 0 and Item 1 from string to dictionary (Figure 4-18).

Key	Type	Value
▼ Root	Dictionary	(1 item)
▶ sections	Array	(0 items)

Figure 4-16. Changing the type from string to array

Key	Type	Value
▼ Root	Dictionary	(1 item)
▼ sections	Array	(0 items)

Figure 4-17. Click the disclosure triangle to open the array

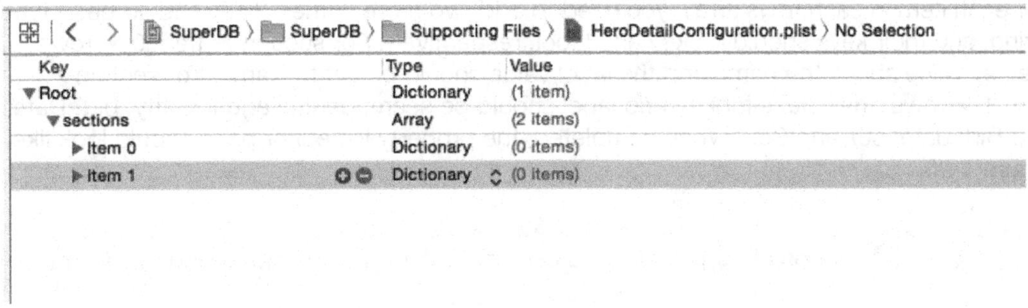

Figure 4-18. Adding two dictionary items

Remember that you were going to create an array where each item in the array represented a section of your table view? You've created those two items. Item 0 is the first section of HeroDetailController table view; Item 1 is the second.

Now you create the rows array under each section to hold the row information for each section. Next to Item 0 there should be a disclosure triangle. Open it and click the + next to Item 0. This will create a new row with key New Item, of type string, under Item 0. Change the key to rows and change the type to array. Open the disclosure triangle next to rows and click the + button. This will create another Item 0, this time under rows. Change the type from string to dictionary. Repeat this procedure, adding a rows item under the Item 1 header. This time, create three items under this second rows item. Your property list editor should look like Figure 4-19.

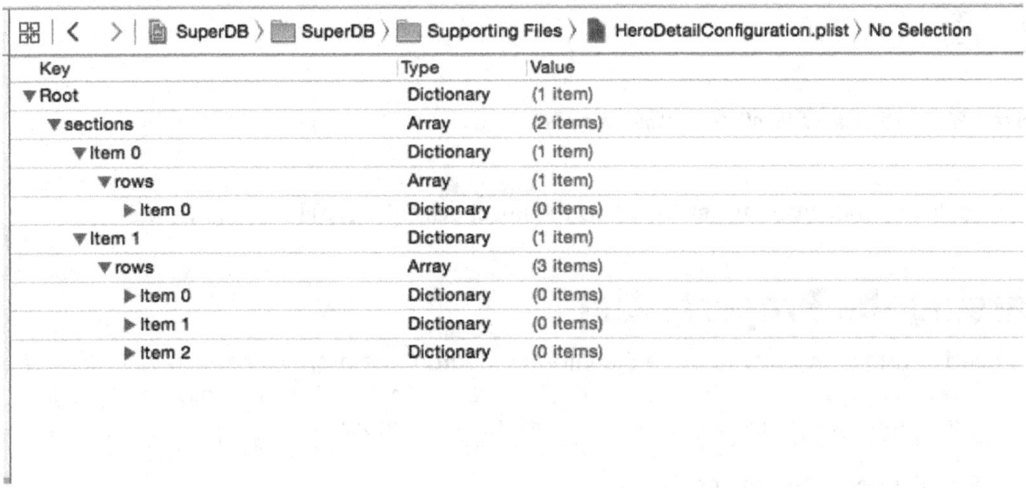

Figure 4-19. HeroDetailConfiguration.plist

For each item in each rows array, you need to add two more entries. They should be of type string, and their keys should be key and label, respectively. For section ➤ Item 0 ➤ rows, the key value should be name and the label value should be set to Name. For section ➤ Item 1 ➤ rows, the values for key and label should be secretIdentity and Identity; birthDate and Birthdate; sex and Sex. When completed, the property list editor pane should look like Figure 4-20.

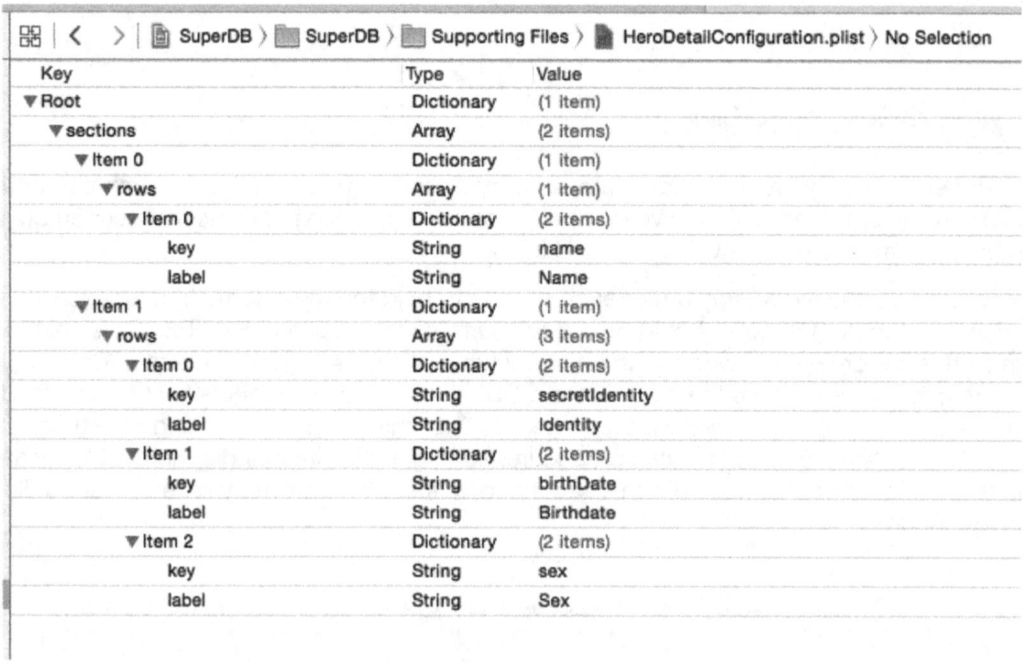

Key	Type	Value
🔲 | < > | 📄 SuperDB ⟩ 📁 SuperDB ⟩ 📁 Supporting Files ⟩ 📄 HeroDetailConfiguration.plist ⟩ No Selection		
▼ Root	Dictionary	(1 item)
▼ sections	Array	(2 items)
▼ Item 0	Dictionary	(1 item)
▼ rows	Array	(1 item)
▼ Item 0	Dictionary	(2 items)
key	String	name
label	String	Name
▼ Item 1	Dictionary	(1 item)
▼ rows	Array	(3 items)
▼ Item 0	Dictionary	(2 items)
key	String	secretIdentity
label	String	Identity
▼ Item 1	Dictionary	(2 items)
key	String	birthDate
label	String	Birthdate
▼ Item 2	Dictionary	(2 items)
key	String	sex
label	String	Sex

Figure 4-20. The completed HeroDetailConfiguration.plist

Now, you'll use this property list to set up the HeroDetailController table view.

Parsing the Property List

You need to add a property to store the information from the property list you just created. Since this property needs to be used by the HeroDetailController internally only, you'll make it a private, via the category in HeroDetailController.m.

```
@interface HeroDetailController ()
@property (strong, nonatomic) NSArray *sections;
@end
```

Next, you need to load the property list and read the sections key. Before the end of viewDidLoad, add the following:

```
NSURL *plistURL = [[NSBundle mainBundle] URLForResource:@"HeroDetailConfiguration"
                                          withExtension:@"plist"];
NSDictionary *plist = [NSDictionary dictionaryWithContentsOfURL:plistURL];
self.sections = [plist valueForKey:@"sections"];
```

You declare a property, sections, of type NSArray, to hold the contents of the sections array in your HeroDetailConfiguration.plist property list. You read in the contents of the property list using the NSDictionary class method dictionaryWithContentsOfURL:. Since you know that this dictionary has only one key/value pair, with a key of sections, you read that value into sections property. You then use that property to lay out the HeroDetailController table view.

You now have the metadata needed to populate your HeroDetailController's table view cells, but you don't have the data. The data should come from the HeroListController in one of two ways: when the user taps a cell and when the user taps the Add (+) button.

Pushing the Details

Before you can send the data down from the HeroListController, you need something to receive it in the HeroDetailController. Add #import "AppDelegate.h" just after the #import <UIKit/UIKit.h> and add the following property to the HeroDetailController interface declaration in HeroDetailController.h:

```
@property (strong, nonatomic) NSManagedObject *hero;
```

Now edit HeroListController.m. Find the addHero: method. Change the line that reads as follows

```
[NSEntityDescription insertNewObjectForEntityForName:[entity name]
                              inManagedObjectContext:managedObjectContext];
```

to the following:

```
NSManagedObject *newHero = [NSEntityDescription insertNewObjectForEntityForName:[entity name]
                                                inManagedObjectContext:managedObjectContext];
```

Then add the following to the end:

```
[self performSegueWithIdentifier:@"HeroDetailSegue" sender:newHero];
```

First, you assign your new Hero instance to the variable newHero. Then you told the HeroListController to execute the segue named HeroDetailSegue and pass newHero as the sender. Where did that segue name, HeroDetailSegue, come from? From you.

Remember the segue you created earlier for when a user taps a cell in the HeroListController? Well, now you're going to get rid of it. Why? Because it doesn't give you the flexibility you need to transition from both a cell and the Add (+) button. You need to create a manual segue and invoke it from code.

Select the SuperDB.storyboard file and find the segue between the HeroListController and the HeroDetailController. Delete it. Control-drag from the HeroListController (the icon in the label) to the HeroDetailController (somewhere in the view). A pop-up menu appears; choose the push menu item. A new segue should appear between the two view controllers; select it. In the Attributes Inspector, give it the identifier HeroDetailSegue (Figure 4-21).

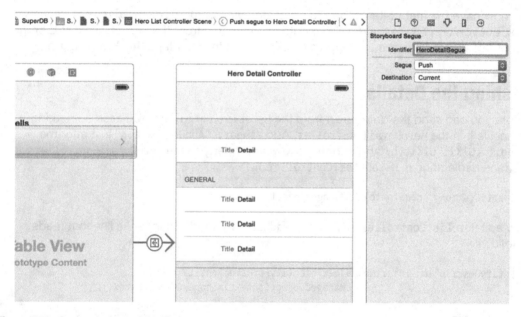

Figure 4-21. Setting the segue identifier

Now you need to connect the HeroListController cells to the HeroDetailSegue. Edit HeroListController.m. Find the method tableView:didSelectRowAtIndexPath: and simply create the function as follows:

```
-(void) tableView:(UITableView *)tableView didSelectRowAtIndexPath:(NSIndexPath *)indexPath
{
NSManagedObject *selectedHero = [self.fetchedResultsController objectAtIndexPath:indexPath];
[self performSegueWithIdentifier:@"HeroDetailSegue" sender:selectedHero];
}
```

You're essentially doing the same thing you did in addHero:, except that the Hero object is coming from the fetched results controller rather than being created. This looks good so far, but you still aren't sending data to the HeroDetailController. You handle that in the UIViewController method prepareForSegue:sender:. Add this method to HeroListController.m (uncomment it from the template code; if it is not present in the template, you can put it anywhere, but you put it after the setEditing:animated: method):

```
- (void)prepareForSegue:(UIStoryboardSegue *)segue sender:(id)sender
{
    // Get the new view controller using [segue destinationViewController].
    // Pass the selected object to the new view controller.
    if ([segue.identifier isEqualToString:@"HeroDetailSegue"])
    {
        if ([sender isKindOfClass:[NSManagedObject class]]) {
            HeroDetailController *detailController = segue.destinationViewController;
            detailController.hero = sender;
        }
        else {
            NSString *message = NSLocalizedString(@"Error trying to show Hero detail",
                                                   @"Error trying to show Hero detail");
            [self showAlert:NSLocalizedString(@"Hero Detail Error", @"Hero Detail Error")
                    message:NSLocalizedString(message, message)
                 buttonText:NSLocalizedString(@"Aw, nuts", @"Aw, nuts")
                    handler:^(UIAlertAction *alert) {
                      [self dismissButtonOnAlertController:alert];
                    }];
        }
    }
}
```

Note that prepareForSegue:sender: is called by performSegueWithName:sender: internally. It's a hook Apple gives you to set things up correctly before showing the HeroDetailController.

By the way, Xcode should have complained about HeroDetailController and detailController.hero. Add the following #import at the top of HeroListController.m:

```
#import "HeroDetailController.h"
```

Showing the Details

You're sending the Hero object down from HeroListController to the HeroDetailController. Now you're ready to show the details. Edit HeroDetailController.m and find tableView:c ellForRowAtIndexPath:. Remember, it is commented, so it won't show up in the jump bar function menu. Uncomment it and replace the body with this:

```
static NSString *CellIdentifier = @"HeroDetailCell";
UITableViewCell *cell = [tableView dequeueReusableCellWithIdentifier:CellIdentifier];
if (cell == nil)
cell = [[UITableViewCell alloc] initWithStyle:UITableViewCellStyleValue2
                  reuseIdentifier:CellIdentifier];

// Configure the cell...
NSUInteger sectionIndex = [indexPath section];
NSUInteger rowIndex = [indexPath row];

NSDictionary *section = [self.sections objectAtIndex:sectionIndex];
NSArray *rows = [section objectForKey:@"rows"];
NSDictionary *row = [rows objectAtIndex:rowIndex];
cell.textLabel.text = [row objectForKey:@"label"];
cell.detailTextLabel.text = [self.hero valueForKey:[row objectForKey:@"key"]];

return cell;
```

Build and run the app. You get your list of heroes. Tap one to see the details; your detail view should look like Figure 4-22.

Figure 4-22. Detail view for a new hero

Editing the Details

Look back at Figure 4-2 and compare it to Figure 4-22. Note that the left image in Figure 4-2 has an Edit button on the right side of the navigation bar, and Figure 4-2 specifies that you have an Edit mode for the detail view, as shown in the right image. Let's add the Edit button and implement the Edit mode in the HeroDetailController.

Editing Mode in the Detail View

Compare the two images in Figure 4-2. How do they differ? First, the Edit button in the left image has been replaced with a Save button in the right image. Also, the Save button is highlighted. The Back button has been replaced with a Cancel button. The cells in the right image appear to be indented. While it appears to be a lot of changes, it's actually not that much effort to implement.

First, add the Edit button to the navigation bar. Select HeroDetailController.m and find the viewDidLoad method. Uncomment the following line:

```
self.navigationItem.rightBarButtonItem = self.editButtonItem;
```

Run the application and drill down to the detail view. There's the Edit button on the right side of the navigation bar. If you click it, the view should change to look like Figure 4-23.

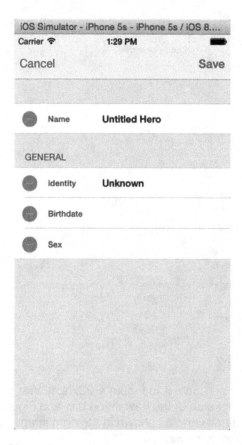

Figure 4-23. *The detail view in editing mode*

Note that the Edit button has automatically changed into a Done button and is highlighted. If you tap Done, it will revert into the Edit button. This is fine, but you really want the Done button to read Save. That's a little more work.

As you've seen, the editButtonItem method gives you an instance of a UIBarButton that toggles between Edit and Done when pressed. It also toggles the editing property in your HeroDetailController (which inherits the property from UITableViewController) between NO and YES. The button also invokes the setEditing:animated: callback.

You want to replace the Done with Save. To accomplish this, you need to replace the Edit button with a Save button. While you're at it, add a specific method to handle the saving, which you'll use later. First, you need to add a property for the Save button and a callback method. Since you access the Save button only inside HeroDetailController, you can make it a private property. And since the callback is used only by the Save button, you can make that a private declaration as well. Edit HeroDetailController.m and add it to the category.

```
@interface HeroDetailController ()
@property (strong, nonatomic) NSArray *sections;
@property (strong, nonatomic) UIBarButtonItem *saveButton;
- (void)save;
@end
```

Now you need to create an instance of a Save button and assign it to this variable. Add the following to viewDidLoad in HeroDetailController.m, right after the Edit button code in viewDidLoad you just uncommented.

```
self.saveButton = [[UIBarButtonItem alloc] initWithBarButtonSystemItem:UIBarButtonSystemItemSave
                                             target:self
                                             action:@selector(save)];
```

Now, you need to switch between the Edit and Save buttons. But where do you call this method? Remember, when the Edit button is pressed, it invokes the setEditing:animated: method. Override the default setEditing:animated: method and have yours switch the buttons.

```
- (void)setEditing:(BOOL)editing animated:(BOOL)animated
{
    [super setEditing:editing animated:animated];
    self.navigationItem.rightBarButtonItem = (editing) ? self.saveButton : self.editButtonItem;
}
```

And you need to add the save method (put it at the bottom of the file, just before the @end).

```
#pragma mark - (Private) Instance Methods

- (void)save
{
    [self setEditing:NO animated:YES];
}
```

Save your work and run the application. Navigate down the detail view and tap the Edit button. It should toggle between Edit and Save as you toggle in and out of editing mode. Now, let's fix it so the Back button changes into a Cancel button.

The process is almost identical to what you did for the Edit/Save buttons: declare a property and callback method and toggle the button in the navigation bar. However, you also need an property to store the Back button. Add the following to the `HeroDetailController` category:

```
@property (strong, nonatomic) UIBarButtonItem *backButton;
@property (strong, nonatomic) UIBarButtonItem *cancelButton;
- (void)cancel;
```

Assign the `backButton` to the left navigation bar button and create an instance of the Cancel button in `viewDidLoad`.

```
self.backButton = self.navigationItem.leftBarButtonItem;
self.cancelButton = [[UIBarButtonItem alloc] initWithBarButtonSystemItem:UIBarButtonSystem
                                                                           ItemCancel
                                                          target:self
                                                          action:@selector(cancel)];
```

Modify `setEditing:animated:` to toggle the Back and Cancel buttons.

```
self.navigationItem.leftBarButtonItem = (editing) ? self.cancelButton : self.backButton;
```

Finally, add the `cancel` callback method. For now, it's identical to the save method, but you'll be changing that soon.

```
- (void)cancel
{
    [self setEditing:NO animated:YES];
}
```

Run the application again. When you hit the Edit button in the detail view, the Back button should switch to Cancel. If you press the Cancel button, you should exit editing mode.

Now you want to eliminate those red buttons that appear to the right of each cell in editing mode. When you click those buttons, they rotate, and a Delete button will appear in the appropriate cell. This isn't really relevant for the detail view, you can't delete an attribute (you can, however, clear it, or set its value to nil). So, you don't want this button to appear at all. Add this method to `HeroDetailController.m` (somewhere with the other table view delegate methods):

```
- (UITableViewCellEditingStyle)tableView:(UITableView *)tableView
        editingStyleForRowAtIndexPath:(NSIndexPath *)indexPath
{
    return UITableViewCellEditingStyleNone;
}
```

Running application shows that the red buttons are gone. You are able to toggle the detail view in and out of editing mode, but you still can't edit anything. There's still a bit of work ahead of you to add this functionality.

Creating a Custom UITableViewCell Subclass

Let's look at the Contacts application. When you edit a contact's attributes, an accessory view appears, with a keyboard (Figure 4-24), allowing for inline editing. You're going to emulate this functionality in your SuperDB application. This is going to require you to develop a custom UITableViewCell subclass.

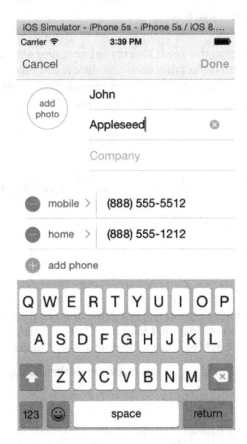

Figure 4-24. *Editing in the Contacts application*

Let's look at the current layout of the table view cell. Currently, you set two parts of the cell: the textLabel and the detailTextLabel (Figure 4-25). Both parts are static text; you can assign the values programmatically, but you are unable to interact with them via the user interface. The iOS SDK does not give you a class where you can assign the textLabel statically but edit the detailTextLabel portion. That's what you have to build.

Figure 4-25. *Current breakdown of the table view cell*

The key component is replacing the detailTextLabel property with a UITextField. This will give you the ability to edit within the table view cell. Since you replaced one portion of the table view cell, you have to replace the textLabel as well. Since that text is static, you'll use a UILabel. In principle, your custom table view cell should look like Figure 4-26.

Figure 4-26. *Breakdown of your custom table view cell*

Let's get started.

Single-click the SuperDB group in the Navigator pane and create a new file. Choose Cocoa Touch Class under the Source templates. Make this class a subclass of UITableViewCell. Let's name the class SuperDBEditCell. Click Next and then Create.

You need a UILabel and a UITextField. Add those properties to SuperDBEditCell.h.

```
@interface SuperDBEditCell : UITableViewCell

@property (strong, nonatomic) UILabel *label;
@property (strong, nonatomic) UITextField *textField;

@end
```

Now add the appropriate initialization code. Edit SuperDBEditCell.m and add the initWithStyle:reuseIdentifier:, as follows:

```
-(id)initWithStyle:(UITableViewCellStyle)style reuseIdentifier:(NSString *)reuseIdentifier{

    self = [super initWithStyle:style reuseIdentifier:reuseIdentifier];
    if (self) {
self.selectionStyle = UITableViewCellSelectionStyleNone;

self.label = [[UILabel alloc] initWithFrame:CGRectMake(12.0, 15.0, 67.0, 15.0)];
self.label.backgroundColor = [UIColor clearColor];
```

```
self.label.font = [UIFont boldSystemFontOfSize:[UIFont smallSystemFontSize]];
self.label.textAlignment = NSTextAlignmentRight;
self.label.textColor = kLabelTextColor;
self.label.text = @"label";
[self.contentView addSubview:self.label];

self.textField = [[UITextField alloc] initWithFrame:CGRectMake(93.0, 13.0, 170.0, 19.0)];
self.textField.backgroundColor = [UIColor clearColor];
self.textField.clearButtonMode = UITextFieldViewModeWhileEditing;
self.textField.enabled = NO;
self.textField.font = [UIFont boldSystemFontOfSize:[UIFont systemFontSize]];
self.textField.text = @"Title";
[self.contentView addSubview:self.textField];
}
return self;
}
```

Note that kLabelTextColor is a constant that you calculated, so the label will have the same color as before. Add this #define before the @implementation directive:

```
#define kLabelTextColor [UIColor colorWithRed:0.321569f green:0.4f blue:0.568627f alpha:1.0f]
```

Now you need to adjust the HeroDetailController to use SuperDBEditCell. But before you do that, you need to fix the configuration in SuperDB.storyboard.

Open SuperDB.storyboard and select the first table view cell in the HeroDetailController. Open the Identity Inspector and change the Class field to SuperDBEditCell. Switch to the Attributes Inspector and change the Style to Custom. Repeat this for the three other table view cells.

Open HeroDetailController.m. Add this #import as the second #import directive:

```
#import "SuperDBEditCell.h"
```

Then find tableView:cellForRowAtIndexPath: and edit it to read as follows:

```
static NSString *CellIdentifier = @"SuperDBEditCell";
SuperDBEditCell *cell = [tableView dequeueReusableCellWithIdentifier:CellIdentifier];
if (cell == nil)
cell = [[SuperDBEditCell alloc] initWithStyle:UITableViewCellStyleValue2
                            reuseIdentifier:CellIdentifier];

// Configure the cell...
NSUInteger sectionIndex = [indexPath section];
NSUInteger rowIndex = [indexPath row];

NSDictionary *section = [self.sections objectAtIndex:sectionIndex];
NSArray *rows = [section objectForKey:@"rows"];
NSDictionary *row = [rows objectAtIndex:rowIndex];
cell.label.text = [row objectForKey:@"label"];
cell.textField.text = [[self.hero valueForKey:[row objectForKey:@"key"]] description];

return cell;
```

Save and run the app. It should behave exactly as before you created your custom table view cell. Now you can turn on the ability to edit.

Override the setEditing: method in SuperDBEditCell.m.

```
- (void)setEditing:(BOOL)editing animated:(BOOL)animated
{
    [super setEditing:editing animated:animated];
    self.textField.enabled = editing;
}
```

Save and run the app again. Navigate to the detail view and enter editing mode. Tap over the Unknown Hero of the Identity row. You should see the keyboard input view appear on the bottom of the screen, and a cursor should appear at the end of Unknown Hero. Tap another row. The cursor should appear in that row.

Let's edit the Identity row. Tap over the Unknown Hero to activate the keyboard input view. Tap the x button at the right end of the cell. This should erase Unknown Hero. Now type **Super Cat** and tap Save. You should exit editing mode, and your hero's new identity should read Super Cat. Tap Back to return to the list view.

Wait. What happened? You renamed your hero Super Cat, but the list view still shows Unknown Hero. If you click the Unknown Hero row, the detail view also still shows Unknown Hero. Why weren't your changes saved?

Remember when you added the Save button to the detail view? You also added a callback, save, to be invoked when the Save button was tapped. Let's look at the callback again.

```
- (void)save
{
    [self setEditing:NO animated:YES];
}
```

Note that this method *doesn't save anything*! All it does is turn off editing mode. Let's figure out how to save your changes for real.

Saving Your Changes

Let's review your detail view. The detail view is a table view managed by your HeroDetailController. The HeroDetailController also has a reference to your Hero object, which is an NSManagedObject. Each row in the table view is your custom table view cell class, SuperDBEditCell. Depending on which row you need, you assign a different hero attribute to display.

Now, to save the changes you make, the Save button invokes the save method. This is the point where you need to save the changes to your NSManagedObject. You will modify your SuperDBEditCell class to know what attribute it is displaying. In addition, you will define a property, value, to tell you the new data in the cell.

First, add your properties to SuperDBEditCell.h.

```
@property (strong, nonatomic) NSString *key;
@property (strong, nonatomic) id value;
```

Next, edit SuperDBEditCell.m to define an property override methods for the value property.

```
#pragma mark - Property Overrides

- (id)value
{
    return self.textField.text;
}

- (void)setValue:(id)aValue
{
    self.textField.text = aValue;
}
```

Modify HeroDetailController.m to assign the key name to each cell inside tableView: cellForRowAtIndexPath.

```
cell.key = [row objectForKey:@"key"];
```

Finally, iterate over each cell on save to update the hero's attributes in the save method after the setEditing line.

```
[self setEditing:NO animated: YES];

for (SuperDBEditCell *cell in [self.tableView visibleCells])
    [self.hero setValue:[cell value] forKey:[cell key]];

NSError *error;
if (![self.hero.managedObjectContext save:&error])
    NSLog(@"Error saving: %@", [error localizedDescription]);

[self.tableView reloadData];
```

Save and run the application. Navigate down to the detail view and enter editing mode. Change the Identity to Super Cat and tap Save. Tap the Back button to return to the list view. You should see that the hero's identity is now displaying Super Cat.

> **Note**   Not really. You would now face a crash, which is because birthDate is expecting an NSDate, but what is actually being passed to it is a string from the textField. We will fix that.

Now you're going to work on specialized input views for the birthdate and sex attributes.

Specialized Input Views

Note that when the user taps the Birthdate or Sex row in the detail view, the keyboard input view is displayed. You could allow the user to enter the birthdate or sex via the keyboard and validate the input, but there is a better way. You can create subclasses of SuperDBEditCell to handle those special cases.

DatePicker SuperDBEditCell Subclass

Single-click the SuperDB group in the Navigator pane and create a new file. Select Objective-C class and make it a subclass of SuperDBEditCell. Name the class SuperDBDateCell and create the files. Edit SuperDBDateCell.m to read as follows:

```objc
#import "SuperDBDateCell.h"

static NSDateFormatter *__dateFormatter = nil;

@interface SuperDBDateCell ()
@property (strong, nonatomic) UIDatePicker *datePicker;
- (IBAction)datePickerChanged:(id)sender;
@end

@implementation SuperDBDateCell

+ (void)initialize
{
    __dateFormatter = [[NSDateFormatter alloc] init];
    [__dateFormatter setDateStyle:NSDateFormatterMediumStyle];
}

- (id)initWithStyle:(UITableViewCellStyle)style reuseIdentifier:(NSString *)reuseIdentifier
{
    self = [super initWithStyle:style reuseIdentifier:reuseIdentifier];
    if (self) {
        // Initialization code
        self.textField.clearButtonMode = UITextFieldViewModeNever;

        self.datePicker = [[UIDatePicker alloc] initWithFrame:CGRectZero];
        self.datePicker.datePickerMode = UIDatePickerModeDate;
[self.datePicker addTarget:self
                action:@selector(datePickerChanged:)
            forControlEvents:UIControlEventValueChanged];
        self.textField.inputView = _datePicker;
    }

    return self;
}
```

```
#pragma mark - SuperDBEditCell Overrides

- (id)value
{
    if (self.textField.text == nil || [self.textField.text length] == 0)
        return nil;
    return self.datePicker.date;
}

- (void)setValue:(id)value
{
    if (value != nil && [value isKindOfClass:[NSDate class]]) {
        [self.datePicker setDate:value];
        self.textField.text = [__dateFormatter stringFromDate:value];
    }
    else {
        self.textField.text = nil;
    }
}

#pragma mark - (Private) Instance Methods

- (IBAction)datePickerChanged:(id)sender
{
    NSDate *date = [self.datePicker date];
    self.value = date;
    self.textField.text = [__dateFormatter stringFromDate:date];
}

@end
```

What have you done here? You defined a local static variable __dateFormatter of type
NSDateFormatter. You're doing this because creating an NSDateFormatter is an expensive
operation, and you don't want to have to create a new instance every time you want to
format a an NSDate object. You could have made it a private property of SuperDBDateCell
and lazily created it, but that would mean you would create a new one for every instance of
SuperDBDateCell. By making it a local static variable, you have to create only one instance
for the lifetime of the SuperDB application.

Next, you declared a private UIDatePicker property, datePicker, and a callback for
datePicker, datePickerChanged.

In the SuperDBDateCell @implementation, you defined a class method, +initialize.
This is a special class method inherited from NSObject. The SuperDB application will call
SuperDBDateCell +initialize exactly one time, before any call to the SuperDBDateCell
class or an instance. This is where you initialize the local static __dateFormatter to hold an
NSDateFormatter instance.

You added some custom initialization code to initWithStyle:reuseIdentifier:. This is where you instantiate the datePicker property and assign it to the textField inputView property. Normally inputView is nil. This tells iOS to use the keyboard input view for the textField. By assigning it an alternate view, you're telling iOS to show the alternate view when editing the textField.

SuperDBDateCell overrides the value property to make sure you display and return an NSDate, rather than an NSString. This is where you use the __dateFormatter to convert the date to a string and then assign it to the textField text property.

Finally, you implement the datePicker's callback for when you change the date via the UI. Every time you change the date in the datePicker, you update the textField to reflect that change.

Using the DatePicker SuperDBEditCell Subclass

Let's review how the table view cells are created. In the HeroDetailController, you created the cells in the tableView:cellForRowAtIndexPath: method. When you first wrote this method, you created an instance UITableViewCell. Later, you replaced this with an instance of your custom subclass, SuperDBEditCell. Now you've created another subclass for a specific IndexPath, the IndexPath displaying the birthDate attribute. How can you tell your application which custom subclass to use? That's right, you'll add that information to your property list: HeroDetailController.plist.

Single-click HeroDetailController.plist. Expand all the disclosure triangles so you can see all the elements. Navigate down to sections ➤ Item 0 ➤ rows ➤ Item 0 ➤ key. Single-click the key row so that it is highlighted. Click the + button next to key. Rename this row from New Item to **class**. In the value column, type **SuperDBEditCell**. Repeat this for all the key rows under sections ➤ Item 1. They should all have the value SuperDBEditCell, except for the class row below the birthDate key. That should have a value of SuperDBDateCell (Figure 4-27).

Key	Type	Value
88 | < > | SuperDB › SuperDB › Supporting Files › HeroDetailConfiguration.plist › No Selection		
▼ Root	Dictionary	(1 item)
▼ sections	Array	(2 items)
▼ Item 0	Dictionary	(1 item)
▼ rows	Array	(1 item)
▼ Item 0	Dictionary	(3 items)
key	String	name
class	String	SuperDBEditCell
label	String	Name
▼ Item 1	Dictionary	(1 item)
▼ rows	Array	(3 items)
▼ Item 0	Dictionary	(3 items)
key	String	secretIdentity
class	String	SuperDBEditCell
label	String	Identity
▼ Item 1	Dictionary	(3 items)
key	String	birthDate
class	String	SuperDBDateCell
label	String	Birthdate
▼ Item 2	Dictionary	(3 items)
key	String	sex
class	String	SuperDBEditCell
label	String	Sex

Figure 4-27. *HeroDetailController.plist after adding the table view cell class key*

You need to modify tableView:cellForRowAtIndexPath: to make use of the information you just placed in the property list. Open HeroDetailController.m and edit tableView:cellForRowAtIndexPath: to appear like this:

```
- (UITableViewCell *)tableView:(UITableView *)tableView cellForRowAtIndexPath:
(NSIndexPath *)indexPath
{
    NSUInteger sectionIndex = [indexPath section];
    NSUInteger rowIndex = [indexPath row];
    NSDictionary *section = [self.sections objectAtIndex:sectionIndex];
    NSArray *rows = [section objectForKey:@"rows"];
    NSDictionary *row = [rows objectAtIndex:rowIndex];

    NSString *cellClassname = [row valueForKey:@"class"];
    SuperDBEditCell *cell = [tableView dequeueReusableCellWithIdentifier:cellClassname];
    if (cell == nil) {
        Class cellClass = NSClassFromString(cellClassname);
        cell = [cellClass alloc];
        cell = [cell initWithStyle:UITableViewCellStyleValue2 reuseIdentifier:cellClassname];
    }

    // Configure the cell...
    cell.key = [row objectForKey:@"key"];
    cell.value = [self.hero valueForKey:[row objectForKey:@"key"]];
    cell.label.text = [row objectForKey:@"label"];

    return cell;
}
```

Save and run the application. Navigate down to the detail view and enter editing mode. Click the `Birthdate` cell, next to the label. The accessory input view should appear and should be a date picker set to today's date. When you change the date in the date picker, the date should change in the table view cell.

There's one more input to take care of. This version of your application uses the string attribute editor to solicit the sex (sorry, we couldn't resist!) of the superhero. This means that there is no validation on the input other than that it's a valid string. A user could type M, Male, MALE, or Yes, Please, and they would all be happily accepted by the application. That means, later, if you want to let the user sort or search their heroes by gender, you could have problems because the data won't be structured in a consistent manner. You'll tackle that problem next.

Implementing a Selection Picker

As you saw earlier, you could have enforced a specific sex spelling by using a regular expression, putting up an alert if the user typed something besides Male or Female. This would have prevented values other than the ones you want from getting entered, but this approach is not all that user friendly. You don't want to annoy your user. Why make them type anything at all? There are only two possible choices here. Why not present a selection list and let the user just tap the one they want? Hey, that sounds like a great idea! You're no doubt glad you thought of it. Let's implement it now, shall you?

Again, create a new Objective-C class and make it a subclass of `SuperDBEditCell`. Name the class `SuperDBPickerCell`, after the fact that you will be using a `UIPickerView`. Most of what you do will be similar to what you did for `SuperDBDateCell`, but there are some key differences.

Edit the interface definition in `SuperDBPickerCell.h` to read as follows:

```
@interface SuperDBPickerCell : SuperDBEditCell <UIPickerViewDataSource,
UIPickerViewDelegate>

@property (strong, nonatomic) NSArray *values;

@end
```

The property is named `pickerValues`, which will hold the possible selections. You also added the `UIPickerViewDataSource` and `UIPickerViewDelegate` protocols to `SuperDBPickerCell`.

Now, let's edit the implementation of `SuperDBPickerCell` in `SuperDBPickerCell.m`.

```
@interface SuperDBPickerCell ()
@property (strong, nonatomic) UIPickerView *pickerView;
@end
```

```objc
@implementation SuperDBPickerCell

- (id)initWithStyle:(UITableViewCellStyle)style reuseIdentifier:(NSString *)reuseIdentifier
{
    self = [super initWithStyle:style reuseIdentifier:reuseIdentifier];
    if (self) {
        self.textField.clearButtonMode = UITextFieldViewModeNever;

        self.pickerView = [[UIPickerView alloc] initWithFrame:CGRectZero];
        self.pickerView.dataSource = self;
        self.pickerView.delegate = self;
        self.pickerView.showsSelectionIndicator = YES;
        self.textField.inputView = self.pickerView;
    }

    return self;
}

#pragma mark UIPickerViewDataSource Methods

- (NSInteger)numberOfComponentsInPickerView:(UIPickerView *)pickerView
{
    return 1;
}

- (NSInteger)pickerView:(UIPickerView *)pickerView numberOfRowsInComponent:(NSInteger)
component
{
    return [self.values count];
}

#pragma mark - UIPickerViewDelegate Methods

- (NSString *)pickerView:(UIPickerView *)pickerView
             titleForRow:(NSInteger)row
            forComponent:(NSInteger)component
{
    return [self.values objectAtIndex:row];
}

- (void)pickerView:(UIPickerView *)pickerView
      didSelectRow:(NSInteger)row
       inComponent:(NSInteger)component
{
    self.value = [self.values objectAtIndex:row];
}
```

```
#pragma mark - SuperDBEditCell Overrides

- (void)setValue:(id)value
{
    if (value != nil) {
        NSInteger index = [self.values indexOfObject:value];
        if (index != NSNotFound) {
            self.textField.text = value;
        }
    }
    else {
        self.textField.text = nil;
    }
}

@end
```

SuperDBPickerCell is conceptually identical to SuperDBDateCell. Rather than using an NSDatePicker, you use a UIPickerView. To tell the pickerView what to display, you need to have SuperDBDateCell conform to the protocols UIPickerViewDataSource and UIPickerViewDelegate. Rather than having a callback on the pickerView to indicate when the picker value has changed, you use the delegate method pickerView:didSelectRow:. Since you're storing the value as a string, you don't need to override the implementation of the value accessor method. However, you do need to override the value mutator.

You need to tell the application to use this new class for the Sex attribute. Edit the class row in the property list, HeroDetailConfiguration.plist. Change the value from SuperDBEditCell to SuperDBPickerCell. Make sure you are changing the right row. The label row should read Sex, and the attribute row should read sex.

If you run the application now and try to edit the Sex attribute, you should see the picker wheel appear on the bottom on of the screen. However, there are no values to choose from. If you look back at the code you just added, the picker wheel gets its information from the values property. But you never set this. Again, you could hard-code this in the SuperDBPickerCell object, but that would limit the usefulness of this object. Instead, you'll add a new item to the property list.

Just like you did earlier with the class item, you need to add a new key, which you'll call values. Unlike the class key, you'll only add it to the item with the sex key. Edit the HeroDetailConfiguration.plist and open all the nodes. For the last item, find the row with the key label. Click the + button on that row. Name the new item **values** and change its type to array. Add two string items to the values array and give them the values Male and Female. See Figure 4-28.

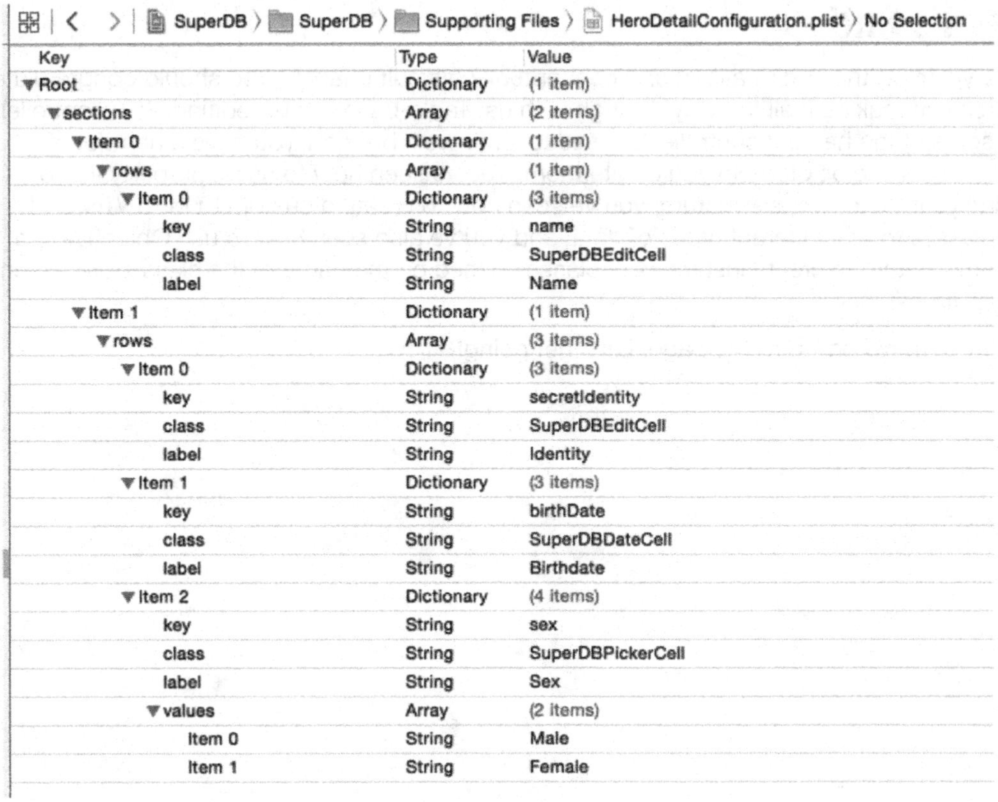

SuperDB › SuperDB › Supporting Files › HeroDetailConfiguration.plist › No Selection

Key	Type	Value
▼Root	Dictionary	(1 item)
▼sections	Array	(2 items)
▼Item 0	Dictionary	(1 item)
▼rows	Array	(1 item)
▼Item 0	Dictionary	(3 items)
key	String	name
class	String	SuperDBEditCell
label	String	Name
▼Item 1	Dictionary	(1 item)
▼rows	Array	(3 items)
▼Item 0	Dictionary	(3 items)
key	String	secretIdentity
class	String	SuperDBEditCell
label	String	Identity
▼Item 1	Dictionary	(3 items)
key	String	birthDate
class	String	SuperDBDateCell
label	String	Birthdate
▼Item 2	Dictionary	(4 items)
key	String	sex
class	String	SuperDBPickerCell
label	String	Sex
▼values	Array	(2 items)
Item 0	String	Male
Item 1	String	Female

Figure 4-28. *HeroDetailController.plist with values for the sex item*

Now you need to pass the contents of values to table view cell when `tableView:cellForRowAtIndexPath:` is in the `HeroDetailController`. Open `HeroDetailController.m` and add the following to `tableView:cellForRowAtIndexPath:` before the other cell configuration code:

```
NSArray *values = [row valueForKey:@"values"];
if (values != nil) {
    // TODO clean this up - ugh
    [cell performSelector:@selector(setValues:) withObject:values];
}
```

Build and run the app. Navigate down to the detail view and tap the Edit button. Tap the Sex cell, and the picker view should appear with the choices Male and Female. Set the value, tap Save, and the Sex cell should be populated.

Devil's End

Well, you're at the end of a long and conceptually difficult chapter. You should congratulate yourself on making it all the way through with us. Table-based detail editing view controllers are some of the hardest controller classes to write well, but now you have a handful of tools in your toolbox to help you create them. You've seen how to use a property list to define your table view's structure, you've seen how to create a custom UITableViewCell subclasses to edit different types of data, and you've also seen how to use Objective-C's dynamic nature to create instances of classes based on the name of the class stored in an NSString instance.

Ready to move on? Turn the page. Let's get going!

Chapter 5

Preparing for Change: Migrations and Versioning

By now you have mastered a great deal of the Core Data architecture and functionality by building a fully functioning, albeit somewhat simple, Core Data application. You've now got enough Core Data chops to build a solid app, send it to your testers, and then send it on to the App Store.

But what happens if you change your data model and send a new version of your application to testers who already have the previous version? Consider the SuperDB app. Let's say you decide to add a new attribute to the Hero entity; make one of the existing, currently optional attributes required; and then add a new entity. Can you just send the program to your users or will this cause problems with their data?

As things stand right now, if you make changes to your data model, the existing data sitting in the user's persistent store on their iPhone will be unusable in the new version of your application. Your application will crash on launch. If you launch the new version from Xcode, you will see a big, scary error message like the following:

```
2012-07-17 17:33:56.641 SuperDB[11233:c07] Unresolved error Error Domain=NSCocoaErrorDomain
Code=134100 "The operation couldn't be completed. (Cocoa error 134100.)" UserInfo=0x80a3b30 {metadata={
    NSPersistenceFrameworkVersion = 409;
    NSStoreModelVersionHashes =     {
        Hero = <0fe30005 4578f63c 124e2af7 3798fb56 7a194f27 f9281223 bd265ee3 d985d2fc>;
    };
    NSStoreModelVersionHashesVersion = 3;
    NSStoreModelVersionIdentifiers =     (
        ""
    );
    NSStoreType = SQLite;
    NSStoreUUID = "719284D9-793C-48A7-8F3E-C633CD4F0402";
    "_NSAutoVacuumLevel" = 2;
}, reason=The model used to open the store is incompatible with the one used to create the store}, {
```

```
metadata =      {
    NSPersistenceFrameworkVersion = 409;
    NSStoreModelVersionHashes =          {
        Hero = <0fe30005 4578f63c 124e2af7 3798fb56 7a194f27 f9281223 bd265ee3 d985d2fc>;
    };
    NSStoreModelVersionHashesVersion = 3;
    NSStoreModelVersionIdentifiers =          (
        ""
    );
    NSStoreType = SQLite;
    NSStoreUUID = "719284D9-793C-48A7-8F3E-C633CD4F0402";
    "_NSAutoVacuumLevel" = 2;
};
reason = "The model used to open the store is incompatible with the one used to create the store";
}
```

If this happens in development, it's not usually a big deal. If nobody else has a copy of your app and you don't have any irreplaceable data stored in it, you can just select Reset Content and Settings from the iPhone Simulator menu in the simulator or uninstall the application from your iPhone using Xcode's Organizer window, and Core Data will create a new persistent store based on the revised data model the next time you install and run your application.

If, however, you have given the application to others, they will be stuck with an unusable application on their iPhone unless they uninstall and re-install the application, thereby losing all of their existing data.

As you probably imagine, this is not something that makes for particularly happy customers. In this chapter, you'll learn how to version your data model. Then you'll learn about Apple's mechanism for converting data between different data model versions, which are called *migrations*. You'll see the difference between the two types of migrations: lightweight migrations and standard migrations. Then you will set up the SuperDB Xcode project to use lightweight migrations so that the changes you make in the next few chapters won't cause problems for your (admittedly nonexistent) users.

At the end of this chapter, the SuperDB application will be all set up and ready for new development, including changes to your data model, without having to worry about your users losing their data when you ship a new version.

About Data Models

When you create a new Xcode project using a template that supports Core Data, you are provided with a single data model in the form of an .xcdatamodel file in your project. In Chapter 2, you saw how this file was loaded into an instance of NSManagedObjectModel at runtime in the application delegate's managedObjectModel method. To understand versioning and migrations, it's important to look a little deeper under the hood to see what's going on.

Data Models Are Compiled

The .xcdatamodel class in your project does not get copied into your application's bundle the way other resources do. The data model file contains a lot of information that your application doesn't need. For example, it contains information about the layout of the objects in Xcode's model editor's diagram view (Figure 5-1), which is only there to make your life easier. Your application doesn't care about how those rounded rectangles are laid out, so there's no reason to include that information inside your application bundle.

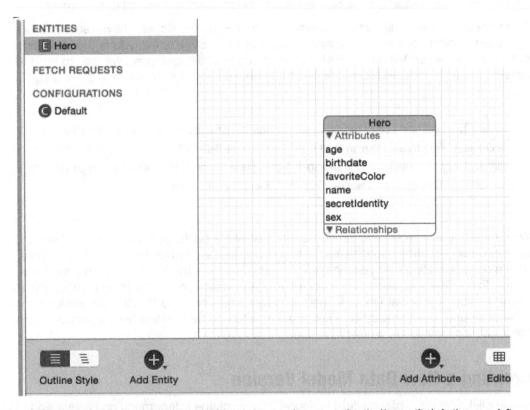

Figure 5-1. *Certain information, such as that the rounded rectangle representing the Hero entity is in the upper-left corner and that the disclosure triangles next to Attributes and Relationships are expanded, is stored in the .xcdatamodel file but not in the .mom file*

Instead, your .xcdatamodel files get compiled into a new type of file with an extension of .mom, which stands for managed object model (sorry, Mom). This is a much more compact binary file that contains just the information that your application needs. This .mom file is what is actually loaded to create instances of NSManagedObjectModel.

Data Models Can Have Multiple Versions

You most likely understand what versioning means in a general sense. When a company releases a new version of a piece of software with new features, it typically has a new number or designation. For example, you are working on a specific version of Xcode (for us, it's 8.1) and a specific version of Mac OS X (for us it's 10.10, also known as Yosemite).

These are called *marketing version identifiers* or *numbers* because they are primarily intended to tell customers the difference between various released versions of the software. Marketing versions are incremented when a new version of the program is released to customers.

There are other, finer-grained forms of versioning used by developers, however. If you've ever used a concurrent versioning system such as CVS, SVN, or Git, you're probably aware of how this all works. Versioning software keeps track of the changes over time to all of the individual source code and resource files that make up your project (among other things).

> **Note**   This book won't cover regular version control, but it's a good thing to know about if you're a developer. Fortunately, there are a lot of resources on the Web for learning how to install and use different version-control software packages. A good place to start is the Wikipedia page on version control at `http://en.wikipedia.org/wiki/Revision_control`.

Xcode integrates with several version-control software packages, but it also has some built-in version-control mechanisms, including one that's intended for use with Core Data data models. Creating new versions of your data models is the key to keeping your users happy. Every time you release a version of your application to the public, you should create a new version of your data model. This will create a new copy so that the old version can be kept around to help the system figure out how to update the data from a persistent store made with one version to a newer version.

Creating a New Data Model Version

Single-click `SuperDB.xcdatamodeld` in Xcode. Now click the Editor menu and select Add Model Version. You will be asked to name this new version. The default values Xcode presents to you (Figure 5-2) are fine. Just click Finish.

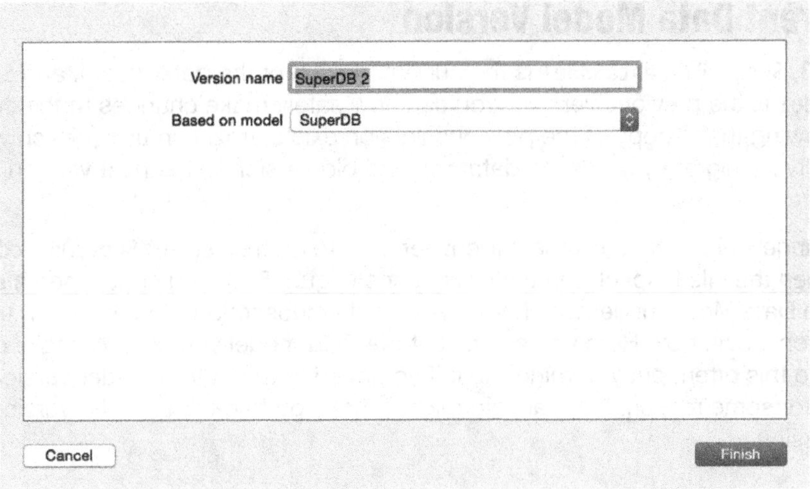

Version name SuperDB 2

Based on model SuperDB

Cancel   Finish

Figure 5-2. Naming the new data model version

You just added a new version of your data model. Once you click Finish, the SuperDB.xcdatamodeld file will gain a disclosure triangle next to it. It will be opened to reveal two different versions of your data model (Figure 5-3).

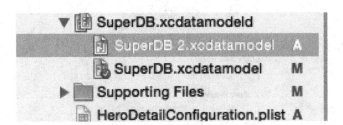

Figure 5-3. A versioned data model contains the current version, marked with a green check mark on its icon, along with every previous version

The icon for one of the versions will have a green check mark on it. This indicates the current version (in your case, SuperDB.xcdatamodel), which is the one your application will use. By default, when you create a new version, you actually create a copy of the original. However, the new version keeps the *same file name* as the original, whereas the name of the copy is appended with an incrementally larger number. This file represents what your data model looked like when you created the new version, and it should be left untouched.

The fact that the higher number is the older file might seem a little weird, but as more versions accumulate, the numbering will make more sense. The next time you create a new version, the old version will be named SuperDB 3.xcdatamodel, and so on. The numbering makes sense for all the noncurrent versions, since each version will have a number one higher than the previous one. By keeping the name of the current model the same, it's easy to tell which is the one you can change.

The Current Data Model Version

In Figure 5-3, SuperDB.xcdatamodel is the current version of the data model, and SuperDB
2.xcdatamodel is the previous version. You can now safely make changes to the current
version, knowing that a copy of the previous version exists, frozen in time, which will give
you the ability to migrate your users' data from the old version to the next version when you
release it.

You can change which version is the current version. To do this, select SuperDB.xcdatamodeld
and then open the File Inspector in the Utility pane (Figure 5-4). You should see a section
named Core Data Model under which you will find the subsection Model Version that has
a Current drop-down box. Here you can select the data model you want to make current.
You won't do this often, but you might do it if you need to revert to an older version of the
application for some reason. You can use migrations to go back to an older version or move
to a new version.

Figure 5-4. The File Identity pane for a data model

Data Model Version Identifiers

Although you can assign version identifiers like 1.1 or Version A to data models by selecting the specific data model version in the Navigation pane and bringing up the File Inspector (Figure 5-4), this identifier is purely for your own use and is completely ignored by Core Data.

Instead, Core Data performs a mathematical calculation called a *hash* on each entity in your data model file. The hash values are stored in your persistent store. When Core Data opens your persistent store, Core Data uses these hash values to ensure that the version of your data stored in the store is compatible with the current data model.

Since Core Data does its version validation using the stored hash values, you don't need to worry about incrementing version numbers for versioning to work. Core Data will just know which version a persistent store was created for by looking at the stored hash value and comparing it to the hash calculated on the current version of the data model.

Migrations

As you saw at the beginning of the chapter, when Core Data detects that the persistent store in use is incompatible with the current data model, it throws an exception. The solution is to provide a migration to tell Core Data how to move data from the old persistent store to a new one that matches the current data model.

Lightweight vs. Standard

There are two different types of migrations supported by Core Data. The first, called a *lightweight migration*, is available only in the case of relatively straightforward modifications to your data model. If you add or remove an attribute from an entity or add or delete an entity from the data model, for example, Core Data is perfectly capable of figuring out how to migrate the existing data into the new model. In the case of a new attribute, it simply creates storage for that attribute but doesn't populate it with data for the existing managed objects. In a lightweight migration, Core Data actually analyzes the two data models and creates the migration for you.

If you make a change that's not straightforward and thus can't be resolved by the lightweight migration mechanism, then you have to use a standard migration. A standard migration involves creating a mapping model and possibly writing some code to tell Core Data how to move the data from the old persistent store to the new one.

Standard Migrations

The changes you will be making to the SuperDB application in this book are all pretty straightforward, and an in-depth discussion of standard migrations is beyond the scope of this book. Apple has documented the process fairly thoroughly in the developer documentation, though, so you can read more about standard migrations at `https://developer.apple.com/library/ios/documentation/Cocoa/Conceptual/ CoreDataVersioning/Articles/Introduction.html`.

Setting Up Your App to Use Lightweight Migrations

On the other hand, you will be using lightweight migrations a lot through the rest of the book. In every remaining Core Data chapter, you will create a new version of your data model and let lightweight migrations handle moving the data. However, lightweight migrations are not turned on by default, so you need to make some changes to your application delegate to enable them.

Edit AppDelegate.m and find the persistentStoreCoordinator method. Replace this line:

```
if (![_persistentStoreCoordinator
        addPersistentStoreWithType:NSSQLiteStoreType
                  configuration:nil
                            URL:storeURL
                        options:nil
                          error:&error]) {
```

with these lines:

```
NSDictionary *options = @{NSMigratePersistentStoresAutomaticallyOption:@YES,
                          NSInferMappingModelAutomaticallyOption:@YES};
if (![_persistentStoreCoordinator
        addPersistentStoreWithType:NSSQLiteStoreType
                  configuration:nil
                            URL:storeURL
                        options:options
                          error:&error]) {
```

The way to turn on lightweight migrations is to pass a dictionary into the options argument when you call the addPersistentStoreWithType:configuration:URL:options:error: method to add your newly created persistent store to the persistent store coordinator. In that dictionary, you use two system-defined constants, NSMigratePersistentStoresAutomaticallyOption and NSInferMappingModelAutomaticallyOption, as keys in the dictionary and store an NSNumber under both of those keys that holds an Objective-C BOOL value of YES. By passing in a dictionary with these two values when you add the persistent store to the persistent store coordinator, you indicate to Core Data that you want it to attempt to automatically create migrations if it detects a change in the data model version and, if it's able to create the migrations, to automatically use those migrations to migrate the data to a new persistent store based on the current data model.

And that's it. With these changes, you are ready to start making changes to your data model without fear (well, maybe not completely without fear). By using lightweight migrations, you limit the complexity of the changes you're able to make. For example, you won't be able to split up an entity into two different entities or move attributes from one entity to another, but the majority of changes you'll need to make outside of major refactoring can be handled by lightweight migrations. Plus, once you set up your project the way you've done in this chapter, that functionality is basically free.

Time to Migrate On

After a couple of long, conceptually difficult chapters, taking a break to set up your project to use migrations gave you a nice breather, but don't underestimate the importance of migrations. The people who use your applications are trusting you to take a certain amount of care with their data. Putting some effort into making sure that your changes don't cause major problems for your users is important.

Any time you put out a new release of your application with a new data model version, make sure you test the migration thoroughly. This is true regardless of whether you're using the lightweight migrations you set up in this chapter or the heavier-duty standard migrations.

Migrations, especially lightweight migrations, are relatively easy to use, but they hold the potential for causing your users significant inconvenience, so don't get lulled into a false sense of security by how easy they are to use. Test every migration thoroughly with as much realistic data as you can.

And with that warning out of the way, let's continue adding functionality to the SuperDB application. Up next? Custom managed objects for fun and profit.

Chapter 6

Custom Managed Objects

At the moment, the Hero entity is represented by instances of the class NSManagedObject. Thanks to key-value coding, you have the ability to create entire data models without ever having to create a class specifically designed just to hold your application's data.

This approach has some drawbacks, however. For one thing, when using key-value coding with managed objects, you use NSString constants to represent your attributes in code, but these constants are not checked in any way by the compiler. If you mistype the name of an attribute, the compiler won't catch it. It can also be a little tedious having to use valueForKey: and setValue:forKey: all over the place instead of just using properties and dot notation.

Although you can set default values for some types of data model attributes, you can't, for example, set conditional defaults such as defaulting a date attribute to today's date. For some types of attributes, there's no way at all to set a default in the data model. Validation is similarly limited. Although you can control certain elements of some attributes, such as the length of a string or max value of a number, there's no way to do complex or conditional validation or to do validation that depends on the values in multiple attributes.

Fortunately, NSManagedObject can be subclassed, just like other Objective-C classes, and that's the key to doing more advanced defaulting and validation. It also opens the door to adding additional functionality to your entity by adding methods. You can, for example, create a method to return a value calculated from one or more of the entity's attributes.

In this chapter, you'll create a custom subclass of NSManagedObject for your Hero entity. Then, you'll use that subclass to add some additional functionality. You'll also add two new attributes to Hero. One is the hero's age. Instead of storing the age, you'll calculate it based on their birthdate. As a result, you won't need Core Data to create space in the persistent store for the hero's age, so you'll use the transient attribute type and then write an accessor method to calculate and return the hero's age. The transient attribute type tells Core Data not to create storage for that attribute. In your case, you'll calculate the hero's age as needed at runtime.

The second attribute you'll add is the hero's favorite color. Now, there is no attribute type for colors, so you'll implement something called a transformable attribute. Transformable attributes use a special object called a *value transformer* to convert custom objects to instances of NSData so they can be stored in the persistent store. You'll write a value transformer that will let you save UIColor instances this way. In Figure 6-1, you can see what the detail editing view will look like at the end of the chapter with the two new attributes in place.

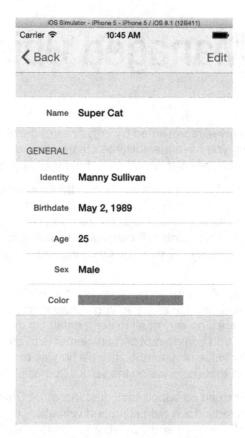

Figure 6-1. The Hero detail view as it will look at the end of the chapter

Of course, you don't have an attribute editor for colors, so you'll have to write one to let the user select the hero's favorite color. You'll just create a simple, slider-based color chooser (Figure 6-2).

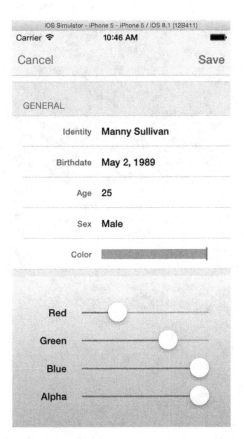

Figure 6-2. The simple, slider-based color attribute editor

Because there's no way to set a default color in the data model, you'll write code to default the favorite color attribute to white. If you don't do that, then the color will be nil when the user goes to edit it the first time, which will cause problems.

Finally, you'll add validation to the date field to prevent the user from selecting a birthdate that occurs in the future, and you'll tweak your attribute editors so that they notify the user when an entered attribute has failed validation. You'll give the user the option to go back and fix the attribute or to just cancel the changes they made (Figure 6-3).

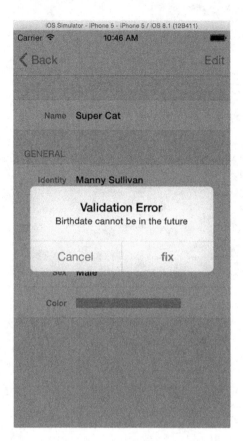

Figure 6-3. *When attempting to save an attribute that fails validation, the user will have the option of fixing the problem or canceling their changes*

Although you'll be adding validation only to the Birthdate field, the reporting mechanism you'll write will be generic and reusable if you add validation to another field. You can see an example of the generic error alert in Figure 6-4.

Figure 6-4. Since your goal is generally to write reusable code, your validation mechanism will also enforce validations done on the data model, such as minimum length

There's a fair amount of work to do, so let's get started. You'll continue working with the same SuperDB application from the previous chapter. Make sure that you created a new version of your data model and that you turned on lightweight migrations, as shown in the previous chapter.

Updating the Data Model

The first order of business is to add your two new attributes to the data model. Make sure that the disclosure triangle next to SuperDB.xcdatamodeld in the SuperDB folder in the Navigator pane is expanded, and single-click the current version of the data model, the one with the green check mark icon on it.

Once the model editor comes up, first make sure you are in table view mode. Then, select the Hero entity in the component pane (Figure 6-5).

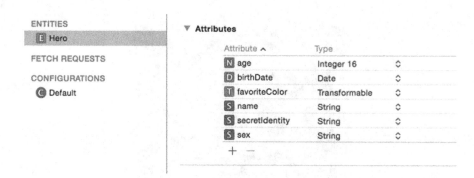

Figure 6-5. Back in the model editor

Adding the Age Attribute

Click the plus icon labeled Add Attribute in the lower right of the data model. Change the new attribute's name to **age**. In the model editor, uncheck Optional and check Transient. That will let Core Data know that you don't need to store a value for this attribute. In your case, since you're using SQLite for your persistent store, this will tell Core Data not to add a column for age to the database table used to store hero data. Change the attribute type to Integer 16; you're going to calculate age as a whole number. That's all you have to do for now for the age attribute. Of course, as things stand, you can't do anything meaningful with this particular attribute because it can't store anything, and you don't yet have any way to tell it how to calculate the age. That will change in a few minutes, when you create a custom subclass of NSManagedObject.

Adding the Favorite Color Attribute

Add another attribute. This time, call the new attribute **favoriteColor** and set the attribute type to Transformable. Once you've changed the Type pop-up to Transformable, you should notice a new text field labeled Name, with a grayed-out value of Value Transformer Name (Figure 6-6).

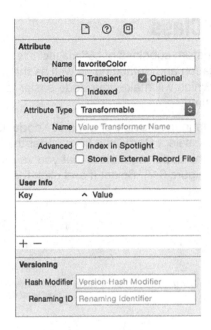

Figure 6-6. *Making the favoriteColor attribute a transformable attribute*

The value transformer name is the key to using transformable attributes. You'll learn about value transformers in more depth in just a few minutes, but you'll populate this field now to save yourself a trip back to the model editor later. This field is where you need to put the name of the value transformer class that will be used to convert whatever object represents this attribute into an NSData instance for saving in the persistent store, and vice versa. If you leave the field blank, Core Data will use the default value transformer, NSKeyedUnarchiveFromDataTransformerName. The default value transformer will work with a great many objects by using NSKeyedArchiver and NSKeyedUnarchiver to convert any object that conforms to the NSCoding protocol into an instance of NSData.

Adding a Minimum Length to the Name Attribute

Next, let's add some validation to ensure that your name attribute is at least one character long. Single-click the name attribute to select it. In the model editor, enter **1** in the text field next to the Validation label to specify that the value entered into this attribute must be at least one character long. The Min. Length check box should automatically check itself. This may seem like a redundant validation, since you already unchecked Optional in a previous chapter for this attribute, but the two do not do exactly the same thing. Because the Optional check box is unchecked, the user will be prevented from saving if name is nil. However, your application takes pains to ensure that name is never nil. For example, you give name a default value. If the user deletes that value, the text field will still return an empty string instead of nil. Therefore, to ensure that an actual name is entered, you're going to add this validation.

Save the data model.

Creating the Hero Class

It's now time to create your custom subclass of NSManagedObject. This will give you the flexibility to add custom validation and defaulting as well as the ability to use properties instead of key-value coding, which will make your code easier to read and give you additional checks at compile time.

Single-click the SuperDB group in the Navigator pane of Xcode. Create a new file. When the New File Assistant appears, select Core Data from under the iOS heading in the left pane; then look for an icon in the upper-right pane that you've probably never seen before: NSManagedObject subclass (Figure 6-7). Select it and click the Next button.

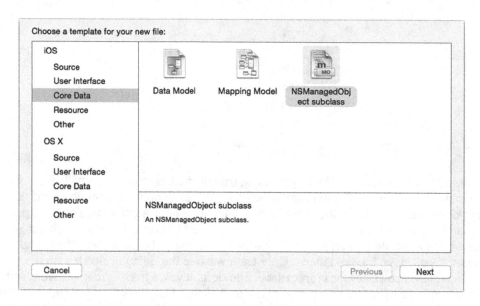

Figure 6-7. Selecting the NSManagedObject subclass template

Next, you will be prompted to select the entities you want to manage (Figure 6-8). Check Hero and click Next.

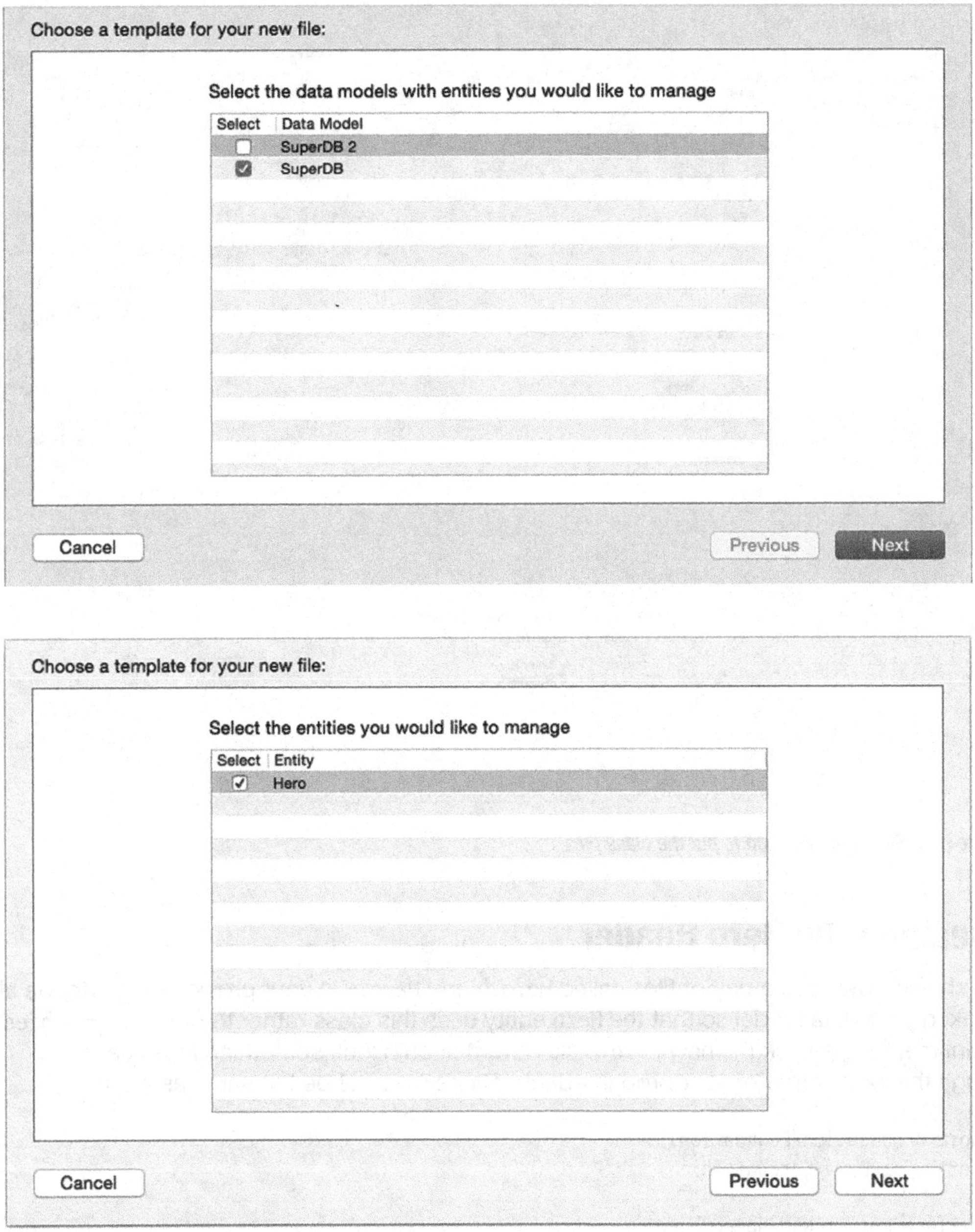

Choose a template for your new file:

Select the data models with entities you would like to manage

Select	Data Model
☐	SuperDB 2
☑	SuperDB

Cancel   Previous   **Next**

Choose a template for your new file:

Select the entities you would like to manage

Select	Entity
☑	Hero

Cancel   Previous   Next

Figure 6-8. *Select the Hero entity*

Finally, you will be prompted where to save the generated class files (Figure 6-9). Leave the "Use scalar properties for primitive data types" box unchecked and make sure that Language is set to Objective-C. The default location should be fine, so just click Create.

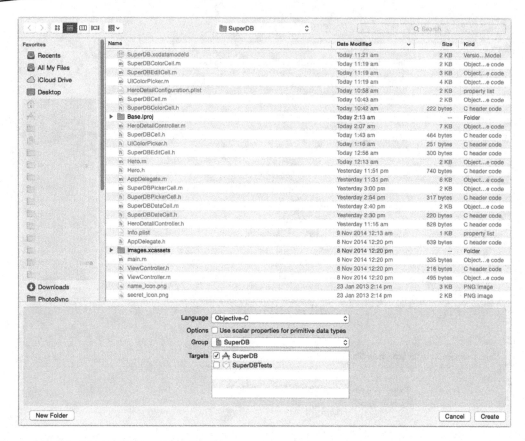

Figure 6-9. *Select the location to put the class files*

Tweaking the Hero Header

You should now have a pair of files called Hero.h and Hero.m in your project folder. Xcode also tweaked your data model so that the Hero entity uses this class rather than NSManagedObject at runtime. Single-click the new Hero.h file now. It should look something look like this, though the exact order of your property declarations may not be the same as ours:

```
#import <Foundation/Foundation.h>
#import <CoreData/CoreData.h>

@interface Hero : NSManagedObject

@property (nonatomic, retain) NSDate * birthDate;
@property (nonatomic, retain) NSString * name;
@property (nonatomic, retain) NSString * secretIdentity;
@property (nonatomic, retain) NSString * sex;
@property (nonatomic, retain) id favoriteColor;
@property (nonatomic, retain) NSNumber * age;

@end
```

> **Caution**   If your Hero.h file does not include declarations of age and favoriteColor, chances
> are you did not save properly somewhere along the way. If so, select Hero.h and Hero.m in your
> project file and press Delete, being sure the files are moved to the trash. Then go back, make sure
> your attributes were properly created in your data model, make sure the data model was saved,
> and then re-create Hero.h and Hero.m.

You need to make two quick changes here. First, you want to make age read-only. You're
not going to allow people to set a hero's age; you're just going to calculate it based on the
birthdate. You also want to change favoriteColor from the generic ID to UIColor to indicate
that your favoriteColor attribute is, in fact, an instance of UIColor. This will give you some
additional type safety by letting the compiler know what type of object represents the
favoriteColor attribute. You also need to add a couple of constants that will be used in your
validation methods.

Add the following after #imports but before the @interface declaration:

```
#import <UIKit/UIKit.h>

#define kHeroValidationDomain @"com.oz-apps.SuperDB.HeroValidationDomain"
#define kHeroValidationBirthdateCode 1000
#define kHeroValidationNameOrSecretIdentityCode 1001
```

Then change the age and favoriteColor property declarations.

```
@property (nonatomic, retain) UIColor *favoriteColor;
@property (nonatomic, retain, readonly) NSNumber * age;
```

Don't worry too much about the constants. You'll learn about error domains and error codes
in a few moments. Switch to Hero.m. You've got a bit more work to do in the implementation
file. Before you do that, let's talk about what you're going to do.

Defaulting

One of the most common Core Data tasks that requires you to subclass NSManagedObject is
setting conditional default values for attributes or setting the default value for attribute types
that can't be set in the data model, such as default values for transformable attributes.

The NSManagedObject method awakeFromInsert is designed to be overridden by subclasses
for the purpose of setting default values. It gets called immediately after a new instance of
an object is inserted into a managed object context and before any code has a chance to
make changes to or use the object.

In your case, you have a transformable attribute called favoriteColor that you want to default to white. To accomplish that, add the following method before the @end declaration in Hero.m:

```
- (void)awakeFromInsert
{
    self.favoriteColor = [UIColor colorWithRed:1.0 green:1.0 blue:1.0 alpha:1.0];
    [super awakeFromInsert];
}
```

Notice the use of the @dynamic keyword in Hero.m. This tells the compiler not to generate accessors and mutators for the property that follows. The idea here is that the accessors and mutators will be provided by the superclass at runtime. Don't worry too much about the specifics; just know that this bit of complexity is required in order for Core Data to work properly.

> **Tip**   Notice that you didn't use [UIColor whiteColor] for the default. The reason you used the colorWithRed:green:blue:alpha: factory method is because it always creates an RGBA color. UIColor supports several different color models. Later, you're going to be breaking UIColor down into its separate components (one each for red, green, blue, and alpha) in order to save it in the persistent store. You're also going to let the user select a new color by manipulating sliders for each of these components. The whiteColor method, however, doesn't create a color using the RGBA color space. Instead, it creates a color using the grayscale color model, which represents colors with only two components, gray and alpha.

Simple enough. You just create a new instance of UIColor and assign it to favoriteColor. Another common usage of awakeFromInsert is for defaulting date attributes to the current date. You *could*, for example, default the birthdate attribute to the current date by adding the following line of code to awakeFromInsert:

```
self.birthdate = [NSDate date];
```

Validation

Core Data offers two mechanisms for doing attribute validation in code; one that's intended to be used for single-attribute validations, and one that's intended to be used when a validation depends on the value of more than one attribute. Single-attribute validations are relatively straightforward. You might want to make sure that a date is valid, a field is not nil, or that a number attribute is not negative. Multifield validations are a little more complex. Let's say that you have a Person entity, and it has a string attribute called legalGuardian where you keep track of the person who is legally responsible and able to make decisions for a person if they are a minor. You might want to make sure this attribute is populated, but you only want to do that for minors, not for adults. Multi-attribute validation will let you make the attribute required if the person's age attribute is less than 18 but not otherwise.

Single-Attribute Validations

NSManagedObject provides a method for validating single attributes called validateValue:forKey:error:. This method takes a value, a key, and an NSError handle. You could override this method and perform validation by returning YES or NO based on whether the value is valid. If it doesn't pass, you would also be able to create an NSError instance to hold specific information about what is not valid and why. You could do that. But don't. As a matter of fact, Apple specifically states you *shouldn't* do this. You never actually need to override this method because the default implementation uses a very cool mechanism to dynamically dispatch error handling to special validation methods that aren't defined in the class.

For example, let's say you have a field called birthdate. NSManagedObject will, during validation, automatically look for a method on your subclass called validateBirthdate:error:. It will do this for every attribute, so if you want to validate a single attribute, all you have to do is declare a method that follows the naming convention of validateXXX:error: (where XXX is the name of the attribute to be validated), returning a BOOL that indicates whether the new value passed validation.

Let's use this mechanism to prevent the user from entering dates that occur in the future. Before the @end declaration in Hero.m, add the following method:

```
-(BOOL) validateBirthDate:(id *)ioValue error:(NSError *__autoreleasing *)outError {
{
    NSDate *date = *ioValue;
    if ([date compare:[NSDate date]] == NSOrderedDescending) {
        if (outError != NULL) {
            NSString *errorStr = NSLocalizedString(@"Birthdate cannot be in the future",
                                          @"Birthdate cannot be in the future");
            NSDictionary *userInfoDict = [NSDictionary dictionaryWithObject:errorStr
                                                        forKey:NSLocalizedDescriptionKey];
            NSError *error = [[NSError alloc] initWithDomain:kHeroValidationDomain
                                                code:kHeroValidationBirthdateCode
                                          userInfo:userInfoDict];

            *outError = error;
        }
        return NO;
    }
    return YES;
}
```

> **Tip** Are you wondering why you're passing a pointer to a pointer to an NSError rather than just a pointer? Pointers to pointers allow a pointer to be passed by reference. In Objective-C methods, arguments, including object pointers, are passed by value, which means that the called method gets its own copy of the pointer that was passed in. So if the called method wants to change the pointer, as opposed to the data the pointer points to, you need another level of indirection. That's why you have the pointer to the pointer.

As you can see from the preceding method, you return NO if the date is in the future and YES if the date is in the past. If you return NO, you take some additional steps. You create a dictionary and store an error string under the key NSLocalizedDescriptionKey, which is a system constant that exists for this purpose. You then create a new instance of NSError and pass that newly created dictionary as the NSError's userInfo dictionary. This is the standard way to pass back information in validation methods and pretty much every other method that takes a handle to an NSError as an argument.

Notice that when you create the NSError instance, you use the two constants you defined earlier, kHeroValidationDomain and kHeroValidationBirthdateCode.

```
NSError *error = [[NSError alloc] initWithDomain:kHeroValidationDomain
                                  code:kHeroValidationBirthdateCode
                                  userInfo:userInfoDict];
```

> **Tip**   Notice that you don't call super in the single-attribute validation methods. It's not that these methods are defined as abstract; it's that they simply don't exist. These methods are created dynamically at runtime, so not only is there no point in calling super, there's actually no method on super to call.

Every NSError requires an error domain and an error code. Error codes are integers that uniquely identify a specific type of error. An error domain defines the application or framework that generated the error. For example, there's an error domain called NSCocoaErrorDomain that identifies errors created by code in Apple's Cocoa frameworks. You defined your own error domain for your application using a reverse DNS-style string and assigned that to the constant kHeroValidationDomain. You'll use that domain for any error created as a result of validating the Hero object. You could also have chosen to create a single domain for the entire SuperDB application, but by being more specific, your application will be easier to debug.

By creating your own error domains, you can be as specific as you want to be. You also avoid the problem of searching through long lists of system-defined constants, looking for just the right code that covers a specific error. kHeroValidationBirthdateCode is the first code you've created in your domain, and the value of 1000 is arbitrary; it would have been perfectly valid to choose 0, 1, 10000, or 34848 for this error code. It's your domain; you can do what you want.

nil vs. NULL

In your validation methods, you may have noticed that you're comparing outError to NULL to see if you've been provided a valid pointer, rather than comparing to nil as you typically do. Both nil and NULL serve the same purpose (to represent empty pointers), and in fact, they are defined to the same thing: the number zero. In terms of your code functioning, nil and NULL are 100 percent interchangeable.

That being said, you should endeavor to use the right one at the right time. The one you use will be a clue to your future self, as well as any other developers who work with your code, as to what you are doing.

When you are checking an Objective-C object pointer, compare to nil. With any other C pointers, use NULL. In this case, you're dealing with a pointer to a pointer, so you use NULL. If a pointer doesn't directly reference an Objective-C object, NULL is the appropriate comparison value, even if the pointer it references points to an object.

Multiple-Attribute Validations

When you need to validate a managed object based on the values of multiple fields, the approach is a little different. After all the single-field validation methods have fired, another method will be called to let you do more complex validations. There are actually two such methods: one that is called when an object is first inserted into the context, and another when you save changes to an existing managed object.

When inserting a new managed object into a context, the multiple-attribute method you use is called validateForInsert:. When updating an existing object, the validation method you implement is called validateForUpdate:. In both cases, you return YES if the object passes validation and NO if there's a problem. As with single-field validation, if you return NO, you should also create an NSError instance that identifies the specifics of the problem encountered.

In many instances, the validation you want to do at insert and at update are identical. In those cases, do not copy the code from one and paste it into the other. Instead, create a new validation method and have both validateForInsert: and validateForUpdate: call that new validation method.

In your application, you don't have a need for any multiple-attribute validations (yet!), but let's say, hypothetically, that instead of making both name and secretIdentity required, you only wanted to require one of the two. You could accomplish that by making both name and secretIdentity optional in the data model and then using the multiple-attribute validation methods to enforce it. To do that, you would add the following three methods to your Hero class:

```
-(BOOL) validateNameOrSecretIdentity:(NSError *__autoreleasing *)outError {
{
    if ((0 == [self.name length]) && (0 == [self.secretIdentity length])) {
        if (outError != NULL) {
            NSString *errorStr = NSLocalizedString(@"Must provide name or secret identity.",
                                        @"Must provide name or secret identity.");
            NSDictionary *userInfoDict = [NSDictionary dictionaryWithObject:errorStr
                                        forKey:NSLocalizedDescriptionKey];
            NSError *error = [[NSError alloc] initWithDomain:kHeroValidationDomain
                                        code:kHeroValidationNameOrSecretIdentityCode
                                        userInfo:userInfoDict];
            *outError = error;
        }
    }
    return YES;
}
```

```
-(BOOL)validateForInsert:(NSError *__autoreleasing *)outError {
{
    return [self validateNameOrSecretIdentity:outError];
}

-(BOOL) validateForUpdate:(NSError *__autoreleasing *)outError {
{
    return [self validateNameOrSecretIdentity:outError];
}
```

Virtual Accessors

At the beginning of the chapter, you added a new attribute called age to your data model. You don't need to store the hero's age, however, because you can calculate it based on the hero's birthdate. Calculated attributes like this are often referred to as *virtual accessors*. They look like accessors, and as far as other objects are concerned, they can be treated just like the other attributes. The fact that you're calculating the value at runtime rather than retrieving it from the persistent store is simply an implementation detail.

As your Hero object stands right now, the age accessor will always return nil because you've told your data model not to create storage space for it in the persistent store and have made it read only. To make it behave correctly, you must implement the logic to calculate age in a method that looks like an accessor (which is why it's called a virtual accessor). To do that, add the following method to Hero.m, just before @end:

```
- (NSNumber *)age
{
    if (self.birthDate == nil)
        return nil;

    NSCalendar *gregorian = [[NSCalendar alloc] initWithCalendarIdentifier:
    NSCalendarIdentifierGregorian];
    NSDateComponents *components = [gregorian components:NSCalendarUnitYear
                                        fromDate:self.birthdate
                                          toDate:[NSDate date]
                                         options:0];
    NSInteger years = [components year];
    return [NSNumber numberWithInteger:years];
}
```

Note the check you put in the beginning in the method. If you haven't set your hero's birthdate, you don't want to calculate the age.

Now any code that uses the age property accessor will be returned an NSNumber instance with the calculated age of the superhero.

Adding Validation Feedback

In Chapter 4, you created a class named SuperDBEditCell that encapsulates the common functionality shared by the various table view cells. The SuperDBEditCell class does not include code designed to save the managed object; it just concerns itself with the display. You did store the attribute that each SuperDBEditCell instance displays. But now you want to add validation feedback when the edited attribute fails validation, and you don't want to duplicate functionality across subclasses.

What you want to do is have each instance of SuperDBEditCell (or subclass) validate the attribute it is handling. You want to perform the validation when the table view cell loses focus (that is, you move to another cell) and when the user attempts to save. If the edited value does not pass validation, you should pop up an alert window telling your user the validation error and present two buttons: Cancel, reverting the value, or Fix, letting the user edit the cell. To handle this, you need to have SuperDBEditCell respond to the UITextFieldDelegate protocol. Finally, if the user taps the Cancel button on the navigation bar, you will undo all the changes they've made.

First, edit SuperDBEditCell.h, and change the @interface declaration to read as follows:

```
@interface SuperDBEditCell : UITableViewCell <UITextFieldDelegate>
```

Next, you need to add a property to your NSManagedObject.

```
@property (strong, nonatomic) NSManagedObject *hero;
```

And you also need to add the line #import <CoreDate/CoreDate.h> just after the first #import line.

Finally, you need a validate method to invoke when you want the validation to occur.

```
- (IBAction)validate;
```

Switch to SuperDBEditCell.m, and add the validate method you just declared.

```
#pragma mark - Instance Methods

-(IBAction)validate {
    id val = self.value;
    NSError *error;
    if (![self.hero validateValue:&val forKey:self.key error:&error]) {
        NSString *message = nil;
        if ([[error domain] isEqualToString:@"NSCocoaErrorDomain"]) {
            NSDictionary *userInfo = [error userInfo];
            message = [NSString stringWithFormat:NSLocalizedString(
                    @"Validation error on: %@\rFailure Reason: %@",
                    @"Validation error on: %@\rFailure Reason: %@"),
                    [userInfo valueForKey:@"NSValidationErrorKey"],
                    [error localizedFailureReason]];
        } else {
            message = [error localizedDescription];
            UIAlertController *alert = [UIAlertController
```

```
                          alertControllerWithTitle:NSLocalizedString(@"Validation Error",
                                                                      @"Validation Error")
                                    message:message
                              preferredStyle:UIAlertControllerStyleAlert];
        UIAlertAction *buttonCancel = [UIAlertAction
                      actionWithTitle:NSLocalizedString(@"Cancel", @"Cancel")
                                style:UIAlertActionStyleCancel
                              handler:^(UIAlertAction *action) {
            [self setValue:[self.hero valueForKey:self.key]];
        }];
        UIAlertAction *buttonFix = [UIAlertAction
                      actionWithTitle:NSLocalizedString(@"Fix", @"Fix")
                                style:UIAlertActionStyleDefault
                              handler:^(UIAlertAction *action) {
            [self.textField becomeFirstResponder];
        }];
        [alert addAction:buttonCancel];
        [alert addAction:buttonFix];

        [[[[[UIApplication sharedApplication]delegate]window]rootViewController]
                             presentViewController:alert animated:YES completion:nil];
        }
    }
}
```

You need the textField delegate method textField:didEndEditing: to call your validate method.

```
#pragma mark UITextFieldDelegate methods

- (void)textFieldDidEndEditing:(UITextField *)textField
{
    [self validate];
}
```

Finally, you need your cell's textField to know about its new delegate. In SuperDBEditCell's initWithStyle:reuseIdentifier: method, just before the textField is added to the cell's contentView, add this:

```
self.textField.delegate = self;
```

What have you done here? First, you made sure the NSTextField delegate was set to self in initWithStyle:reuseIdentifier:. Then, you added the validate method. Basically, your validate calls validateValue:forKey:error: on your NSManagedObject. If this validation fails, you parse the NSError object and create a UIAlertView. Next, you defined a textFieldDidEndEditing: delegate method. This method gets invoked when the NSTextField in your SuperDBEditCell class exits editing mode. This happens when the user taps from a cell to another cell or when the user taps Save or Back on the navigation bar. This handler method gets called when the user taps a button on the UIAlertController you display on validation error. Depending on which button was tapped, Cancel or Fix, you either revert the value or move the focus to the table view cell.

Now you just need to pass your Hero object down from HeroDetailController to the SuperDBEditCell. Edit HeroDetailController.m and find the tableView:cellForRowAtIndexPath:. Just before all the other cell configurations, add this:

```
cell.hero = self.hero;
```

Updating the Detail View

Looking at Figure 6-2, you see that you need two more cells in the General section of the table view. Before you go any further, let's update the detail view.

Open SuperDB.storyboard and find the HeroDetailController. Select the second table view section by clicking in an area outside the table view cells (next to the General label is a good place). Open the Attributes Inspector in the Utility pane, and change the Rows field from 3 to 5. The second section of the table view should now show five rows. That's all you need to do in the storyboard editor. Easy, right?

Now let's take a look at Figure 6-2 again. The order of the labels in the second section are Identity, Birthdate, Age, Sex, and Favorite Color. When you last ran the application, the section labels were Identity, Birthdate, and Sex. Not only do you need to add Age and Favorite Color, you need to reorder things so that Age comes before Sex. Fortunately, since your cells are configured from a property list, this should be (relatively) simple.

Open HeroDetailCofiguration.plist. Navigate down to Root ➤ Sections ➤ Item 1 ➤ rows ➤ Item 1. If the disclosure triangle next to the last Item 1 is open, close it. Item 1 and Item 2 should be right next to each other. If the Item 2 disclosure triangle is open, close it as well. Now select the Item 1 row and click the (+) button next to the Item 1 label. A new row should have been inserted between Item 1 and Item 2. Item 2 is renamed to Item 3. The new Item 2 has a type of string with no value.

Change the new Item 2's type to Dictionary, and open its disclosure triangle. This is the configuration for your Age cell. Click the (+) button next to the new Item 2 three times to add three rows. Keep all three rows as type string and give them the following key/value pairs: key/age, class/SuperDBEditCell, label/Age.

Now add a row after Item 3, repeat the process, adding three rows with type string to the new Item 4. The key/value pairs will be the following: key/favoriteColor, class/ SuperDBEditCell, label/Color.

Build and run the app. Navigate down to the detail view.

The app should have crashed. Why?

Well, you're assigning the age attribute to the textField's text property. Age will be an instance of NSNumber, and textField.text will expect an NSString. You could subclass SuperDBEditCell to handle NSNumbers, but you probably won't need it. It's far easier to change this method in SuperDBEditCell.m.

```
- (void)setValue:(id)aValue
{
    if ([aValue isKindOfClass:[NSString class]])
        self.textField.text = aValue;
    else
        self.textField.text = [aValue description];
}
```

If you were showing a lot of NSNumbers, you probably wouldn't do this, but this works for now.

Try building and running the app again. If you add a new hero, you should see something like Figure 6-10.

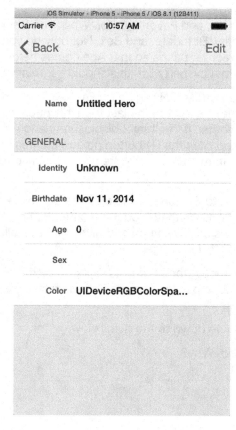

Figure 6-10. The Hero detail view

There's a problem with the Age cell. For one, in Edit mode, you can tap inside the Age cell, and it will get focus and show the keyboard input. Second, when you try to save from Edit mode, the app will crash. Let's fix this.

Refactoring SuperDBEditCell

The Age cell is editable by default. There is a table view data source method, `tableView:canEditRowAtIndexPath:`, that determines whether a specific table view cell is editable. By default, this method is provided in the `UITableViewController` template but commented out. As a result, the table view assumes all cells are editable. Clearly, you need this method to return NO for the Age cell index path. Unfortunately, by specifying a cell as uneditable, the cell won't indent in Edit mode. That may be OK, but you'd like your Age cell to indent even if you can't edit it.

The app crash is because of these lines of code in the `HeroDetailController` save method:

```
for (SuperDBEditCell *cell in [self.tableView visibleCells])
    [self.hero setValue:[cell value] forKey:[cell key]];
```

When you try to set the value in the `Hero` entity's attribute of age, you'll get an exception crash. Remember, you declared age to be transient in your data model. That means the value of age is calculated, and there's no way to set it. You need a way to check whether you should save the value in the cell.

First, you need to define an uneditable version of `SuperDBEditCell`. But rather than do that, let's make a superclass of `SuperDBEditCell`, called `SuperDBCell`, that uses a `textField` but doesn't allow it to be enabled for editing. This seems like a good time to try Xcode's refactoring capabilities.

Xcode Refactoring Options

Open Edit ➤ Refactor in Xcode. You should see the submenu in Figure 6-11.

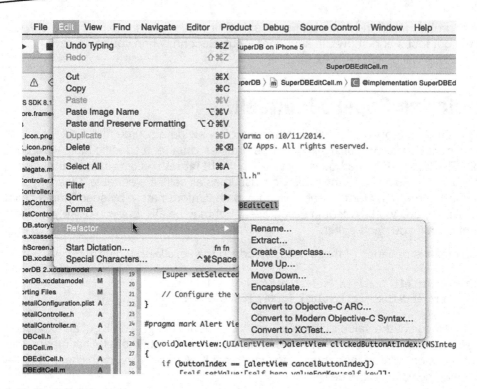

Figure 6-11. *Xcode Refactor menu*

Before you continue, let's quickly review what refactoring is and what each menu item does. Refactoring is restructuring code without changing its external behavior. Typically, you refactor some code (usually a method) to improve some nonfunctional attribute (i.e., reduce complexity, improve readability). This is not undertaken as a random "rewrite" of the code. Rather, it's a disciplined approach of small changes.

Note   An excellent resource on refactoring patterns is Martin Fowler's *Refactoring: Improving the Design of Existing Code* (Addison-Wesley, 1999). Not only does it explain the process behind refactoring, but it outlines several refactoring techniques.

Xcode's refactoring options are as follows:

- *Rename*: Renames symbols so they indicate more clearly their purpose and make the source easier to read. Examples of symbols are the name of a class, method, or function. Unfortunately, methods declared in a protocol cannot be renamed.

- *Extract*: Extracts code you select in Xcode into a new method or function.

- *Create Superclass*: Defines a superclass for the class currently selected in Xcode.

- *Move Up*: Moves the selected method, property, or instance variable from a class to the superclass, provided both are defined in your project.

- *Move Down*: The opposite of Move Up, moves the selected symbol from a class to a subclass, provided both are defined in your project.

- *Encapsulate*: Encapsulates an instance variable and create the appropriate accessors.

- *Convert to Objective-C ARC*: Assists in converting legacy projects to use Automatic Reference Counting.

- *Convert to Modern Objective-C Syntax*: Updates code to use more modern Objective-C features like the new Literals syntax (arrays, dictionaries, Booleans).

This was just a brief introduction to the Refactor menu items to familiarize yourself with what's available in Xcode for future projects. Let's get back to the SuperDB app.

You'll use the Create Superclass option. Open `SuperDBEditCell.h` and highlight the class name, `SuperDBEditCell`, after the `@interface` declaration. Select Edit ➤ Refactor ➤ Create Superclass. Xcode should present a pop-up for what to call the superclass (Figure 6-12). Name the class `SuperDBCell`, select the "Create files for new superclass" option, and click Preview. You should see a File Merge pop-up that shows all the changes it will make to create the superclass `SuperDBCell` (Figure 6-13).

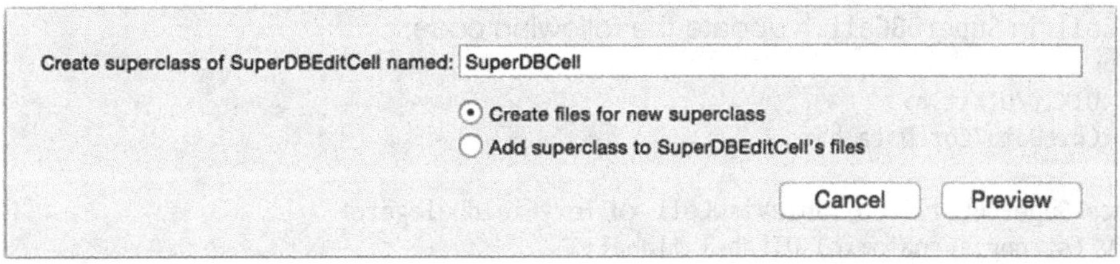

Figure 6-12. Create Superclass pop-up

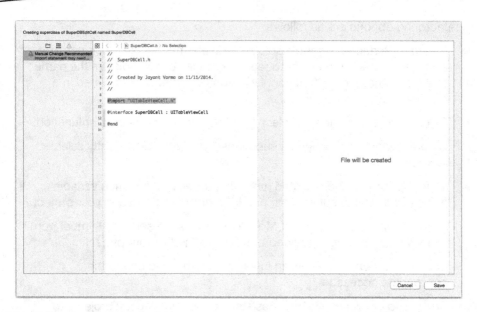

Figure 6-13. Refactoring file merge preview

This particular preview doesn't show much, other than the creation of the SuperDBCell interface and implementation files. Click Save. Xcode may ask if it should take a snapshot. Whether you use snapshots or not is up to you. We use them occasionally, but we prefer using a revision control system like Git.

Moving Code Around

Now, Xcode didn't do everything you wanted. It did create the files for SuperDBCell, and it did make SuperDBEditCell a subclass of SuperDBCell, but it didn't do much else. Remember you wanted to make SuperDBCell the same as SuperDBEditCell, but the textField wasn't going to ever been enabled.

Let's start with the SuperDBCell interface file. You'll move most of SuperDBEditCell into SuperDBCell. In SuperDBCell.h update the following code:

```
#import <UIKit/UIKit.h>
#import <CoreData/CoreData.h>

@interface SuperDBCell : UITableViewCell <UITextFieldDelegate>
@property (strong, nonatomic) UILabel *label;
@property (strong, nonatomic) UITextField *textField;

@property(strong, nonatomic) NSString *key;
@property(strong, nonatomic) id value;

@property(strong, nonatomic) NSManagedObject *hero;
@end
```

As a result, SuperDBEditCell.h will change as well.

```
#import <UIKit/UIKit.h>
#import <CoreData/CoreData.h>
#import "SuperDBCell.h"

@interface SuperDBEditCell : SuperDBCell <UITextFieldDelegate>

- (IBAction)validate;

@end
```

Next, you adjust the SuperDBCell implementation.

```
#import "SuperDBCell.h"

#define kLabelTextColor [UIColor colorWithRed:0.321569f green:0.4f blue:0.568627f alpha:1.0f]

@implementation SuperDBCell

- (id)initWithStyle:(UITableViewCellStyle)style reuseIdentifier:(NSString *)reuseIdentifier
{
    self = [super initWithStyle:style reuseIdentifier:reuseIdentifier];
    if (self) {
        // Initialization code
        self.selectionStyle = UITableViewCellSelectionStyleNone;

        // TODO - use Auto Layout to adjust sizes
        self.label = [[UILabel alloc] initWithFrame:CGRectMake(12.0, 15.0, 67.0, 15.0)];
        self.label.backgroundColor = [UIColor clearColor];
        self.label.font = [UIFont boldSystemFontOfSize:[UIFont smallSystemFontSize]];
        self.label.textAlignment = NSTextAlignmentRight;
        self.label.textColor = kLabelTextColor;
        self.label.text = @"label";
        [self.contentView addSubview:self.label];

        self.textField = [[UITextField alloc] initWithFrame:CGRectMake(93.0, 13.0, 170.0, 19.0)];
        self.textField.backgroundColor = [UIColor clearColor];
        self.textField.clearButtonMode = UITextFieldViewModeWhileEditing;
        self.textField.enabled = NO;
        self.textField.font = [UIFont boldSystemFontOfSize:[UIFont systemFontSize]];
        self.textField.text = @"Title";
        [self.contentView addSubview:self.textField];
    }
    return self;
}
```

```
#pragma mark - Property Overrides

- (id)value
{
    return self.textField.text;
}

- (void)setValue:(id)newValue
{
    if ([newValue isKindOfClass:[NSString class]])
        self.textField.text = newValue;
    else
        self.textField.text = [newValue description];
}

@end
```

You moved most of the initWithStyle:reuseIdentifier: code from SuperDBEditCell to SuperDBCell. Note that you disabled the textField.

```
self.textField.enabled = NO;
```

Also, you did not declare SuperDBCell to be the textField delegate. SuperDBCell does not have a setEditing:animated: method; it doesn't need one. The only reason SuperDBEditCell had one was to enable and disable the textField.

As a result of the SuperDBCell implementation, you need to change SuperDBEditCell.m. First, you update initWithStyle:reuseIdentifier:.

```
- (id)initWithStyle:(UITableViewCellStyle)style reuseIdentifier:(NSString *)reuseIdentifier
{
    self = [super initWithStyle:style reuseIdentifier:reuseIdentifier];
    if (self) {
        // Initialization code
        self.textField.delegate = self;
    }
    return self;
}
```

Next, you delete the value property accessor and mutator. While you're at it, you can delete the #define at the top of the file since you moved it to SuperDBCell.m.

Your "refactoring" is complete, but you still need to make some changes.

Editable Property

The SuperDB app crashes when you try to save an edited Hero since it tries to save the value in the Age cell. You want the HeroDetailController's save method to skip the Age cell when updating its Hero instance.

You could weave some Core Data wizardry and ask the Hero instance to check whether the cell's attribute key is transient or not. That seems like a lot of work just to know something you can infer pretty reliably. Remember, you created the SuperDBCell class to handle those fields that are uneditable (and probably don't need to be updated). So, what you want is for SuperDBCell to return YES on some query and SuperDBEditCell to return NO (or vice versa). Let's just define a method, isEditable, in SuperDBCell to return NO. You'll override the method in SuperDBEditCell to return YES.

Add this to SuperDBCell.h:

```
- (BOOL)isEditable;
```

And add its implementation to SuperDBCell.m.

```
#pragma mark - Instance Methods

- (BOOL)isEditable
{
    return NO;
}
```

Override the method in SuperDBEditCell.m.

```
#pragma mark - SuperDBCell Overrides

- (BOOL)isEditable
{
    return YES;
}
```

Now you need to use this method in HeroDetailController.m. Update the appropriate code in the save method.

```
for (SuperDBEditCell *cell in [self.tableView visibleCells]) {
    if ([cell isEditable])
        [self.hero setValue:[cell value] forKey:[cell key]];
}
```

Finally, you need to update your HeroDetailConfiguration.plist to have the Age cell use SuperDBCell. Open HeroDetailConfiguration.plist, navigate to Root ➤ sections ➤ Item 1 ➤ rows ➤ Item 2 ➤ class, and change its value to SuperDBCell.

Build and run the app. Navigate to the detail view and enter Edit mode. Try to tap the Age cell. You can't because it's not editable.

Creating a Color Table View Cell

Now that you've completed your color value transformer, let's think about how you can enter your hero's favorite color. Look back at Figure 6-1. You have a table view cell that displays a band of your hero's favorite color. When the user chooses the favorite color cell in Edit mode, you want to display a color picker (Figure 6-2). The color picker is not available via the iOS SDK, like the date and value pickers you used in Chapter 4. You're going to have to build one from scratch.

Custom Color Editor

Single-click the SuperDB folder in the navigation pane and create a new file using Cocoa Touch Class. When prompted, name the class UIColorPicker and make it a subclass of UIControl. UIControl is the base class for control objects such as buttons and sliders. Here you define a subclass of UIControl that encapsulates four sliders. The only property you need UIColorPicker to declare is its color.

```
@property (strong, nonatomic) UIColor *color;
```

Every other property can be declared privately in a category in the implementation file, UIColorPicker.m.

```
@interface UIColorPicker ()
@property (strong, nonatomic) UISlider *redSlider;
@property (strong, nonatomic) UISlider *greenSlider;
@property (strong, nonatomic) UISlider *blueSlider;
@property (strong, nonatomic) UISlider *alphaSlider;
- (IBAction)sliderChanged:(id)sender;
- (UILabel *)labelWithFrame:(CGRect)frame text:(NSString *)text;
-(UISlider *)createSliderWithAction:(CGRect) frame function:(SEL) theFunc;

@end
```

You also declared two (private) methods. One is the callback for when the sliders change (siderChanged:). The other is a convenience method for creating the picker view.

Add the following initialization code:

```
-(id) initWithFrame:(CGRect)frame {

  self = [super initWithFrame:frame];
    if(self){
        [self labelWithFrame:CGRectMake(20, 40, 60, 24) text:@"Red"];
        [self labelWithFrame:CGRectMake(20, 80, 60, 24) text:@"Green"];
        [self labelWithFrame:CGRectMake(20, 120, 60, 24) text:@"Blue"];
        [self labelWithFrame:CGRectMake(20, 160, 60, 24) text:@"Alpha"];
```

```
        self.redSlider = [self createSliderWithAction:CGRectMake(100, 40, 190, 24)];
        self.greenSlider = [self createSliderWithAction:CGRectMake(100, 80, 190, 24)];
        self.blueSlider = [self createSliderWithAction:CGRectMake(100, 120, 190, 24)];
        self.alphaSlider = [self createSliderWithAction:CGRectMake(100, 160, 190, 24)];
    }
    return self;
}
```

Here you are laying out the appearance of your color picker. You place the sliders in the view with the initWithFrame: method. Here is the code for the createSliderWithAction: method:

```
-(UISlider *) createSliderWithAction:(CGRect)frame function:(SEL)theFunc {
    UISlider *slider = [[UISlider alloc]initWithFrame:frame];
    [slider addTarget:self action:theFunc forControlEvents:UIControlEventValueChanged];
    [self addSubview:slider];
    return slider;
}
```

You need to override the color property mutator in order to set the slider values correctly.

```
#pragma mark - Property Overrides
-(void)setColor:(UIColor *)color {
    _color = color;
    const CGFloat *components = CGColorGetComponents(color.CGColor);
    [_redSlider setValue:components[0]];
    [_greenSlider setValue:components[1]];
    [_blueSlider setValue:components[2]];
    [_alphaSlider setValue:components[3]];
}
```

Now you can implement your (private) instance methods. First, implement sliderChanged.

```
#pragma mark - (Private) Instance Methods

-(IBAction)sliderChanged:(id)sender{
    _color = [UIColor colorWithRed:_redSlider.value green:_greenSlider.value
                                    blue:_blueSlider.value alpha:_alphaSlider.value];

    [self sendActionsForControlEvents:UIControlEventValueChanged];
}
```

Next, implement labelWithFrame:text.

```
-(UILabel *)labelWithFrame:(CGRect)frame text:(NSString *)text{
    UILabel *label = [[UILabel alloc]initWithFrame:frame];

    [label setUserInteractionEnabled:NO];
    [label setBackgroundColor:[UIColor clearColor]];
    [label setFont:[UIFont boldSystemFontOfSize:[UIFont systemFontSize]]];
    [label setTextAlignment:NSTextAlignmentRight];
```

```
    [label setTextColor:[UIColor darkTextColor]];
    [label setText:text];
    [self addSubview:label];

    return label;
}
```

Now that you've created your custom color picker, you need to add a custom table view cell class to use it.

Custom Color Table View Cell

Since you have a custom picker view, you're going to need to subclass `SuperDBEditCell`, like you did for `SuperDBDateCell` and `SuperDBPickerCell`. But how are you going to display a `UIColor` value in your `SuperDBEditableCell` class? You could create a string that displays the four values of the color (red, green, blue, and alpha). For most end users, those numbers are meaningless. Your users are going to expect to see the actual color when they're viewing the hero detail. You don't have a mechanism to display colors in a table view cell.

If you build a complicated table view cell subclass to display the color, are you going to use it elsewhere in the application? The likely answer is no. So, while you could spend time and effort building this class, don't. Here's a simpler solution: populate the text field with an `NSString` with a special Unicode character that displays as a solid rectangle. Then add code to change the font color of the text to make it appear in your hero's favorite color.

Create a new Cocoa Touch Class as a subclass of `SuperDBEditCell` and name it `SuperDBColorCell`. Add the Color Picker class as the (private) property to `SuperDBColorCell.m`.

```
#import "UIColorPicker.h"

@interface SuperDBColorCell ()
@property (strong, nonatomic) UIColorPicker *colorPicker;
- (void)colorPickerChanged:(id)sender;
- (NSAttributedString *)attributedColorString;
@end
```

You also add a (private) instance method, `attributedColorString`, that returns an `NSAttributedString`. An attributed string is a string that also has information on how to format itself. Prior to iOS 6, attributed strings were extremely limited. Now, you're able to use them with `UIKit` objects. You'll see why you want this method soon.

Define the `initWithStyle:reuseIdentifier:` method as follows:

```
- (id)initWithStyle:(UITableViewCellStyle)style reuseIdentifier:(NSString *)reuseIdentifier
{
    self = [super initWithStyle:style reuseIdentifier:reuseIdentifier];
    if (self) {
        // Initialization code
        self.colorPicker = [[UIColorPicker alloc] initWithFrame:CGRectZero];
```

```
[self.colorPicker addTarget:self
                     action:@selector(colorPickerChanged:)
           forControlEvents:UIControlEventValueChanged];
        self.textField.inputView = self.colorPicker;
    }
    return self;
}
```

This should be pretty straightforward. Like the other SuperDBEditCell subclasses, you've instantiated your picker object and set it as the textField's inputView.

Next, override SuperDBEditCell's value accessor and mutator.

```
#pragma mark - SuperDBEditCell Overrides

- (id)value
{
    return self.colorPicker.color;
}

- (void)setValue:(id)value
{
  if (value != nil && [value isKindOfClass:[UIColor class]]) {
        [super setValue:value];
        self.colorPicker.color = value;
    }
    else {
        self.colorPicker.color = [UIColor colorWithRed:1.0 green:1.0 blue:1.0 alpha:1.0];
    }
    self.textField.attributedText = self.attributedColorString;
}
```

In setValue: make note of this line:

```
self.textField.attributedText = self.attributedColorString;
```

Rather than setting the textField's text property, you using the new attributedText property. This tells the textView that you're using an attributed string and to use the attributes you've defined to format the string. You also set the Color Picker to white if the Hero has no color attribute defined.

Add the colorPicker callback method.

```
#pragma mark - (Private) Instance Methods

- (void)colorPickerChanged:(id)sender
{
    self.textField.attributedText = self.attributedColorString;
}
```

Again, you're telling the `textField` to update itself. But with what?

Finally, add the following code:

```
- (NSAttributedString *)attributedColorString
{
    NSString *block = [NSString stringWithUTF8String:"\u2588\u2588\u2588\u2588\u2588\u2588\
                                                      u2588\u2588\u2588\u2588"];
    UIColor *color = self.colorPicker.color;
    NSDictionary *attrs = @{NSForegroundColorAttributeName:color,
                    NSFontAttributeName:[UIFont boldSystemFontOfSize:[UIFont systemFontSize]]};
    NSAttributedString *attributedString =
        [[NSAttributedString alloc] initWithString:block attributes:attrs];
    return attributedString;
}
```

First, you define a string with a bunch of Unicode characters in it. `\u2588` is the Unicode character for a block character. All you've done is to make a string of ten block characters. Next, you ask the `colorPicker` to tell you its color. Then you use that color and the system bold font (15pt) to define a dictionary. The keys you use are `NSForegroundColorAttributeName` and `NSFontAttributeName`. These keys are specifically defined for UIKit-attributed string support. As you can infer from their names, `NSForegroundColorAttributeName` sets the foreground (or text) color of the string, and `NSFontAttributeName` allows you to define the font you want for the string. Finally, you instantiate the attributed string with the Unicode string block and the attributes dictionary.

You could have use the `textField`'s regular `text` property and just set the `textColor` as needed, but we thought this brief demonstration of attributed strings might pique your curiosity. Attributed strings are extremely flexible and powerful and are worth your time to investigate.

> **Note**   To learn more about attributed strings, check out Apple's Attributed String Programming
> Guide at `http://developer.apple.com/library/mac/#documentation/Cocoa/`
> `Conceptual/AttributedStrings/AttributedStrings.html`.

Cleaning Up the Picker

You have one more step before you can use your new Color Picker. First, you need to update the configuration property list to use the `SuperDBColorCell`. Open `HeroDetailController.plist` and drill down to Root ➤ sections ➤ Item 1 ➤ rows ➤ Item 4 ➤ class. Change its value from `SuperDBEditCell` to `SuperDBColorCell`.

All set? Let's build and run. Navigate down the detail view. Tap the Edit button and tap the Color cell.

That's weird. You didn't get the Color Picker to appear at all. But the Color cell has a cursor and clear text button (Figure 6-14).

Figure 6-14. Weird color cell appearance

You're probably getting tired of us having you build and run the app when we know things won't work. Think of it as an exercise in actual development. Many times you'll think you've gotten everything right, only to find things don't work when you run the app. That's when you have to (unit) test, debug, or think your way through to a solution.

Anyway, there's a reason why the Color Picker didn't appear. Edit SuperDBColorCell.m and find initWithStyle:reuseIdentifier:. In the initializer code, you created the Color Picker like this:

```
self.colorPicker = [[UIColorPicker alloc] initWithFrame:CGRectZero];
```

You made the size of the Color Picker a zero-sized CGRect. For all you know, it could be appearing. But since its size is zero, there's nothing to see. Didn't you do this with the Date Picker and Picker View? Yes, you did, but those classes have hooks inside of them to resize themselves accordingly. Since you built the Color Picker from scratch, you have to call those hooks manually.

First, you need to initialize the Color Picker with a nonzero CGRect. Use a default size to start.

```
self.colorPicker = [[UIColorPicker alloc] initWithFrame:CGRectMake(0, 0, 320, 216)];
```

Switch to UIColorPicker.m and add this method after the initWithFrame: method:

```
- (void)willMoveToSuperview:(UIView *)newSuperview
{
    self.frame = newSuperview.bounds;
}
```

Now when you run it and try to edit the Color cell, you should see something like Figure 6-15.

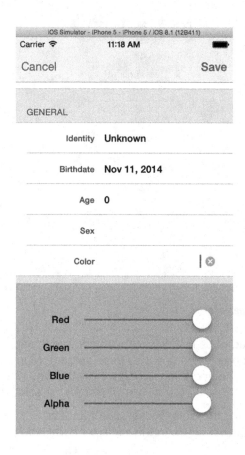

Figure 6-15. The Color Picker

Well, it works, but it doesn't look very pretty. You can fix that with some graphical magic. You should still be editing UIColorPicker.m. Add the following #import:

```
#import "QuartzCore/CAGradientLayer.h"
```

Now add the following #defines:

```
#define kTopBackgroundColor    [UIColor colorWithRed:0.98 green:0.98 blue:0.98 alpha:1.0]
#define kBottomBackgroundColor [UIColor colorWithRed:0.79 green:0.79 blue:0.79 alpha:1.0]
```

Look for a commented-out `drawRect:` method and uncomment it. If you deleted it, don't worry; just make it look like this:

```
- (void)drawRect:(CGRect)rect
{
    CAGradientLayer *gradient = [CAGradientLayer layer];
    gradient.frame = self.bounds;
gradient.colors = [NSArray arrayWithObjects:(__bridge id)[kTopBackgroundColor CGColor],
                                    (__bridge id)[kBottomBackgroundColor CGColor], nil];
    [self.layer insertSublayer:gradient atIndex:0];
}
```

We want to point out the `drawRect:` method. This method is used to set the background color of the Color Picker and give it a smooth color transition.

One last thing: you want to turn off the Clear Text button in the Color Cell. It's pretty simple. In `SuperDBColorCell.m`, add this line to the initialization code in `initWithStyle:reuseIdentifier:`

```
self.textField.clearButtonMode = UITextFieldViewModeNever;
```

Build and run the app. Navigate down and edit the Color cell. That's much better (Figure 6-16)!

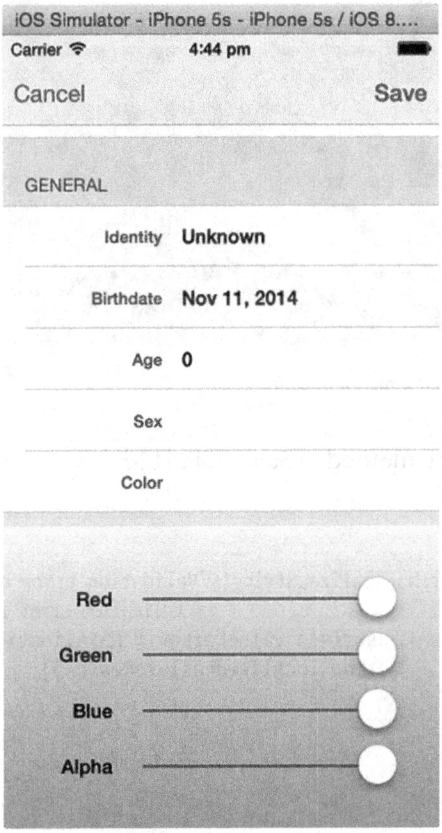

Figure 6-16. *Color Picker with a gradient background*

One More Thing

Run the app, and add a new hero. Enter Edit mode and clear out the Name field. Now tap the Identity field. As expected, the validation alert dialog will appear. However, it will not display the proper failure reason (Figure 6-17).

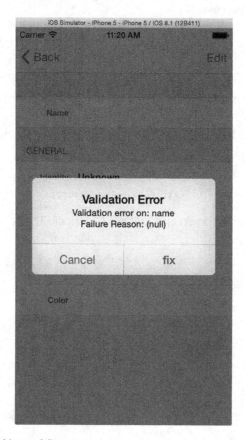

Figure 6-17. *Validation dialog without a failure reason*

Looking back at the `validate` method in `SuperDBEditCell.m`, you see the message is populated like this:

```
message =
    [NSString stringWithFormat:NSLocalizedString(@"Validation error on: %@\rFailure Reason: %@",
                                    @"Validation error on: %@, Failure Reason: %@)"),
                        [userInfo valueForKey:@"NSValidationErrorKey"],
                        [error localizedFailureReason]];
```

The method call to the NSError instance

```
[error localizedFailureReason]
```

is returning nil. Prior to iOS 4, Core Data used to populate the localizedFailureReason.
Since then, it doesn't. You need to provide a simple fix for this that you can customize.

NSError provides a method, code, that will return an integer error code. The value of this code
is defined depending on the origination of the error.

> **Note**   To learn more about how NSError and error codes work, read the Error Handling
> Programming Guide at https://developer.apple.com/library/ios/#documentation/
> Cocoa/Conceptual/ErrorHandlingCocoa/ErrorHandling/ErrorHandling.html.
> Specifically, read the chapter entitled "Error Objects, Domains, and Codes."

The error code you get here is defined in the Core Data header file CoreDataErrors.h.

> **Note**   CoreDataError.h is documented by Apple at https://developer.apple.com/
> library/ios/#documentation/Cocoa/Reference/CoreDataFramework/
> Miscellaneous/CoreData_Constants/Reference/reference.html.

You happen to know that the error code value you're getting is 1670. This is assigned the
enumeration of NSValidationStringTooShortError. You could put some logic to handle this
specific error code, and you'd be set, but we did a little more work for you.

Find the file CoreDataErrors.plist in the Book Downloads package. This is a simple plist file
we've created that maps the Core Data error code to a simple error message. Add this file to
the SuperDB project, making sure to make a copy.

You could make a CoreDataError class to handle the loading of this plist, but you'll take
an easier route for expediency's sake. First, declare a static dictionary at the top of
SuperDBEditCell.m, right before the @implementation declaration.

```
static NSDictionary *__CoreDataErrors;
```

Populate this dictionary in the class initializer. This will go right after the @implementation
declaration.

```
+ (void)initialize
{
NSURL *plistURL = [[NSBundle mainBundle] URLForResource:@"CoreDataErrors"
                                          withExtension:@"plist"];
    __CoreDataErrors = [NSDictionary dictionaryWithContentsOfURL:plistURL];
}
```

Now, you need to edit the `validate` method to use this dictionary. Find the line that begins with this:

```
if ([[error domain] isEqualToString:@"NSCocoaErrorDomain"]) {
```

and edit the `if` block to read as follows:

```
if ([[error domain] isEqualToString:@"NSCocoaErrorDomain"]) {
        NSString *errorCodeStr = [NSString stringWithFormat:@"%d", [error code]];
        NSString *errorMessage = [_CoreDataErrors valueForKey:errorCodeStr];
        NSDictionary *userInfo = [error userInfo];
        message =
            [NSString stringWithFormat:NSLocalizedString(@"Validation error on:
                                                %@\rFailure Reason: %@",
                        @"Validation error on:%@, Failure Reason: %@)"),
                        [userInfo valueForKey:@"NSValidationErrorKey"],
                        errorMessage];
}
```

Build and run the app. Erase the `Hero`'s name and try to move to another field. The validation alert dialog should look like Figure 6-4.

You can edit the string values in `CoreDataErrors.plist` to customize the error message however you like. Let's hope Apple restores this functionality soon.

Color Us Gone

By now, you should have a good grasp on just how much power you gain from subclassing and subclassing `NSManagedObject` specifically. You saw how to use it to do conditional defaulting and both single-field and multifield validation. You also saw how to use custom managed objects to create virtual accessors. You saw how to politely inform your user when they've entered an invalid attribute that causes a managed object to fail validation, and you saw how to use transformable attributes and value transformers to store custom objects in Core Data.

This was a dense chapter, but you should really be starting to get a feel for just how flexible and powerful Core Data can be. You have one more chapter on Core Data before you move on to other parts of the iOS 8 SDK. When you're ready, turn the page to learn about relationships and fetched properties.

Chapter 7

Relationships, Fetched Properties, and Expressions

Welcome to the final chapter on Core Data. So far, your application includes only a single entity, Hero. In this chapter, we'll show you how managed objects can incorporate and reference other managed objects through the use of relationships and fetched properties. This will give you the ability to make applications of much greater complexity than your current SuperDB application.

That's not the only thing you're going to do in this chapter, however. You'll also turn your HeroDetailController into a generic managed object controller. By making the controller code even more generic, you'll make the controller subclasses smaller and easier to maintain. You'll extend the configuration property list to allow you to define additional entity views.

You have a lot to do in this chapter, so no dallying. Let's get started.

Expanding Your Application: Superpowers and Reports

Before we talk about the nitty-gritty, let's quickly look at the changes you're going to make to the SuperDB application in this chapter. On the surface, the changes look relatively simple. You'll add the ability to specify any number of superpowers for each hero and also add a number of reports that show other superheroes that meet certain criteria, including heroes who are either younger or older than this hero or who are the same sex or the opposite sex (Figure 7-1).

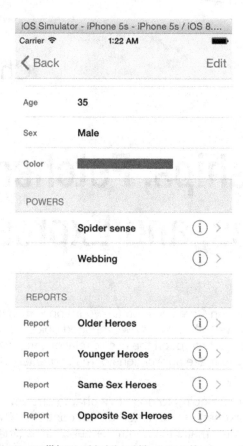

Figure 7-1. *At the end of this chapter, you'll have added the ability to specify any number of superpowers for each hero, as well as provided a number of reports that let you find other heroes based on how they relate to this hero*

The powers will be represented by a new entity that you'll create and imaginatively call Power. When users add or edit a power, they will be presented with a new view (Figure 7-2), but in reality, under the hood, it will be a new instance of the same object used to edit and display heroes.

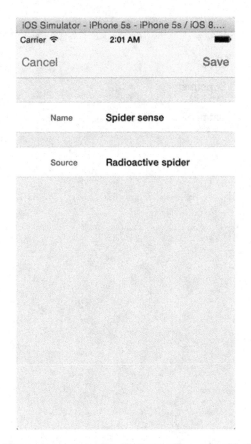

Figure 7-2. *The new view for editing powers is actually an instance of the same object used to edit heroes*

When users drill down into one of the reports, they will get a list of the other heroes that meet the selected criteria (Figure 7-3).

Figure 7-3. The Reports section on your hero will let you find other heroes who meet certain criteria in relation to the hero you're currently editing. Here, for example, you're seeing all the heroes who were born before Spiderman

Tapping any of the rows will take you to another view where you can edit that hero, using another instance of the same generic controller class. Your users will be able to drill down an infinite number of times (limited only by memory), all courtesy of a single class.

Before you start implementing these changes, you need to understand a few concepts and then make some changes to your data model.

Relationships

We introduced the concept of Core Data relationships in Chapter 2. Now we will go into more detail and show how they can be used in applications. The relationship is one of the most important concepts in Core Data. Without relationships, entities would be isolated. There would be no way to have one entity contain another entity or reference another entity.

Let's look at a hypothetical header file for a simple example of an old-fashioned data model class to give you a familiar point of reference:

```
#import <UIKit/UIKit.h>

@class Address;

@interface Person : NSObject

@property (strong, nonatomic) NSString *firstName;
@property (strong, nonatomic) NSString *lastName;
@property (strong, nonatomic) NSDate *birthdate;
@property (strong, nonatomic) UIImage *image;
@property (strong, nonatomic) Address *address;
@property (strong, nonatomic) Person *mother;
@property (strong, nonatomic) Person *father;
@property (strong, nonatomic) NSMutableArray *children;

@end
```

Here you have a class that represents a single person. You have instance variables to store a variety of information about that person and properties to expose that information to other objects. There's nothing earth-shattering here. Now, let's think about how you could re-create this object in Core Data.

The first four instance variables—firstName, lastName, birthDate, and image—can all be handled by built-in Core Data attribute types, so you could use attributes to store that information on the entity. The two NSString instances would become String attributes, the NSDate instance would become a Date attribute, and the UIImage instance would become a Transformable attribute, handled in the same way as UIColor in the previous chapter.

After that, you have an instance of an Address object. This object probably stores information such as street address, city, state or province, and postal code. That's followed by two Person instance variables and a mutable array designed to hold pointers to this person's children. Most likely, these arrays are intended to hold pointers to more Person objects.

In object-oriented programming, including a pointer to another object as an instance variable is called *composition*. Composition is an incredibly handy device because it lets you create much smaller classes and reuse objects, rather than have data duplicated.

In Core Data, you don't have composition per se, but you do have relationships, which essentially serve the same purpose. Relationships allow managed objects to include references to other managed objects of a specific entity, known as *destination entities*, or sometimes just destinations. Relationships are Core Data properties, just as attributes are. As such, they have an assigned name, which serves as the key value used to set and retrieve the object or objects represented by the relationship. Relationships are added to entities in Xcode's data model editor in the same way attributes are added. You'll see how to do this in a few minutes. There are two basic types of relationships: to-one relationships and to-many relationships.

To-One Relationships

When you create a to-one relationship, you are saying that one object can contain a pointer to a single managed object of a specific entity. In your example, the Person entity has a single to-one relationship to the Address entity.

Once you've added a to-one relationship to an object, you can assign a managed object to the relationship using key-value coding (KVC). For example, you might set the Address entity of a Person managed object like so:

```
NSManagedObject *address = [NSEntityDescription
                        insertNewObjectForEntityForName:@"Address"
                              inManagedObjectContext:thePerson.managedObjectContext];
[thePerson setValue:address forKey:@"address"];
```

Retrieving the object can also be accomplished using KVC, just with attributes:

```
NSManagedObject *address = [thePerson valueForKey:@"address"];
```

When you create a custom subclass of NSManagedObject, as you did in the previous chapter, you can use Objective-C properties and dot notation to get and set those properties. The property that represents a to-one relationship is an instance of NSManagedObject or a subclass of NSManagedObject, so setting the address looks just like setting attributes.

```
NSManagedObject *address = [NSEntityDescription
                        insertNewObjectForEntityForName:@"Address"
                              inManagedObjectContext:thePerson.managedObjectContext];
thePerson.address = address;
```

And retrieving a to-one relationship becomes as follows:

```
NSManagedObject *address = thePerson.address;
```

In almost every respect, the way you deal with a to-one relationship in code is identical to the way you've been dealing with Core Data attributes. You use KVC to get and set the values using Objective-C objects. Instead of using Foundation classes that correspond to different attribute types, you use NSManagedObject or a subclass of NSManagedObject that represents the entity.

To-Many Relationships

To-many relationships allow you to use a relationship to associate multiple managed objects to a particular managed object. This is equivalent to using composition with a collection class such as NSMutableArray or NSMutableSet in Objective-C, as with the children instance variable in the Person class you looked at earlier. In that example, you used an NSMutableArray, which is an editable, ordered collection of objects. That array allows you to add and remove objects at will. If you want to indicate that the person represented by an instance of Person has children, you just add the instance of Person that represents that person's children to the children array.

In Core Data, it works a little differently. To-many relationships are unordered. They are represented by instances of NSSet, which is an unordered, immutable collection that you can't change, or by NSMutableSet, an unordered collection that you can change. Here's how getting a to-many relationship and iterating over its contents might look with an NSSet:

```
NSSet *children = [thePerson valueForKey:@"children"];
for (NSManagedObject *oneChild in children) {
    // do something
}
```

> **Note** Do you spot a potential problem from the fact that to-many relationships are returned as an unordered NSSet? When displaying them in a table view, it's important that the objects in the relationship are ordered consistently. If the collection is unordered, you have no guarantee that the row you tap will bring up the object you expect. You'll see how to deal with that a little later in the chapter.

On the other hand, if you want to add or remove managed objects from a to-many relationship, you must ask Core Data to give you an instance of NSMutableSet by calling mutableSetValueForKey: instead of valueForKey:, like so:

```
NSManagedObject *child = [NSEntityDescription insertNewObjectForEntityForName:@"Person"
                              inManagedObjectContext:thePerson.managedObjectContext];
NSMutableSet *children = [thePerson mutableSetValueForKey:@"children"];

[children addObject:child];
[children removeObject:child];
```

If you don't need to change which objects a particular relationship contains, use valueForKey:, just as with to-one arrays. Don't call mutableSetValueForKey: if you don't need to change which objects make up the relationship because it incurs slightly more overhead than just calling valueForKey:.

In addition to using valueForKey: and mutableSetValueForKey:, Core Data also provides special methods, created dynamically at runtime, that let you add and delete managed objects from a to-many relationship. There are four of these methods per relationship. Each method name incorporates the name of the relationship. The first allows you to add a single object to a relationship

```
- (void)addXXXObject:(NSManagedObject *)value;
```

where XXX is the capitalized name of the relationship and value is either an NSManagedObject or a specific subclass of NSManagedObject. In the Person example you've been working with, the method to add a child to the children relationship looks like this:

```
- (void)addChildrenObject:(Person *)value;
```

The method for deleting a single object follows a similar form.

```
- (void)removeXXXObject:(NSManagedObject *)value;
```

The dynamically generated method for adding multiple objects to a relationship takes the following form:

```
- (void)addXXX:(NSSet *)values;
```

The method takes an instance of NSSet containing the managed objects to be added. So, the dynamically created method for adding multiple children to your Person managed object is as follows:

```
- (void)addChildren:(NSSet *)values;
```

Finally, here's the method used to remove multiple managed objects from a relationship:

```
- (void)removeXXX:(NSSet *)values;
```

Remember that these methods are generated for you when you declare a custom NSManagedObject subclass. When Xcode encounters your NSManagedObject subclass declaration, it creates a category on the subclass that declares the four dynamic methods using the relationship name to construct the method names. Since the methods are generated at runtime, you won't find any source code in your project that implements the methods. If you never call the methods, you'll never see the methods. As long as you've already created the to-many relationship in your model editor, you don't need to do anything extra to access these methods. They are created for you and ready to be called.

> **Note** There's one tricky point associated with the methods generated for to-many relationships. Xcode declares the four dynamic methods when you first generate the NSManagedObject subclass files from the template. If you have an existing data model with a to-many relationship and a subclass of NSManagedObject, what happens if you decide to add a new to-many relationship to that data model? If you add the to-many relationship to an existing NSManagedObject subclass, you need to add the category containing the dynamic methods yourself, which is what you'll do a little later in the chapter.

There is absolutely no difference between using these four methods and using mutableSetValueForKey:. The dynamic methods are just a little more convenient and make your code easier to read.

Inverse Relationships

In Core Data, every relationship can have an inverse relationship. A relationship and its inverse are two sides of the same coin. In your Person object example, the inverse relationship for the children relationship might be a relationship called parent. A relationship does not need to be the same kind as its inverse. A to-one relationship, for example, can have an inverse relationship that is to-many. In fact, this is pretty common. If you think about it in real-world terms, a person can have many children. The inverse is that a child can have only one biological mother and one biological father, but the child can have multiple parents and guardians. So, depending on your needs and the way you modeled the relationship, you might choose to use either a to-one or a to-many relationship for the inverse.

If you add an object to a relationship, Core Data will automatically take care of adding the correct object to the inverse relationship. So, if you had a person named Steve and added a child to Steve, Core Data would automatically make the child's parent Steve.

Although relationships are not required to have an inverse, Apple generally recommends that you always create and specify the inverse, even if you won't need to use the inverse relationship in your application. In fact, the compiler will actually warn you if you fail to provide an inverse. There are some exceptions to this general rule, specifically when the inverse relationship will contain an extremely large number of objects, since removing the object from a relationship triggers its removal from the inverse relationship. Removing the inverse will require iterating over the set that represents the inverse, and if that's a very large set, there could be performance implications. But unless you have a specific reason not to do so, you should model the inverse because it helps Core Data ensure data integrity. If you have performance issues as a result, it's relatively easy to remove the inverse relationship later.

> **Note**   You can read more about how the absence of inverse relationships can cause integrity problems at https://developer.apple.com/library/mac/#documentation/Cocoa/ Conceptual/CoreData/Articles/cdRelationships.html.

Fetched Properties

Relationships allow you to associate managed objects with specific other managed objects. In a way, relationships are sort of like iTunes playlists where you can put specific songs into a list and then play them later. If you're an iTunes user, you know that there are things called Smart Playlists, which allow you to create playlists based on criteria rather than a list of specific songs. You can create a Smart Playlist, for example, that includes all the songs by a specific artist. Later, when you buy new songs from that artist, they are added to that Smart Playlist automatically because the playlist is based on criteria and the new songs meet those criteria.

Core Data has something similar. There's another type of attribute you can add to an entity that will associate a managed object with other managed objects based on criteria, rather than associating specific objects. Instead of adding and removing objects, fetched properties work by creating a predicate that defines which objects should be returned. Predicates, as you may recall, are objects that represent selection criteria. They are primarily used to sort collections and fetch results.

> **Tip** If you're rusty on predicates, *Learn Objective-C on the Mac,* by Scott Knaster, Waqar Maliq, and Mark Dalrymple devotes an entire chapter to the little beasties.

Fetched properties are always immutable. You can't change their contents at runtime. The criteria are usually specified in the data model (a process that you'll look at shortly), and then you access the objects that meet that criteria using properties or KVC.

Unlike to-many relationships, fetched properties are ordered collections and can have a specified sort order. Oddly enough, the data model editor doesn't allow you to specify how fetched properties are sorted. If you care about the order of the objects in a fetched property, you must actually write code to do that, which you'll look at later in this chapter.

Once you've created a fetched property, working with it is pretty straightforward. You just use valueForKey: to retrieve the objects that meet the fetched property's criteria in an instance of NSArray.

```
NSArray *olderPeople = [person valueForKey:@"olderPeople"];
```

If you use a custom NSManagedObject subclass and define a property for the fetched property, you can also use dot notation to retrieve objects that meet the fetched property's criteria in an NSArray instance, like so:

```
NSArray *olderPeople = person.olderPeople;
```

Creating Relationships and Fetched Properties in the Data Model Editor

The first step in using relationships or fetched properties is to add them to your data model. Let's add the relationship and fetched properties you'll need in your SuperDB application now. If you look back at Figure 7-1, you can probably guess that you're going to need a new entity to represent the heroes' powers, as well as a relationship from your existing Hero entity to the new Power entity you're going to create. You'll also need four fetched properties to represent the four different reports.

Delete Rules

Every relationship, regardless of its type, has something called a *delete rule*, which specifies what happens when one object in the relationship is deleted. There are four possible delete rules:

- *Nullify*: This is the default delete rule. With this delete rule, when one object is deleted, the inverse relationship is just updated so that it doesn't point to anything. If the inverse relationship is a to-one relationship, it is set to `nil`. If the inverse relationship is a to-many relationship, the deleted object will be removed from the inverse relationship. This option ensures that there are no references to the object being deleted but does nothing more.

- *No Action*: If you specify a delete rule of No Action, when you delete one object from a relationship, nothing happens to the other object. Instances where you would use this particular rule are extremely rare and are generally limited to one-way relationships with no inverse. This action is rarely used because the other object's inverse relationship would end up pointing to an object that no longer exists.

- *Cascade*: If you set the delete rule to Cascade, when you delete a managed object, all the objects in the relationship are also removed. This is a more dangerous option than Nullify, in that deleting one object can result in the deletion of other objects. You would typically choose Cascade when a relationship's inverse relationship is to-one and the related object is not used in any other relationships. If the object or objects in the relationship are used only for this relationship and not for any other reason, then you probably do want a Cascade rule so that you don't leave orphaned objects sitting in the persistent store taking up space.

- *Deny*: This delete rule option will actually prevent an object from being deleted if there are any objects in this association, making it the safest option in terms of data integrity. The Deny option is not used frequently, but if you have situations where an object shouldn't be deleted as long as it has any objects in a specific relationship, this is the one you would choose.

Expressions and Aggregates

Another use of expressions is to aggregate attributes without loading them all into memory. If you want to get the average, median, minimum, or maximum for a specific attribute, such as the average age of your heroes or count of female heroes, you can do that (and more) with an expression. In fact, that's how you should do it. To understand why, you need to know a little about the way Core Data works under the hood.

The fetched results controller you're using in `HeroListController` contains objects for all of the heroes in your database, but it doesn't have all of them fully loaded into memory as managed objects. Core Data has a concept of a fault. A fault is sort of like a stand-in for a managed object. A fault object knows a bit about the managed object it's standing in for, such as its unique ID and perhaps the value of one attribute being displayed, but it's not a fully managed object.

A fault turns into a full-fledged managed object when something triggers the fault. Triggering a fault usually happens when you access an attribute or key that the fault doesn't know about. Core Data is smart enough to turn a fault into a managed object when necessary, so your code usually doesn't need to worry about whether it's dealing with a fault or a managed object.

However, it's important to know about this behavior so you don't unintentionally cause performance problems by triggering faults unnecessarily.

Most likely, the faults in your fetched results controller don't know anything about the sex attribute of Hero. So, if you were to loop through the heroes in your fetched results controller to get a count of the female heroes, you would be triggering every fault to become a managed object. That's inefficient because it uses a lot more memory and processing power than necessary. Instead, you can use expressions to retrieve aggregate values from Core Data without triggering faults.

Here's an example of how to use an expression to retrieve the average birth date calculated for all female heroes in your application (you can't use age in a fetch request because it's a transient attribute that isn't stored):

```
NSExpression *ex = [NSExpression expressionForFunction:@"average:"
                           arguments:@[[NSExpression expressionForKeyPath:@"birthdate"]]];
NSPredicate *pred = [NSPredicate predicateWithFormat:@"sex == 'Female'"];

NSExpressionDescription *ed = [[NSExpressionDescription alloc] init];
[ed setName:@"averageBirthdate"];
[ed setExpression:ex];
[ed setExpressionResultType:NSDateAttributeType];

NSArray *properties = [NSArray arrayWithObject:ed];

NSFetchRequest *request = [[NSFetchRequest alloc] init];
[request setPredicate:pred];
[request setPropertiesToFetch:properties];
[request setResultType:NSDictionaryResultType];

NSEntityDescription *entity = [NSEntityDescription entityForName:@"Hero"
                                    inManagedObjectContext:context];
[request setEntity:entity];

NSArray *results = [context executeFetchRequest:request error:nil];
NSDate *date = [results objectAtIndex:0];
NSLog(@"Average birthdate for female heroes: %@", date);
```

Aggregate expressions are relatively new to Core Data. As of this writing, the process of using expressions to obtain aggregates is not thoroughly documented, but the preceding code sample, along with the API documentation for NSExpression and NSExpressionDescription, should get you pointed in the right direction for working with aggregates.

Adding the Power Entity

Before you start making changes, create a new version of your data model by single-clicking the current version in the Groups & Files pane (the one with the green check mark) and then selecting Add Model Version from the Data Model submenu of the Editor menu. This ensures that the data you collected using the previous data models migrate properly to the new version you'll be creating in this chapter.

Click the current data model to bring up the model editor. Using the plus icon in the lower-left corner of the model editor's entity pane, add a new entity and call it **Power**. You can leave all the other fields at their default values (Figure 7-4).

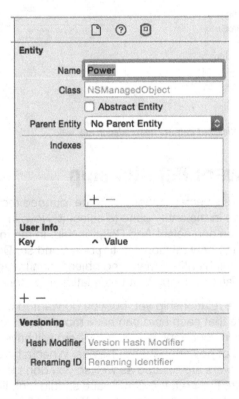

Figure 7-4. Rename the new entity Power and leave the other fields at their default values

If you look back at Figure 7-2, you can see that the Power object has two fields: one for the name of the power and another that identifies the source of this particular power. In the interest of keeping things simple, the two attributes will just hold string values.

With Power selected in the property pane, add two attributes using the property pane. Call one of them **name**, uncheck the Optional check box, set its Type to String, and give it a Default value of New Power. Give the second one a name of **source** and set its Type to String as well.

Leave Optional checked. There is no need for a default value. Once you're finished, you should have two rounded rectangles in the model editor's diagram view (Figure 7-5).

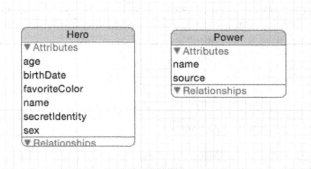

Figure 7-5. You now have two entities, but they are not related in any way

Creating the Powers Relationship

Right now, the Power entity is selected. Single-click the rounded rectangle that represents the Hero entity or select Hero in the entity pane to select it. Now, in the properties pane, click and hold the plus button and select Add Relationship. In the model editor's detail pane, change the name of the new relationship to powers and set Destination to Power. The Destination field specifies which entity's managed objects can be added to this relationship, so by selecting Power, you are indicating that this relationship stores powers.

You can't specify the inverse relationship yet, but you do want to check the To-Many Relationship box to indicate that each hero can have more than one power. Also, change the delete rule to Cascade. In your application, every hero will have his or her own set of powers—there's no sharing of powers between heroes. When a hero is deleted, you want to make sure that hero's powers are deleted as well so you don't leave orphaned data in the persistent store. Once you're finished, the detail pane should look like Figure 7-6, and the diagram view should have a line drawn between the Hero and Power entities to represent the new relationship (Figure 7-7).

Relationship

Name	powers
Properties	☐ Transient ☑ Optional
Destination	Power
Inverse	No Inverse Relationship
Delete Rule	Cascade
Type	To Many
Arrangement	☐ Ordered
Count	Unbounded ☐ Minimum
	Unbounded ☐ Maximum
Advanced	☐ Index in Spotlight
	☐ Store in External Record File

User Info

Key	^ Value

+ −

Versioning

Hash Modifier	Version Hash Modifier
Renaming ID	Renaming Identifier

Figure 7-6. *The detail pane view of the powers relationship*

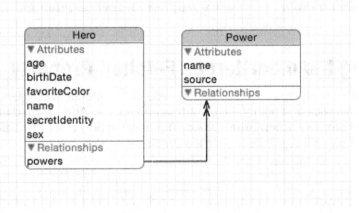

Figure 7-7. *Relationships are represented in the diagram view by lines drawn between rounded rectangles. A single arrowhead represents a to-one relationship, and a double arrowhead (as shown here) represents a to-many relationship*

Creating the Inverse Relationship

You won't actually need the inverse relationship in your application, but you're going to follow Apple's recommendation and specify one. Since the inverse relationship will be to-one, it doesn't present any performance implications. Select the Power entity again, and add a relationship to it using the property pane. Name this new relationship **hero**, and select a Destination entity of Hero. If you look at your diagram view now, you should see two lines representing the two different relationships you've created.

Next, click the Inverse pop-up menu and select powers. This indicates that the relationship is the inverse of the one you created earlier. Once you've selected it, the two relationship lines in the diagram view will merge together into a single line with arrowheads on both sides (Figure 7-8).

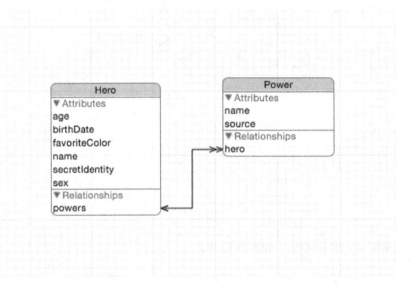

Figure 7-8. Inverse relationships are represented as a single line with arrowheads on both sides, rather than two separate lines

Creating the olderHeroes Fetched Property

Select the Hero entity again so that you can add some fetched properties to it. In the property pane, click and hold the plus button and choose Add Fetched Property. Call the new fetched property olderHeroes. Notice that there is only one other field that can be set on the detail pane: a big white box called Predicate (Figure 7-9).

Figure 7-9. The detail pane showing a fetched property

What Is a Predicate?

A predicate is a statement that returns a Boolean value. Think of them as like a conditional statement within an if or while. They are intended to be used against a set of objects, whether Cocoa or Core Data. Predicates are not dependent on the specific data being searched but rather provide an abstract way of defining a query to filter data. At its simplest, a predicate compares two values using an operator. An example operator would be == to test whether two values are equal. There are more sophisticated operators that allow for string comparison (using LIKE or CONTAINS). Predicates can be joined to format a compound predicated. Typically, predicates are joined with an AND or an OR operator.

There are two special variables you can use in the predicate of a fetched property: $FETCH_SOURCE and $FETCHED_PROPERTY. $FETCH_SOURCE refers to the specific instance of a managed object. $FETCHED_PROPERTY is a description of the entity property being fetched.

You can read more detail in Apple's Predicate Programming Guide https://developer. apple.com/library/ios/documentation/Cocoa/Conceptual/Predicates/Predicates.pdf).

Tip   Both relationships and fetched properties can use their own entity as the destination.

So, you need to define a predicate that finds all the heroes who are older (in other words, have an earlier `birthDate`) than the `Hero` in the detail view. You need to compare your Hero's `birthDate` against all the other `Hero` entities. If `$FETCH_SOURCE` is your `Hero` entity, your predicate will be as follows:

```
$FETCH_SOURCE.birthDate > birthDate
```

Enter this formula into the Predicate field in the Attributes Inspector. Remember, a date is really just an integer; the later the date, the greater the value.

Creating the youngerHeroes Fetched Property

Add another fetched property named `youngerHeroes`. The destination will be `Hero` again, and the predicate should be the same as the previous one, except the operator will be `<` instead of `>`. Type the following for the `youngerHeroes` predicate in the Attributes Inspector:

```
$FETCH_SOURCE.birthDate < birthDate
```

One thing to be aware of is that a fetched property retrieves all matching objects, potentially including the object on which the fetch is being performed. This means it is possible to create a result set that, when executed on Super Cat, returns Super Cat.

Both the `youngerHeroes` and `olderHeroes` fetched properties automatically exclude the hero being evaluated. Heroes cannot be older or younger than themselves; their birth date will always exactly equal their own birth date, so no hero will ever meet the two criteria you just created.

Let's now add a fetched property that has slightly more complex criteria.

Creating the sameSexHeroes Fetched Property

The next fetched property you're going to create is called `sameSexHeroes`, which it returns all heroes who are the same sex as this hero. You can't just specify to return all heroes of the same sex, however, because you don't want this hero to be included in the fetched property. Super Cat is the same sex as Super Cat, but users will not expect to see Super Cat when they look at a list of the heroes who are the same sex as Super Cat.

Create another fetched property, naming it `sameSexHeroes`. Open the model editor. Make sure Destination is set to Hero. For the Predicate field, type the following:

```
($FETCH_SOURCE.sex == sex) AND ($FETCH_SOURCE != SELF)
```

It's pretty clear what the left side of this compound predicate is doing. But what are you doing on the right side? Remember, a fetched property predicate will return all matching objects, including the object that owns the fetched property. In this case, you asked for all heroes of a certain sex, and your hero in the detail view will match that criteria. You need to exclude that specific hero.

You could just compare names and exclude heroes with the same name as yours. That might work, except for the fact that two heroes might have the same name. Maybe using name isn't the best idea. But what value is there that uniquely identifies a single hero? There isn't one, really.

Fortunately, predicates recognize a special value called SELF, which returns the object being compared. The $FETCH_SOURCE variable represents the object where the fetch request is happening. Therefore, to exclude the object where the fetch request is firing, you just need to require it to return only objects where $FETCH_SOURCE != SELF.

Creating the oppositeSexHeroes Fetched Property

Create a new fetched property called oppositeSexHeroes and enter the predicate as follows:

```
$FETCH_SOURCE.sex != sex
```

Make sure you save your data model before continuing.

Adding Relationships and Fetched Properties to the Hero Class

Since you created a custom subclass of NSManagedObject, you need to update that class to include the new relationship and fetched properties. If you had not made any changes to the Hero class, you could just regenerate the class definition from your data model, and the newly generated version would include properties and methods for the relationships and fetched properties you just added to your data model. Since you have added validation code, you need to update it manually. Single-click Hero.h and add the following code before @interface:

```
@class Power;
```

Add the following code after the other properties:

```
@property (nonatomic, retain) NSSet *powers;

@property (nonatomic, readonly) NSArray *olderHeroes;
@property (nonatomic, readonly) NSArray *youngerHeroes;
@property (nonatomic, readonly) NSArray *sameSexHeroes;
@property (nonatomic, readonly) NSArray *oppositeSexHeroes;
```

Add the following code after @end:

```
@interface Hero (PowerAccessors)
- (void)addPowersObject:(Power *)value;
- (void)removePowersObject:(Power *)value;
- (void)addPowers:(NSSet *)value;
- (void)removePowers:(NSSet *)value;
@end
```

Save the file. Switch to Hero.m and make the following changes (after the other @dynamic declarations):

```
@dynamic powers;
@dynamic olderHeroes, youngerHeroes, sameSexHeroes, oppositeSexHeroes;
```

Updating the Detail View

Looking at Figure 7-1, you have two new table view sections to add to your detail view: Powers and Reports. Unfortunately, it won't be as easy as adding new cells to the General section was in Chapter 6. It turns out that you can't use the storyboard editor to set things up for you. The reason is that the Powers section is dynamically data driven. You don't know how many rows are in the Powers section until you have a Hero entity to inspect. All the other sections have a fixed set of rows.

You start by converting HeroDetailController to be more data-driven in its current configuration. Open SuperDB.storyboard and find the HeroDetailController. Select the table view and open the Attributes Inspector. Change the table view's Content field from Static Cells to Dynamic Prototypes. The detail view should change to a single table view cell with a section header of Prototype Cells (Figure 7-10).

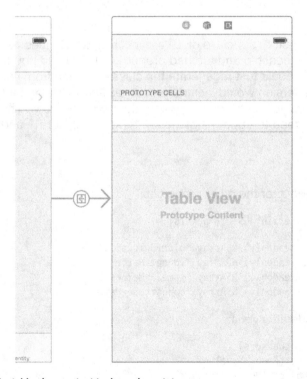

Figure 7-10. Changing the table view content to dynamic prototypes

Select the one table view cell that remains and change the Utility pane to the Attributes Inspector. In the Identifier field, delete it so that it is empty.

Now open HeroDetailController.m. Look for the methods numberOfSectionsInTableView: and tableView:numberOfRowsInSection:. You can't use the jump bar to find them because you commented them out, but if you look for the label "Table view data source," it should place you near the right place. Uncomment the methods, and change their bodies to read as follows:

```
- (NSInteger)numberOfSectionsInTableView:(UITableView *)tableView
{
    return self.sections.count;
}

- (NSInteger)tableView:(UITableView *)tableView numberOfRowsInSection:(NSInteger)section
{
    NSDictionary *sectionDict = [self.sections objectAtIndex:section];
    NSArray *rows = [sectionDict objectForKey:@"rows"];
    return rows.count;
}
```

You're simply using your configuration information to determine how many sections your table view has and how many rows are in each section.

Now, your configuration information doesn't contain the Header value. If you ran the app now, the detail view would look like Figure 7-11.

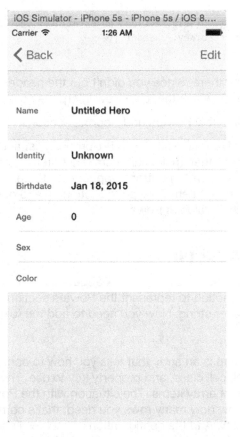

Figure 7-11. Detail view with no general section header

Add the header information to your configuration plist. Edit HeroDetailConfiguration.plist and navigate to Root ➤ Section ➤ Item 1. Open Item 1, select the Item 1 row, and add a new item. Give the item a key of header and a value of General. Keep the type as String (Figure 7-12).

Key	Type	Value
▼ Root	Dictionary	(1 item)
▼ sections	Array	(2 items)
▶ Item 0	Dictionary	(1 item)
▼ Item 1	Dictionary	(2 items)
header	String	General
▶ rows	Array	(5 items)

Figure 7-12. Adding the general section header to the property list

Now head back over to HeroDetailController.m. Add the following method (we put it after tableView:numberOfRowsInSection:):

```
- (NSString *)tableView:(UITableView *)tableView titleForHeaderInSection:(NSInteger)section
{
    NSDictionary *sectionDict = [self.sections objectAtIndex:section];
    return [sectionDict objectForKey:@"header"];
}
```

The General label should be there. Since you didn't put the header item in the first section, objectForKey: will return nil, which the table view interprets as no header label.

Now you're ready to add the new Powers and Reports sections.

Head back to the HeroDetailConfiguration.plist property list and select the Sections item. Open the Sections item; then make sure Item 0 and Item 1 are both closed. Hover the pointer over Item 1 until the (+) and (-) buttons appear next to Item 1. Click the (+) button. A new Item 2 should appear. Set Item 2's type to Dictionary and open it. Add a new row to Item 2. Name it **header** with a value of Powers.

Rethinking Configuration

Before you go further, take a step back and think about your detail configuration property list. You just added a new section to represent the Powers section. You added a header item to contain the Section Header string. Now you need to add the rows item, right?

Probably not.

Remember that the rows item is an array that tells you how to configure each cell in the section plus what label, cell class, and property key to use. The number of cells is determined by the number of array items. The situation with the Powers section is almost the opposite. You don't know how many rows you need; that's coming from the Powers relationship of the Hero entity. And the configuration of each cell should be identical.

There are a couple of approaches you can take. Let's discuss two ideas.

For the Powers section, you'll make the rows item a dictionary. The dictionary will contain three String items. The keys will be key, class, and label. These are the same keys you are using for each item when rows is an Array. You can infer that when the rows item is a dictionary, the section is data-driven; but when the rows item is an Array, the section is configuration-driven.

Here's another approach. For each section, along with the header item, you define an item titled dynamic, which will be a Boolean type. If YES, then the section is data-driven; if NO, the section is configuration-driven. For all cases, rows will be an array, but for dynamic sections, it will contain only one entry. If there is no dynamic item, it is the same as dynamic being set to NO.

Either approach will work. There are probably many more ideas we could toss around, but that's not where we're heading with this. Regardless of the approach you take, it's going to require adding a lot of code to handle this logic—code that, so far, you've put inside the HeroDetailController class. Adding this parsing logic may belong inside the HeroDetailController but, as it gets more complicated, will only muddy your code. You're going to refactor your application to pull the property list–handling code out of HeroDetailController into a new class, HeroDetailConfiguration. Then you'll choose which approach to take to handle the data-driven Powers section.

Create a new Cocoa Touch Class file. Make it a subclass of NSObject and name it HeroDetailConfiguration.

Looking at HeroDetailController, you see that you put the sections array inside a private category. You'll do the same for HeroDetailConfiguration. Open HeroDetailConfiguration.m and add the following before the @implmentation:

```
@interface HeroDetailConfiguration ()
@property (strong, nonatomic) NSArray *sections;
@end
```

Next you need to create your initializer. You want it to open the property list and parse the contents into the sections array.

```
- (id)init
{
    self = [super init];
    if (self) {
        // Initialization Code
        NSURL *plistURL = [[NSBundle mainBundle] URLForResource:@"HeroDetailConfiguration"
                                                  withExtension:@"plist"];
        NSDictionary *plist = [NSDictionary dictionaryWithContentsOfURL:plistURL];
        self.sections = [plist valueForKey:@"sections"];
    }
    return self;
}
```

Now let's go back to HeroDetailController.m and see where to use the sections array. The following methods access the HeroDetailController sections array:

```
numberOfSectionsInTableView:
tableView:numberOfRowsInSection:
tableView:titleForHeaderInSection:
tableView:cellForRowAtIndexPath:
```

You can use this to design your methods for HeroDetailConfiguration. Right off the bat, you can see the three methods needed.

```
numberOfSections
numberOfRowsInSection:
headerInSection:
```

Define the methods in HeroDetailConfiguration.h.

```
- (NSInteger)numberOfSections;
- (NSInteger)numberOfRowsInSection:(NSInteger)section;
- (NSString *)headerInSection:(NSInteger)section;
```

Now let's implement them in HeroDetailConfiguration.m. It should be pretty straightforward.

```
- (NSInteger)numberOfSections
{
    return self.sections.count;
}

- (NSInteger)numberOfRowsInSection:(NSInteger)section
{
    NSDictionary *sectionDict = [self.sections objectAtIndex:section];
    NSArray *rows = [sectionDict objectForKey:@"rows"];
    return rows.count;
}

- (NSString *)headerInSection:(NSInteger)section
{
    NSDictionary *sectionDict = [self.sections objectAtIndex:section];
    return [sectionDict objectForKey:@"header"];
}
```

The implementations should be pretty much the same as what you implemented before in the HeroDetailController.

Now you need to look at what you're doing in HeroDetailController tableView:cellForRow AtIndexPath:. The heart of the what's needed is at the beginning of the method.

```
NSUInteger sectionIndex = [indexPath section];
NSUInteger rowIndex = [indexPath row];
NSDictionary *section = [self.sections objectAtIndex:sectionIndex];
NSArray *rows = [section objectForKey:@"rows"];
NSDictionary *row = [rows objectAtIndex:rowIndex];
```

Essentially, you get the row dictionary for a specific index path. And that's what you need your HeroDetailConfiguration object to do for you: give you a row dictionary for an index path. So, the method you want would be something like this:

```
- (NSDictionary *)rowForIndexPath:(NSIndexPath *)indexPath;
```

Let's add it to HeroDetailConfiguration.h. And let's stub the body in HeroDetailConfiguration.m.

Before you worry about handling the issue of implementing the Powers section, just replicate the functionality you already have in place. In this case, you just add the five lines of code from the beginning of HeroDetailController tableView:cellForRowAtIndexPath: and put them in your new method.

```
- (NSDictionary *)rowForIndexPath:(NSIndexPath *)indexPath
{
    NSUInteger sectionIndex = [indexPath section];
    NSUInteger rowIndex = [indexPath row];
    NSDictionary *section = [self.sections objectAtIndex:sectionIndex];
    NSArray *rows = [section objectForKey:@"rows"];
    NSDictionary *row = [rows objectAtIndex:rowIndex];
    return row;
}
```

> **Note** If you find the compiler complaining about indexPath not having a selector section or row, then you need to add the line #import <UIKit/UIKit.h> to HeroDetailController.h.

Now let's edit HeroDetailController.m to use your new HeroDetailConfiguration class. First, add the #import at the top (right after the SuperDBEditCell #import).

```
#import "HeroDetailConfiguration.h"
```

Replace the sections Property declaration with one for HeroDetailConfiguration.

```
@property (strong, nonatomic) NSArray *sections;
@property (strong, nonatomic) HeroDetailConfiguration *config;
```

Replace the sections initialization code in viewDidLoad with config initialization.

```
    NSURL *plistURL = [[NSBundle mainBundle] URLForResource:@"HeroDetailController"
        withExtension:@"plist"];
    NSDictionary *plist = [NSDictionary dictionaryWithContentsOfURL:plistURL];
    self.sections = [plist valueForKey:@"sections"];
    self.config = [[HeroDetailConfiguration alloc] init];
```

Replace the code in numberOfSectionsInTableView.

```
- (NSInteger)numberOfSectionsInTableView:(UITableView *)tableView
{
    return self.sections.count;
    return [self.config numberOfSections];
}
```

Replace the code in tableView:numberOfRowsInSection:.

```
- (NSInteger)tableView:(UITableView *)tableView numberOfRowsInSection:(NSInteger)section
{
    NSDictionary *sectionDict = [self.sections objectAtIndex:section];
    NSArray *rows = [sectionDict objectForKey:@"rows"];
    return row.count;
    return [self.config numberOfRowsInSection:section];
}
```

Replace the code in tableView:titleForHeaderInSection:.

```
- (NSString *)tableView:(UITableView *)tableView titleForHeaderInSection:(NSInteger)section
{
    NSDictionary *sectionDict = [self.sections objectAtIndex:section];
    return [sectionDict objectForKey:@"header"];
    return [self.config headerInSection:section];
}
```

Finally, replace the code in tableView:cellForRowAtIndexPath:.

```
    NSUInteger sectionIndex = [indexPath section];
    NSUInteger rowIndex = [indexPath row];
    NSDictionary *section = [self.sections objectAtIndex:sectionIndex];
    NSArray *rows = [section objectForKey:@"rows"];
    NSDictionary *row = [rows objectAtIndex:rowIndex];
    NSDictionary *row = [self.config rowForIndexPath:indexPath];
```

At this point, your app should behave just like it did before you started this refactoring.

Encapsulation and Information Hiding

Before you move on to handling the Power section (you'll get there soon, promise!), let's look at HeroDetailController tableView:cellForRowAtIndexPath: once more. Your HeroDetailConfiguration is returning a row dictionary. In turn, you are using that information throughout the remainder of the method.

```
NSDictionary *row = [self.config rowForIndexPath:indexPath];
NSString *cellClassname = [row objectForKey:@"class"];
...
NSArray *values = [row valueForKey:@"values"];
...
```

```
cell.key = [row objectForKey:@"key"];
cell.value = [self.hero valueForKey:[row objectForKey:@"key"]];
cell.label.text = [row objectForKey:@"label"];
```

While it's probably fine to keep things this way, you most likely want to replace these calls with a method in HeroDetailConfiguration. Why? In short, because of two concepts: encapsulation and information hiding. Information hiding is the idea of hiding the implementation details. Imagine that you change how you store your configuration information. In that case, you'd have to change the way you populate your table view cell. By putting the specific access calls inside HeroDetailConfiguration, you don't have to worry if your configuration storage mechanism changes. You can freely change the internal implementation without having to worry about your table view cell code. Encapsulation is the idea that you placed all the configuration access code into a single object, HeroDetailConfiguration, rather peppering the access code all over your view controllers.

Looking at the calls to objectForKey: on the row dictionary, you probably want methods like these:

```
- (NSString *)cellClassnameForIndexPath:(NSIndexPath *)indexPath;
- (NSArray *)valuesForIndexPath:(NSIndexPath *)indexPath;
- (NSString *)attributeKeyForIndexPath:(NSIndexPath *)indexPath;
- (NSString *)labelForIndexPath:(NSIndexPath *)indexPath;
```

Add them to HeroDetailConfiguration.h and then add their implementations to HeroDetailConfiguration.m.

```
- (NSString *)cellClassnameForIndexPath:(NSIndexPath *)indexPath
{
    NSDictionary *row = [self rowForIndexPath:indexPath];
    return [row objectForKey:@"class"];
}

- (NSArray *)valuesForIndexPath:(NSIndexPath *)indexPath
{
    NSDictionary *row = [self rowForIndexPath:indexPath];
    return [row objectForKey:@"values"];
}

- (NSString *)attributeKeyForIndexPath:(NSIndexPath *)indexPath
{
    NSDictionary *row = [self rowForIndexPath:indexPath];
    return [row objectForKey:@"key"];
}

- (NSString *)labelForIndexPath:(NSIndexPath *)indexPath
{
    NSDictionary *row = [self rowForIndexPath:indexPath];
    return [row objectForKey:@"label"];
}
```

Finally, replace the code in HeroDetailController tableView:cellForRowAtIndexPath: with the new methods.

```
NSDictionary *row = [self.config rowForIndexPath:indexPath];
NSString *cellClassname = [row objectForKey:@"class"];
NSString *cellClassname = [self.config cellClassnameForIndexPath:indexPath];
    ...
NSArray *values = [row valueForKey:@"values"];
NSArray *values = [self.config valuesForIndexPath:indexPath];
    ...
cell.key = [row objectForKey:@"key"];
cell.value = [self.hero valueForKey:[row objectForKey:@"key"]];
cell.label.text = [row objectForKey:@"label"];
cell.key = [self.config attributeKeyForIndexPath:indexPath];
cell.value = [self.hero valueForKey:[self.config attributeKeyForIndexPath:indexPath]];
cell.label.text = [self.config labelForIndexPath:indexPath];
```

If you wanted, you could keep refactoring your code, but this is a good point to move on.

Data-Driven Configuration

Now you're ready to tackle the whole point of this refactoring. It's time to set up the property list to handle the data-driven Powers section. We detailed two possible approaches earlier. You're going to take the approach that has you add a dynamic Boolean item and keeps the row item as an array. For items where dynamic is YES, the row item array will have only one element. If there are more, you're going to ignore them.

Open HeroDetailConfiguration.plist, and navigate to Root ➤ sections ➤ Item 2. If the disclosure triangle is closed, open it. Select the item named header, and add an two items after it. Name the first item **dynamic**, set its type to Boolean, and give it a value of YES. Name the second item **rows**, and set its type to Array. Add a dictionary to the rows Array and give the dictionary three items. Give the three Dictionary items the names of **key**, **class**, and **label**. Leave the type of all three items as String. Set the key value to powers; set the class to SuperDBCell. Leave the label value blank.

Your property list editor should look something like Figure 7-13.

Key	Type	Value
▼ Root	Dictionary	(1 item)
▼ sections	Array	(3 items)
▶ Item 0	Dictionary	(1 item)
▶ Item 1	Dictionary	(2 items)
▼ Item 2	Dictionary	(3 items)
header	String	Powers
dynamic	Boolean	YES
▼ rows	Array	(1 item)
▼ Item 0	Dictionary	(3 items)
key	String	powers
class	String	SuperDBEditCell
label	String	

Figure 7-13. The Power section property list configuration

Now you need the HeroDetailConfiguration to use this new dynamic item.

First, you need to define a method to check whether the section you are looking at is dynamic or not. Let's add that method declaration to HeroDetailConfiguration.h.

```
- (BOOL)isDynamicSection:(NSInteger)section;
```

Let's add the implementation to HeroDetailConfiguration.m.

```
- (BOOL)isDynamicSection:(NSInteger)section
{
    BOOL dynamic = NO;

    NSDictionary *sectionDict = [self.sections objectAtIndex:section];
    NSNumber *dynamicNumber = [sectionDict objectForKey:@"dynamic"];
    if (dynamicNumber != nil)
        dynamic = [dynamicNumber boolValue];

    return dynamic;
}
```

By default, you'll assume that a section is not dynamic if there's no dynamic entry in the configuration property list section.

Now, you need to update the rowForIndexPath: method to handle dynamic sections. You just need to change one line.

```
NSUInteger rowIndex = [indexPath row];
NSUInteger rowIndex = ([self isDynamicSection:sectionIndex]) ? 0 : [indexPath row];
```

While you're here, add the following method declaration to HeroDetailConfiguration.h:

```
- (NSString *)dynamicAttributeKeyForSection:(NSInteger)section;
```

(You're cheating a little here because you know that this method will make your life easier in a little bit.) The implementation in HeroDetailConfiguration.m will look like this:

```
- (NSString *)dynamicAttributeKeyForSection:(NSInteger)section
{
    if (![self isDynamicSection:section])
        return nil;

    NSIndexPath *indexPath = [NSIndexPath indexPathForRow:0 inSection:section];
    return [self attributeKeyForIndexPath:indexPath];
}
```

If the section is not dynamic, you'll return nil. Otherwise, you create an index path and use the existing functionality.

Adding Powers

Now you can move on to updating the HeroDetailController to use this new configuration setup. In HeroDetailController.m, edit tableView:numberOfRowsInSection: like so:

```
- (NSInteger)tableView:(UITableView *)tableView numberOfRowsInSection:(NSInteger)section
{
    NSInteger rowCount = [self.config numberOfRowsInSection:section];
    if ([self.config isDynamicSection:section]) {
        NSString *key = [self.config dynamicAttributeKeyForSection:section];
        NSSet *attributeSet = [self.hero mutableSetValueForKey:key];
        rowCount = attributeSet.count;
    }

    return rowCount;
}
```

You ask the HeroDetailConfiguration to tell you the number of rows in the section. If the section is dynamic, you read the row configuration to determine what property to use from your Hero entity. That property will be a Set, so you need to convert it to an Array to get its size.

Well, you still don't have any powers in your Hero entity. So you need a way to add new powers to your Hero. Clearly, you should do that when you're editing the Hero's details. If you run the app, navigate to the detail view and tap the Edit button, the Powers section is still blank. Go back to the Address Book application: when you need a new address, a cell appears with a green (+) button to add a new address (Figure 7-14). You need to mimic that behavior.

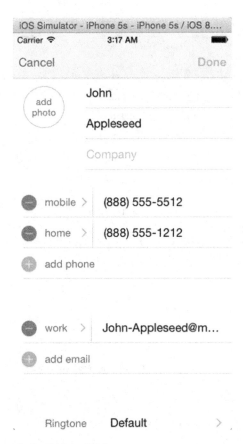

Figure 7-14. Adding a new address in the Address Book app

Open HeroDetailController.m and find the tableView:numberOfRowsInSection: method you just modified. Change this line:

rowCount = attributeSet.count;

to this:

rowCount = (self.editing) ? attributeSet.count+1 : attributeSet.count;

However, this is not enough. You need to have the table view refresh when you enter Edit mode. In setEditing:animated:, add this line after the call to super:

[self.tableView reloadData];

If you run the app now and edit your hero's details (Figure 7-15), there are two issues. First, the new cell in the Powers section has a strange value. Second, if you watch closely while entering and exiting Edit mode, the transition no longer seems smooth. The cells seem to jump. Everything works, but it isn't a good user experience.

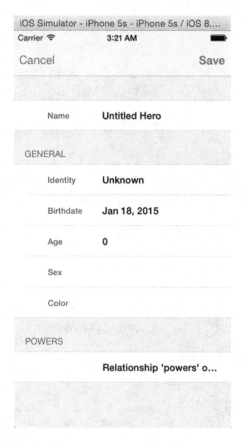

Figure 7-15. *First step to adding new powers*

Let's take a look at fetched results controller delegate methods in the HeroListController. When the updates begin, you call the beginUpdates method on the table view. Then you insert or delete rows with insertRowsAtIndexPath:withRowAnimation: and deleteRowsAtIndexPath:withRowAnimation:. Finally, when the updates are complete, you call endUpdates on the table view. You need to do something similar with the Powers section when entering and leaving Edit mode.

In the private category at the top of HeroDetailController.m, add the new method declaration, as shown here:

```
- (void)updateDynamicSections:(BOOL)editing;
```

And call it from setEditing:animated:.

```
- (void)setEditing:(BOOL)editing animated:(BOOL)animated
{
    [self.tableView beginUpdates];
    [self updateDynamicSections:editing];
    [super setEditing:editing animated:animated];
    [self.tableView endUpdates];
```

```
    self.navigationItem.rightBarButtonItem = (editing) ? self.saveButton : self.editButtonItem;
    self.navigationItem.leftBarButtonItem = (editing) ? self.cancelButton : self.backButton;
}
```

Here's the implementation:

```
- (void)updateDynamicSections:(BOOL)editing
{
    for (NSInteger section = 0; section < [self.config numberOfSections]; section++) {
        if ([self.config isDynamicSection:section]) {
            NSIndexPath *indexPath;
            NSInteger row = [self tableView:self.tableView numberOfRowsInSection:section];
            if (editing) {
                indexPath = [NSIndexPath indexPathForRow:row inSection:section];
                [self.tableView insertRowsAtIndexPaths:@[indexPath]
                                withRowAnimation:UITableViewRowAnimationAutomatic];
            }
            else {
                indexPath = [NSIndexPath indexPathForRow:row-1 inSection:section];
                [self.tableView deleteRowsAtIndexPaths:@[indexPath]
                                withRowAnimation:UITableViewRowAnimationAutomatic];
            }
        }
    }
}
```

Now the addition and removal of a cell to Powers section when entering and exiting Edit mode looks much smoother.

Way back in Chapter 4 when you first wrote the HeroDetailController, you implemented the table view delegate method of tableView:editingStyleForRowAtIndexPath:.

```
- (UITableViewCellEditingStyle)tableView:(UITableView *)tableView
        editingStyleForRowAtIndexPath:(NSIndexPath *)indexPath
{
    return UITableViewCellEditingStyleNone;
}
```

If you recall, this turns off the appearance of the Delete button next to table view cell when the detail view enters Edit mode. Now you want it to show the appropriate button next to the Power section cells.

```
- (UITableViewCellEditingStyle)tableView:(UITableView *)tableView
        editingStyleForRowAtIndexPath:(NSIndexPath *)indexPath
{
    UITableViewCellEditingStyle editStyle = UITableViewCellEditingStyleNone;
    NSInteger section = [indexPath section];
    if ([self.config isDynamicSection:section]) {
        NSInteger rowCount = [self tableView:self.tableView numberOfRowsInSection:section];
```

```
        if ([indexPath row] == rowCount-1)
            editStyle = UITableViewCellEditingStyleInsert;
        else
            editStyle = UITableViewCellEditingStyleDelete;
    }
    return editStyle;
}
```

For the Insert button to work, you need to implement the table view data source method
`tableView:commitEditingStyle:forRowAtIndexPath:`. This method already exists in
HeroDetailController.m, but is commented it out. You can find it in the table view data
source section of the jump bar. Uncomment it, and modify it so it looks like this:

```
- (void)tableView:(UITableView *)tableView
        commitEditingStyle:(UITableViewCellEditingStyle)editingStyle
        forRowAtIndexPath:(NSIndexPath *)indexPath
{
    NSString *key = [self.config attributeKeyForIndexPath:indexPath];
    NSMutableSet *relationshipSet = [self.hero mutableSetValueForKey:key];
    NSManagedObjectContext *managedObjectContext = [self.hero managedObjectContext];

    if (editingStyle == UITableViewCellEditingStyleDelete) {
        // Delete the row from the data source
        NSManagedObject *relationshipObject =
            [[relationshipSet allObjects] objectAtIndex:[indexPath row]];
        [relationshipSet removeObject:relationshipObject];
    }
    else if (editingStyle == UITableViewCellEditingStyleInsert) {
        NSEntityDescription *entity = [self.hero entity];
        NSDictionary *relationships = [entity relationshipsByName];
        NSRelationshipDescription *destRelationship = [relationships objectForKey:key];
        NSEntityDescription *destEntity = [destRelationship destinationEntity];

        NSManagedObject *relationshipObject =
            [NSEntityDescription insertNewObjectForEntityForName:[destEntity name]
                                        inManagedObjectContext:managedObjectContext];
        [relationshipSet addObject:relationshipObject];
    }

    NSError *error = nil;
    if (![managedObjectContext save:&error]) {
        // need to make HeroDetailController a UIAlertViewDelegate
        UIAlertController *alert = [UIAlertController
            alertControllerWithTitle:NSLocalizedString(
                @"Error saving entity",
                @"Error saving entity")
                        message:[NSString stringWithFormat:NSLocalizedString(
                                    @"Error was: %@, quitting",
                                    @"Error was: %@, quitting"), [error localizedDescription]]
                    preferredStyle:UIAlertControllerStyleAlert];
```

```
    UIAlertAction *cancelButton = [UIAlertAction
                        actionWithTitle:NSLocalizedString(@"Aw, Nuts",@"Aw, Nuts")
                                  style:UIAlertActionStyleCancel handler:nil];
    [alert addAction:cancelButton];
    [self presentViewController:alert animated:YES completion:nil];
    }

    if (editingStyle == UITableViewCellEditingStyleDelete) {
        // Delete the row from the data source
        [tableView deleteRowsAtIndexPaths:@[indexPath]
                    withRowAnimation:UITableViewRowAnimationFade];
    }
    else if (editingStyle == UITableViewCellEditingStyleInsert) {
        // Create a new instance of the appropriate class, insert it into the array,
        // and add a new row to the table view
        [tableView insertRowsAtIndexPaths:@[indexPath]
                    withRowAnimation:UITableViewRowAnimationAutomatic];
    }
}
```

Every time you get a new Powers cell, it displays some strange String: Relationship
'powers'.... That's because it's displaying the results of a valueForKey: call on the Hero
entity, with a key of powers. You need to update your tableView:cellForRowAtIndexPath: to
handle dynamic sections. Replace the following:

```
cell.value = [self.hero valueForKey:[self.config attributeKeyForIndexPath:indexPath]];
```

with the following:

```
if ([self.config isDynamicSection:[indexPath section]]) {
    NSString *key = [self.config attributeKeyForIndexPath:indexPath];
    NSMutableSet *relationshipSet = [self.hero mutableSetValueForKey:key];
    NSArray *relationshipArray = [relationshipSet allObjects];
    if ([indexPath row] != [relationshipArray count]) {
        NSManagedObject *relationshipObject = [relationshipArray objectAtIndex:[indexPath row]];
        cell.value = [relationshipObject valueForKey:@"name"];
        cell.accessoryType = UITableViewCellAccessoryDetailDisclosureButton;
        cell.editingAccessoryType = UITableViewCellAccessoryDetailDisclosureButton;
    }
    else {
        cell.label.text = nil;
        cell.textField.text = @"Add New Power...";
    }
}
else {
    cell.value = [self.hero valueForKey:[self.config attributeKeyForIndexPath:indexPath]];
}
```

Notice that for a dynamic cell, you set the accessoryType and editingAccessoryType. This is the blue arrow button on the cell's right edge. Also, you handle the case for when you add an additional cell in Edit mode.

Now you need to add a power view so that you can edit the name and source of your Hero's new powers.

Refactoring the Detail View Controller

You have a new managed object that you want to display and edit. You could make a new table view controller class specifically to handle displaying a Power entity. It would a pretty simple class, and you could implement it quickly. Sometimes when developing, you might do that. It's not necessarily the most elegant solution, but it might the most expedient. And sometimes you just need to get it working.

But since this a book and you're working through this example, it makes sense to refactor your HeroDetailController into a more generic ManagedObjectController. Later you can use this refactored controller to implement the views for the fetched properties of the Hero entity. You laid the foundation for this work when you moved the view controller configuration into a property list. Since then, you've tried to implement generic solutions in the HeroDetailController. Ideally, that work paid off.

First, you'll rename the HeroDetailConfiguration class to ManagedObjectConfiguration. You won't change the name of the property list because that's still specific for displaying the Hero entity. Next, you'll create the ManagedObjectController class. You'll move most of the logic from the HeroDetailController to the ManagedObjectController. The only HeroDetailController will be a thin subclass that knows the name of the configuration property list to load.

Let's get started.

Renaming the Configuration Class

The HeroDetailConfiguration class name worked because it was used by the HeroDetailController. Now that you're renaming the Controller class, you should rename the configuration class. Open HeroDetailConfiguration.h, and highlight the class name in the Editor pane. Select the Edit ➤ Refactor ➤ Rename menu, and rename the class to ManagedObjectConfiguration (Figure 7-16). Click Preview and review the changes Xcode made. It should change the interface and implementation files, as well as the references in HeroDetailController. When you're ready, click Save.

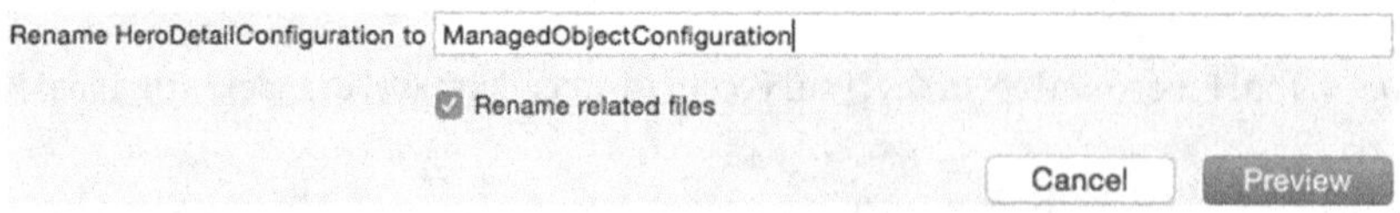

Rename HeroDetailConfiguration to ManagedObjectConfiguration

☑ Rename related files

Cancel   Preview

Figure 7-16. The Rename refactoring pane

There's a code change you need to make. In the ManagedObjectConfiguration init method, the configuration property list is loaded like this:

```
NSURL *plistURL = [[NSBundle mainBundle] URLForResource:@"ManagedObjectConfiguration"
                                 withExtension:@"plist"];
```

Remember, you're keeping the current configuration property list name as HeroDetailConfiguration.plist. If you hard-code that name, you won't have really done anything useful. You need to change the initializer from a simple init method to something like this:

```
- (id)initWithResource:(NSString *)resource;
```

Add that declaration to the ManagedObjectController.h file, inside the @interface. Then you can change the init method to the following:

```
- (id)init
- (id)initWithResource:(NSString *)resource
{
    self = [super init];
    if (self) {
        // Initialization Code
        NSURL *plistURL = [[NSBundle mainBundle] URLForResource:@"ManagedObjectConfiguration"
                                         withExtension:@"plist"];
        NSURL *plistURL = [[NSBundle mainBundle] URLForResource:resource withExtension:@"plist"];
        NSDictionary *plist = [NSDictionary dictionaryWithContentsOfURL:plistURL];
        self.sections = [plist valueForKey:@"sections"];
    }
    return self;
}
```

Now you need to change this line in the HeroDetailController viewDidLoad method:

```
self.config = [[ManagedObjectConfiguration alloc] init];
```

to

```
self.config = [[ManagedObjectConfiguration alloc] initWithResource:@"HeroDetailConfiguration"];
```

> **Note** Why make this change if you're just going to refactor HeroDetailController? Well, one of the big keys with refactoring is making small changes and checking things still work. You wouldn't want to make a lot of changes just to find things don't work. Another key to successful refactoring is writing unit tests. Then you have a repeatable set of tests that will help ensure you haven't make drastic changes you don't expect. You'll learn about unit tests in Chapter 15.

At this point, your app should still be working, but you've made only a minor change. The big one is coming up next.

Refactoring the Detail Controller

You could just create a new class named ManagedObjectController and move most of the code from HeroDetailController to your new class. But this is adding a layer of complexity (moving code), which could lead to a mistake being made. It's easier to rename the HeroDetailController, clean up the code to be more generic, and then implement a new HeroDetailController class.

Open HeroDetailController.h and rename the class to ManagedObjectController, using Edit ➤ Refactor   Rename. Review the proposed changes by Xcode. You'll notice that Xcode is changing SuperDB.storyboard, which is just an XML file internally. You'll just need to have faith that Xcode knows what it's doing. Click Save. You may want to build and run the app just to check it's still working.

Refactoring the Hero Instance Variable

In your ManagedObjectController class, you have an instance variable called hero. That variable name is no longer representative of what that variable holds, so let's refactor it as well. Open ManagedObjectController.h and rename the hero property to managedObject. Now you must make the changes in the rest of the app.

> **Note**   Why not use the Xcode refactor option? You could have, but it's not so good at renaming instance variables. When we tried it, it wanted to make changes to both the data model and the storyboard. That's just wrong. We could have unchecked those changes in the File Preview pane and saved the changes. But Xcode doesn't rename the other occurrences, so you have to do it manually anyway.

Open ManagedObjectController.m and find all occurrences of the following:

self.hero

and change them to the following:

self.managedObject

Lastly, edit HeroListContoller.m, and change this line in prepareForSegue:sender:

detailController.hero = sender;

to the following:

detailController.managedObject = sender;

Save your work and check the app.

A Little More Abstraction

While you're working on ManagedObjectController, take this opportunity to add some discrete functionality. Specifically, when you add or remove powers, you put the code to do this in tableView:commitEditingStyle:forRowAtIndexPath:. Let's split this code into specific methods to add and remove Relationship objects. Add the following method declarations to ManagedObjectController.h:

```
- (NSManagedObject *)addRelationshipObjectForSection:(NSInteger)section;
- (void)removeRelationshipObjectInIndexPath:(NSIndexPath *)indexPath;
```

Before you implement these methods, add a new private method. Find the private category in ManagedObjectController.m and add this line:

```
- (void)saveManagedObjectContext;
```

Then, add the implementation.

```
- (void)saveManagedObjectContext
{
    NSError *error;
    if (![self.managedObject.managedObjectContext save:&error]) {
        // need to make HeroDetailController a UIAlertViewDelegate
        UIAlertController *alert = [UIAlertController
            alertControllerWithTitle:NSLocalizedString(
                @"Error saving entity",
                @"Error saving entity")
                        message:[NSString stringWithFormat:NSLocalizedString(
                                @"Error was: %@, quitting",
                                @"Error was: %@, quitting"), [error localizedDescription]]
                    preferredStyle:UIAlertControllerStyleAlert];
        UIAlertAction *cancelButton = [UIAlertAction
                            actionWithTitle:NSLocalizedString(@"Aw, Nuts",@"Aw, Nuts")
                                    style:UIAlertActionStyleCancel handler:nil];
        [alert addAction:cancelButton];
        [self presentViewController:alert animated:YES completion:nil];
    }
}
```

Does this look familiar? It should; it's essentially the code in the save method. So, update the following lines in the save method from these:

```
NSError *error;
if (![self.managedObject.managedObjectContext save:&error])
    NSLog(@"Error saving: %@", [error localizedDescription]);
```

to these:

```
[self saveManagedObjectContext];
```

Now you can add the new method implementations (we added them just for the @end in
ManagedObjectController.m).

```
#pragma mark - Instance Methods

- (NSManagedObject *)addRelationshipObjectForSection:(NSInteger)section
{
    NSString *key = [self.config dynamicAttributeKeyForSection:section];
    NSMutableSet *relationshipSet = [self.managedObject mutableSetValueForKey:key];

    NSEntityDescription *entity = [self.managedObject entity];
    NSDictionary *relationships = [entity relationshipsByName];
    NSRelationshipDescription *destRelationship = [relationships objectForKey:key];
    NSEntityDescription *destEntity = [destRelationship destinationEntity];

    NSManagedObject *relationshipObject =
        [NSEntityDescription insertNewObjectForEntityForName:[destEntity name]
                                      inManagedObjectContext:self.managedObject.
                                      managedObjectContext];
    [relationshipSet addObject:relationshipObject];
    [self saveManagedObjectContext];
    return relationshipObject;
}

- (void)removeRelationshipObjectInIndexPath:(NSIndexPath *)indexPath
{
    NSString *key = [self.config dynamicAttributeKeyForSection:[indexPath section]];
    NSMutableSet *relationshipSet = [self.managedObject mutableSetValueForKey:key];
    NSManagedObject *relationshipObject =
        [[relationshipSet allObjects] objectAtIndex:[indexPath row]];
    [relationshipSet removeObject:relationshipObject];
    [self saveManagedObjectContext];
}
```

Finally, change tableView:commitEditingStyle:forRowAtIndexPath:.

```
- (void)tableView:(UITableView *)tableView
        commitEditingStyle:(UITableViewCellEditingStyle)editingStyle
        forRowAtIndexPath:(NSIndexPath *)indexPath
{
    if (editingStyle == UITableViewCellEditingStyleDelete) {
        // Delete the row from the data source
        [tableView deleteRowsAtIndexPaths:@[indexPath]
        withRowAnimation:UITableViewRowAnimationFade];
    }
    else if (editingStyle == UITableViewCellEditingStyleInsert) {
        // Create a new instance of the appropriate class, insert it into the array,
        // and add a new row to the table view
        [tableView insertRowsAtIndexPaths:@[indexPath]
                        withRowAnimation:UITableViewRowAnimationAutomatic];
    }
}
```

You're not adding or removing the Relationship object anymore. All you're doing is adding
or removing table view cells. You'll see why soon.

A New HeroDetailController

Now you want to create a new HeroDetailController to replace the one you renamed to the ManagedObjectController. Create a new Cocoa Touch Class file, name it HeroDetailController, and make it a subclass of ManagedObjectController. Before you modify the HeroDetailController, you need to make some changes to the ManagedObjectController. You need to move the property that holds the configuration information from the private category to the @interface declaration. Edit ManagedObjectController.h and declare the configuration property (you also need to declare the ManagedObjectConfiguration).

```
#import <UIKit/UIKit.h>

@class ManagedObjectConfiguration;

@interface ManagedObjectController : UITableViewController

@property (strong, nonatomic) ManagedObjectConfiguration *config;
@property (strong, nonatomic) NSManagedObject *managedObject;

- (NSManagedObject *)addRelationshipObjectForSection:(NSInteger)section;
- (void)removeRelationshipObjectInIndexPath:(NSIndexPath *)indexPath;

@end
```

Since you moved the configuration, you need to delete the declaration in ManagedObjectController.m.

```
@interface ManagedObjectController ()
@property (strong, nonatomic) ManagedObjectConfiguration *config;
@property (nonatomic, strong) UIBarButtonItem *saveButton;
```

You also need to delete the assignment in viewDidLoad.

```
- (void)viewDidLoad
{
    [super viewDidLoad];
    ...
    self.config = [[ManagedObjectConfiguration alloc] initWithResource:@"HeroDetailConfiguration"];
}
```

Now you can update HeroDetailController. All you need to do is load your configuration property list. Your HeroDetailController.m should look like this:

```
#import "HeroDetailController.h"
#import "ManagedObjectConfiguration.h"

@implementation HeroDetailController
```

```
- (void)viewDidLoad
{
    [super viewDidLoad];
    // Do any additional setup after loading the view.
    self.config = [[ManagedObjectConfiguration alloc]
    initWithResource:@"HeroDetailConfiguration"];
}

@end
```

Now you need to tell your storyboard to use this HeroDetailController. Open SuperDB.
storyboard and select the ManagedObjectController scene. Select the View Controller
icon and open the Identity Inspector. Change the class from ManagedObjectController to
HeroDetailController.

> **Note**   How did this change? It happened when you used the rename refactoring. When Xcode
> showed you the change in SuperDB.storyboard, this was the change it was making.

And that should do it. You're ready to create a power view.

The Power View Controller

You'll start by creating the new power view controller in SuperDB.storyboard. Open SuperDB.
storyboard and add a new table view controller to the right of the hero detail controller. Your
storyboard should look something like Figure 7-17.

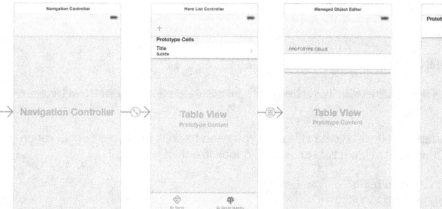

Figure 7-17. *Adding a table view controller to SuperDB.storyboard*

Select the table view controller and in the Identity Inspector change the class to
PowerViewController. Next select the table view in the scene, and in the Attributes
Inspector, change the style from Plain to Grouped.

The last thing you need to do is define the segue between the HeroDetailController to your
new PowerViewController. Control-drag from the HeroDetailController icon (in the label
bar) to the PowerViewController scene. When the Manual Segue pop-up appears, select
Push. Select the segue, and give it the name **PowerViewSegue** in the Attributes Inspector.

Now you need to create the PowerViewController class and configuration. Create
a new Cocoa Touch Class file, named PowerViewController, as a subclass of
ManagedObjectController. Edit PowerViewController.m.

```
#import "PowerViewController.h"
#import "ManagedObjectConfiguration.h"

@implementation PowerViewController

- (void)viewDidLoad
{
    [super viewDidLoad];
    // Do any additional setup after loading the view.
    self.config = [[ManagedObjectConfiguration alloc] initWithResource:@"PowerViewConfiguration"];
}

@end
```

Essentially, this is the same as HeroDetailController.m. Instead of loading the
HeroDetailConfiguration property list, you load the PowerViewConfiguration
property list. Let's create this property list. Create a new property list file and name it
PowerViewConfiguration.plist. You need a configuration property list with two sections.
Each section has no header label and one row each. In the end, your property list should
look like Figure 7-18.

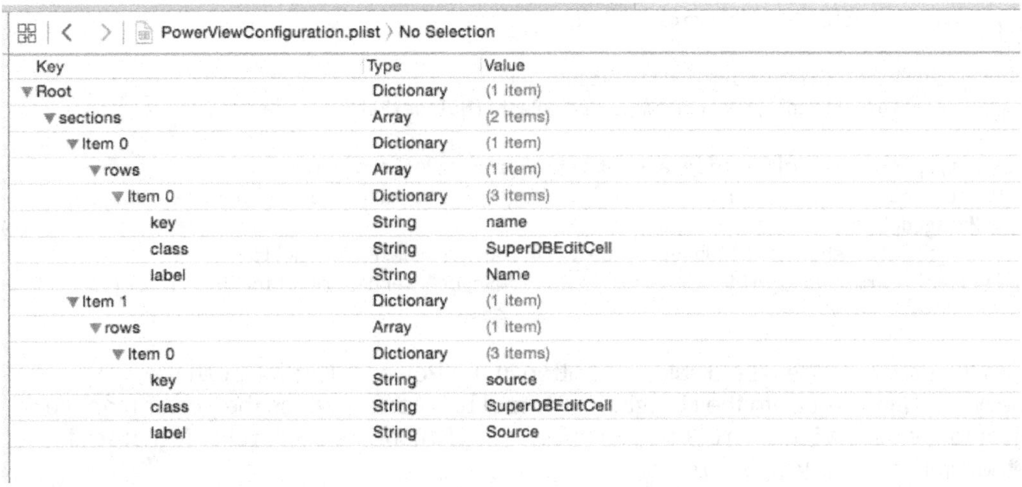

Key	Type	Value
▼ Root	Dictionary	(1 item)
▼ sections	Array	(2 items)
▼ Item 0	Dictionary	(1 item)
▼ rows	Array	(1 item)
▼ Item 0	Dictionary	(3 items)
key	String	name
class	String	SuperDBEditCell
label	String	Name
▼ Item 1	Dictionary	(1 item)
▼ rows	Array	(1 item)
▼ Item 0	Dictionary	(3 items)
key	String	source
class	String	SuperDBEditCell
label	String	Source

Figure 7-18. Power view configuration

Navigating to the PowerViewController

Your PowerViewController is defined and configured. You've defined the segue to transition from the HeroDetailController to PowerViewController. Now you need to execute the PowerViewSegue when the user adds a new power or selects a power in Edit mode. Open HeroDetailController.m, and add the following table view data source method:

```
#pragma mark - Table view data source

- (void)tableView:(UITableView *)tableView
        commitEditingStyle:(UITableViewCellEditingStyle)editingStyle
        forRowAtIndexPath:(NSIndexPath *)indexPath
{
    if (editingStyle == UITableViewCellEditingStyleDelete)
        [self removeRelationshipObjectInIndexPath:indexPath];
    else if (editingStyle == UITableViewCellEditingStyleInsert) {
        NSManagedObject *newObject = [self addRelationshipObjectForSection:[indexPath
        section]];
        [self performSegueWithIdentifier:@"PowerViewSegue" sender:newObject];
    }

    [super tableView:tableView commitEditingStyle:editingStyle forRowAtIndexPath:indexPath];
}
```

Since you added this method, you added the logic to remove a power as well. Remember when you changed this method in ManagedObjectController? You only added and removed the table view cells. We said you were going to handle adding and removing powers to the Hero entity later. Well, here it is. Pretty simple, right? Finally, you call the super method (which is in the ManagedObjectController).

One last thing you need to do is handle when you want to view an existing power. After the HeroDetailController tableView:commitEditingStyle:forRowAtIndexPath:, add this table view delegate method:

```
#pragma mark - Table view delegate

- (void)tableView:(UITableView *)tableView
        accessoryButtonTappedForRowWithIndexPath:(NSIndexPath *)indexPath
{
    NSString *key = [self.config attributeKeyForIndexPath:indexPath];
    NSMutableSet *relationshipSet = [self.managedObject mutableSetValueForKey:key];
    NSManagedObject *relationshipObject =
        [[relationshipSet allObjects] objectAtIndex:[indexPath row]];
    [self performSegueWithIdentifier:@"PowerViewSegue" sender:relationshipObject];
}
```

When the user taps the blue disclosure button in the Power cell, it will push the PowerViewController onto the NavigationController stack. To pass the power managed object to the PowerViewController, you need to implement the prepareForSegue:sender: method in HeroDetailController.m.

```
- (void)prepareForSegue:(UIStoryboardSegue *)segue sender:(id)sender
{
    if ([segue.identifier isEqualToString:@"PowerViewSegue"]) {
        if ([sender isKindOfClass:[NSManagedObject class]]) {
            ManagedObjectController *detailController = segue.destinationViewController;
            detailController.managedObject = sender;
    }
    else {
        UIAlertController *alert = [UIAlertController
            alertControllerWithTitle:NSLocalizedString(
                @"Power Error",
                @"Power Error")
                            message:[NSString stringWithFormat:NSLocalizedString(
                                    @"Error trying to show Power detail",
                                    @"Error trying to show Power detail"),
                                    [error localizedDescription]]
                    preferredStyle:UIAlertControllerStyleAlert];
        UIAlertAction *cancelButton = [UIAlertAction
                        actionWithTitle:NSLocalizedString(@"Aw, Nuts",@"Aw, Nuts")
                                style:UIAlertActionStyleCancel handler:nil];
        [alert addAction:cancelButton];
        [self presentViewController:alert animated:YES completion:nil];
    }
}
```

That's it. The Power section and view are all set. Now let's look into displaying fetched properties.

Fetch Properties

Look back at Figure 7-1. Below the Powers section is another section titled Reports that shows four cells. Each cell holds a fetched property and accessory disclosure button. Tapping the disclosure button will show the results of the fetched property (Figure 7-3). Let's get this working.

Looking at Figure 7-3, you can see that it's a simple table view that displays the hero's name and secret identity. You need to create a new table view controller for the report display. Create a new Cocoa Touch Class file named HeroReportController; make it a subclass of UITableViewController. Select HeroReportController.h, and add new property to hold the list of heroes you want to display.

```
@property (strong, nonatomic) NSArray *heroes;
```

Switch to HeroReportController.m. You need to import your Hero header at the top of the file.

```
#import "Hero.h"
```

Next, adjust the table view data source methods.

```
- (NSInteger)numberOfSectionsInTableView:(UITableView *)tableView
{
    // Return the number of sections.
    return 1;
}

- (NSInteger)tableView:(UITableView *)tableView numberOfRowsInSection:(NSInteger)section
{
    // Return the number of rows in the section.
    return self.heroes.count;
}

- (UITableViewCell *)tableView:(UITableView *)tableView
        cellForRowAtIndexPath:(NSIndexPath *)indexPath
{
    static NSString *CellIdentifier = @"HeroReportCell";
    UITableViewCell *cell = [tableView dequeueReusableCellWithIdentifier:CellIdentifier
                                                            forIndexPath:indexPath];

    // Configure the cell...
    Hero *hero = [self.heroes objectAtIndex:[indexPath row]];
    cell.textLabel.text = hero.name;
    cell.detailTextLabel.text = hero.secretIdentity;

    return cell;
}
```

Let's lay out your HeroReportController in your storyboard. Open SuperDB.storyboard. Select a table view controller from the Object Library in the Utility pane, and drop it below the PowerViewController. Select this new table view controller and open the Identity Inspector. Change the class to HeroReportController. Next, select the table view in the new table view controller, and open the Attributes Inspector. Change the Selection field from Single Selection to No Selection. Finally, select the table view cell. In the Attributes Inspector, change the Style to Subtitle; enter HeroReportCell for the Identifier; and change the Selection field to None.

Now Control-drag from the HeroDetailController view controller to the new table view controller. When the Manual Segue pop-up appears, select Push. Select the new segue, and in the Attributes Inspector, name it ReportViewSegue.

Next, you need to edit HeroDetailConfiguration property list to add the Reports section. Navigate to Root ➤ sections ➤ Item 2. Make sure the Item 2 disclosure triangle is closed. Select the Item 2 row and add an new item. Item 3 should appear. Change Item 3 from String to Dictionary. Open the Item 3 disclosure triangle and add two subitems. Name the first one **header**, and give it a value of Reports. Name the second **rows** and make it an Array. You're going to add four items to the rows Array, each one representing the report you want to view. By the time you're done, it should look like Figure 7-19.

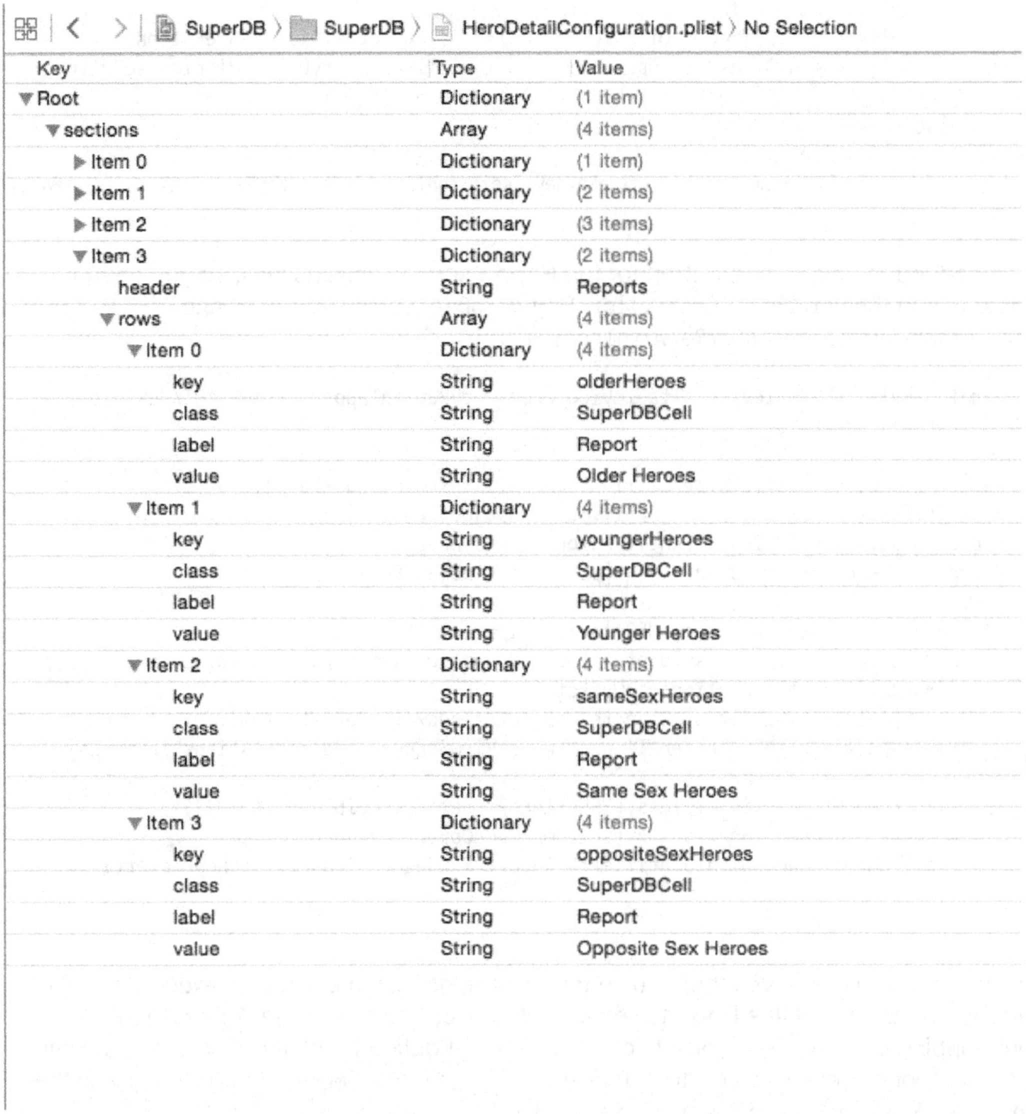
SuperDB 〉 SuperDB 〉 HeroDetailConfiguration.plist 〉 No Selection

Key	Type	Value
▼Root	Dictionary	(1 item)
▼sections	Array	(4 items)
▶Item 0	Dictionary	(1 item)
▶Item 1	Dictionary	(2 items)
▶Item 2	Dictionary	(3 items)
▼Item 3	Dictionary	(2 items)
header	String	Reports
▼rows	Array	(4 items)
▼Item 0	Dictionary	(4 items)
key	String	olderHeroes
class	String	SuperDBCell
label	String	Report
value	String	Older Heroes
▼Item 1	Dictionary	(4 items)
key	String	youngerHeroes
class	String	SuperDBCell
label	String	Report
value	String	Younger Heroes
▼Item 2	Dictionary	(4 items)
key	String	sameSexHeroes
class	String	SuperDBCell
label	String	Report
value	String	Same Sex Heroes
▼Item 3	Dictionary	(4 items)
key	String	oppositeSexHeroes
class	String	SuperDBCell
label	String	Report
value	String	Opposite Sex Heroes

Figure 7-19. *Adding the reports configuration*

Notice that you've added a new item for these row items: value. This is so you can use a static value for your report section cells. Open `ManagedObjectController.m` and navigate to `tableView:cellForRowAtIndexPath:`. Replace the nondynamic table view cell configuration code.

```
else {
    cell.value =
        [self.managedObject valueForKey:[self.config attributeKeyForIndexPath:indexPath]];
    NSString *value = [[self.config rowForIndexPath:indexPath] objectForKey:@"value"];
    if (value != nil) {
```

```
            cell.value = value;
            cell.accessoryType = UITableViewCellAccessoryDetailDisclosureButton;
            cell.editingAccessoryType = UITableViewCellAccessoryDetailDisclosureButton;
    }
    else
            cell.value =
                [self.managedObject valueForKey:[self.config attributeKeyForIndexPath:indexPath]];
}
```

You've added the disclosure button for the Report section cells as well, so you need to handle that in the HeroDetailController. Edit HeroDetailController.m, and modify tableVi ew:accessoryButtonTappedForRowWithIndexPath:.

```
- (void)tableView:(UITableView *)tableView accessoryButtonTappedForRowWithIndexPath:
(NSIndexPath *)indexPath
{
    NSString *key = [self.config attributeKeyForIndexPath:indexPath];
    NSEntityDescription *entity = [self.managedObject entity];
    NSDictionary *properties = [entity propertiesByName];
    NSPropertyDescription *property = [properties objectForKey:key];

    if ([property isKindOfClass:[ NSRelationshipDescription class]]) {
        NSMutableSet *relationshipSet = [self.managedObject mutableSetValueForKey:key];
        NSManagedObject *relationshipObject =
            [[relationshipSet allObjects] objectAtIndex:[indexPath row]];
        [self performSegueWithIdentifier:@"PowerViewSegue" sender:relationshipObject];
    }
    else if ([property isKindOfClass:[NSFetchedPropertyDescription class]]) {
        NSArray *fetchedProperties = [self.managedObject valueForKey:key];
        [self performSegueWithIdentifier:@"ReportViewSegue" sender:fetchedProperties];
    }
}
```

Now you need to check whether you've tapped a relationship cell (the Powers section) or a fetched property cell (the Reports section). You're calling the segue, ReportViewSegue, when tapping on a fetched property cell. You haven't defined that segue yet, but you will in just a second. Before you do that, let's update prepareForSegue:sender: to handle the ReportViewSegue. After the PowerViewSegue check, add this:

```
else if ([segue.identifier isEqualToString:@"ReportViewSegue"]) {
    if ([sender isKindOfClass:[NSArray class]]) {
        HeroReportController *reportController = segue.destinationViewController;
        reportController.heroes = sender;
    }
    else {
UIAlertController *alert = [UIAlertController
                    alertControllerWithTitle:NSLocalizedString(@"Power Error",
                                                               @"Power Error")
                                     message:NSLocalizedString(@"Error trying to show Power",
                                                               @"Error trying to show Power")
                              preferredStyle:UIAlertControllerStyleAlert];
```

```
UIAlertAction *OKButton = [UIAlertAction
                          actionWithTitle:NSLocalizedString(@"Aw Nuts",
                                                            @"Aw Nuts")
                                    style:UIAlertActionStyleDefault
                                  handler:nil];
[alert addAction:OKButton];
[self presentViewController:alert animated:YES completion:nil];
    }
}
```

Finally, since you're using the HeroReportController, you need to import its header file at the top of HeroDetailController.m.

```
#import "HeroReportController.h"
```

Build and run SuperDB. Add a few different heroes with different birthdays and of different sex. Drill down the report and see the results when looking for older, younger, same sex, and opposite sex heroes. Create a new hero, but don't set the sex. See what happens. The sexless hero will appear on the opposite sex report but not on the same sex report. We'll leave it you to reason out why and how you might fix this.

Wonderful to the Core

This chapter and the previous chapters have given you a solid foundation in the use of Core Data. Along the way, we provided some information about how to design complex iPhone applications so that they can be maintained and expanded without writing unnecessary code or repeating the same logic in multiple places. We demonstrated just how much benefit you can get from taking the time to write code generically. We showed you how to look for opportunities to refactor your code to make it smaller, more efficient, easier to maintain, and just generally more pleasant to be around.

We could go on for several more chapters about Core Data and not exhaust the topic. But Core Data is not the only new framework introduced since iOS SDK 3. At this point, you should have a solid enough understanding of Core Data to be able to, armed with Apple's documentation, take your explorations even further.

Now it's time to leave our friend Core Data behind and explore some of the other aspects of iOS SDK.

Chapter 8

Behind Every iCloud

With iOS 5, Apple introduced iCloud, the latest in its line of Internet-based tools and services. To the end user, iCloud extends Apple's previous MobileMe offerings of e-mail, contact management, and Find My iPhone, with iOS backup and restore, iTunes Match, Photo Stream, and Back to My Mac. With iOS 8, iCloud got a major overhaul and now includes a new framework called CloudKit. This provides you with authentication, private and public databases, structures, and asset storage services.

For all the bells and whistles that Apple has built, at its heart iCloud is a cloud-based storage and synchronization service. Its main purpose is to allow users to access their content across all their devices: iPhone, iPad, or Mac. Best of all, Apple has given iOS developers a set of APIs for accessing iCloud. This lets you build apps that can take advantage of the same iCloud features as Apple without having to invest in building an extensive server infrastructure. Even better, you don't have to learn a new complicated SDK. Rather than providing a new iCloud framework, Apple added new classes to existing frameworks, primarily Foundation and UIKit, and extended existing classes to enable iCloud access.

The basic idea behind iCloud is to have a single place where apps can store and access data. Changes made by one instance of your app on one device can be instantly propagated to another instance of the app running on another device. At the same time, iCloud provides an authoritative copy of your application's data. This data can be used to restore your application's state on a new device, providing a seamless user experience as well as backup data. The data with CloudKit is separate and is public data that is shared between all users of their apps. This data is stored like on a shared disk drive that can be accessed from other devices as well.

Data Storage with iCloud

There are a few different ways to store your data in iCloud.

- *iOS Backup*: This is a global device configuration that backs up your iOS device to iCloud.

- *Key-Value Data Storage*: This is used for storing small amounts of infrequently changing data used by your application.

- *Document Storage*: This is used for storing user documents and application data.

- *Core Data with iCloud*: This puts your application's persistent backing store on iCloud.

Before we discuss these storage mechanisms in detail, let's review how iCloud and iOS work together.

iCloud Basics

Inside your iCloud application there is a ubiquity container. Depending on the storage type used, you may explicitly define the URL for this container or iOS will create one for you. The ubiquity container is where iCloud data is stored by your application. iOS will synchronize the data between your device and iCloud. This means that any changes your application makes to data in the ubiquity container will be sent to iCloud. Conversely, any changes in iCloud will be sent to your application's ubiquity container on your device.

Now, iOS doesn't send the entire data file back and forth from iCloud for every change. Internally, iOS and iCloud break up your application's data into smaller chunks of data. When changes occur, only the chunks that have changed are synchronized with iCloud. On iCloud, your application data is versioned, keeping track of each set of changes.

In addition to breaking up your application's data into chunks, iOS and iCloud will send the data file's metadata. Since the metadata is relatively small and important, the metadata is sent all the time. In fact, iCloud will know a data file's metadata before the actual data is synchronized. This is especially important with iOS. Since an iOS device may be space and bandwidth constrained, iOS won't necessarily automatically download data from iCloud until it needs it. But since iOS has the metadata, it knows when its copy is out of date with iCloud.

Note   Interestingly, if iOS detects another iOS device on the same WiFi network, rather than sending data up to iCloud and down to the other device, iOS will simply transfer the data from one device to the other.

---

iCloud Backup

Backup is an iOS system service offered by iCloud. It automatically backs up your iOS device daily over WiFi. Everything in your application's home directory is backed up. The application bundle, caches directory, and temp directory are ignored by iOS. Since the data is transmitted over WiFi and sent to Apple's iCloud data center, you should try to keep your application's data as small as possible. The more data, the longer the backup time and the more iCloud storage your users will consume.

> **Note**   If you've used up your iCloud storage capacity (at the time of this writing, 5GB by default), iOS will ask you if you want to buy more storage. Regardless, you'll need to figure out how your application will handle the case if iCloud is full.

When designing your application's data storage policy, keep the following in mind:

- User-generated data, or data that cannot be re-created by your application, should be stored in the Documents directory. From there it will be automatically backed up to iCloud.

- Data that can be downloaded or re-created by your application should live in Library/Caches.

- Data that is temporary should be stored in the tmp directory. Remember to delete these files when they are no longer needed.

- Data that your application needs to persist, even in low storage situations, should be flagged with the NSURLIsExcludedFromBackupKey attribute. Regardless of where you put these files, they will not be deleted by Backup. It's your application's responsibility to manage these files.

You can set NSURLIsExcludedFromBackupKey via the setResource:forKey:error: method in NSURL.

```
NSURL *url = [[NSBundle mainBundle] URLForResource:@"" withExtension:@""];
NSError *error = nil;
BOOL success = [url setResourceValue:@YES forKey:NSURLIsExcludedFromBackupKey error:&error];
```

Enabling iCloud in Your Application

To use iCloud data storage within your application, you need to perform two tasks. First, you need to enable the application's entitlements and enable them for iCloud. Second, you need to create an iCloud-enabled provisioning profile. This is done via the iOS Provisioning Portal that you access via the Apple Developer Center web site. We'll go over the specifics of enabling your application later in this chapter, when you extend your SuperDB application to use iCloud.

When entitlements are enabled in your application, Xcode expects to find an .entitlements file within your project directory. This .entitlements file is simply a property list of key-values pairs. These key-value pairs configure additional capabilities or security features of your application. For iCloud access, the .entitlements file specifies the keys to define ubiquity identifiers for the iCloud key-value and document ubiquity containers.

Key-Value Data Storage

As the name suggests, iCloud key-value data storage is a simple key-value storage mechanism integrated with iCloud. Conceptually, it's similar to NSUserDefaults. Like NSUserDefaults, the only allowable data types are those supported by property lists. It is best to use it for data with values that are infrequently updated. Placing your application's preferences or settings in it would be a good use case. You shouldn't use key-value data storage in place of NSUserDefaults. You should keep writing configuration information to NSUserDefault and write shared data to key-value data storage. This way your application still has configuration information if iCloud is unavailable.

There are a number of limitations on the key-value data storage that you need to keep in mind. First, there is a 1MB maximum storage limit per value. Keys have a separate 1MB per-key limit. Furthermore, each application is allowed a maximum of 1,024 separate keys. As a result, you will need to be judicious about what you put in key-value data storage.

Key-value data is synced with iCloud at periodic intervals. The frequency of these intervals is determined by iCloud, so you don't have much control over this. As a result, you shouldn't use the key-value data storage for time-sensitive data.

Key-value data storage handles data conflicts by always choosing the latest value for each key.

To use key-value data storage, you use the default NSUbiquitousKeyValueStore. You access values using the appropriate *ForKey: and set*ForKey: methods, similar to NSUserDefaults. You will also need to register for notifications about changes to the store via iCloud. To synchronize data changes, you call the synchronize method. You can also use the synchronize method as a check to see whether iCloud is available. You might initialize your application to use key-value data storage like this:

```
NSUbiquitousKeyValueStore *kv_store = [NSUbiquitousKeyValueStore defaultStore];

// register for KV Data Storage changes from iCloud
[[NSNotificationCenter defaultCenter] addObserver:self
                                selector:@selector (storeDidChange:)
                                    name:NSUbiquitousKeyValueStoreDidChange
                                                    ExternallyNotification
                                  object:self.kv_store];
BOOL avail = [self.kv_store synchronize];
if (avail) {
// iCloud is available
    ...
}
else {
    // iCloud is NOT available
}
```

The synchronize method does not push data to iCloud. It simply notifies iCloud that new data is available. iCloud will determine when to retrieve the data from your device.

Document Storage

For iCloud document storage, a document is a custom subclass of UIDocument. UIDocument is an abstract class that is used to store your application's data, either as a single file or as a file bundle. A file bundle is a directory that behaves as a single file. To manage a file bundle, use the NSFileWrapper class.

Before we describe iCloud Document Storage, let's look at UIDocument.

UIDocument

UIDocument eases the development of document-based applications by giving a number of features for "free."

- *Background reading and writing of data*: Keeps your application's UI responsive

- *Conflict detection*: Helps you resolve differences between document versions

- *Safe-saving*: Makes sure your document is never in a corrupted state

- *Automated saves*: Makes life easier for your users

- *Automatic iCloud integration*: Handles all interchanges between your document and iCloud

If you want to build a single file document, you would create a simple UIDocument subclass.

```
@interface MyDocument : UIDocument

@property (strong, nonatomic) NSString *text;

@end
```

There are a number of methods you need to implement in your UIDocument subclass. First, you need to be able to load the document data. To do this, you override the loadFromContents:ofType:error: method.

```
-(BOOL)loadFromContents:(id)contents
                ofType:(NSString *)typeName
                error:(NSError *__autoreleasing *)outError {
    if ([contents length] > 0) {
        self.text = [[NSString alloc] initWithData:(NSData *)contents
                    encoding:NSUTF8StringEncoding];
    } else {
        self.text = @"";
    }
```

```
//Update the view here

return YES;
}
```

The contents parameter is defined as id. If your document is a file bundle, the content will be of type NSFileWrapper. For your single document file case, the content is an NSData object. This is a simple implementation; it never fails. If you implemented a failure case and returned NO, you should create an error object and give it a meaningful error message. You also want to put code in place to update the UI once the data is successfully loaded. You also never check the content type. Your application could support multiple data types, and you have to use the typeName parameter to handle the different data loading scenarios.

When you close your application or when auto-save is invoked, the UIDocument method contentForType:error: is called. You need to override this method as well.

```
-(id) contentsForType:(NSString *)typeName error:(NSError *__autoreleasing *)outError {
    if(!self.text) {
        self.text = @"";
    }

    NSData *data = [self.text dataUsingEncoding:NSUTF8StringEncoding
                    allowLossyConversion:NO];
    return data;
}
```

If your document is stored as a file bundle, you return an instance of NSFileWrapper rather than the NSData object for a single file. That's all you need to do to ensure your data gets saved; UIDocument will handle the rest.

UIDocument needs a file URL to determine where to read and write data. The URL will define the document directory, file name, and possibly file extension. The directory can be either a local (application sandbox) directory or a location in the iCloud ubiquity container. The file name should be generated by your application, optionally allowing the user to override the default value. While using a file extension might be optional, it's probably a good idea to define one (or more) for your application. You pass this URL to the initWithFileURL method of your UIDocument subclass to create a document instance.

```
MyDocument *doc = [[MyDocument alloc] initWithFileURL:aURL];
...
[doc saveToURL:doc.fileURL forSaveOperation:UIDocumentSaveForCreating
                    completionHandler:^(BOOL success) {
    if(success) {
        // handle successful save
    } else {
        // handle failed save
    }
}];
```

Once you have created a UIDocument instance, you create the file using the saveToURL:forSaveOperation:completionHandler: method. You use the value UIDocumentSaveForCreating to indicate that you are saving the file for the first time. The completionHandler: parameter takes a block. The block takes a BOOL parameter to tell you whether the save operation was successful.

You don't just need to create documents; your application may need to open and close existing documents. You still need to call initWithFileURL to create a document instance, but then you call openWithCompletionHandler: and closeWithCompletionHandler: to open and close your document.

```
MyDocument *doc = [[MyDocument alloc] initWithFileURL:aURL];
...
[doc openWithCompletionHandler:^(BOOL success) {
    if(success) {
        // handle successful save
    } else {
        // handle failed save
    }
}];


//Work on Document


[doc closeWithCompletionHandler:nil];
```

Both methods take a block to execute on completion. Like the saveToURL:forSave Operation:completionHandler: method, the block has a BOOL parameter to tell you whether the open/close succeeded or failed. You're not required to pass a block. In the previous example code, you pass nil to closeWithCompletionHandler: to indicate you don't do anything after the document is closed.

To delete a document, you could simply use the NSFileManager removeItemAtURL: and pass in the document file URL. However, you should do what UIDocument does for reading and writing and perform the delete operation in the background.

```
MyDocument *doc = [[MyDocument alloc]initWithFileURL:aURL];
...
// Close the document
...
dispatch_async(dispatch_get_global_queue(DISPATCH_QUEUE_PRIORITY_DEFAULT, 0), ^{
    NSFileCoordinator *fileCoordinator = [[NSFileCoordinator alloc]
                                        initWithFilePresenter:nil];
    [fileCoordinator coordinateWritingItemAtURL:aURL options:NSFileCoordinatorWritingFor
     Deleting error:nil byAccessor:^(NSURL *newURL) {
        NSFileManager *fileManager = [[NSFileManager alloc] init];
        [fileManager removeItemAtURL:newURL error:nil];
    }];
});
```

First, you dispatch the entire delete operation to a background queue via the dispatch_async function. Inside the background queue, you create an NSFileCoordinator instance. NSFileCoordinator coordinates file operations between processes and objects. Before any file operation is performed, it sends messages to all the NSFilePresenter protocol objects that have registered themselves with the file coordinator. Delete the document file by invoking the NSFileCoordinator method coordinateWritingItemAtURL:options:error: byAccessor:. The accessor is a block operation that defines the actual file operation you want performed. It's passed an NSURL parameter, representing the location of the file. Always use the block parameter NSURL, not the NSURL passed to coordinateWritingItemAtURL:.

Before performing an operation on your UIDocument subclass, you probably want to check the documentState property. The possible states are defined as follows:

- UIDocumentStateNormal: The document is open and has no issues.

- UIDocumentStateClosed: The document is closed. If the document is in this state after opening, it indicates there may be a problem with the document.

- UIDocumentStateInConflict: There are versions of this document in conflict. You may need to write code to allow your user to resolve these conflicts.

- UIDocumentStateSavingError: The document could not be saved because of some error.

- UIDocumentStateEditingDisabled: The document cannot be edited; either your application or iOS will not permit it.

You can check the document state using a simple bitwise operator.

```
MyDocument *doc = [[MyDocument alloc] initWithFileURL:aURL];
...
if(doc.documentState & UIDocumentStateClosed) {
    // Document state is Closed
}
```

UIDocument also provides a notification named UIDocumentStateChangedNotification that you can use to register an observer.

```
MyDocument *doc = [[MyDocument alloc] initWithFileURL:aURL]];
...

    [[NSNotificationCenter defaultCenter] addObserver:self selector:@
      selector(documentStateChanged:) name:UIDocumentStateChangedNotification object:doc];
```

Your observer class would implement the method documentStateChanged: to check the document state and handle each state accordingly.

To perform automated saves, UIDocument periodically invokes the method hasUnsavedChanges, which returns a BOOL depending on whether your document has changed since the last save. The frequency of these calls is determined by UIDocument and cannot be adjusted. Generally, you don't override hasUnsavedChanges. Rather, you do one of two things: register the NSUndoManager via the UIDocument undoManager property to register for undo/redo operations or call the updateChangeCount: method every time a trackable change is made to your document. For your document to work with iCloud, you must enable the automated saves feature.

UIDocument with iCloud

Using iCloud document storage requires an adjustment to the normal UIDocument process to use a Documents subdirectory of your application's ubiquity container. To get the ubiquity container URL, you pass the document identifier into the NSFileManager method URLForUbiquityContainerIdentifer:, passing nil as the argument.

```
id iCloudToken = [[NSFileManager defaultManager] ubiquityIdentityToken];
if (iCloudToken) {
    // Have cloud Access
    NSURL *ubiquityURL = [[NSFileManager defaultManager] URLForUbiquityContainerIdentifier:nil];
    NSURL *ubiquityDocURL = [ubiquityURL URLByAppendingPathComponent:@"Documents"];
} else {
    // No iCloud Access
}
```

By using nil in URLForUbiquityContainerIdentifer:, NSFileManager will use the ubiquity container ID defined in the application's entitlements file. We'll cover this in the "Entitlements" section later, but for now, just try to follow along. If you want to use the ubiquity container identifier explicitly, it's a combination of your ADC Team ID and App ID.

```
NSString *ubiquityContainer = @"HQ7JAY4X53.com.ozapps.iCloudAppID";
NSURL *ubiquityURL = [[NSFileManager defaultManager]
                        URLForUbiquityContainerIdentifier:ubiquityContainer];
```

Notice the use of the NSFileManager method ubiquityIdentityToken to check for iCloud availability. This method returns a unique token tied to the user's iCloud account. Depending on your application, if iCloud access is unavailable, you should inform the user and either work with local storage or exit the application.

NSMetadataQuery

Earlier, we stated that iCloud and iOS don't automatically sync documents in an application's ubiquity container. However, a document's metadata is synced. For an iCloud document storage application, you can't simple use the file contents of the Documents directory in your ubiquity container to know what documents are available for your application. Rather, you have to perform a metadata query using the NSMetadataQuery class.

Early in your application life cycle you need to instantiate an NSMetadataQuery and configure it to look for the appropriate documents in the Documents subdirectory of the ubiquity container.

```
self.query = [[NSMetadataQuery alloc]init];
[self.query setSearchScopes:@[NSMetadataQueryUbiquitousDocumentsScope]];
NSString *filePattern = @"*.txt";
[self.query setPredicate:[NSPredicate predicateWithFormat:@"%K LIKE %K",
                          NSMetadataItemFSNameKey, filePattern]];
```

This example assumes that you have a query property and it's configured to look for all files with the .txt extension.

After creating the NSMetadataQuery object, you need to register for its notifications.

```
[[NSNotificationCenter defaultCenter]
    addObserver:self
      selector:@selector(processFiles:)
          name:NSMetadataQueryDidFinishGatheringNotification
        object:nil];
[[NSNotificationCenter defaultCenter]
    addObserver:self
      selector:@selector(processFile:)
          name:NSMetadataQueryDidUpdateNotification
        object:nil];
[self.query startQuery];
```

NSMetadataQueryDidFinishGatheringNotification is sent when the query object has finished its initial information loading query. NSMetadataQueryDidUpdateNotification is sent when the contents of the Documents subdirectory have changed and they affect the results of the query. Finally, you start the query.

When a notification is sent, the processFiles: method is invoked. It might look something like this:

```
-(void) processFiles:(NSNotification *) aNotification {
    NSMutableArray *files = [[NSMutableArray alloc]init];

    //disable query during processing
    [self.query disableUpdates];

    NSArray *queryResults = [self.query results];

    for(NSMetadataItem *result in queryResults) {
        NSURL *fileURL = [result valueForAttribute:NSMetadataItemURLKey];
        NSNumber *aBool = nil;

        //exclude hidden files
        [fileURL getResourceValue:&aBool forKey:NSURLIsHiddenKey error:nil];
        if(aBool && ![aBool boolValue])
            [files addObject:fileURL];
    }
```

```
//do something with the files in the array

//re-enable the query
[self.query enableUpdates];
}
```

First, you disable the query updates to prevent notifications from being sent while you're processing. In this example, you simply get a list of files in the Documents subdirectory and add them to an array. You make sure to exclude any hidden files in the directory. Once you have the array of files, you use them in your application (perhaps to update a table view of file names). Finally, you reenable the query to receive updates.

You've only skimmed the surface of how to use iCloud document storage. There are a lot of document life-cycle issues that your document-based application should handle to be effective.

> **Note** For more information, read Apple's documentation. Check the iCloud chapter of the iOS App Programming Guide first (https://developer.apple.com/library/ios/#documentation/iPhone/Conceptual/iPhoneOSProgrammingGuide/AppArchitecture/AppArchitecture.html#//apple_ref/doc/uid/TP40007072-CH3-SW21).
>
> Then read the iCloud Design Guild (https://developer.apple.com/library/ios/#documentation/General/Conceptual/iCloudDesignGuide)
>
> and the document-based App Programming Guide for iOS (https://developer.apple.com/library/ios/#documentation/General/Conceptual/iCloudDesignGuide).

Core Data with iCloud

Using Core Data with iCloud is a fairly simple process. You place your persistent store in your application's ubiquity container. However, you don't want your persistent store to be synchronized with iCloud. That would create unnecessary overhead. Rather, you want to synchronize the transactions between applications. When another instance of your application receives the transaction data from iCloud, it reapplies every operation performed on the persistent store. This helps ensure that the different instances are updated with the same set of operations.

Even though you don't want to synchronize the persistent store with iCloud, Apple recommends that you place the data file in the ubiquity container within a folder with the extension .nosync. This tells iOS not to synchronize the contents of this folder but will keep the data associated with the correct iCloud account.

```
// Assume we have an instance of NSPersistentStoreCoordinator *persistentStoreCoordinator

NSString *dataFileName = @"iCloudCoreDataApp.sqlite";
NSString *dataDirectoryName = @"Data.nosync";
NSString *logsDirectoryName = @"Logs";
```

```
__block NSPersistentStoreCoordinator *psc = _persistentStoreCoordinator;
dispatch_async(dispatch_get_global_queue(DISPATCH_QUEUE_PRIORITY_DEFAULT, 0), ^{

    // Get Ubiquity Identity Token to check of iCloud access
    NSFileManager *fileManager = [NSFileManager defaultManager];
    id ubiquityToken = [fileManager ubiquityIdentityToken];
    NSURL *ubiquityURL = [fileManager URLForUbiquityContainerIdentifier:nil];
    if (ubiquityToken && ubiquityURL) {
        // Have iCloud Access
        NSString *dataDir = [[ubiquityURL path]
                              stringByAppendingPathComponent:dataDirectoryName];
        if([fileManager fileExistsAtPath:dataDir] == NO) {
            NSError *fileSystemError;
            [fileManager createDirectoryAtPath:dataDir
                    withIntermediateDirectories:YES
                                     attributes:nil
                                          error:&fileSystemError];
            if (fileSystemError != nil) {
                NSLog(@"Error creating database directory %@", fileSystemError);
                // handle the error
            }
        }

        NSString *ubiquityContainer = [ubiquityURL lastPathComponent];
        NSURL *logsPath = [NSURL fileURLWithPath:[[ubiquityURL path]
                            stringByAppendingPathComponent:logsDirectoryName]];

        NSDictionary *options = @{
                NSMigratePersistentStoresAutomaticallyOption:@YES,
                    NSInferMappingModelAutomaticallyOption:@YES,
                    NSPersistentStoreUbiquitousContentNameKey:ubiquityContainer,
                    NSPersistentStoreUbiquitousContentURLKey:logsPath };

        NSString *dataPath = [dataDir stringByAppendingPathComponent:dataFileName];
        [psc performBlockAndWait:^{
            NSError *error = nil;
            [psc addPersistentStoreWithType:NSSQLiteStoreType
                              configuration:nil
                                        URL:[NSURL fileURLWithPath:dataPath]
                                    options:options
                                      error:&error];
        }];
    }
    else {
        // No iCloud Access
    }
});
```

Notice that you perform your persistent store operations in a background queue so that
your iCloud access does not block your application UI. Most of the example here defines
your data directory path, Data.nosync, and the log directory path, Logs. The actually
persistent store creation is similar to what you've done earlier. You added two key-value

pairs to the options dictionary: `NSPersistentStoreUbiquitousContentNameKey` with your ubiquity container ID and `NSPersistentStoreUbiquityContentURLKey` with the transaction log directory path. Core Data and iCloud will use `NSPersistentStoreUbiquityContentURLKey` to synchronize the transaction logs.

Now you need to register to observe a notification when changes are received from iCloud. Generally, you don't want to put this when you create the persistent store coordinator; rather, you do it when creating the managed object context.

```
[[NSNotificationCenter defaultCenter]
    addObserver:self
        selector:@selector(mergeChangesFromUbiquitousContent:)
            name:NSPersistentStoreDidImportUbiquitousContentChangesNotification
          object:coordinator];
```

The implementation of `mergeChangesFromUbiquitousContent:` will have to handle the merging of content between iCloud and local persistent store. Fortunately, for all but the most complicated models, Core Data makes this relatively painless.

```
-(void)mergeChangesFromUbiquitousContent:(NSNotification *)aNotification {
    NSManagedObjectContext *cotext = [self managedObjectContext];
    [context performBlock:^{
        [context mergeChangesFromContextDidSaveNotification:aNotification];

        //Send a notification to refresh the UI, if necessary
    }];
}
```

Enhancing SuperDB

You're going to enhance the Core Data SuperDB application and place the persistent store in iCloud. Based on your review of the iCloud APIs, this should be a fairly straightforward process. Remember, you can't run iCloud apps on the simulator (yet), so you need to tether your device to your development machine. Additionally, since you need a provisioning profile, you need an Apple Developer Center account.

Make a copy of the SuperDB project from Chapter 6. If you haven't completed Chapter 6, that's OK. You can copy the project from this book's download archive and start from there.

Entitlements

You will need an entitlements file for your applications. Earlier you had to create this file yourself and set up the key-value entries. Figure 8-1 shows the entitlements file for the SuperDB app. To create this file, you just have to switch on a required capability and the entitlements file is automatically created by Xcode. You will do that in the next section.

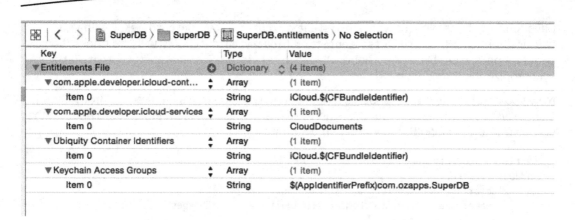

Figure 8-1. The entitlement section of the target Summary Editor

Enabling iCloud and Creating the Relevant Files

You need to create the entitlements file, an iCloud-enabled provisioning profile, App IDs, and so on. This is now a matter of simply selecting a box. However, the prerequisite is that you need to be registered with Apple's Developer Program.

Go to the project properties and click the target SuperDB. On the Capabilities tab, look for iCloud and switch it on (see Figure 8-2).

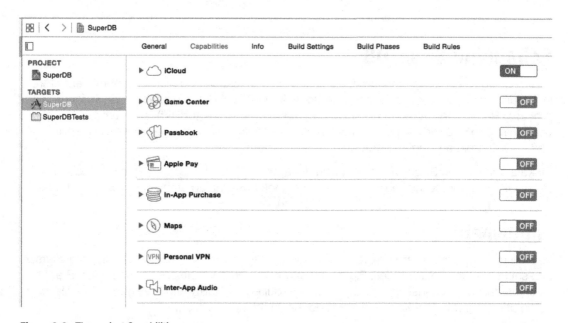

Figure 8-2. The project Capabilities screen

Xcode will select or prompt you for the relevant team account to use and create the relevant entitlements file, certificates, and so on. Select the appropriate services that you need to enable for this application. There are no settings for the key-value storage; for iCloud Documents, you need to select the appropriate container. This is created by default as iCloud.$(CFBundleIdentifier). In this case, the bundle identifier is com.ozapps.SuperDB, so the container is identified as iCloud.com.ozapps.SuperDB (see Figure 8-3).

Figure 8-3. The project with iCloud enabled

Whew. That was easy and less work to get iCloud activated for your application than it was in the past.

Updating the Persistent Store

In the SuperDB Xcode project window, open AppDelegate.m and find the persistentStoreCoordinator method. You need to rewrite it to check and use an iCloud persistent store if possible or fall back to a local persistent store. The beginning of the method remains the same: you check whether you've already created an instance of your persistent store coordinator; if not, you instantiate one.

```
- (NSPersistentStoreCoordinator *)persistentStoreCoordinator
{
    if (_persistentStoreCoordinator != nil) {
        return _persistentStoreCoordinator;
    }

    _persistentStoreCoordinator = [[NSPersistentStoreCoordinator alloc]
                        initWithManagedObjectModel:[self managedObjectModel]];
```

You dispatch the following code to a background queue so as not to block the main thread. The following code is similar to the example provided in the "Core Data with iCloud" section earlier. Review that section for a detailed explanation.

```
__block NSPersistentStoreCoordinator *psc = _persistentStoreCoordinator;
dispatch_async(dispatch_get_global_queue(DISPATCH_QUEUE_PRIORITY_DEFAULT, 0), ^{
    __block NSPersistentStore *newStore = nil;

    NSString *dataFile = @"SuperDB.sqlite";
    NSString *dataDir = @"Data.nosync";
    NSString *logsDir = @"Logs";
    __block NSError *error = nil;

    NSFileManager *fileManager = [NSFileManager defaultManager];
    id ubiquityToken = [fileManager URLForUbiquityContainerIdentifier:nil];
    NSURL *ubiquityURL = [fileManager URLForUbiquityContainerIdentifier:nil];
    if(ubiquityToken && ubiquityURL) {
        NSString *dataDirPath = [[ubiquityURL path] stringByAppendingPathComponent:dataDir];
        if([fileManager fileExistsAtPath:dataDirPath] == NO) {
            NSError *fileSystemError;
            [fileManager createDirectoryAtPath:dataDirPath
                    withIntermediateDirectories:YES
                                     attributes:nil error:&fileSystemError];
            if(fileSystemError != nil) {
                NSLog(@"Error creating database directory %@", fileSystemError);
            }
        }

        NSURL *logsURL = [NSURL fileURLWithPath:[[ubiquityURL path]
                                    stringByAppendingPathComponent:logsDir]];
        NSDictionary *options = @{
                NSMigratePersistentStoresAutomaticallyOption:@YES,
                    NSInferMappingModelAutomaticallyOption:@YES,
                    NSPersistentStoreUbiquitousContentNameKey:[ubiquityURL lastPathComponent],
                    NSPersistentStoreUbiquitousContentURLKey:logsURL
                };

        [psc performBlockAndWait:^{
            NSURL *dataFileURL = [NSURL fileURLWithPath:[dataDirPath
                                    stringByAppendingPathComponent:dataFile]];
            newStore = [psc addPersistentStoreWithType:NSSQLiteStoreType
                                         configuration:nil
                                                   URL:dataFileURL
                                               options:options
                                                 error:&error];
        }];
    }
});
```

If for some reason you don't have access to iCloud, you can fall back to using the local persistent store coordinator.

```
} else {
    NSURL *storeURL = [[self applicationDocumentsDirectory] URLByAppendingPathComponent:dataFile];
    NSDictionary *options = @{
            NSMigratePersistentStoresAutomaticallyOption:@YES,
            NSInferMappingModelAutomaticallyOption:@YES
    };

    [psc performBlockAndWait:^{
        [psc addPersistentStoreWithType:NSSQLiteStoreType configuration:nil URL:storeURL
                                                    options:options error:&error];
    }];
}
```

You need to check whether you actually have a new persistent store coordinator.

```
if(!newStore) {
    /*
    Replace this implementation with the code to handle the error appropriately

    abort() causes the application to generate a crash log and terminate.
    This should not be used in a shipping application though it can be useful
    during development.
    */

    NSLog(@"Unresolved error %@, %@", error, [error userInfo]);
    abort();
}
```

Once complete, you send a notification on the main thread that you've loaded the persistent store coordinator. You use this notification to update the UI, if necessary.

```
    dispatch_async(dispatch_get_main_queue(), ^{
        [[NSNotificationCenter defaultCenter] postNotificationName:@"DataChanged"
                                                    object:self userInfo:nil];
    });
});

    return _persistentStoreCoordinator;
}
```

Updating the Managed Object Context

You need to register to receive notifications when the data in the ubiquity container changes. You do that in the managedObjectContext method of the AppDelegate. The additions are in bold.

```
- (NSManagedObjectContext *)managedObjectContext
{
    if (_managedObjectContext != nil) {
        return _managedObjectContext;
    }

    NSPersistentStoreCoordinator *coordinator = [self persistentStoreCoordinator];
    if (coordinator != nil) {
        _managedObjectContext = [[NSManagedObjectContext alloc] init];
        [_managedObjectContext setPersistentStoreCoordinator:coordinator];
        [[NSNotificationCenter defaultCenter]
                addObserver:self
                    selector:@selector(mergeChangesFromUbiquitousContent:)
                        name:NSPersistentStoreDidImportUbiquitousContentChangesNotification
                    object:coordinator];
    }
    return _managedObjectContext;
}
```

You've told the Notification Center to invoke the AppDelegate method mergeChangesFromUbiquitousContent:, so you need to implement that method. First, add the method declaration to the interface file, AppDelegate.h, before the @end declaration.

```
- (void)mergeChangesFromUbiquitousContent:(NSNotification *)notification;
```

Then, add the implementation to the bottom of AppDelegate.m, just before the @end.

```
#pragma mark - Handle Changes from iCloud to Ubiquitous Container

-(void)mergeChangesFromUbiquitousContent:(NSNotification *)aNotification {
    NSManagedObjectContext *context = [self managedObjectContext];
    [context performBlock:^{
        [context mergeChangesFromContextDidSaveNotification:aNotification];
        //Send a notification to refresh the UI, if necessary
        NSNotification *refreshNotification = [NSNotification notificationWithName:
        @"DataChanged" object:self userInfo:[aNotification userInfo]];
        [[NSNotificationCenter defaultCenter] postNotification:refreshNotification];
    }];
}
```

This method first merges the changes into your managed object context. Then it sends a DataChanged notification. You used that notification earlier when you created the persistent store coordinator. It's intended to notify you when the UI should be updated. Let's do that.

Updating the UI on DataChanged

Open HeroListController.m in the Xcode editor and find the viewDidLoad method. Just before the end of the method, register for the DataChanged notification.

```
[[NSNotificationCenter defaultCenter]
        addObserver:self
          selector:@selector(updateReceived:)
              name:@"DataChanged"
            object:nil];
```

While you're at it, be a good iOS programmer and unregister it in the didReceiveMemoryWarning method.

```
[[NSNotificationCenter defaultCenter] removeObserver:self];
```

When the DataChanged notification is received, the updateReceived: method will be invoked. So, you need to declare and implement it, so add the method declaration to HeroListController.h, before the @end.

```
- (void)updateReceived:(NSNotification *)notification;
```

Now, add the implementation to HeroListController.m, again before the @end.

```
- (void)updateReceived:(NSNotification *)notification
{
    NSError *error;
    if (![self.fetchedResultsController performFetch:&error]) {
        NSLog(@"Error performing fetch: %@", [error localizedDescription]);
    }
    [self.heroTableView reloadData];
}
```

Essentially, it just refreshes the data and table view.

Testing the Data Store

Build and run the app. Since you're starting with a new persistent store, there should be no entries. Add a new hero, edit the details, and save. Now quit the application (and/or stop it in Xcode). On your device, tap and hold the SuperDB app icon until it begins to shake. Delete the app. You should receive an alert dialog to tell you that the local data will be lost, but the iCloud data will be kept. Tap Delete.

Now run the app again. Wait a few moments, and the Hero list should update to include the hero you added earlier. Even though you deleted the app (and its local data), iCloud was able to synchronize and restore the persistent store.

Keep Your Feet on the Ground

While developing an application for iCloud, there may be times when you want to view or even delete the data in iCloud. There are a few ways you can view and manage the data your application is putting in iCloud.

- *Via Mac*: Open System Preferences and choose iCloud. Click the Manage button on the lower right.

- *Via iOS*: Use the Settings app and navigate to iCloud Storage & Backup Manage Storage.

- *Via the Web (view only)*: Navigate to `http://developer.icloud.com/` and log in. Click the Documents icon.

Those are just the basics of building an iCloud-enabled application for iOS. For any application, there are many things to keep in mind, but here are some key things to remember:

- How will your app behave if iCloud is not available?

- If you allow "offline" use, how will your application synchronize with iCloud?

- How will your application handle conflicts? This will be highly dependent on your data model.

- Try to design your data/document model to minimize the data transfer between your device and iCloud.

Ideally you've gotten a good taste of what it means to enable iCloud in your app. Let's head back to Earth and have some fun building a game.

Chapter 9

Peer-to-Peer Over Bluetooth Using Multipeer Connectivity

Game Kit has to be one of the coolest frameworks available for people interested in developing games on the iOS SDK. Game Kit classes provide three different technologies: GameCenter, Peer-to-Peer Connectivity, and In Game Voice. With iOS 7, Apple introduced a new framework called Multipeer Connectivity. This chapter will focus on Peer-to-Peer Connectivity using Multipeer Connectivity. We won't be covering any of Game Kit functionality in this chapter.

Peer-to-Peer Connectivity

Multipeer Connectivity makes it easy to wirelessly connect multiple iOS devices, either via Bluetooth or WiFi. Bluetooth is a wireless networking option built into all but the first-generation iPhone and iPod touch. Multipeer Connectivity allows any supported devices to communicate with any other supported devices that are within range. For Bluetooth, this is roughly 30 feet (about 10 meters) of each other. You might build a social networking app that allows people to easily transfer contact information over Bluetooth. In fact, the amazing application FireChat is built upon Multipeer Connectivity. Some other apps that allow iPhones to be used like a CB radio also uses Multipeer Connectivity as their core. The good part about Multipeer Connectivity is that it does not require the presence of a network and can connect over Bluetooth or can use a network, if one is present.

Peer-to-Peer Connectivity relies on two components.

- The *session* allows iPhone OS devices running the same application to easily send information back and forth over Bluetooth without writing any networking code.

- The *browser* provides an easy way to find other devices without writing any networking or discovery (Bonjour) code.

Under the hood, Multipeer Connectivity sessions leverage Bonjour, Apple's technology for zero-configuration networking and device discovery. As a result, devices using Multipeer Connectivity are capable of finding each other on the network without the user needing to enter an IP address or domain name.

This Chapter's Application

In this chapter, you'll explore Multipeer Connectivity by writing a simple networked game. You'll write a two-player version of tic-tac-toe (Figure 9-1) that will use Multipeer Connectivity to let people on two different iOS devices play against each other over Bluetooth. You won't be implementing online play over the Internet or local area network in this chapter.

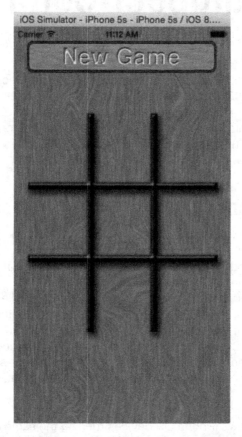

Figure 9-1. You'll use a simple game of tic-tac-toe to learn the basics of Game Kit

When users launch your application, they will be presented with an empty tic-tac-toe board and a single button labeled New Game. (For the sake of simplicity, you're not going to implement a single-device mode to let two players play on the same device.) When the user presses the New Game button, the application will start looking for Bluetooth peers using the peer picker (Figure 9-2).

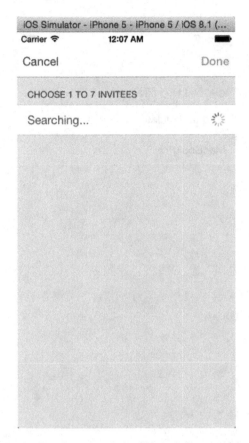

Figure 9-2. *When the user presses the New Game button, it will launch the peer picker to look for other devices running the tic-tac-toe game*

If another device within range runs the TicTacToe application and the user also presses the New Game button, the two devices will find each other, and the peer picker will present a dialog to the users, letting them choose among the available peers (Figure 9-3).

Figure 9-3. When another device within range starts a game, the two devices will show up in each other's peer picker dialog

After one player selects a peer, the iPhone will attempt to make a connection (Figure 9-4). Once the connection is established, the other person will be asked to accept or refuse the connection (Figure 9-5). If the connection is accepted, the two applications will negotiate to see who goes first. Each side will randomly select a number, the numbers will be compared, and the highest number will go first. Once that decision is made, play will commence (Figure 9-6) until someone wins (Figure 9-7).

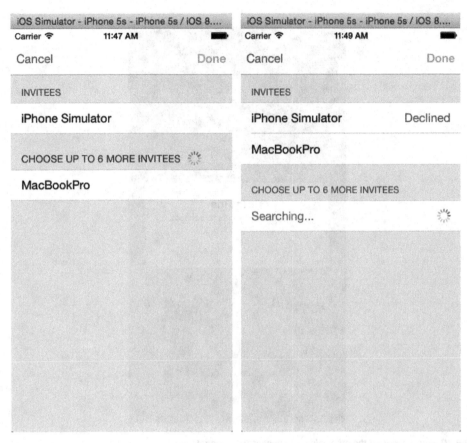

Figure 9-4. Establishing a connection with a selected peer. The status will change once accepted and connected or when declined

Figure 9-5. Dialog requesting the other player to accept the connection

Figure 9-6. The user whose turn it is can tap any available space. That space will get an X or an O on both users' devices

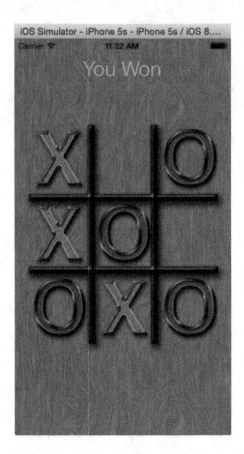

Figure 9-7. We have a winner!

If the connection is lost for whatever reason, the iPhone will report the lost connection to the user (Figure 9-8).

Figure 9-8. Lost connection alert

Network Communication Models

Before we look at how Multipeer Connectivity works, let's talk generally about communication models used in networked programs so that we're all on the same page in terms of terminology.

Client-Server Model

You're probably familiar with the client-server model because it is the model used by the World Wide Web. Machines called *servers* listen for connections from other machines, referred to as *clients*. The server then takes actions based on the requests received from the clients. In the context of the Web, the client is usually a web browser, and there can be any number of clients attaching to a single server. The clients never communicate with each other directly but direct all communications through the server. Most massively multiplayer online role-playing games (MMORPGs) like World of Warcraft also use this model. Figure 9-9 represents a client-server scenario.

Figure 9-9. The client-server model features one machine acting as a server with all communications—even communications between clients—going through the server

In the context of an iPhone application, a client-server setup is where one phone acts as a server and listens for other iPhones running the same program. The other phones can then connect to that server. If you've ever played a game where one machine "hosts" a game and others then join the game, that game is almost certainly using a client-server model.

A drawback with the client-server model is that everything depends on the server, which means that the game cannot continue if anything happens to the server. If the user whose phone is acting as the server quits, crashes, or moves out of range, the entire game is ended. Since all the other machines communicate through the central server, they lose the ability to communicate if the server is unavailable. This is generally not an issue with client-server games where the client is a hefty server farm connected to the Internet by redundant high-speed lines, but it certainly can be an issue with mobile games.

Peer-to-Peer Model

In the peer-to-peer model, all the individual devices (called *peers*) can communicate with each other directly. A central server may be used to initiate the connection or to facilitate certain operations, but the main distinguishing feature of the peer-to-peer model is that peers can talk to each other directly and can continue to do so even in the absence of a server (Figure 9-10).

Figure 9-10. In the peer-to-peer model, peers can talk to each other directly and can continue to do so even in the absence of a server

The peer-to-peer model was popularized by file-sharing services like BitTorrent. A centralized server is used to find other peers that have the file you are looking for, but once the connection is made to those other peers, they can continue, even if the server goes offline.

The simplest and probably the most common implementation of the peer-to-peer model on the iPhone is when you have two devices connected to each other. This is the model used in head-to-head games, for example. Multipeer Connectivity makes this kind of peer-to-peer network exceedingly simple to set up and configure, as you'll see in this chapter.

> **Note**   With Multipeer Connectivity there is an upper limit of eight devices that can connect. That is actually seven, with the eighth being your own. The browser displays how many more peers you can invite and connect to.

Hybrid Client-Server/Peer-to-Peer

The client-server and peer-to-peer models of network communication are not mutually exclusive, and it is possible to create programs that utilize a hybrid of both. For example, a client-server game might allow certain communications to go directly from client to client without going through the server. In a game that has a chat window, it might allow messages intended for only one recipient to go directly from the machine of the sender to the machine of the intended recipient, while any other kind of chat would go to the server to be distributed to all clients.

You should keep these different networking models in mind as we discuss the mechanics of making connections and transferring data between application nodes. *Node* is a generic term that refers to any computer connected to an application's network. A client, server, or peer is a node. The game you will be writing in this chapter will use a simple, two-machine, peer-to-peer model.

The Multipeer Connectivity Peer

It does not take much to figure out that the core building block of Multipeer Connectivity is a *peer*. It is used to identify the device in this connection. With earlier technology, it was two devices that would connect, one being the server or the host and the other the client. Now to identify each device in this connectivity, you use the peerID. This is created using the MCPeerID object and takes a display name, which is how this peer appears to other peers. You can create a peerID and assign it a display name like so:

```
NSString *deviceName = @"iMac";  //[[UIDevice currentDevice] name];
MCPeerID *peerID = [[MCPeerID alloc]initWithDisplayName: deviceName];
```

> **Note**   Since the peer names follow the Bonjour API, these have to be no longer than 15 characters in length. So while you can see the name iPhone Simulator, that is invalid and would not connect. You cannot assign a unique name to every instance, so you could get the device name and use the first 15 characters or devise your own methodology. For the purpose of this chapter, we are running the project between a iMac and a MacBookPro running in the iPhone simulator and therefore the devices are named so respectively.

The Multipeer Connectivity Session

The key to Multipeer Connectivity is the *session*, represented by the class MCSession. The session represents your end of a network connection with one or more other iPhones. Regardless of whether you are acting as a client, a server, or a peer, an instance of MCSession will represent the connections you have with other phones. You will use MCSession whether you employ the peer picker or write your own code to find machines to connect to and let the user select from them.

> **Note**   As you make your way through the next few pages, don't worry too much about where each of these elements is implemented. This will all come together in the project you create in this chapter.

You will also use MCSession to send data to connected peers. You will implement session delegate methods to get notified of changes to the session, such as when another node connects or disconnects, as well as to receive data sent by other nodes.

Creating the Session

To use a session, you must first create allocate and initialize a MCSession object, like so:

```
MCSession *theSession = [[MCSession alloc]initWithPeer:peerID];
```

You pass just the peerID when initializing a session. Easy as that, this provides the *display name*. This is a name that will be provided to the other nodes to uniquely identify your phone. You cannot pass in nil or have the displayname as nil or blank. If multiple devices are connected, this will allow the other users to see which devices are available and connect to the correct one. In Figure 9-4, you can see an example of where the unique identifier is used. In that example, one other device is advertising itself with the same session identifier, using a display name of MacBookPro.

After you create a session, it won't actually start advertising its availability or looking for other available nodes. You do that by creating an MCAdvertiserAssistant object, like so:

```
assistant = [[MCAdvertiserAssistant alloc]
            initWithServiceType:@"oz-appsgame"
                discoveryInfo:nil session:session];
```

You pass three parameters to the MCAdvertiserAssistant when creating and initializing it.

The first argument is a session identifier, which is a string that is unique to your application. This is used to prevent your application's sessions from accidentally connecting to sessions from another program. Since the session identifier is a string, it can be anything, though there are a couple of limitations.

- It cannot exceed 15 characters in length.
- It has to have valid ASCII characters, which include lowercase letters, numbers, and hyphens.
- As recommended by Apple, the game from oz-apps is coded as oz-appsgame.

> **Note**   For more information on serviceType, you can see the Bonjour API at https://developer.apple.com/bonjour.

By assigning session identifiers in this manner, rather than by just randomly picking a word or phrase, you are less likely to accidentally choose a session identifier that is used by another application on the App Store. It would have been better if reverse DNS could be used, but that's the limitation.

The second argument is `discoveryInfo`. This is a dictionary object with key-value pair data that can be sent to another peer for identification. This can be `nil`; however, if you would want to connect to only certain peers, you can send credentials, and so on, in this data, and the peer at the other end can use it for identifying and authorizing this peer.

The last argument is an `MCSession` object, the session you created.

Finding and Connecting to Other Sessions

Even after creating the `MCAdvertiserAssistant`, the peer is not searchable nor does it advertise its availability. You need to simply invoke the start method.

```
[assistant start];
```

In fact, if another peer was configured to browse and connect, you would see this peer in the browser list. If the other peer tried to connect, a dialog would pop up requesting permission to connect, and if you give it permission to connect, the session would be connected.

Listening for Other Sessions

If you had set only the `MCAdvertiserAssistant`, then your device would be advertising its presence but unable to browse or search for other peers. If you want to search for other peers, you need to use the `MCBrowserViewController`. This provides a standard GUI with all the functionality required to browse and connect with other peers. There is a limit of eight peers with Multipeer Connectivity, with the eighth being this peer (so seven other peers).

To create the `ViewController`, you can do so like this where the `nearbyBrowser` is an object that we have not spoken about earlier:

```
browser = [[MCBrowserViewController alloc] initWithBrowser: nearbyBrowser session:session];
```

The `nearbyBrowser` is an `MCNearbyServiceBroswer` object that is used to browse peers that are nearby. You can create a `nearbyBrowser` object like so where you use our `peerID` object and the service name specified earlier:

```
MCNearbyServiceBrowser nearbyBrowser = [[MCNearbyServiceBrowser alloc]
                    initWithPeer:peerID serviceType:@"oz-appsgame"];
```

To display the `browserViewController`, you need to present it like so:

```
[self presentViewController:browser animated:YES completion:nil];
```

If you run your app with just this much code, you can find the browser displayed, searching for peers.

Any peer configured to advertise the serviceType name that you specified will show up in this browser list when they are in the vicinity of the browser. See Figure 9-3.

If you were to tap a peer displayed in the browser, it will send a request to that peer to connect, and upon approving the connection, the peer will connect. The connected peers show up as connected. However, when you press the Cancel or Done button, nothing happens. To handle the browser buttons, you need to make your class handle the MCBrowserViewControllerDelegate. It has two methods that you need to manage: browserViewControllerDidFinish: and browserWasCancelled:. The first is called when you press the Done button, and the second is called when Cancel is pressed. All you need to do is call the dismissViewControllerAnimated: method in both of the methods, like so:

```
[self dismissViewControllerAnimated:YES completion:nil];
```

Most important when working with delegates created in code, do not forget to set the delegate as follows:

```
browser.delegate = self;
```

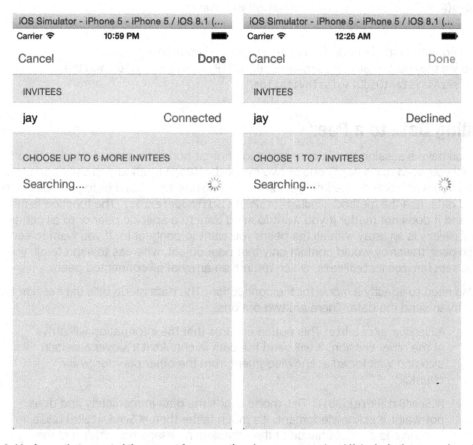

Figure 9-11. A peer that accepted the request for connection shows connected and if the invitation was rejected, shows declined

Connecting Peers

There are three states that a device can be in with regard to peer connectivity; these are defined in the MCSessionState enumeration as follows:

```
MCSessionStateNotConnected      // not in the session
MCSessionStateConnecting        // connecting to this peer
MCSessionStateConnected         // connected to the session
```

These are self-explanatory, and all devices are in the MCSessionStateNotConnected state when they start the application. The state changes to MCSessionStateConnecting when the user taps a peer in the browser, and then depending on the outcome (if the request was accepted or rejected), the state changes to MCSessionStateConnected or MCSessionStateNotConnected.

The function session:didChangeState is a method in the MCSessionDelegate.

```
-(void) session:(MCSession *)session peer:(MCPeerID *)peerID didChangeState:(MCSessionState)
state {
    NSLog(@"%@ -> state %d", peerID.displayName, state);
}
```

When a node tries to connect, the MCAdvertiserAssistantDelegate is notified via the method advertiserAssistantWillPresentInvitation and the advertiserAssistantDidDismissInvitation.

Sending Data to a Peer

Once you have a session that is connected to another node, it's easy to send data to that node. All you need to do is call one of two methods. Which method you call depends on whether you want to send the information to all connected sessions or to just specific ones. To send data, use the method sendData:toPeers:withMode:error:. The function is the same, and it does not matter if you want to send data to a specific peer or to all connected peers. toPeers is an array with all the peers you want to connect to. If you want to send to a specific peer, the array would contain only that peer object, whereas to send to all, you can use the session.connectedPeers, which returns an array of all connected peers.

You also need to specify a *mode* for the connection. The data mode tells the session how it should try to send the data. There are two options.

- MCSendDataReliable: This option ensures that the information will arrive at the other session. It will send the data in chunks if it's over a certain size and wait for an acknowledgment from the other peer for every chunk.

- MCSendDataUnreliable: This mode sends the data immediately and does not wait for acknowledgment. It's much faster than MCSendDataReliable, but there is a small chance of the complete message not arriving at the other node.

Usually, the MCSendDataReliable data mode is the one you'll want to use, though if you have a program where speed of transmission matters more than accuracy, then you should consider MCSendDataUnreliable.

Here is what it looks like when you send data to a single peer:

```
NSError *error = nil;
if (![self.session sendData:theData
                   toPeers:[NSArray arrayWithObject:peerID]
                 withMode:MCSessionSendDataReliable
                     error:&error]){
    NSLog(@"error in sending %@", [error localizedDescription]);
}
```

And here's what it looks like to send data to all connected peers:

```
NSError *error = nil;
if (![session sendData:packet
             toPeers:session.connectedPeers
            withMode:MCSessionSendDataReliable
              error:&error])
{
    NSLog(@"error in sending %@", [error localizedDescription]);
}
```

Packaging Up Information to Send

Any information that you can get into an instance of NSData can be sent to other peers. There are two basic approaches to doing this for use in Multipeer Connectivity. The first is to use archiving and unarchiving, just as you did in the archiving section of *Beginning iPhone Development*.

With the archiving/unarchiving method, you define a class to hold a single packet of data to be sent. That class will contain instance variables to hold whatever types of data you might need to send. When it's time to send a packet, you create and initialize an instance of the packet object, and then you use NSKeyedArchiver to archive the instance of that object into an instance of NSData, which can be passed to sendData:toPeers:withDataMode:error: or to sendDataToAllPeers:withDataMode:error:. You'll use this approach in this chapter's example. However, this approach incurs a small amount of overhead, since it requires the creation of objects to be passed, along with archiving and unarchiving those objects.

Although archiving objects is the best approach in many cases, because it is easy to implement and it fits well with the design of Cocoa Touch, there may be some cases where applications need to constantly send a lot of data to their peers, and this overhead might be unacceptable. In those situations, a faster option is to just use a static array (a regular old C array, not an NSArray) as a local variable in the method that sends the data.

You can copy any data you need to send to the peer into this static array and then create an NSData instance from that static array. There's still some object creation involved in creating the NSData instance, but it's one object instead of two, and you don't have the overhead of archiving. Here's a simple example of sending data using this faster technique:

```
NSUInteger packetData[2];
packetData[0] = foo;
packetData[1] = bar;
NSData *packet = [NSData dataWithBytes:packetData length:2 * sizeof(packetData)];

NSError *error = nil;
if (![session sendData:packet
                toPeers:session.connectedPeers
            withMode:MCSessionSendDataReliable
                error:&error])
{
    NSLog(@"error in sending %@", [error localizedDescription]);
}
```

Receiving Data from a Peer

When a session receives data from a peer, the session passes the data to a method called receiveData:fromPeer, and this method will be called any time new data comes in from a peer. There's no need to acknowledge receipt of the data or worry about waiting for the entire packet. You can just use the provided data as is appropriate for your program. All the gnarly aspects of network data transmission are handled for you. Every call to sendData:toP eers:withMode:error: made by other peers who specify your peer identifier will result in one call of the data receive handler.

Here's an example of a data receive handler method that would be the counterpart to the earlier send example:

```
-(void) session:(MCSession *)session didReceiveData:(NSData *)data fromPeer:(MCPeerID *)
peerID {

    NSString *sender = peerID.displayName;
    NSString *textData = [[NSString alloc]initWithData: data encoding: NSUTF8StringEncoding];
    NSLog(@"%@ said %@", sender, textData);
}
```

You'll look at receiving archived objects when you build this chapter's example.

Closing Connections

When you're finished with a session, before you release the session object, it's important to do a little cleanup. Before releasing the session object, you must make the session unavailable, disconnect it from all of its peers, set the data receive handler to nil, and set the session delegate to nil. Here's what the code in your dealloc method (or any other time you need to close the connections) might look like:

```
[self.session disconnect];
self.session.delegate = nil;
self.session = nil;
self.peerID = nil;
```

Handling a Peer Connection

Earlier, the onus was on the developer to connect to the peer and manage the connection. Now it is all encapsulated and done by the Multipeer Connectivity API. When the user has selected a peer in the browser and the other authorizes the connection, the connection is made. If you want to display something in the code, you can do so via the delegate methods that will be called. You do not have to anymore store the *peer identifier*, which is a string that identifies the device to which you're connected, as the MCSession object has an array of all connected peers. However, you need to save a reference to the session so you can use it to send data and to disconnect the session later.

Well, that's enough discussion. Let's start building the application.

Creating the Project

You know the drill. Fire up Xcode if it's not already open and create a new project. Use the Single View Application template and call the project **TicTacToe**. Once the project is open, look in the project archives that accompany this book, in the folder Chapter_9-TicTacToe. Find the image files called wood_button.png, board.png, O.png, and X.png, and copy them into the Supporting Files group of your project. There's also an icon file called icon.png, which you can copy into your project if you want to use it.

Turning Off the Idle Timer

The first thing you want to do is to turn off the *idle timer*. The idle timer is what tells your iPhone to go to sleep if the user has not interacted with it in a while. Because the user won't be tapping the screen during the opponent's turn, you need to turn this off to prevent the phone from going to sleep if the other user takes a while to make a move. Generally speaking, you don't want networked applications to go to sleep because sleeping breaks the network connection. Most of the time, with networked iPhone games, disabling the idle timer is the best approach.

Expand the TicTacToe group in the Navigator pane in Xcode and single-click AppDelegate.m. Add the following line of code to applicationDidFinishLaunchingWithOptions:, before the method returns, to disable the idle timer:

```
[[UIApplication sharedApplication] setIdleTimerDisabled:YES];
```

Note   There may be rare times when you want to leave the idle timer functioning and just close your sessions when the app goes to sleep, but closing sessions on sleep is not quite as straightforward as it would seem. The application delegate method `applicationWillResignActive:` is called before the phone goes to sleep, but unfortunately, it's also called at other times. In fact, it's called any time that your application loses the ability to respond to touch events. That makes it close to impossible to differentiate between when the user has been presented a system alert, such as from a push notification or a low-battery warning (which won't result in broken connections), and when the phone is actually going to sleep. So, until Apple provides a way to differentiate between these scenarios, your best bet is to simply disallow sleep while a networked program is running.

Importing the Multipeer Connectivity Framework

Multipeer Connectivity is not one of the frameworks that is automatically linked by the Xcode project template, so you need to manually link it yourself in order to access the session and peer picker methods. Select the TicTacToe project at the top of the Navigator pane. Next, select the TicTacToe target in the Project Editor. Select the Build Phases tab and expand the Link Binary With Libraries (3 items) section. Click the + button on the lower left. Select `MultipeerConnectivity.framework` from the dialog that appears and then click Add.

`MultipeerConnectivity.framework` will appear in the Navigator pane, at the top of the project groups. Let's clean it up by dragging it into the Frameworks group.

Designing the Interface

Now you'll design your game's user interface. Since tic-tac-toe is a relatively simple game, you'll design your user interface in Interface Builder, rather than by using OpenGL ES.

Each space on the board will be a button. When the user taps a button that hasn't already been selected (which you determine by seeing whether the button has an image assigned), you set the image to either `X.png` or `O.png` (which you added to your project a few minutes ago). You then send that information to the other device. You're also going to use the button's tag value to differentiate the buttons and make it easier to determine when someone has won. You assign each of the buttons that represents a space on the board with a sequential tag, starting in the upper-left corner. You can see which space will have which tag value by looking at Figure 9-12. This way, you can identify which button was pressed without having a separate action method for each button.

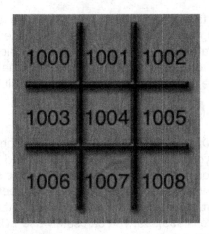

Figure 9-12. Assign each game space button a tag value

Defining Application Constants

When referring to specific buttons on the tic-tac-toe board, you could use the tag values you defined in Figure 9-12 (and will have to in Interface Builder), but it would be better to use a set of mnemonic constants. You'll also define some constants for the current game state and whether the user is an *X* or an *O*.

You could stick these constant definitions in various header and implementation files throughout the application, but it might be easier to stick them in a single file. Let's do that.

Select the TicTacToe group in the Navigator pane and create a new file. Select the Source section under iOS in the template chooser dialog. Choose Header File and click Next. Save the file as TicTacToe.h. Select TicTacToe.h; it should look like this:

```
#ifndef TicTacToe_TicTacToe_h
#define TicTacToe_TicTacToe_h

#endif
```

Those macros (#ifndef, #define, #endif), are C language hooks to make sure you include TicTacToe.h only once. You don't really need to worry about that in Objective-C because the #import macro takes care of that for you. You can delete those lines.

Now, you need to define some constants of your own. First, you defined a constant to represent the Multipeer Connectivity session ID.

```
#define kTicTacToeSessionID @"oz-tictactoe"
```

Next, you defined a constant for use with encoding and decoding data packets through Multipeer Connectivity.

```
#define kTicTacToeArchiveKey @"com.oz-apps.TicTacToe"
```

When the application connects to another device, you have the application decide which player goes first by generating a random number and having the higher number go first. You define the number generator with the macro dieRoll(), which will generate a number between 0 and 999,999. You're using a large number here so that the chance of both devices rolling the same value (which would require a re-roll) will be extremely low.

```
#define dieRoll() (arc4random() % 1000000)
```

You also define a constant, kDiceNotRolled, that will identify when the die has not yet been rolled. Remember that you're storing both your die roll and your opponent's die roll in NSInteger instance variables. On the iPhone, NSInteger is the same as an int. You use the value INT_MAX to identify when those values have not yet been determined. INT_MAX is the largest value that an int can hold on the platform. Since the largest number the dieRoll() macro will generate is 999,999, you can safely use INT_MAX to identify when a die hasn't been rolled because INT_MAX currently equals 2,147,483,647 on iOS. If INT_MAX ever changes, it will likely get bigger, not smaller.

```
#define kDiceNotRolled INT_MAX
```

You need some enumerations. GameState will be your definition to an enumerated list of the different game states.

```
typedef enum GameStates {
    kGameStateBeginning,
    kGameStateRollingDice,
    kGameStateMyTurn,
    kGameStateYourTurn,
    kGameStateInterrupted,
    kGameStateDone
} GameState;
```

BoardSpace is the enumerated list that you defined in Figure 9-12. Note that you defined the first enumeration, kUpperLeft, to 1000. Each subsequent enumeration is incremented up from there.

```
typedef enum BoardSpaces {
    kUpperLeft = 1000,
    kUpperMiddle,
    kUpperRight,
    kMiddleLeft,
    kMiddleMiddle,
    kMiddleRight,
    kLowerLeft,
    kLowerMiddle,
    kLowerRight
} BoardSpace;
```

`PlayerPiece` is a simple enumeration to let you know what piece the player is assigned.

```
typedef enum PlayerPieces {
    kPlayerPieceUndecided,
    kPlayerPieceO,
    kPlayerPieceX
} PlayerPiece;
```

Finally, you define an enumerated list to list the different kind of packet types the application will exchange via Game Kit.

```
typedef enum PacketTypes {
    kPacketTypeDieRoll,
    kPacketTypeAck,
    kPacketTypeMove,
    kPacketTypeReset,

} PacketType;
```

Now that you've defined these constants, you can start by working on the application view.

Designing the Game Board

Select `Main.Storyboard` in the Navigator. Xcode will open it in Interface Builder. There will be one view controller in Interface Builder. Find the image view in the Object Library and drag it into the view. Because it's the first object you're adding to the view, it should resize to take up the full view. Place it so that it fills the entire view and then bring up the Attributes Inspector in the Utility pane. At the top of the Attributes Inspector, set the Image field to `board.png`, which is one of the images you added to your project earlier.

Next, drag a button from the library to the top of the view. The exact placement doesn't matter yet. After it's placed, use the Attributes Inspector to change the button type from system to custom. Delete the button label text, *Button*, either in Interface Builder or via the Attributes Inspector. In the Image field of the Attributes Inspector, select `wood_button.png` and then select Editor ➤ Size to Fit Content (or press ⌘=) to change the button's size to match the image you assigned to it. Now use the blue guidelines to center the button in the view and place it against the top blue margin so it looks like Figure 9-13.

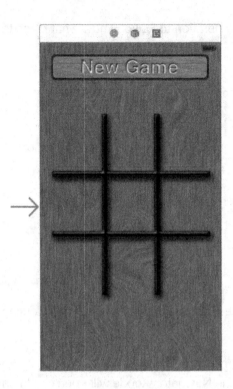

Figure 9-13. Your interface after sizing and placing the button

Look again in the library for a label and drag it to the view. Center the label on top of gameButton. Resize the label so it runs from the left blue margin to the right blue margin horizontally and from the top blue margin down to just above the tic-tac-toe board. It will overlap the button you just added, and that's fine because the label will display text only when the button isn't visible. Use the Attributes Inspector to center the text and to increase the size of the font to 60 points. Feel free to also set the text to a nice bright color if you want. Once you have the label the way you want it, delete the label text, *Label*, so that it doesn't display anything at application start.

Now, you need to add a button for each of the nine game spaces and assign them each a tag value so that your code will have a way to identify which space on the board each button represents. Drag nine buttons to the view, and use the Attributes Inspector to change their type to Custom. Use the size inspector to place them in the locations specified in Table 9-1, and use the Attributes Inspector to assign them the listed tag value. Here's one shortcut to consider: create one, set its size and attributes, and then start making copies.

Table 9-1. *Game Space Locations, Sizes, and Tags*

Game Space	X	Y	Width	Height	Tag
Upper Left	24	122	86	98	1000
Upper Middle	120	122	86	98	1001
Upper Right	217	122	86	98	1002
Middle Left	24	230	86	98	1003
Middle	120	230	86	98	1004
Middle Right	217	230	86	98	1005
Lower Left	24	336	86	98	1006
Lower Middle	120	336	86	98	1007
Lower Right	217	336	86	98	1008

You've defined your interface, so now let's connect it to your controller. While still in Interface Builder, change the editor from Standard to Assistant view in the toolbar. The Editor pane should split horizontally, with Interface Builder on the left and the Source Code Editor, open to ViewController.h, on the right. You want to add outlets for the New Game button and label you placed on top of it. If you Control-drag from the middle of the New Game button, the Outlet pop-up should automatically set the Type field to UILabel. That means you're adding an outlet for the label. Name it **feedbackLabel** and click Connect.

You need to add an outlet for the New Game button you created as well, but it's essentially blocked by the feedbackLabel. Open the disclosure triangle on the bottom left of the Interface Builder Editor pane, and expand the Object Dock on the left (Figure 9-14). In the Objects group, underneath the view (if it's not open, open it), find the New Game button object named Button. Control-drag from Button to just below the feedbackLabel outlet and create a new outlet. Name it **gameButton** and click Connect.

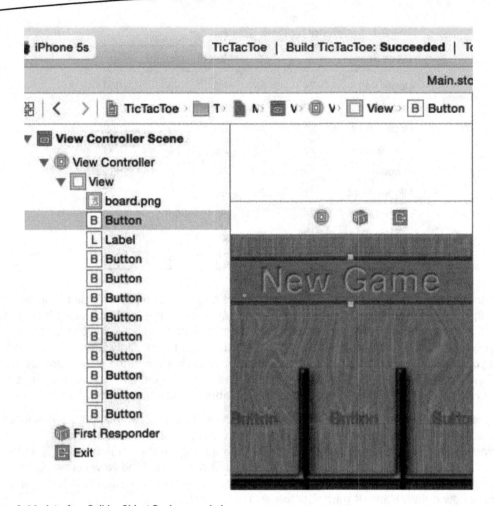

Figure 9-14. Interface Builder Object Dock, expanded

You need to connect an action when the New Game button is pressed. Control-drag from the Button in the Object Dock to just above the @end in ViewController.h. Create a new action named **gameButtonPressed** (Figure 9-15).

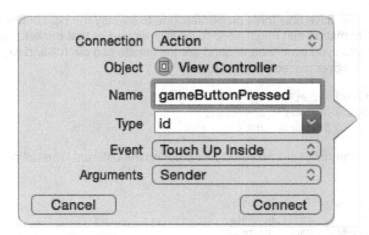

Figure 9-15. Creating the gameButtonPressed action

Now you need to connect an action to the nine game space buttons. You don't need to define outlets for them, though, just the actions. Control-drag from the upper-left button to the just below the action, gameButtonPressed, you just created. Create a new action named **gameSpacePressed**. Now, Control-drag from every other game space button to the gameSpacePressed method declaration. The whole method declaration should highlight, and a pop-up label should appear called Connect Action. Make the connections.

Close the Assistant Editor and save the storyboard.

Creating the Packet Object

You need to define how you'll have your game communicate with other instances of itself. You could use something simple like an array, where you know what each element represents, or a dictionary, where you know what keys to use. Rather than doing that, you'll define a specific class, Packet, that will be used to send information back and forth between the two nodes, via Multipeer Connectivity. We alluded to this earlier when you created the enum PacketType in TicTacToe.h.

Select the TicTacToe group in the Navigator pane and create a new Cocoa class with a class name of Packet, as a subclass of NSObject. Ensure that the language is Objective-C.

Once the files are created, select Packet.h and open it in the editor. First, you need to add the TicTacToe.h header file.

```
#import "TicTacToe.h"
```

You need Packet to conform to the NSCoding protocol so that you can archive it into an NSData instance to send through the Multipeer Connectivity session.

```
@interface Packet : NSObject <NSCoding>
```

The Packet class will have only three properties: one to identify the type of packet and two others to hold information that might need to be sent as part of that packet. The only other pieces of information you ever need to send are the results of a die roll and which space on the game board a player placed an *X* or *O*.

```
@property (nonatomic) PacketType type;
@property (nonatomic) NSUInteger dieRoll;
@property (nonatomic) BoardSpace space
```

Then you need a handful of init methods for creating the different types of packets you will send.

```
-(id)initWithType:(PacketType)aPacketType
          dieRoll:(NSUInteger) aDieRoll
            space:(BoardSpace) aBoardSpace;
-(id)initDieRollPacket;
-(id)initDieRollPacketWithRoll:(NSUInteger) aDieRoll;
-(id)initMovePacketWithSpace:(BoardSpace) aBoardSpace;
-(id)initAckPacketWithDieRoll:(NSUInteger) aDieRoll;
-(id)initResetPacket;
```

That's it. Save Packet.h and move to Packet.m.

First, you implement the init methods you declared in the interface file.

```
-(id) initWithType:(PacketType)aPacketType
          dieRoll:(NSUInteger)aDieRoll
            space:(BoardSpace)aBoardSpace {
    self = [super init];
    if (self) {
        self.type = aPacketType;
        self.dieRoll = aDieRoll;
        self.space = aBoardSpace;
    }
    return self;
}

-(id) initDieRollPacket {
    int roll = dieRoll();
    return [self initWithType:kPacketTypeDieRoll dieRoll:roll space:0];
}

-(id) initDieRollPacketWithRoll:(NSUInteger)aDieRoll {
    return [self initWithType:kPacketTypeDieRoll dieRoll:aDieRoll space:0];
}

-(id) initMovePacketWithSpace:(BoardSpace)aBoardSpace {
    return [self initWithType:kPacketTypeMove dieRoll:0 space:aBoardSpace];
}
```

```
-(id) initAckPacketWithDieRoll:(NSUInteger)aDieRoll {
    return [self initWithType:kPacketTypeAck dieRoll:aDieRoll space:0];
}

-(id) initResetPacket {
    return [self initWithType:kPacketTypeReset dieRoll:0 space:0];
}
```

Every other initializer is just a wrapped call to initWithType:dieRoll:space: with the BoardSpace being zero (undefined).

You also need to make Packet conform the NSCoding protocol, adding encodeWithCoder: and initWithCoder: methods.

```
#pragma mark - NSCoder (Archiving) methods

-(void) encodeWithCoder:(NSCoder *)aCoder {
    [aCoder encodeInt:[self type] forKey:@"type"];
    [aCoder encodeInteger:[self dieRoll] forKey:@"dieRoll"];
    [aCoder encodeInt:[self space] forKey:@"space"];
}

-(id) initWithCoder:(NSCoder *)aDecoder {
    if (self = [super init]) {
        [self setType:[aDecoder decodeIntForKey:@"type"]];
        [self setDieRoll:[aDecoder decodeIntegerForKey:@"dieRoll"]];
        [self setSpace:[aDecoder decodeIntForKey:@"space"]];
    }
    return self;
}
```

Packet is a fairly straightforward class. There shouldn't be anything in its implementation that you haven't seen before. Save Packet.m. Next, you'll write your view controller and finish up your application.

Setting Up the View Controller Header

You declared two outlets and two actions to your view controller via Interface Builder. Now you'll complete your implementation of your view controller, including making it work with Multipeer Connectivity. Open ViewController.h in the editor.

The first thing you need to do is import the Multipeer Connectivity and TicTacToe headers so that the compiler knows about the objects and methods from Multipeer Connectivity and the constants you defined earlier.

```
#import <MultipeerConnectivity/MultipeerConnectivity.h>
#import "TicTacToe.h"
```

After that, you tell the compiler that there is a class called `Packet`. A `@class` declaration doesn't cause the compiler to look for the class header file—it's just a promise that a class really exists, so it's OK to declare it this way.

```
@class Packet;
```

Your controller class needs to conform to a few protocols. Your controller will be the delegate of the Multipeer Connectivity peer browser and session, so you conform your class to the three protocols used to define the delegate methods for each of these jobs.

```
@interface ViewController : UIViewController
                <MCBrowserViewControllerDelegate, MCSessionDelegate>
```

You need to add some instance variables (ivars). First, you'll add the braces right after the `@interface` declaration.

```
{
}
```

You need an ivar to keep track of the current game state.

```
GameState _state;
```

Because you don't know whether you will roll the die or receive your opponent's die roll first, you need variables to hold them both. Once you have both, you can compare them and start the game.

```
NSInteger _myDieRoll;
NSInteger _opponentDieRoll;
```

Once you know who goes first, you can store whether you're O or X in this instance variable.

```
PlayerPiece _playerPiece;
```

Finally, you have two more Booleans to keep track of whether you've received the opponent's die roll and whether your opponent has acknowledged receipt of yours. You don't want to begin the game until you have both die rolls and you know your opponent has both as well. When both of these are YES, you'll know it's time to start the actual game play.

```
BOOL _dieRollReceived;
BOOL _dieRollAcknowledged;
```

You already have two outlet properties, `feedbackLabel` and `gameButton`, that you created via Interface Builder. You also need properties for the Multipeer Connectivity session and to hold the peer identifier of the one connected node.

```
@property (nonatomic, strong) MCSession *session;
@property (nonatomic, strong) MCPeerID *peerID;
@property (nonatomic, strong) MCBrowserViewController *browser;
@property (nonatomic, strong) MCNearbyServiceBrowser *nearbyBrowser;
@property (nonatomic, strong) MCAdvertiserAssistant *assistant;
```

You load both of the images representing the two game pieces when your view is loaded and keep a reference to them.

```
@property (nonatomic, strong) UIImage *xPieceImage;
@property (nonatomic, strong) UIImage *oPieceImage;
```

Finally, you declare a bunch of methods that you need in your game. We'll discuss the specific methods in more detail when you implement them in your controller. You add them before the two actions, gameButtonPressed: and gameSpacePressed:, that you added via Interface Builder.

```
-(void) resetBoard;
-(void) startNewGame;
-(void) resetDieState;
-(void) startGame;
-(void) sendPacket:(Packet *)packet;
-(void) sendDieRoll;
-(void) checkForEndGame;
```

That's all you need in this file. Save it and open ViewController.m.

Implementing the Tic-Tac-Toe View Controller

There's a lot of code to add to ViewController.m, so let's get started.

First, you need to import the header file Packet.h.

```
#import "Packet.h"
```

Initialize the piece images and set your current die roll to kDiceNotRolled in viewDidLoad (after the call to super).

```
_myDieRoll = kDiceNotRolled;
self.oPieceImage = [UIImage imageNamed:@"O.png"];
self.xPieceImage = [UIImage imageNamed:@"X.png"];

NSString *DeviceName = @"MyName" ;//[[UIDevice currentDevice]name];
self.peerID = [[MCPeerID alloc] initWithDisplayName: DeviceName];
self.session = [[MCSession alloc] initWithPeer: self.peerID];
```

At the bottom of your implementation file are the two action methods. You need to implement them. First, edit gameButtonPressed:.

```
#pragma mark - Game Specific Actions

- (IBAction)gameButtonPressed:(id)sender {
    _dieRollAcknowledged = NO;
    _dieRollRecieved = NO;

    _gameButton.hidden = YES;
```

```
    if (self.assistant == nil)
        self.assistant = [[MCAdvertiserAssistant alloc]
                              initWithServiceType:kTicTacToeSessionID
                                   discoveryInfo:nil
                                         session:self.session];
    [self.assistant start];

    if (self.nearbyBrowser == nil)
        self.nearbyBrowser = [[MCNearbyServiceBrowser alloc]
                                  initWithPeer:self.peerID
                                   serviceType:kTicTacToeSessionID];

    if (self.browser == nil)
        self.browser = [[MCBrowserViewController alloc]
                            initWithBrowser:self.nearbyBrowser
                                    session:self.session];
    self.browser.delegate = self;
    [self presentViewController:self.browser animated:YES completion:nil];
}
```

You need to also create the delegate methods to handle the MCBrowserViewControllerDelegate.
After the viewDidLoad function, you can type the following:

```
#pragma mark - MCBrowserViewController Delegate Methods

-(void) browserViewControllerDidFinish:(MCBrowserViewController *)browserViewController {
    [self dismissViewControllerAnimated:YES completion:nil];
}

-(void) browserViewControllerWasCancelled:(MCBrowserViewController *)browserViewController {
    _gameButton.hidden = NO;

    [self dismissViewControllerAnimated:YES completion:nil];
}
```

This is the callback for when the user presses the New Game button. You set _
dieRollReceived and _dieRollAcknowledged to NO because you know neither of these things
has happened yet for the new game. Next, you hide the button because you don't want
your player to request a new game while you're looking for peers or playing the game. Then
you create an instance of MCBrowserViewController, set self as the delegate, and show the
peer browser controller. That's all you need to do to kick off the process of letting the user
select another device to play against. The peer browser will handle everything and then call
delegate methods when you need to take some action.

Now, add the callback for when the user presses one of the game space buttons.

```
- (IBAction)gameSpacePressed:(id)sender
{
    UIButton *buttonPressed = sender;
    if (_state == kGameStateMyTurn && [buttonPressed imageForState:UIControlStateNormal] == nil) {
        [buttonPressed setImage:((_playerPiece == kPlayerPieceO) ? self.oPieceImage
                                                                 : self.xPieceImage)
                       forState:UIControlStateNormal];
```

```
        _feedbackLabel.text = NSLocalizedString(@"Opponent's Turn", @"Opponent's Turn");
        _state = kGameStateYourTurn;

        Packet *packet = [[Packet alloc] initMovePacketWithSpace:buttonPressed.tag];
        [self sendPacket:packet];

        [self checkForGameEnd];
    }
}
```

The first thing you do is cast sender to a UIButton. You know sender will always be an instance of UIButton, and doing this will prevent you from needing to cast sender every time you use it. Next, you check the game state. You don't want to let the user select a space if it's not that player's turn. You also check to make sure that the button pressed has no image already assigned. If it has an image assigned to it, then there's already either an *X* or an *O* in the space this button represents, and the user is not allowed to select it. If the space has no image assigned and it is your turn, you set the image to whichever image is appropriate for your player, based on whether you went first or second. The piece variable will get set later when you compare die rolls. You set the feedback label to inform the users that it's no longer their turn and change the state to reflect that as well. You must inform the other device that you've made your move, so you create an instance of Packet, passing the tag value from the button that was pressed to identify which space the player selected. You use the method called sendPacket:, which you'll look at in a moment, to send the instance of Packet to the other node. At the last step, you check to see whether the game is over. The method checkForGameEnd determines whether either player won or whether there are no spaces on the board, which would mean it's a tie.

Before you implement the methods you defined your interface file, you need think about the protocol declarations you made. You defined ViewController to conform to the protocols MCBrowserControllerDelegate and MCSessionDelegate. Let's tackle them in order, starting with MCBrowserControllerDelegate.

Multipeer Connectivity Peer-To-Peer Delegate Methods

When the Multipeer Connectivity browser displays itself, it requires a configured peer to identify yourself, a serviceType on which to connect, and a session. The two delegate methods that you need to configure are when the user taps Cancel or when the user taps Done after connecting with another peer. You already configured the code earlier. The methods are called browserViewControllerDidFinish and browserViewControllerWasCancelled.

This code is fine, but there is one thing glaringly missing. You have code to browse another peer, but you do not have code to advertise yourself on the serviceType. So, to advertise this device, you use the MCAdvertiserAssistant object and start advertising. Add this code to the end of the gameButtonPressed code:

```
if (self.assistant == nil)
    self.assistant = [[MCAdvertiserAssistant alloc]
                        initWithServiceType:kTicTacToeSessionID
                            discoveryInfo:nil
                                session:self.session];
[self.assistant start];
```

This will ensure that another peer that is browsing would be able to see/find this device. You set up the assistant to advertise the device with the name you used to initialize the MCPeerID object and the serviceType as defined in the kTicTacToeSessionID defined in the TicTacToe.h header file. Lastly, you also supply it the configured session and then start the advertising using the start method. When you have connected or do not need to advertise anymore, you can use the stop method.

Add the method to handle the connection of the peer in the browserViewControllerDidFinish method.

```
-(void) browserViewControllerDidFinish:(MCBrowserViewController *)browserViewController {
    [self dismissViewControllerAnimated:YES completion:nil];
    self.browser.delegate = nil;
    self.browser = nil;

    [self.assistant stop];
    self.assistant = nil;

    [self.nearbyBrowser stopBrowsingForPeers];
    self.nearbyBrowser = nil;

    [self startNewGame];
}
```

Next, you add this delegate method to handle user cancels.

```
-(void) browserViewControllerWasCancelled:(MCBrowserViewController *)browserViewController {
    _gameButton.hidden = NO;

    [self dismissViewControllerAnimated:YES completion:nil];
}
```

You just unhide the New Game button.

Multipeer Connectivity Session Delegate Methods

Now, you need to implement the Multipeer Connectivty session delegate methods. These methods are mostly used for data transfer and exchange. You need to implement these methods even if you are not using them. However, you will start with the session:peer:didChangeState.

```
#pragma mark - Multipeer Connectivity Session Delegate Methods

-(void) session:(MCSession *)session
          peer:(MCPeerID *)peerID
didChangeState:(MCSessionState)state {
    if (state == MCSessionStateNotConnected){
    }
}
```

For the other delegate methods, you simply need to define the methods without any code implementation (for now).

```
-(void) session:(MCSession *)session
       didFinishReceivingResourceWithName:(NSString *)resourceName
                                fromPeer:(MCPeerID *)peerID
                                   atURL:(NSURL *)localURL
                               withError:(NSError *)error {

}

-(void) session:(MCSession *)session
       didReceiveStream:(NSInputStream *)stream
               withName:(NSString *)streamName
               fromPeer:(MCPeerID *)peerID {

}

-(void) session:(MCSession *)session
       didStartReceivingResourceWithName:(NSString *)resourceName
                                fromPeer:(MCPeerID *)peerID
                            withProgress:(NSProgress *)progress {

}
```

Multipeer Connectivity Data Receive Handler

Before you go on, there is one more method you need to implement: didReceiveData:fromPeer. This method is invoked when data is received by the device.

```
-(void) session:(MCSession *)session didReceiveData:(NSData *)data fromPeer:(MCPeerID *)
peerID {
    NSKeyedUnarchiver *unarchiver = [[NSKeyedUnarchiver alloc] initForReadingWithData:data];
    Packet *packet = [unarchiver decodeObjectForKey:kTicTacToeArchiveKey];

    //NSLog(@"We got the packet of type %u from %@", packet.type, peerID.displayName);

    switch (packet.type) {
    case kPacketTypeDieRoll: {
        _opponentDieRoll = packet.dieRoll;
        Packet *ack = [[Packet alloc] initAckPacketWithDieRoll:_opponentDieRoll];
        [self sendPacket:ack];
        _dieRollRecieved = YES;
        break;
    }
    case kPacketTypeAck: {
        if (packet.dieRoll != _myDieRoll) {
            //TODO: Check this
            NSLog(@"Ack packet doesn't match your die roll (mine: %lu, send: %ld",
            (unsigned long)packet.dieRoll, (long)_myDieRoll);
        }
        _dieRollAcknowledged = YES;
        break;
    }
```

```
        case kPacketTypeMove: {
            dispatch_async(dispatch_get_main_queue(), ^{
                UIButton *aButton = (UIButton *) [self.view viewWithTag:[packet space]];
                [aButton setImage:((_playerPiece == kPlayerPieceO) ?
                                                    self.xPieceImage:
                                                    self.oPieceImage)
                        forState:UIControlStateNormal];
                _state = kGameStateMyTurn;
                _feedbacklabel.text = NSLocalizedString(@"Your Turn", @"Your Turn");
                [self checkForEndGame];
            });
            break;
        }
        case kPacketTypeReset: {
            if (_state == kGameStateDone)
              [self resetDieState];
            break;
        }
        default:
            break;
    }

    if (_dieRollRecieved == YES && _dieRollAcknowledged == YES)

        dispatch_async(dispatch_get_main_queue(), ^{
            [self startGame];
        });

}
```

This is your data receive handler. This method is called whenever you receive a packet from the other node. The first thing you do is unarchive the data into a copy of the original Packet instance that was sent. Then you use a switch statement to take different actions based on the type of packet you received. If it's a die roll, you store your opponent's value, send back an acknowledgment of the value, and set dieRollReceived to YES. If you've received an acknowledgment, make sure the number returned is the same as the one you sent. This is just a consistency check. It shouldn't ever happen that the number is not the same. If it did, it might be an indication of a problem with your code, or it could mean that someone is cheating. Although we doubt that anyone would bother cheating at tic-tac-toe, people have been known to cheat in some networked games, so you might want to consider validating any information exchanged with peers. Here, you're just logging the inconsistency and moving on. In your real-world applications, you might want to take more serious action if you detect a data inconsistency of this nature.

If the packet is a move packet, which denotes that the other player chose a space, you update the appropriate space with an X or O image, and you change the state and label to reflect the fact that it's now your player's turn. You also check to see whether the other player's move resulted in the game being over. When you receive a reset packet, all you do is change the game state to kGameStateDone so that if a die roll comes in before you've realized the game is over, you don't discard it. If you received a packet and both dieRollReceived and dieRollAcknowledged are now YES, you know it's time to start the game.

One thing to note is the strange blocks in dispatch_async. The callbacks from Multipeer Connectivity are called on another queue, whereas all UI updates are made on the main queue. If you do not dispatch this on the main queue (in other words, remove the enclosing dispatch_async), the updates to the GUI would not be visible, and it would seem like the application is not working properly.

Finally, you add the code to manage whether the peer was disconnected. In the session:peer:didChangeState function, update this code.

```
if (state == MCSessionStateNotConnected){
    UIAlertController *alert = [UIAlertController
              alertControllerWithTitle:@"Error Connecting"
                               message:@"Unable to establish connection"
                         preferredStyle:UIAlertControllerStyleAlert];
    UIAlertAction *cancel = [UIAlertAction
                    actionWithTitle:@"Bummer"
                               style:UIAlertActionStyleDestructive
                             handler:^(UIAlertAction *action) {
                  [self resetBoard];
                  _gameButton.hidden = NO;
              }];
    [alert addAction:cancel];
[self presentViewController:alert animated:YES completion:nil];
}
```

You reset the game board and unhide the New Game button.

Implementing Tic-Tac-Toe Methods

The method startNewGame is simple. It just calls a method to reset the board and then calls another method to roll the die and send the result to the other node. Both of these actions can happen at times other than game start. For example, you reset the board if the connection is lost, and you send the die roll if both nodes roll the same number.

```
#pragma mark - Instance methods

-(void) startNewGame {
    [self resetBoard];
    [self sendDieRoll];
}
```

Resetting the board involves removing the images from all of the buttons that represent spaces on the game board. Rather than declaring nine outlets—one to point at each button—you just loop through the nine tag values and retrieve the buttons from your content view using viewWithTag:. You also blank out the feedback label. And you send a packet to the other node telling it that you're resetting. This is done just to make sure that if you follow up with another die roll, the other machine knows not to overwrite it. The fact that network communication happens asynchronously means you can't rely on things always happening in a specific order, as you can with a program running on only one device. It's possible that you'll send the die roll before the other device has finished determining who won. By sending a reset packet, you tell the other node that there may be another die roll coming for a new game, so make sure it's in the right state to accept that new roll. If you didn't do something like this, it might store your die roll and then overwrite the rolled value when it resets its own board, which would cause a hang because the other device would then be waiting for a die roll that would never arrive. You also need to reset the player's game piece. Because the game is over, you don't know whether the player will be *X* or *O* for the next game.

```
- (void)resetBoard
{
    for (int i = kUpperLeft; i <= kLowerRight; i++) {
        UIButton *aButton = (UIButton *)[self.view viewWithTag:i];
        [aButton setImage:nil forState:UIControlStateNormal];
    }
    self.feedbackLabel.text = @"";
    Packet *packet = [[Packet alloc] initResetPacket];
    [self sendPacket:packet];
    _playerPiece = kPlayerPieceUndecided;
}
```

Resetting the die state is nothing more than setting dieRollReceived and dieRollAcknowledged to NO and setting both your die roll and the opponent's die roll to kDiceNotRolled.

```
- (void)resetDieState
{
    _dieRollReceived = NO;
    _dieRollAcknowledged = NO;
    _myDieRoll = kDiceNotRolled;
    _opponentDieRoll = kDiceNotRolled;
}
```

startGame is called once you have received your opponent's die roll and have also gotten an acknowledgment that it has received yours. First, you make sure you don't have a tie. If you do have a tie, you kick off the die-rolling process again. Otherwise, you set state, piece, and the feedbackLabel's text based on whether it's your turn or the opponent's turn to go first. Then you reset the die state. It may seem odd to do it here, but at this point, you're finished with the die rolling for this game, and because you may receive your opponent's die roll before your code has realized the game is over, you reset now to ensure that the die rolls are not accidentally reused in the next game.

```
- (void)startGame
{
    if (_myDieRoll == _opponentDieRoll) {
        _myDieRoll = kDiceNotRolled;
        _opponentDieRoll = kDiceNotRolled;
        [self sendDieRoll];
        _playerPiece = kPlayerPieceUndecided;
    }
```

```
    else if (_myDieRoll < _opponentDieRoll) {
        _state = kGameStateYourTurn;
        _playerPiece = kPlayerPieceX;
        self.feedbackLabel.text = NSLocalizedString(@"Opponent's Turn", @"Opponent's Turn");

    }
    else {
        _state = kGameStateMyTurn;
        _playerPiece = kPlayerPieceO;
        self.feedbackLabel.text = NSLocalizedString(@"Your Turn", @"Your Turn");
    }
    [self resetDieState];
}
```

sendDieRoll: checks your die roll property. If you haven't rolled yet, it initializes a Packet that rolls the die for you and sets your die roll to the value of the packet's die roll. If you have a die roll, you initialize a Packer with that die roll value. Finally, you send the die roll Packet off to your opponent.

```
- (void)sendDieRoll
{
    Packet *rollPacket;
    _state = kGameStateRollingDice;
    if (_myDieRoll == kDiceNotRolled) {
        rollPacket = [[Packet alloc] initDieRollPacket];
        _myDieRoll = rollPacket.dieRoll;
    }
    else {
        rollPacket = [[Packet alloc] initDieRollPacketWithRoll:_myDieRoll];
    }
    [self sendPacket:rollPacket];

}
```

sendPacket: sends a packet to the other device (duh!). It takes an instance of Packet and archives it into an instance of NSData. It then uses the session's sendDataToAllPeers:withDat aMode:error: method to send it across the wire—well, across the wireless, in this case.

```
- (void)sendPacket:(Packet *)packet
{
    NSMutableData *data = [[NSMutableData alloc] init];
    NSKeyedArchiver *archiver = [[NSKeyedArchiver alloc] initForWritingWithMutableData:data];
    [archiver encodeObject:packet forKey:kTicTacToeArchiveKey];
    [archiver finishEncoding];

    NSError *error = nil;
    if (![self.session sendData:data toPeers:self.session.connectedPeers
                    withMode:MCSessionSendDataReliable error:&error]) {
        // You would some do real error handling
        NSLog(@"Error sending data: %@", [error localizedDescription]);
    }
}
```

The checkForGameEnd method just checks all nine spaces to see whether they have *X* or *O* in them and then looks for three in a row. It does this by first declaring a variable called moves to keep track of how many moves have happened. This is how it will tell whether there's a tie. If there have been nine moves and no one has won, then there are no available spaces left on the board, so it's a tie. Next, you declare an array of nine UIImage pointers. You'll pull the images out of the nine buttons representing spaces on the board and put them in this array to make it easier to check whether a player won. If you find three in a row, you'll store one of the three images in this variable so you know which player won the game. Next, you loop through the buttons by tag, as you did in the resetBoard method earlier, storing the images from the buttons in the array you declared earlier. The next big chunk of code just checks to see whether there are three of the same images in a row anywhere. If it finds three in a row, it stores one of the three images in winningImage. When it completes the check, it will know which player, if any, has won. If there wasn't a winner, then you check to see whether any spaces are left on the board by looking at moves. If no spaces remain, then you know the game is over, and the cat won.

Note In tic-tac-toe, a tie is also called a "cat's game." The expression "the cat won" refers to a tie.

If any of the preceding code set the state to kGameStateDone, then you use performSelector: withObject:afterDelay: to start a new game after the user has had time to read who won.

```
- (void)checkForGameEnd
{
    NSInteger moves = 0;

    UIImage     *currentButtonImages[9];
    UIImage     *winningImage = nil;

    for (int i = kUpperLeft; i <= kLowerRight; i++) {
        UIButton *oneButton = (UIButton *)[self.view viewWithTag:i];
        if ([oneButton imageForState:UIControlStateNormal])
            moves++;
        currentButtonImages[i - kUpperLeft] = [oneButton imageForState:UIControlStateNormal];
    }

    // Top Row
    if (currentButtonImages[0] == currentButtonImages[1]
        && currentButtonImages[0] == currentButtonImages[2]
        && currentButtonImages[0] != nil)
        winningImage = currentButtonImages[0];

    // Middle Row
    else if (currentButtonImages[3] == currentButtonImages[4]
            && currentButtonImages[3] == currentButtonImages[5]
            && currentButtonImages[3] != nil)
        winningImage = currentButtonImages[3];
```

```objc
// Bottom Row
else if (currentButtonImages[6] == currentButtonImages[7]
        && currentButtonImages[6] == currentButtonImages[8]
        && currentButtonImages[6] != nil)
    winningImage = currentButtonImages[6];

// Left Column
else if (currentButtonImages[0] == currentButtonImages[3]
        && currentButtonImages[0] == currentButtonImages[6]
        && currentButtonImages[0] != nil)
    winningImage = currentButtonImages[0];

// Middle Column
else if (currentButtonImages[1] == currentButtonImages[4]
        && currentButtonImages[1] == currentButtonImages[7]
        && currentButtonImages[1] != nil)
    winningImage = currentButtonImages[1];

// Right Column
else if (currentButtonImages[2] == currentButtonImages[5]
        && currentButtonImages[2] == currentButtonImages[8]
        && currentButtonImages[2] != nil)
    winningImage = currentButtonImages[2];

// Diagonal starting top left
else if (currentButtonImages[0] == currentButtonImages[4]
        && currentButtonImages[0] == currentButtonImages[8]
        && currentButtonImages[0] != nil)
    winningImage = currentButtonImages[0];

// Diagonal starting top right
else if (currentButtonImages[2] == currentButtonImages[4]
        && currentButtonImages[2] == currentButtonImages[6]
        && currentButtonImages[2] != nil)
    winningImage = currentButtonImages[2];

if (winningImage == self.xPieceImage) {
    if (_playerPiece == kPlayerPieceX) {
        self.feedbackLabel.text = NSLocalizedString(@"You Won!", @"You Won!");
        _state = kGameStateDone;
    }
    else {
        self.feedbackLabel.text = NSLocalizedString(@"Opponent Won!", @"Opponent Won!");
        _state = kGameStateDone;
    }
}
else if (winningImage == self.oPieceImage) {
    if (_playerPiece == kPlayerPieceO){
        self.feedbackLabel.text = NSLocalizedString(@"You Won!", @"You Won!");
        _state = kGameStateDone;
    }
```

```
        else {
            self.feedbackLabel.text = NSLocalizedString(@"Opponent Won!", @"Opponent Won!");
            _state = kGameStateDone;
        }

    }
    else {
        if (moves >= 9) {
            self.feedbackLabel.text = NSLocalizedString(@"Cat Wins!", @"Cat Wins!");
            _state = kGameStateDone;
        }
    }

    if (_state == kGameStateDone)
        [self performSelector:@selector(startNewGame) withObject:nil afterDelay:3.0];
}
```

Hold on. You're not done yet. You need to back up and adjust the didReceiveMemoryWarning method. You need to disconnect from your peers.

```
[self.session disconnect];
self.session.delegate = nil;
self.peerID = nil;
```

Trying It

This app currently relies on Bluetooth connections or WiFi to work since you're using Multipeer Connectivity and the peer browser. As a result, you need to have two devices that have at least iOS 7 or greater. Since it is a multiplayer game, you need to have two instances running; one can be the simulator, and the other can be a simulator on another Mac or can be run on a physical device. To build and run on a physical device, you would need to be part of the Apple iOS Developer Program.

You can also run this with two devices provisioned for development. You should be able to connect two iOS devices to your computer at the same time. Xcode will display a drop-down menu in the Debug area to select which device to view.

If you do experience problems running Xcode with two devices, you need to build and run on one device, quit, unplug that device, and then plug in the other device and do the same thing. Once you've done that, you will have the application on both devices. You can run it on both devices, or you can launch it from Xcode on one device so you can debug and read the console feedback.

Note   Detailed instructions for installing applications on a device are available at http://developer.apple.com/ios in the developer portal, which is available only to paid iPhone SDK members.

You should be aware that debugging—or even running from Xcode without debugging—will slow down the program running on the connected iOS device, and this can have an effect on network communications. Underneath the hood, all of the data transmissions back and forth between the two devices check for acknowledgments and have a timeout period. If they don't receive a response in a certain amount of time, they will disconnect. So, if you set a breakpoint, chances are that you will break the connection between the two devices when it reaches the breakpoint. This can make figuring out problems in your Multipeer Connectivity application tedious. You often will need to use alternatives to breakpoints, such as `NSLog()` or breakpoint actions, so you don't break the network connection between the devices. We'll talk more about debugging in Chapter 15.

Game On!

This was another long chapter under your belt, and you should now have a pretty firm understanding of Multipeer Connectivity networking. You saw how to use the peer picker to let your user select another iPhone or iPod touch to which to connect. You saw how to send data by archiving objects, and you got a little taste of the complexity that is introduced to your application when you start adding network multiuser functionality. There are plenty of uses and wonderful things that one can do with Multipeer Connectivity since it is easy to implement. The bulk of the complexity in this chapter is providing the communication between the devices for the TicTacToe game.

Chapter 10

Map Kit

iPhones have always had a way to determine where in the world they are. Even though the original iPhone didn't have GPS, it did have a Maps application and was able to represent its approximate location on the map by using cell phone triangulation or by looking up its WiFi IP address in a database of known locations. In the beginning of iOS development, there was no way to leverage this functionality within your own applications. It was possible to launch the Maps application to show a specific location or route, but it wasn't possible using only Apple-provided APIs to show map data without leaving your application.

That changed with Map Kit. Applications now have the ability to show maps, including the user's current location, and even drop pins and show annotations on those maps. Map Kit's functionality isn't limited to just showing maps, either. It includes a feature called *reverse geocoding*, which allows you to take specific coordinates and turn them into a physical address. Your application can use those coordinates to find out not just where the person is located but, frequently, the actual address associated with that location. You can't always get down to the street address, but you can almost always get the city and state or province no matter where in the world your user is. In this chapter, you'll look at the basics of adding Map Kit functionality to any application.

> **Note** The application you build in this chapter will run just fine in the iPhone simulator; however, the simulator won't report your actual location. Instead, it returns the address of Apple's San Francisco Store at Stockton Street in San Francisco, California. You can change the location the simulator uses via the Location Simulator on the Debug pane jump bar in Xcode.

This Chapter's Application

This chapter's application will start by showing a map of where you are located. Figure 10-1 shows Australia because one of the authors lives there. Other than the map, your interface will be empty except for a single button with the imaginative title of Go. When the button is pressed, the application will determine your current location, zoom the map to show that location, and drop a pin to mark the location (Figure 10-2).

Figure 10-1. The MapMe application will start by showing a map of where you are

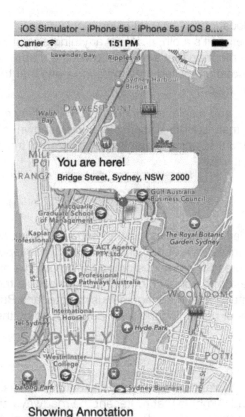

Showing Annotation

Figure 10-2. After determining the current location, the map will zoom in to that location and annotate it

You will then use Map Kit's reverse geocoder to determine the address of your current location, and you'll add an annotation to the map to display the specifics of that location.

Despite its simplicity, this application leverages most of the basic Map Kit functionality. Before you start building your project, let's explore Map Kit and see what makes it tick.

Overview and Terminology

Although Map Kit is not particularly complex, it can be a bit confusing. Let's start with a high-level view and nail down the terminology; then you can dig down into the individual components.

To display map-related data, you add a map view to one of your application's views. Map views can have a delegate, and that delegate is usually the controller class responsible for the view in which the map view resides. That's the approach you'll use for this chapter's application. Your application will have a single view and a single view controller. That single view will contain a map view, along with a few other items, and your single view controller will be the map view's delegate.

Map views keep track of locations of interest using a collection of *annotations*. Any time you see an icon on a map, whether it's a pin, a dot, or anything else, it's an annotation. When an annotation is in the part of the map that's being shown, the map view asks its delegate to provide a view for that annotation (called an *annotation view*) that the map view will draw at the specific location on the map.

Annotations are selectable, and a selected annotation will display a *callout*, which is a small view that floats above the map like the You are Here! view shown in Figure 10-2. If the user taps an annotation view and that annotation view is selectable, the map view will display the callout associated with that view.

The Map View

The core element of the Map Kit framework is the *map view* represented by the class MKMapView. The map view takes care of drawing the maps and responding to user input. Users can use all the gestures they're accustomed to, including a pinch in or out to do a controlled zoom, a double-tap to zoom in, or a two-finger double tap to zoom out. You can add a map view to your interface and configure it using Interface Builder. Like many iOS controls, much of the work of managing the map view is done by the map view's delegate.

Map Types

Map views are capable of displaying maps in several different ways. They can display the map as a series of lines and symbols that represent the roadways and other landmarks in the area being shown. This is the default display, and it's known as the *standard map type*. You can also display the map using satellite images by specifying the *satellite map type*, or you can use what's called the *hybrid map type* where the lines representing roadways and landmarks from the standard type are superimposed on top of the satellite imagery of the satellite type. You can see an example of the default map type in Figure 10-2. Figure 10-3 shows the satellite map type, and Figure 10-4 shows the hybrid map type.

Figure 10-3. *The satellite map type shows satellite imagery instead of lines and symbols*

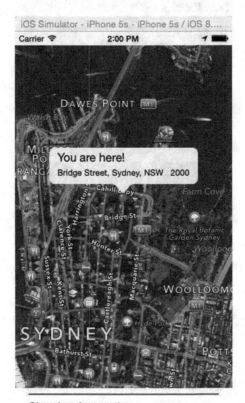

Showing Annotation

Figure 10-4. The hybrid type overlays the lines and symbols of the default type on top of the imagery from the satellite type

You can set the map type in Interface Builder or by setting the map view's `mapType` property to one of the following:

```
self.mapView.mapType = MKMapTypeStandard;
self.mapView.mapType = MKMapTypeSatellite;
self.mapView.mapType = MKMapTypeHybrid;
```

Location Authorization

Prior to iOS 8.0, Apple had a simple form of authorization for location services: either you allowed it or you didn't. If you did not allow the application to access the location services, no data would be returned, and the app could crash. Now with iOS 8.0 onward, there are two options. One is a blanket authorization allowing access just like in the previous versions for background processes. The other option is to provide access only when the application is in use. These permissions are as follows:

- requestAlwaysAuthorization
- requestWhenInUseAuthorization

Earlier you could simply instantiate a `CLLocationManager` instance and the system would request the permissions if the user had not approved or denied access to the application. These functions to request authorization would not work unless you set an entry in the `Info.plist` file. Plus, it is not available in the list of entries found in the drop-down of plist entries when you add a new item. The key to set is called `NSLocationWhenInUseUsageDescription`, and you set the value to a string that will be displayed when the permission dialog is displayed.

```
CLLocationManager *locationManager = [[CLLocationManager alloc]init];
[locationManager requestWhenInUseAuthorization];
```

If you have also set the plist entry, you would see the authorization dialog shown in Figure 10-5.

Figure 10-5. The authorization dialog requesting authorization to access the location services

User Location

Map views will, if configured to do so, use Core Location to keep track of the user's location and display it on the map using a blue dot, much like the way the Maps application does. You won't be using that functionality in this chapter's application, but you can turn it on by setting the map view's showsUserLocation property to YES, like so:

```
mapView.showsUserLocation = YES;
```

If the map is tracking the user's location, you can determine whether their present location is visible in the map view by using the read-only property userLocationVisible. If the user's current location is being displayed in the map view, userLocationVisible will return YES.

You can get the specific coordinates of the user's present location from the map view by first setting showsUserLocation to YES and then accessing the userLocation property. This property returns an instance of MKUserLocation. MKUserLocation is an object and has a property called location, which itself is a CLLocation object. A CLLocation contains a property called coordinate that points to a set of coordinates. This means you can get the actual coordinates from the MKUserLocation object, like so:

```
CLLocationCoordinate2D coords = mapView.userLocation.location.coordinate;
```

Coordinate Regions

A map view wouldn't be much good if you couldn't tell it what to display or find out what part of the world it's currently showing. With map views, the key to being able to do those tasks is the MKCoordinateRegion, a struct that contains two pieces of data that together define the portion of the map to be shown in a map view.

The first member of MKCoordinateRegion is called center. This is another struct of type CLLocationCoordinate2D, which you may remember from the chapter on Core Location in *Beginning iPhone Development*. A CLLocationCoordinate2D contains two floating-point values, a latitude and longitude, and is used to represent a single spot on the globe. In the context of a coordinate region, that spot on the globe is the spot that represents the center of the map view.

The second member of MKCoordinateRegion is called span, and it's a struct of type MKCoordinateSpan. The MKCoordinateSpan struct has two members called latitudeDelta and longitudeDelta. These two numbers are used to set the zoom level of the map by identifying how much of the area around the center should be displayed. These values represent that distance in degrees latitude and longitude. If latitudeDelta and longitudeDelta are small numbers, the map will be zoomed in very close; if they are large, the map will be zoomed out and show a much larger area.

Figure 10-6 shows the MKCoordinateRegion struct graphically.

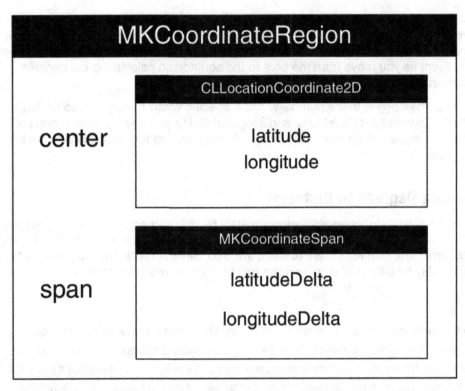

Figure 10-6. *The MKCoordinateRegion represented graphically. It contains two members, both of which are, in turn, structs that own two members*

If you look back at Figure 10-2, the point of the pin you can see is at the coordinates that were passed in MKCoordinateRegion.center. The distance from the top of the map to the bottom of the map was passed in, represented as degrees latitude, using the MKCoordinateRegion.span.latitudeDelta. Similarly, the distance from the left side of the map to the right side of the map was passed in, represented as degrees longitude, as the MKCoordinateRegion.span.longitudeDelta.

> **Tip** If you have trouble remembering which lines are latitude and which are longitude, here's a tip from third-grade geography teacher Mrs. Krabappel (pronounced kruh-bopple). Latitude sounds like altitude, so latitude tells you how high on the globe you are. The equator is a line of latitude. And the Prime Meridian is a line of longitude. Thanks, Mrs. Krabappel!

There are two challenges that this approach presents to the programmer. First, who thinks in degrees latitude or longitude? Although degrees latitude represent roughly the same distance everywhere in the world, degrees longitude vary greatly in the amount of distance they represent as you move from the pole to the equator, so calculating the degrees longitude isn't as straightforward.

The second challenge is that a map view has a specific width-to-height ratio (called an *aspect ratio*), and the `latitudeDelta` and `longitudeDelta` you specify must represent an area with that same aspect ratio. Fortunately, Apple provides tools for dealing with both of these issues.

Converting Degrees to Distance

Each degree of latitude represents approximately 69 miles, or about 111 kilometers, no matter where you are. This makes determining the number to pass in as the `latitudeDelta` of an `MKCoordinateSpan` fairly easy to calculate. You can just divide the lateral distance you want to display by 69 if you're using miles or 111 if you're using kilometers.

> **Note**   Since the earth isn't a perfect sphere (technically speaking, it's close to being an oblate spheroid), there actually is some variation between the amount of distance that 1 degree latitude represents, but it's not enough variation to bother factoring into this calculation, since it's only about a 1 degree variation from pole to equator. At the equator, 1 degree of latitude equals 69.046767 miles or 111.12 kilometers, and the number gets a little smaller as you move toward the poles. We chose 69 and 111 because they're nice round numbers that are within 1 percent of the actual distance pretty much everywhere.

The distance represented by 1 degree longitude, however, is not quite so easy to calculate. To do the same calculation for longitude, you have to take the latitude into account because the distance represented by 1 degree longitude depends on where you are in relation to the equator. To calculate the distance represented by degrees longitude, you have to perform some gnarly math. Fortunately, Apple has done the gnarly math for you and provides a method called `MKCoordinateRegionMakeWithDistance()` that you can use to create a region. You provide coordinates to act as the center, along with the distance in meters for the latitudinal and longitudinal span. The function will look at the latitude in the coordinates provided and calculate both delta values for you in degrees. Here is how you might create a region to show one kilometer on each side of a specific location represented by a `CLLocationCoordinate2D` called center:

```
MKCoordinateRegion viewRegion = MKCoordinateRegionMakeWithDistance(center, 2000, 2000);
```

To show a kilometer on each side of `center`, you must specify 2,000 meters total for each span: 1,000 to the left plus 1,000 to the right and 1,000 to the top plus 1,000 to the bottom. After this call, `viewRegion` will contain a properly formatted `MKCoordinateRegion` that's almost ready for use. All that's left is taking care of the aspect ratio problem.

THE GNARLY MATH

The math to calculate the distance of 1 degree longitude is a bit gnarly, but we thought we'd show those of you who are interested what the man behind the curtain is doing. To calculate the distance for one degree longitude at a given latitude, the calculation is as follows:

$$\frac{\pi}{180°} \times \text{radius of the Earth} \times cos(\text{latitude}°)$$

If Apple didn't provide a function for you, you could create a couple of macros that would accomplish the same thing just by following this formula. The radius of the earth is roughly 3,963.1676 miles, or 6,378.1 kilometers. So, to calculate the distance for 1 degree of longitude at a specific latitude contained in the variable lat, you would do this:

```
double longitudeMiles = ((M_PI / 180.0) * 3963.1676 * cos(latitude));
```

You can do the same calculation to determine the distance of 1 degree longitude in kilometers, like so:

```
double longitudeKilometers = ((M_PI / 180.0) * 6378.1 * cos(latitude));
```

Accommodating Aspect Ratio

In the previous section, we showed how to create a span that showed 1 kilometer on each side of a given location. However, unless the map view is perfectly square, there's no way that the view can show exactly 1 kilometer on each of the four sides of center. If the map view is wider than it is tall, the longitudeDelta will need to be larger than the latitudeDelta. If the map view is taller than it is wide, the opposite is true.

The MKMapView class has an instance method that will adjust a coordinate region to match the map view's aspect ratio. That method is called regionThatFits:. To use it, you just pass in the coordinate region you created, and it will return a new coordinate region that is adjusted to the map view's aspect ratio. Here's how to use it:

```
MKCoordinateRegion adjustRegion = [mapView regionThatFits:viewRegion];
```

Setting the Region to Display

Once you've created a coordinate region, you can tell a map view to display that region by calling the method setRegion:animated:. If you pass YES for the second parameter, the map view will zoom, shift, or otherwise animate the view from its current location to its new location. Here is an example that creates a coordinate region, adjusts it to the map view's aspect ratio, and then tells the map view to display that region:

```
MKCoordinateRegion viewRegion;
MKCoordinateRegion adjustRegion = [mapView regionThatFits:viewRegion];
[_mapView setRegion:adjustRegion animated:YES];
```

The Map View Delegate

As mentioned earlier, map views can have delegates. Map views, unlike table views and pickers, can function without a delegate. On a map view delegate, there are a number of methods you can implement if you need to be notified about certain map-related tasks. They allow you, for example, to get notified when the user changes the part of the map they're looking at, either by dragging to reveal a new section of the map or by zooming to reveal a smaller or larger area. You can also get notified when the map view loads new map data from the server or when the map view fails to do so. The map view delegate methods are contained in the MKMapViewDelegate protocol, and any class that is used as a map view delegate should conform to that protocol.

Map Loading Delegate Methods

Since iOS 6, the Map Kit framework switched from Google Maps to an Apple-provided service to do its job. It doesn't store any map data locally except for temporary caches. Whenever the map view needs to go to Apple's servers to retrieve new map data, it will call the delegate method mapViewWillStartLoadingMap:, and when it has successfully retrieved the map data it needs, it will call the delegate method mapViewDidFinishLoadingMap:. If you have any application-specific processing that needs to happen at either time, you can implement the appropriate method on the map view's delegate.

If Map Kit encounters an error loading map data from the server, it will call the method mapV iewDidFailLoadingMap:withError: on its delegate. At the least, you should implement this delegate method and inform your user of the problem so they aren't sitting there waiting for an update that will never come. Here's a simple implementation of that method that just shows an alert and lets the user know that something went wrong:

```
-(void) mapViewDidFailLoadingMap:(MKMapView *)mapView withError:(NSError *)error {
    UIAlertController *alert = [UIAlertController alertControllerWithTitle:
                                   NSLocalizedString(@"Error loading map", @"Error loading map")
                                   message:[error localizedDescription]
                           preferredStyle:UIAlertControllerStyleAlert];
    UIAlertAction *OKButton = [UIAlertAction actionWithTitle:@"OK"
                               style:UIAlertActionStyleDefault handler:nil];
    [alert addAction:OKButton];
    [self presentViewController:alert animated:YES completion:nil];
}
```

Region Change Delegate Methods

If your map view is enabled, the user will be able to interact with it using the standard iPhone gestures, such as drag, pinch in, pinch out, and double-tap. Doing so will change the region being displayed in the view. There are two delegate methods that will get called whenever this happens, if the map view's delegate implements those methods. As the gesture starts, the delegate method mapView:regionWillChangeAnimated: gets called. When the gesture stops, the method mapView:regionDidChangeAnimated: gets called. You would implement these if you had functionality that needed to happen while the view region was changing or after it had finished changing.

DETERMINING WHETHER COORDINATES ARE VISIBLE

One task that you may need to do quite often in the region change delegate methods is to determine whether a particular set of coordinates are currently visible onscreen. For annotations and for the user's current location (if it is being tracked), the map view will take care of figuring that out for you. Sometimes, however, you need to know whether a particular set of coordinates is currently within the map view's displayed region.

Here's how you can determine that:

```
CLLocationDegrees leftDegrees = mapView.region.center.longitude -
                          (mapView.region.span.longitudeDelta / 2.0);
CLLocationDegrees rightDegrees = mapView.region.center.longitude +
                          (mapView.region.span.longitudeDelta / 2.0);
CLLocationDegrees bottomDegrees = mapView.region.center.latitude -
                          (mapView.region.span.latitudeDelta / 2.0);
CLLocationDegrees topDegrees = mapView.region.center.latitude +
                          (mapView.region.span.latitudeDelta / 2.0);

if (leftDegrees > rightDegrees) { // Int'l Date Line in View
    leftDegrees = -180.0 - leftDegrees;
    if (coords.longitude > 0) // coords to West of Date Line
        coords.longitude = -180 - coords.longitude;
}

if (leftDegrees <= coords.longitude && coords.longitude <= rightDegrees && bottomDegrees <=
coords.latitude && coords.latitude <= topDegrees) {
    // Coordinates are being displayed
}
```

Before moving on to the rest of the map view delegate methods, let's discuss the topic of annotations.

Annotations

Map views offer the ability to tag a specific location with a set of supplementary information. That information, along with its graphic representation on the map, is called an *annotation*. The pin you drop in the application you're going to write (see Figure 10-2) is a form of annotation. The annotation is composed of two components: the *annotation object* and an *annotation view*. The map view will keep track of its annotations and will call out to its delegate when it needs to display any of its annotations.

The Annotation Object

Every annotation must have an annotation object, which is almost always going to be a custom class that you write and that conforms to the protocol MKAnnotation. An annotation object is typically a fairly standard data model object whose job it is to hold whatever data is relevant to the annotation in question. The annotation object has to respond to two methods and implement a single property. The two methods that an annotation object must implement are called title and subtitle, and they are the information that will be displayed in the annotation's callout, the little floating view that pops up when the annotation is selected. Back in Figure 10-4, you can see the title and subtitle displayed in the callout. In that instance, the annotation object returned a title of You are Here! and a subtitle of Bridge Street, Sydney, NSW 2000.

An annotation object must also have a property called coordinate that returns a CLLocationCoordinate2D specifying where in the world (geographically speaking) the annotation should be placed. The map view will use that location to determine where to draw the annotation.

The Annotation View

As we said before, when a map view needs to display any of its annotations, it will call out to its delegate to retrieve an annotation view for that annotation. It does this using the method mapView:viewForAnnotation:, which needs to return an MKAnnotationView or a subclass of MKAnnotationView. The annotation view is the object that gets displayed on the map, not the floating window that gets displayed when the annotation is selected. In Figure 10-4, the annotation view is the pin in the center of the window. It's a pin because you're using a provided subclass of MKAnnotationView called MKPinAnnotationView, which is designed to draw a red, green, or purple pushpin. It includes some additional functionality that MKAnnotationView doesn't have, such as the pin drop animation.

You can subclass MKAnnotationView and implement your own drawRect: method if you have advanced drawing needs for your annotation view. Subclassing MKAnnotationView is often unnecessary, however, because you can create an instance of MKAnnotationView and set its image property to whatever image you want. This opens up a whole world of possibilities without having to ever subclass or add subviews to MKAnnotationView (see Figure 10-7). Code for this is further down.

Showing Annotation

Figure 10-7. By setting the image property of an MKAnnotationView, you can display just about anything on the map. In this example, we've replaced the pin with a surprised cat because that's the way we roll

Adding and Removing Annotations

The map view keeps track of all of its annotations, so adding an annotation to the map is simply a matter of calling the map view's addAnnotation: method and providing an object that conforms to the MKAnnotation protocol.

```
[mapView addAnnotation:annotation];
```

You can also add multiple annotations by providing an array of annotations, using the method addAnnotations:.

```
[mapView addAnnotations:[NSArray arrayWithObjects:annotation1, annotation2, nil]];
```

You can remove annotations either by using the removeAnnotation: method and passing in a single annotation to be removed or by calling removeAnnotations: and passing in an array containing multiple annotations to be removed. All the map view's annotations are accessible using a property called annotations, so if you wanted to remove all annotations from the view, you could to this:

```
[mapView removeAnnotations:mapView.annotations];
```

Selecting Annotations

At any given time, one and only one annotation can be selected. The selected annotation will usually display a *callout*, which is that floating bubble or other view that gives more detailed information about the annotation. The default callout shows the title and subtitle from the annotation. However, you can actually customize the callout, which is just an instance of UIView. You won't be providing custom callout views in this chapter's application, but the process is similar to customizing table view cells the way you did in *Beginning iPhone Development*. For more information on customizing a callout, check the documentation for MKAnnotationView.

> **Note**   Although only a single annotation can currently be selected, MKMapView actually uses an instance of NSArray to keep track of the selected annotations. This may be an indication that at some point in the future map views will support selecting multiple annotations at once. Currently, if you provide a selectedAnnotations array with more than one annotation, only the first object in that array will be selected.

If the user taps an annotation's image (the push pin in Figure 10-4 or the shocked cat in Figure 10-7), it selects that annotation. You can also select an annotation programmatically using the method selectAnnotation:animated: and deselect an annotation programmatically using deselectAnnotation:animated:, passing in the annotation you want to select or deselect. If you pass YES to the second parameter, it will animate the appearance or disappearance of the callout.

Providing the Map View with Annotation Views

Map views ask their delegate for the annotation view that corresponds to a particular annotation using a delegate method called mapView:viewForAnnotation:. This method is called anytime an annotation moves into the map view's displayed region.

Much like the way table view cells work, annotation views are dequeued but not deallocated when they scroll off the screen. Implementations of mapView:viewForAnnotation: should ask the map view if there are any dequeued annotation views before allocating a new one. That means that mapView:viewForAnnotation: is going to look a fair amount like the many tabl eView:cellForRowAtIndexPath: methods you've written. Here's an example that creates an annotation view, sets its image property to display a custom image, and returns it:

```
-(MKAnnotationView *) mapView:(MKMapView *) theMapView
            viewForAnnotation:(id<MKAnnotation>)annotation {
    static NSString *placemarkIdentifier = @"my annotation identifier";
    if ([annotation isKindOfClass:[MyAnnotation class]]){
        MKAnnotationView *annotationView = [mapView
                dequeueReusableAnnotationViewWithIdentifier:placemarkIdentifier];
```

```
    if (annotationView == nil) {
        annotationView = [[MKAnnotationView alloc] initWithAnnotation:annotation
                                       reuseIdentifier:placemarkIdentifier];
        annotationView.image = [UIImage imageNamed:@"shocked_cat.png"];
    } else
        annotationView.annotation = annotation;

    return annotationView;
    }
    return nil;
}
```

There are a few things to notice here. First, notice that you check the `annotation` class to make sure it's an annotation you know about. The Map View delegate gets notified about all annotations, not just the custom one. Earlier, we talked about the `MKUserLocation` object that encapsulated the user's location. Well, that's an annotation also, and when you turn on user tracking for a map, your delegate method gets called whenever the user location needs to be displayed. You could provide your own annotation view for that, but if you return `nil`, the map view will use the default annotation view for it. Generally speaking, for any annotation you don't recognize, your method should return `nil`, and the Map View will probably handle it correctly.

Notice there is an identifier value called `placemarkIdentifier`. This allows you to make sure you're dequeuing the right kind of annotation view. You're not limited to using only one type of annotation view for all of your map's annotations, and the identifier is the way you tell which ones are used for what.

If you did dequeue an annotation view, it's important that you set its annotation property to the annotation that was passed in (annotation in the preceding example). The dequeued annotation view is almost certainly linked to some annotation, not necessarily the one it should be linked to.

Geocoding and Reverse Geocoding

A big feature of Core Location is *geocoding*. Geocoding is the ability to convert from a coordinate (specified as longitude and latitude) and a user-friendly representation of that coordinate. Taking a user-friendly location description (i.e., an address) and converting it to longitude and latitude is called *forward geocoding*. *Reverse geocoding* is converting a longitude and latitude into a user-friendly location description.

Geocoding is handled in Core Location by the `CLGeocoder` class. `CLGeocoder` works asynchronously in the background, querying the appropriate service. In the case of forward geocoding, `CLGeocoder` uses the built-in GPS functionality of your iPhone. For reverse geocoding, `CLGeocoder` queries a large database of coordinate data (in this case, it's Apple's database).

In almost all locations, reverse geocoding will be able to tell you the country and state or province that you're in. The more densely populated the area, the more information you're likely to get. If you're downtown in a large city, you might very well retrieve the street address of the building in which you are located. In most cities and towns, reverse geocoding will, at the least, get you the name of the street you are on. The tricky thing is that you never know for sure what level of detail you're going to get back.

For this chapter's application, you're going to use the reverse geocoding functionality of CLGeocoder. To perform reverse geocoding, you start by creating an instance of CLGeocoder. You then call reverseGeocodeLocation:completionHandler: to perform the geocoding. The completionHandler: argument is a CLGeocodeCompletionHandler type, which is a *block*. A block is an anonymous inline function that encapsulates the lexical scope from where it is executed. For reverseGeocodeLocation:completionHandler:, the completionHandler: block is executed regardless of a successful or failed reverse geocoding attempt.

```
CLGeocoder *geocoder = [[CLGeocoder alloc]init];
[geocoder reverseGeocodeLocation:location
              completionHandler:^(NSArray *placemarks, NSError *error) {
    // process the location or errors
    ...
}]
```

> **Note** You can learn more about blocks from Apple. The documentation on blocks starts here:
> https://developer.apple.com/library/ios/#featuredarticles/Short_Practical_
> Guide_Blocks/_index.html.

If the reverse geocoding succeeds, the completion handler will be invoked with the placemarks array being populated. It should be an array with only one object, of type CLPlacemark. If there was an error during the reverse geocoding or the request was cancelled, then the placemarks array will be nil. In that case, the completion handler will receive an NSError object, detailing the failure.

Table 10-1 maps CLPlacemark's terminology to terms with which you might be more familiar.

Table 10-1. CLPlacement Property Definitions

CLPlacemark Property	Meaning
Thoroughfare	Street address. First line if multiple lines.
subThoroughfare	Street address, second line (e.g., apartment or unit number, box number).
Locality	City.
SubLocality	This might contain a neighborhood or landmark name, though it's often nil.
administrativeArea	State, province, territory, or other similar unit.
subAdministrativeArea	County.
postalCode	ZIP code.
Country	Country.
countryCode	Two-digit ISO country code (see: http://en.wikipedia.org/wiki/ISO_3166-1_alpha-2).

You know what? That's enough talking about Map Kit. Let's start actually using it.

Building the MapMe Application

Let's build an application that shows some of the basic features of the Map Kit. Start by creating a new project in Xcode using the Single View Application template. Call the new project **MapMe**.

Linking the Map Kit and Core Location Frameworks

Before you do any coding, you need to add the Core Location and Map Kit frameworks. Navigate to the Build Phases tab for the MapMe target in the Project Editor. Expand the Link Binary With Libraries (3 items). Click the + on the lower left. Select CoreLocation.framework and MapKit.framework (remember, you can ⌘-click to select multiple frameworks). Click the Add button. The two frameworks should appear in the Navigator pane. You can clean things up a little bit by selecting both the CoreLocation.framework and MapKit.framework and creating a new group from selection and naming it the Frameworks group.

Building the Interface

Select main.storyboard to edit the user interface. Once Interface Builder opens, drag a button from the library to the view. Use the blue guidelines to align the button to the bottom right of the view. Double-click the newly placed button to edit its title and enter **Go**.

Drag a progress view from the library and place it to the left of the button, with the top of the progress view and the top of the button aligned. Resize using the blue guidelines so it extends horizontally from the left margin to the right margin. It will overlap the button, and that's OK.

Next, drag a label from the library over to the view and place it below the progress bar. Resize it horizontally so that it takes up the entire width from the left margin guides to the right margin guides. Now, use the Attributes Inspector to center-align the label's text, and change the font size to 13 so that the text will fit better. Lastly, delete the text *Label*.

Find the map view (Figure 10-8) in the Object Library. Drag the map view to the view. Align the top and left sides of the map view with view. Resize the map view to the width of the window view. Then resize the map view down toward the bottom, until the blue guideline appears, just above the progress bar and button you placed on the bottom earlier (Figure 10-9).

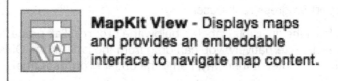

MapKit View - Displays maps and provides an embeddable interface to navigate map content.

Figure 10-8. The map view as it appears in the Object Library (List view)

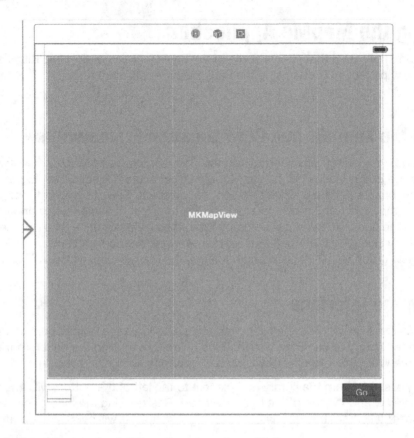

Figure 10-9. *Laying out the map view, just above the progress bar and button*

Now, you make the outlets and action connections. Put the editor in Assistant mode (via the toolbar). The Assistant editor should open ViewController.h to the right of Interface Builder. Control-drag from the Go button to just below the @interface declaration. Be sure you have selected the button, not the (invisible) label. When the Connection pop-up appears, the Type field should be UIButton. Set Connection to Outlet and name it **button**. Next, Control-drag from the Go button again, to just above the @end declaration. This time add an Action, and name it **findMe**.

Now Control-drag from the progress bar to just below the button property you added. Create an outlet named progressBar, making sure that the type is UIProgressView. Using the Attribute Inspector, click in the Hidden check box so that the progress bar will not be visible until you want to report progress to the user.

Next, Control-drag from the (invisible) label to below the progressBar property. You'll have to guess where the label is. Alternatively, you can drag from the label in the Object Dock, like you did in the previous chapter. Either way, name the outlet **progressLabel**.

Finally, Control-drag from the map view to below the progressLabel property declaration. Name this outlet mapView. Control-drag from the map view to the viewController icon on top of the view controller or in the Object Dock. When the Outlets pop-up appears, select delegate.

```
@property (weak, nonatomic) IBOutlet UIButton *button;
@property (weak, nonatomic) IBOutlet UIProgressView *progressBar;
@property (weak, nonatomic) IBOutlet UILabel *progressLabel;
@property (weak, nonatomic) IBOutlet MKMapView *mapView;
- (IBAction)findMe:(id)sender;
```

> **Note**   Most important if you are using the AutoLayout and SizeClasses settings, ensure that
> you have the constraints set; otherwise, the controls might not even show up on the screen. The
> easiest way is to lay them as you want, then select all of them, and finally select Editor ➤ Resolve
> Auto Layout Issues ➤ Add Missing Constraints.

Save the storyboard. Before moving on, put the editor back into Standard mode.

Finishing the View Controller Interface

Select ViewController.h to edit it. For starters, import both the Map Kit and Core Location
header files because you're using both Core Location and Map Kit in this application. You
can alternatively use just @import MapKit; directive that imports the entire framework.

```
#import <UIKit/UIKit.h>
#import <CoreLocation/CoreLocation.h>
```

You need conform your class to the following delegate protocols:

- CLLocationManagerDelegate so you can get notified by Core Location of
  the user's current location

- MKMapKitDelegate because you're going to be your map view's delegate

```
@interface ViewController : UIViewController <CLLocationManagerDelegate, MKMapViewDelegate>
```

Right after the @interface declaration, you declare three instance variables to store the
CLLocationManager, CLGeocoder, and CLPlacemark objects you'll use in the application. You
declare them as instance variable and not properties since you don't need to expose these
objects to your interface.

```
CLLocationManager *manager;
CLGeocoder *geocoder;
CLPlacemark *placemark;
```

> **Note**   Although map views are capable of tracking the user's current location, you're going to track
> the user's location manually using Core Location in this application. By doing it manually, we can
> show you more Map Kit features. If you need to track the user's location in your own applications,
> just let the map view do it for you.

That's it. You declared the outlets and action you need via Interface Builder. Save
ViewController.h. Before you work on the implementation file, you need to work on your
annotation class.

Writing the Annotation Object Class

You need to create a class to hold your annotation object. You'll build a simple one that
stores some address information, which you'll pull from the geocoder. Select the MapMe
group in the Navigator pane. Create a new Cocoa Touch Class file named **MapLocation** and
make it a subclass of NSObject.

Once the new files have been created, single-click MapLocation.h. Once the new files have been
created, single-click MapLocation.h to open the file. First you need to include the Map Kit header.

```
@import MapKit;
```

You need to change MapLocation to adopt the MKAnnotation and NSCoding protocols.

```
@interface MapLocation : NSObject <MKAnnotation, NSCoding>
```

We did say that annotations were pretty standard data model classes, didn't we? We
conformed this to MKAnnotation and also to NSCoding. You're not actually going to use the
archiving functionality, but it's a good habit to conform data model classes to NSCoding.

Next, you need properties to store address data, along with a CLLocationCoordinate2D,
which will be used to track this annotation's location on the map.

```
@property (strong, nonatomic) NSString *street;
@property (strong, nonatomic) NSString *city;
@property (strong, nonatomic) NSString *state;
@property (strong, nonatomic) NSString *zip;
@property (nonatomic, readwrite) CLLocationCoordinate2D coordinate;
```

Notice that you've specifically declared the coordinate property to be readwrite. The
MKAnnotation protocol declares this property as read-only. You could have declared it that way
as well and then just set the coordinate property by using the underlying instance variable, but
you'll use the property to let other classes set your annotation's coordinates. It's OK to redefine
properties to be more permissive than the same property as declared in a protocol to which
you've conformed or as declared in your superclass. You can always redefine a read-only or
write-only property to be read-write, but you must explicitly use the readwrite keyword. Most
of the time, that keyword isn't used because it's the default value and unnecessary.

Save MapLocation.h and switch to the implementation file, MapLocation.m. First you
implement the MKAnnotation protocol methods.

```
#pragma mark - MKAnnotation Protocol Methods

-(NSString *) title {
    return NSLocalizedString(@"You are Here!", @"You are Here!");
}
```

```
-(NSString *) subtitle {
    NSMutableString *result = [NSMutableString string];
    if(self.street)
        [result appendString:self.street];
    if(self.street && (self.city || self.state || self.zip))
        [result appendString:@", "];
    if(self.city)
        [result appendString:self.city];
    if(self.city && self.state)
        [result appendString:@", "];
    if(self.state)
        [result appendString:self.state];
    if(self.zip)
        [result appendFormat:@"  %@", self.zip];

    return result;
}
```

There really shouldn't be anything in the previous code that throws you for a loop. For the MKAnnotation protocol method of title, you just return You are Here!. The subtitle method, however, is a little more complex. Because you don't know which data elements the reverse geocoder will give you, you have to build the subtitle string based on what you have. You do that by declaring a mutable string and then appending the values from your non-nil, nonempty properties.

You need to implement the NSCoder protocol methods.

```
#pragma mark - NSCoder Protocol Methods

-(void) encodeWithCoder:(NSCoder *)aCoder {
    [aCoder encodeObject:self.street forKey:@"street"];
    [aCoder encodeObject:self.city forKey:@"city"];
    [aCoder encodeObject:self.state forKey:@"state"];
    [aCoder encodeObject:self.zip forKey:@"zip"];
}

-(id) initWithCoder:(NSCoder *)aDecoder {
    self = [super init];
    if (self) {
        [self setStreet:[aDecoder decodeObjectForKey:@"street"]];
        [self setCity:[aDecoder decodeObjectForKey:@"city"]];
        [self setState:[aDecoder decodeObjectForKey:@"state"]];
        [self setZip:[aDecoder decodeObjectForKey:@"zip"]];
    }

    return self;
}
```

Everything else here is standard stuff to encode and decode the MapLocation class, so let's move on to implementing the ViewController class. Save MapLocation.m before proceeding.

Implementing the MapMe ViewController

Single-click `ViewController.m`. Start by adding the import of the MapLocation header.

```
#import "MapLocation.h"
```

Next you define some private category methods for handling annotations and reverse geocoding. In the Category interface declaration, add these two method declarations:

```
@interface ViewController ()
-(void) openCallout:(id<MKAnnotation>)annotation;
-(void)reverseGeocode:(CLLocation *)location;
@end
```

Next, set the Map View map type in the `viewDidLoad:` method. Declare all three map types, with two of them commented out. This is just to make it easier for you to change the one you're using and experiment a little. Add these after the call to `super`.

```
self.mapView.mapType = MKMapTypeStandard;
//self.mapView.mapType = MKMapTypeSatellite;
//self.mapView.mapType = MKMapTypeHybrid;
```

Now implement the action method `findMe`, which gets called when the user presses a button.

```
#pragma mark - Action Method

- (IBAction)findMe:(id)sender {
    if (manager == nil)
        manager = [[CLLocationManager alloc] init];
    manager.delegate = self;
    manager.desiredAccuracy = kCLLocationAccuracyBest;

    [manager requestWhenInUseAuthorization];

    [manager startUpdatingLocation];

    self.progressBar.hidden = NO;
    self.progressBar.progress = 0.0;
    self.progressLabel.text = NSLocalizedString(@"Determining Current Location",
    @"Determining Current Location");
    self.button.hidden = YES;
}
```

As discussed, you could have used the map view's ability to track the user's location, but you're going the manual route to learn more functionality. Therefore, you allocate and initialize an instance of `CLLocationManager` to determine the user's location. You set `self` as the delegate and tell the Location Manager you want the best accuracy available, before telling it to start updating the location. Then you unhide the progress bar and set the progress label to tell the user that you are trying to determine the current location. Lastly, you hide the button so the user can't press it again.

> **Note**   You need to call the `requestWhenInUseAuthorization` or the
> `requestAlwaysAuthorization` before you can ask the `CLLocationManager` to start updating
> the location information, and you also need to set the `info.plist` file with the appropriate prompt
> for either of the authorizations. The keys are `NSLocationWhenInUseUsageDelegate` and
> `NSLocationAlwaysUsageDelegate`. You need to set the text that will be displayed when the
> prompt is displayed requesting permissions the first time.

Now, you implement the private category methods you declared in the beginning of
`ViewController.m`.

```
#pragma mark - (Private) Instance Methods

-(void) openCallout:(id<MKAnnotation>)annotation {
    self.progressBar.progress = 1.0;
    self.progressLabel.text = NSLocalizedString(@"Showing Annotation",
                                          @"Showing Annotation");
    [self.mapView selectAnnotation:annotation animated:YES];

    self.button.hidden = YES;
    self.progressBar.hidden = YES;
    self.progressLabel.text = @"";
}
```

You'll use `openCallout:` a little later to select your annotation. You can't select the annotation
when you add it to the map view. You have to wait until it's been added before you can
select it. This method will allow you to select an annotation, which will open the annotation's
callout by using `performSelector:withObject:afterDelay:`. All you do in this method is
update the progress bar and progress label to show that you're at the last step and then use
the `MKMapView`'s `selectAnnotation:animated:` method to select the annotation, which will
cause its callout view to be shown.

You also declared another private method called `reverseGeocode:`. Again, you'll use it a
little later. Given a `CLLocation` instance, it attempts to reverse geocode the location. If it
succeeds, it will create a `MapLocation` annotation and send it to the Map View. If there's an
error, it will pop up an alert dialog.

```
-(void)reverseGeocode:(CLLocation *)location{
    if(!geocoder)
        geocoder = [[CLGeocoder alloc] init];

    [geocoder reverseGeocodeLocation:location
                completionHandler:^(NSArray *placemarks, NSError *error) {
        if(nil != error) {
            UIAlertController *alert = [UIAlertController
        alertControllerWithTitle:NSLocalizedString(@"Error translating coordinates into location",
                                        @"Error translating coordinates into location")
```

```
                    message:NSLocalizedString(@"Geocoder did not recognize coordinates",
                                          @"Geocoder did not recognize coordinates")
              preferredStyle:UIAlertControllerStyleAlert];
            UIAlertAction *OKAction = [UIAlertAction
                    actionWithTitle:@"OK"
                              style:UIAlertActionStyleDefault
                            handler:nil];
            [alert addAction:OKAction];
            [self presentViewController:alert animated:YES completion:nil];
        } else if ([placemarks count] > 0) {
            placemark = [placemarks objectAtIndex:0];

            self.progressBar.progress = 0.5;
            self.progressLabel.text = NSLocalizedString(@"Location Determined",
                                                @"Location Determined");
            MapLocation *annotation = [[MapLocation alloc] init];
            annotation.street = placemark.thoroughfare;
            annotation.city = placemark.locality;
            annotation.state = placemark.administrativeArea;
            annotation.zip = placemark.postalCode;
            annotation.coordinate = location.coordinate;

            [self.mapView addAnnotation:annotation];
        }
    }];
}
```

Next, add the `CLLocationManagerDelegate` methods. To update locations, the method provided was `locationManager:didUpdateToLocation:fromLocation:`, which now has been updated to `locationManger:didUpdateLocations:`, which in turn takes an array of locations instead of the `oldLocation` and `newLocation` that was passed. There will always be at least one item in the array, and the methods `firstObject` and `lastObject` can be used to get the appropriate location.

```
#pragma mark - CLLocationManagerDelegate Methods

-(void) locationManager:(CLLocationManager *)manager didUpdateLocations:(NSArray *)locations
{
    //CLLocation *oldLocation = [locations firstObject];
    CLLocation *newLocation = [locations lastObject];
    if([newLocation.timestamp timeIntervalSince1970] <
       [NSDate timeIntervalSinceReferenceDate] - 60)
        return;

    MKCoordinateRegion viewRegion = MKCoordinateRegionMakeWithDistance(newLocation.
    coordinate, 2000, 2000);
    MKCoordinateRegion adjustedRegion = [self.mapView regionThatFits:viewRegion];
    [self.mapView setRegion:adjustedRegion animated:YES];

    manager.delegate = nil;
    [manager stopUpdatingLocation];
```

```
        self.progressBar.progress = 0.25;
        self.progressLabel.text = NSLocalizedString(@"Reverse Geocoding Location",
                                        @"Reverse Geocoding Location");
        [self reverseGeocode:newLocation];
}
```

First, you check that you're operating with a fresh location, taken within the last minute, and not a cached one. You then use the MKCoordinateRegionMakeWithDistance method to create a region that shows 1 kilometer on each side of the user's current location. You adjust that region to the aspect ratio of your map view and then tell the map view to show that new adjusted region. Now that you've gotten a noncache location, you're going to stop having the location manager give you updates. Location updates are a drain on the battery, so when you don't want any more updates, you should shut the location manager down. Then you update the progress bar and label to let them know where you are in the whole process. This is the first of four steps after the Go button is pressed, so you set progress to 0.25, which will show a bar that is one-quarter blue. Finally, you call the reverseGeocoder: method to convert the new location to an annotation and update the map view.

If the location manager encounters an error, you just show an alert, not the most robust error handling, but it'll do for this.

```
-(void)locationManager:(CLLocationManager *)manager didFailWithError:(NSError *)error{
    NSString *errorType = (error.code == kCLErrorDenied)
                        ? NSLocalizedString(@"Access Denied", @"Access Denied")
                        : NSLocalizedString(@"Unknown Error", @"Unknown Error");

    UIAlertController *alert = [UIAlertController alertControllerWithTitle:
                    NSLocalizedString(@"Error Getting Location", @"Error Getting Location")
                        message:errorType
                    preferredStyle:UIAlertControllerStyleAlert];
    UIAlertAction *OKButton = [UIAlertAction
                            actionWithTitle:@"OK"
                                    style:UIAlertActionStyleDefault
                                    handler:nil];
    [alert addAction:OKButton];
    [self presentViewController:alert animated:YES completion:nil];
}
```

Now, you add the MapView delegate methods.

```
#pragma mark - MKMapViewDelegate Methods

-(MKAnnotationView *) mapView:(MKMapView *) aMapView viewForAnnotation:(id<MKAnnotation>)
annotation {
    static NSString *placemarkIdentifier = @"Map Location Identifier";
    if ([annotation isKindOfClass:[MapLocation class]]) {
        MKPinAnnotationView *annotationView = (MKPinAnnotationView *) [aMapView
                    dequeueReusableAnnotationViewWithIdentifier: placemarkIdentifier];
```

```
        if (nil == annotationView) {
            annotationView = [[MKPinAnnotationView alloc]
                        initWithAnnotation:annotation reuseIdentifier:placemarkIdentifier];
        } else
            annotationView.annotation = annotation;

        annotationView.enabled = YES;
        annotationView.animatesDrop = YES;
        annotationView.pinColor = MKPinAnnotationColorPurple;
        annotationView.canShowCallout = YES;
        [self performSelector:@selector(openCallout:) withObject:annotation afterDelay:0.5];

        self.progressBar.progress = 0.75;
        self.progressLabel.text = NSLocalizedString(@"Creating Annotation",
                                        @"Creating Annotation");
        return annotationView;
    }
    return nil;
}
```

When the map view for which you are the delegate needs an annotation view, it will call `mapView:viewForAnnotation:`. The first thing you do is declare an identifier so you can dequeue the right kind of annotation view; then you make sure the map view is asking you about a type of annotation that you know about. If it is, you dequeue an instance of `MKPinAnnotationView` with your identifier. If there are no dequeued views, you create one. You could also have used `MKAnnotationView` here instead of `MKPinAnnotationView`. In fact, there's an alternate version of this project in the project archive that shows how to use `MKAnnotationView` to display a custom annotation view instead of a pin. If you didn't create a new view, it means you got a dequeued one from the map view. In that case, you have to make sure the dequeued view is linked to the right annotation. Then you do some configuration.

▪ You make sure the annotation view is enabled so it can be selected.

▪ You set `animatesDrop` to YES because this is a pin view, and you want it to drop onto the map the way pins are wont to do.

▪ You set the pin color to purple and make sure that it can show a callout.

▪ After that, you use `performSelector:withObject:afterDelay:` to call that private method you created earlier.

▪ You can't select an annotation until its view is actually being displayed on the map, so you wait half a second to make sure that's happened before selecting. This will also make sure that the pin has finished dropping before the callout is displayed.

▪ You need to update the progress bar and text label to let the user know that you're almost done.

▪ Then you return the annotation view. If the annotation wasn't one you recognize, you return `nil`, and your map view will use the default annotation view for that kind of annotation.

- You implement `mapViewDidFailLoadingMap:withError:` and inform the user if there was a problem loading the map. Again, your error checking in this application is rudimentary; you just inform the user and stop everything.

```objc
-(void) mapViewDidFailLoadingMap:(MKMapView *)mapView withError:(NSError *)error {
    UIAlertController *alert = [UIAlertController alertControllerWithTitle:
                                    NSLocalizedString(@"Error loading map", @"Error loading map")
                                    message:[error localizedDescription]
                                preferredStyle:UIAlertControllerStyleAlert];
    UIAlertAction *OKButton = [UIAlertAction
                            actionWithTitle:@"OK"
                                      style:UIAlertActionStyleDefault
                                    handler:^(UIAlertAction * alert) {
                                        self.progressLabel.text = @"";
                                        self.progressBar.hidden = YES;
                                        self.button.hidden = NO;
                                    }];
    [alert addAction:OKButton];
    [self presentViewController:alert animated:YES completion:nil];
}
```

- Finally, you handle the `alert` method, which is block code. It will hide the progress bar and set the progress label to an empty string. For simplicity's sake, we're just dead-ending the application if a problem occurs. In your apps, you'll probably want to do something a little more user-friendly.

You should now be able to build and run your application, so do that, and try it.

Note   When running in the simulator, you may encounter problems. Try launching the application, but before pressing the Go button, use the Location Simulator in the Debug jump bar to set a location.

Experiment with the code. Change the map type, add more annotations, or try experimenting with custom annotation views.

Go East, Young Programmer

That brings us to the end of the discussion of Map Kit. You saw the basics of how to use Map Kit, annotations, and the reverse geocoder. You saw how to create coordinate regions and coordinate spans to specify what area the map view should show to the user, and you learned how to use Map Kit's reverse geocoder to turn a set of coordinates into a physical address.

Now, armed with your iPhone, Map Kit, and sheer determination, navigate your way one page to the east, err...right, so that we can talk about iOS Messaging.

Chapter 11

Messaging: Mail, Social and iMessage

Since the beginnings of the iOS SDK, Apple has provided the means for developers to send messages. It started with the MessageUI framework, which allowed developers to add support for sending e-mail messages from within their applications. Then, Apple extended the MessageUI framework to include SMS messages. With iOS 5, Apple added support for Twitter with a new Twitter framework, and with iOS 6, Apple migrated from the Twitter framework to the Social framework, adding support for Facebook, Sina Weibo, and Twitter. Let's go over how each messaging system works.

This Chapter's Application

In this chapter, you're going to build an application that lets the user take a picture using their iPhone's camera; or, if they don't have a camera because they're using the simulator, then you'll allow them to select an image from the photo library. They can take the resulting image and send it to a friend via e-mail, SMS, Facebook, or Twitter without leaving the application.

Note While it is possible to send a photo via the Messages application, Apple has not exposed this functionality to developers. This functionality is called Multimedia Messaging Service (MMS). The iOS SDK allows you to use only Short Message Service (SMS) to send text messages. As a result, you'll just be sending a text message in your application.

Your application's interface will be simple (Figure 11-1). It will feature a single button to start the whole thing going. Tapping the button will bring up the camera picker controller, in a manner similar to the sample program in *Beginning iPhone Development*. Once the user has taken or selected an image, they'll be able to crop and/or scale it (Figure 11-2). Assuming the user doesn't cancel, the image picker will return an image, and an activity view will ask the user how they want to send the message (Figure 11-3). Depending on their choice, you'll display the appropriate composition view (Figure 11-4). You'll populate the composition view with text and the selected image (unless it's an SMS message). Finally, once the message is sent, you'll provide some feedback confirming that the message was sent.

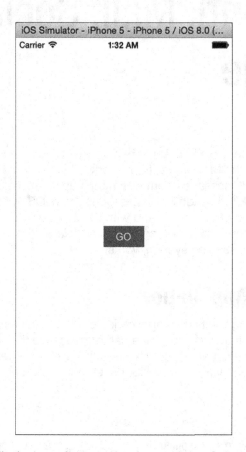

Figure 11-1. The chapter's application has a simple user interface consisting of a button

Figure 11-2. *Users can take a picture with the camera or select an image from their photo library and then crop and scale the image*

Figure 11-3. After selecting and editing the image, you present the message selector view

Figure 11-4. Twitter compose view

Caution   The application in this chapter will run in the simulator, but instead of using the camera, it will allow you to select an image from the simulator's photo library. If you've ever used the Reset Contents and Settings menu item in the simulator, then you have probably lost the photo album's default contents and will have no images available. You can rectify this by launching Mobile Safari in the simulator and navigating to an image on the Web. Make sure the image you are looking at is *not* a link but a static image. This technique will not work with a linked image. Click and hold the mouse button with your cursor over an image, and an action sheet will pop up. One of the options will be Save Image. This will add the selected image to your iPhone's photo library.

In addition, note that you will not be able to send e-mail from within the simulator. You'll be able to create the e-mail, and the simulator will say it sent it, but it's all lies. The e-mail just ends up in the circular file.

The MessageUI Framework

To embed e-mail and SMS services in your application, use the MessageUI framework.
It is one of the smallest frameworks in the iOS SDK. It's composed of two classes,
MFMailComposeViewController and MFMessageComposeViewController, and their
corresponding delegate protocols.

Each class comes with a static method to determine whether the device supports
the service. For MFMailComposeViewController, the method is canSendMail; for
MFMessageComposeViewController, the method is canSendText. It's a good idea to check
whether your device can send an e-mail or SMS message before attempting do so.

```
if ([MFMailComposeViewController canSendMail)] {
    // code to send email
    ...
}
if ([MFMessageComposeViewController canSendText]) {
    // code to send SMS
    ...
}
```

Let's start by reviewing the e-mail class, MFMailComposeViewController.

Creating the Mail Compose View Controller

It's simple to use the MFMailComposeViewController class. You create an instance, set its
delegate, set any properties that you want to prepopulate, and then present it modally.
When the user is done with their e-mail and taps either the Send or Cancel button, the mail
compose view controller notifies its delegate, which is responsible for dismissing the modal
view. Here's how you create a mail compose view controller and set its delegate (your class
must support MFMailComposeViewControllerDelegate):

```
MFMailComposeViewController *mc = [[MFMailComposeViewController alloc] init];
mc.mailComposeDelegate = self;
```

Populating the Subject Line

Before you present the mail compose view, you can preconfigure the various fields of the
mail compose view controller, such as the subject and recipients (To, Cc, and Bcc), as
well as the body and attachments. You can populate the subject by calling the method
setSubject: on the instance of MFMailComposeViewController, like this:

```
[mc setSubject:@"Hello, World!"];
```

Populating Recipients

E-mails can go to three types of recipients. The main recipients of the e-mail are called
the *to* recipients and go on the To line. Recipients who are being copied on the e-mail
go on the Cc line. If you want to include somebody on the e-mail but not let the other

recipients know that person is also receiving the e-mail, you can use the Bcc line, which stands for "blind carbon copy." You can populate all three of these fields when using `MFMailComposeViewController`.

To set the main recipients, use the method `setToRecipients:` and pass in an `NSArray` instance containing the e-mail addresses of all the recipients. Here's an example:

```
[mc setToRecipients:@[@"mihir.m@beta.com"]];
```

Set the other two types of recipients in the same manner, though you'll use the methods `setCcRecipients:` for Cc recipients and `setBccRecipients:` for Bcc recipients.

```
[mc setCcRecipients:@[@"maru@boxes.co.jp"]];
[mc setBccRecipients:@[@"lassie@helpfuldogs.org"]];
```

Setting the Message Body

You can also populate the message body with any text you'd like. You can either use a regular string to create a plain-text e-mail or use HTML to create a formatted e-mail. To supply the mail compose view controller with a message body, use the method `setMessageBody:isHTML:`. If the string you pass in is plain text, you should pass NO as the second parameter, but if you're providing HTML markup in the first argument rather than a plain string, then you should pass YES in the second argument so your markup will be parsed before it is shown to the user.

```
[mc setMessageBody:@"Ohai!!!\n\nKThxBai" isHTML:NO];
[mc setMessageBody:@"<HTML><B>Ohai</B><BR/>I can has cheezburger?</HTML>" isHTML:YES];
```

Adding Attachments

You can also add attachments to outgoing e-mails. To do so, you must provide an instance of `NSData` containing the data to be attached, along with the MIME type of the attachment and the file name to be used for the attachment. *MIME types*, which we discussed briefly in Chapter 9 when we talked about interacting with web servers, are strings that define the type of data being transferred over the Internet. They're used when retrieving from or sending files to a web server, and they're also used when sending e-mail attachments. To add an attachment to an outgoing e-mail, use the method `addAttachmentData:mimeType:fileName:`. Here's an example of adding an image stored in your application's bundle as an attachment:

```
NSString *path = [[NSBundle mainBundle] pathForResource:@"surpriseCat" ofType:@"png"];
NSData *data = [NSData dataWithContentsOfFile:path];
[mc addAttachmentData:data mimeType:@"image/png" fileName:@"surpriseCat"];
```

Presenting the Mail Compose View

Once you've configured the controller with all the data you want populated, you present the controller's view, as you've done before.

```
[self presentViewController:mc animated:YES completion:nil];
```

The Mail Compose View Controller Delegate Method

The mail compose view controller delegate's method is contained in the formal protocol MFMailComposeViewControllerDelegate. Regardless of whether the user sends or cancels and regardless of whether the system was able to send the message, the method mailCom poseController:didFinishWithResult:error: gets called. As with most delegate methods, the first parameter is a pointer to the object that called the delegate method. The second parameter is a *result code* that tells you the fate of the outgoing e-mail, and the third is an NSError instance that will give you more detailed information if a problem was encountered. Regardless of what result code you receive, it is your responsibility in this method to dismiss the mail compose view controller by calling dismissModalViewControllerAnimated:.

If the user taps the Cancel button, your delegate will be sent the result code MFMailComposeResultCancelled. In that situation, the user changed their mind and decided not to send the e-mail. If the user taps the Send button, the result code is going to depend on whether the MessageUI framework was able to successfully send the e-mail. If it was able to send the message, the result code will be MFMailComposeResultSent. If it tried, and failed, the result code will be MFMailComposeResultFailed, in which case you probably want to check the provided NSError instance to see what went wrong. If the message couldn't be sent because there's currently no Internet connection but the message was saved into the Outbox folder to be sent later, you will get a result code of MFMailComposeResultSaved.

Here is a simple implementation of the delegate method that logs what happened:

```
- (void)mailComposeController:(MFMailComposeViewController*)controller
          didFinishWithResult:(MFMailComposeResult)result
                        error:(NSError*)error
{
    switch (result)
    {
        case MFMailComposeResultCancelled:
            NSLog(@"Mail send canceled...");
            break;
        case MFMailComposeResultSaved:
            NSLog(@"Mail saved...");
            break;
        case MFMailComposeResultSent:
            NSLog(@"Mail sent...");
            break;
        case MFMailComposeResultFailed:
            NSLog(@"Mail send error: %@...", [error localizedDescription]);
            break;
        default:
            break;
    }
    [controller dismissViewControllerAnimated:YES completion:nil];
}
```

Message Compose View Controller

MFMessageComposeViewController is similar but simpler than its e-mail counterpart. First, you create an instance and set its delegate.

```
MFMessageComposeViewController *mc = [[MFMessageComposeViewController alloc] init];
mc.messageComposeDelegate = self;
```

Like the Mail composer, it is always suggested that you check whether the device is able to send messages prior to attempting to send one using the canSendText function; this returns a YES or a NO. This is related only to the ability to be able to send text messages via MMS, iMessage, or SMS.

There are a few properties that you can populate: recipients, subject, body, and attachments. Unlike with e-mail, these can be accessed via direct properties on the class, as well as via the method accessors. recipients is an array of strings, where each string is a contact name from your Address Book or phone number. subject is the initial subject of the message, body is the message you want to send, and attachments is an array of dictionaries describing the properties of an attachment.

```
mc.recipients = @[@"Mihir"];
mc.body = @"Hello, Mihir!";
mc.subject = @"My WWDC Trip";
```

The message compose view controller delegate method behaves identically to its e-mail counterpart. There are only three possible results when sending an SMS: cancelled, sent, or failed.

```
- (void)messageComposeViewController:(MFMessageComposeViewController *)controller
                  didFinishWithResult:(MessageComposeResult)result
{
    switch (result)
    {
        case MessageComposeResultCancelled:
            NSLog(@"SMS sending canceled");
            break;
        case MessageComposeResultSent:
            NSLog(@"SMS sent");
            break;
        case MessageComposeResultFailed:
            NSLog(@"SMS sending failed");
            break;
        default:
            NSLog(@"SMS not sent");
            break;
    }
    [controller dismissViewControllerAnimated:YES completion:nil];
}
```

Message Attachments

With iOS 7.0 Apple introduced the functionality to add attatchments to the Messages application. However, before you can attach a message, you would need to confirm if you are allowed to send attachments via MMS or iMessage. The function canSendAttachments returns a YES or NO depending on whether you can include attachments.

You can use addAttachmentData:typeIdentifier:filename: to add file data as the attachment. It is similar to the way you add an attachment to the Mail composer, shown previously. The contents of the file are passed to the function as an NSData object. The only difference is that instead of a MIME type you provide a uniform type identifier (UTI) to this function. A sample UTI looks like public.jpeg or com.myapp.photo and also has constants like kUTTypePNG and kUTTypeJPEG.

```
NSString *path = [[NSBundle mainBundle] pathForResource:@"surpriseCat" ofType:@"png"];
NSData *data = [NSData dataWithContentsOfFile:path];
[mc addAttachmentData:data typeIdentifierkUTTypePNG fileName:@"surpriseCat"];
```

Another method of adding attachments is from a uniform resource locator (URL) using add AttachmentData:withAlternativeFilename:, where you could pass an alternative name to display for that link file name.

Disabling Message Attachments

With an app linked to an older version of iOS, the camera and attachments are not available. With iOS 7.0 and newer, you can disable the camera/attachment buttons using the disableUserAttachments method.

The Social Framework

In iOS 5, Apple tightly integrated with Twitter (www.twitter.com). Basically, your Twitter account was available from the system. As a result, it was easy to send messages (*tweets*) to Twitter or perform Twitter API requests. In iOS 6, Apple abstracted and extended this feature into the Social framework. To access this framework, you need to add the line @import Social; into your project. Along with Twitter, Apple integrated identical functionality for Facebook and Sina Weibo.

SLComposeViewController

SLComposeViewController is similar in design and principle to the e-mail and message view controller classes in the MessageUI framework. However, there isn't a corresponding delegate class. Rather, SLComposeViewController has a completion handler property that can be assigned a block.

To confirm that your application can use a service, you call the static method isAvailableForServiceType:. For example, the check to see whether you can send to Facebook is as follows:

```
if ([SLComposeViewController isAvailableForServiceType:SLServiceTypeFacebook]) {
    // code to send message to Facebook
    ...
}
```

isAvailableForServiceType: takes a String argument of possible service type constants. These service types are defined in the header file SLServiceTypes.h. Currently, Apple defines the following service type constant:

```
NSString *const SLServiceTypeFacebook;
NSString *const SLServiceTypeTwitter;
NSString *const SLServiceTypeSinaWeibo;
```

If you are able to send a send a message to the service, you start by creating an instance of the view controller.

```
SLComposeViewController *composeVC = [SLComposeViewController
                            composeViewControllerForServiceType:SLServiceTypeTwitter];
```

This example would create a view controller for sending a tweet. You're able to set the initial text, add images, and add URLs before presenting the view controller.

```
[composeVC setInitialText:@"Hello, Twitter!"];

UIImage *image = [UIImage imageWithContentsOfFile:@"surpriseCat.png"];
[composeVC addImage:image];

NSURL *url = [NSURL URLWithString:@"http://www.oz-apps.com"];
[composeVC addURL:url];
```

These methods return YES if on success and NO on failure.

There are two convenience methods, removeAllImages and removeAllURLs, to remove any images or URLs you've added.

As mentioned earlier, you don't assign a delegate to handle message completion. Rather, you set the completionHandler property with a block.

```
[composeVC setCompletionHandler:^(SLComposeViewControllerResult result) {
    switch (result) {
        case SLComposeViewControllerResultCancelled:
            NSLog(@"Message cancelled.");
            break;
```

```
        case SLComposeViewControllerResultDone:
            NSLog(@"Message sent.");
            break;
        default:f
            break;
    }
    [self dismissViewControllerAnimated:YES completion:nil];
}];
```

The block accepts one argument, which tells the result of the message. Again, you are expected to dismiss the view controller with a call to dismissViewControllerAnimated:completion:.

SLRequest

SLComposeViewController is fine if you just want to post messages. What if you want to take advantage of the APIs these social media services offer? In that case, you want to use SLRequest, which is basically a wrapper around an HTTP request that handles the authentication between your application and the social media service.

To create a request, you call the class method requestForServiceType:requestMethod: URL:parameters:.

```
SLRequest *request = [SLRequest requestForServiceType:SLServiceTypeFacebook
                                  requestMethod:SLRequestMethodPOST
                                         URL:url
                                  parameters:params];
```

The first argument is the same service type String constant used in SLComposeViewController. requestMethod: is a subset of HTTP actions: GET, POST, and DELETE. Apple has defined an enumeration for this subset: SLRequestMethod.

```
SLRequestMethodGET
SLRequestMethodPOST
SLRequestMethodDELETE
```

URL: is a URL defined by the service provider. This is usually not the public "www" URL of the service. For example, Twitter's URL begins with http://api.twitter.com/. Finally, parameters: is a dictionary of HTTP parameters to send to the service. The contents of the dictionary depend on the service being called.

Once you've composed your request, you send it to the service provider.

```
[request performRequestWithHandler:^(NSData *responseData,
                                  NSHTTPURLResponse *urlResponse,
                                  NSError *error) {
    // Handle the response, process the data or error
    ...
}];
```

The handler is a block that returns the HTTP response object, along with any accompanying data. An error object is returned, which will be non-nil if an error occurred.

> **Note**   This is a pretty short overview of the SLRequest class. You can read more in the class
> documentation at https://developer.apple.com/library/ios/#documentation/
> Social/Reference/SLRequest_Class/Reference/Reference.html.

The Activity View Controller

In iOS 6, Apple introduced a new way to access the various services from within an application:
the activity view controller (UIActivityViewController). In addition to giving applications access
to standard iOS services, such as copy and paste, the activity view controller provides a single
unified interface for applications to send e-mail, send SMS messages, or post content to social
media services. You can even define your own custom service.

Using an activity view controller is simple. Initialize the activity view controller with the items
you want to send (such as text, images, and so on) and push it onto your current view controller.

```
NSString *text = @"some text";
UIImage *image = [[UIImage alloc] initWithContentsOfFile:@"some_image.png"];
NSArray *items = @[ text, image ];

UIActivityViewController *activityVC =
    [[UIActivityViewController alloc] initWithActivityItems:items applicationActivities:nil];

[self presentViewController:activityVC animated:YES completion:nil];
```

That's it. Pretty simple, right?

All the magic happens here:

```
UIActivityViewController *activityVC =
            [[UIActivityViewController alloc] initWithActivityItems:items
                applicationActivities:nil];
```

When you instantiate an activity view controller, you pass it an array of activity items. An
activity item can be any object, and it depends on the application and activity service target.
In the previous example code, the activity items were a string and an image. If you want
to use a custom object as an activity item, have it conform to the UIActivityItemSource
protocol. Then you will have complete control over how your custom object presents its data
to the activity view controller.

applicationActivities: expects an array of UIActivity objects. If passed a value of nil,
then the activity view controller will use a default set of Activity objects. Remember we
said earlier you could define your own custom service? You accomplish that by subclassing
UIActivity to define the communication to your service. Then you pass in your subclass as
part of the array of application activities.

Similarly, you can restrict what you want to display as part of UIActivity. This is simple; you can have an array of the items that you do not want to display and then assign them to the excludeActivityTypes property of UIActivityViewController.

```
NSArray *excludeItems = @[UIActivityTypePostToTwitter, UIActivityTypePostToFacebook,
    UIActivityTypePostToWeibo,UIActivityTypeMessage, UIActivityTypeMail,UIActivityTypePrint,
UIActivityTypeCopyToPasteboard,UIActivityTypeAssignToContact,
UIActivityTypeSaveToCameraRoll,UIActivityTypeAddToReadingList,
UIActivityTypePostToFlickr,UIActivityTypePostToVimeo, UIActivityTypePostToTencentWeibo];
activityVC.excludeActivityTypes = excludeItems;
```

This will therefore show only the AirDrop option and hide all of the others.

For the purposes of this chapter, you're just going to use the default list of application activities. Ready? Let's go!

Building the MessageImage Application

Create a new project in Xcode using the Single View Application template. Call the project **MessageImage**.

Building the User Interface

Look back at Figure 11-1. The interface is pretty simple; it contains a single button labeled Go. When you tap the button, the application will activate your device's camera and allow you to take a picture.

Select Main.storyboard.

From the Object Library, drop a button anywhere onto the view. Double-click the button and give it a title of Go. Enter the assistant editor, which should split the Editor pane, and then open ViewController.h. Control-drag from the Go button to between @interface and @end in ViewController.h. Add a new action and name it selectAndMessageImage. Add constraints to center the button horizontally and vertically via the align button or simply Control-drag from the button downward and select Center Horizontally in Container; similarly, Control-drag to the right and select Center Vertically in Container.

Next, drag a label from the library to the view window. Place the label above the button and set constraints via the align button or simply Control-drag from the label to the left and select Center Horizontally in Container. Next Control-drag from the label to the button and select the Vertical Spacing constraint. In the Attributes Inspector, change the text alignment to centered. Control-drag from the label to above the selectAndMessageImage: action you just created in ViewController.h. Add a new outlet and name it label. Finally, double-click the label and erase the text *Label*.

Save the storyboard.

Taking the Picture

Single-click `ViewController.h`. You need your view controller to conform to two delegate protocols.

```
@interface ViewController : UIViewController <UINavigationControllerDelegate,
                                              UIImagePickerControllerDelegate>
```

This is because the image picker controller you'll be using expects its delegate to conform to both `UINavigationControllerDelegate` and `UIImagePickerControllerDelegate`. You're using the image picker controller so you can use the camera and select an image to send. Now you need to add a property for the image you'll select.

```
@property (strong, nonatomic) UIImage *image;
```

That's all you need for now. Let's move on to the view controller implementation file.

Calling the Camera

Select `ViewController.m` to open it in the editor.

You need to implement the action method when the button is tapped.

```
- (IBAction)selectAndMessageImage:(id)sender
{
    UIImagePickerControllerSourceType sourceType = UIImagePickerControllerSourceTypeCamera;
    if (![UIImagePickerController isSourceTypeAvailable:UIImagePickerControllerSourceTypeCamera]) {
        sourceType = UIImagePickerControllerSourceTypePhotoLibrary;
    }

    UIImagePickerController *picker = [[UIImagePickerController alloc] init];
    picker.delegate = self;
    picker.allowsEditing = YES;
    picker.sourceType = sourceType;
    [self presentViewController:picker animated:YES completion:nil];
}
```

Once the Go button is tapped, you set the image source to be the device's camera. If the camera is not available (if you're running on the simulator), you fall back to using the photo library. You set the image picker delegate to be your view controller and allow the image to be edited. Finally, you display the image picker.

Since you set your view controller to be the image picker's delegate, you can add the delegate methods you need. Add the following after the `selectAndMessageImage:` method:

```
#pragma mark - UIImagePickerController Delegate Methods

- (void)imagePickerController:(UIImagePickerController *)picker
      didFinishPickingMediaWithInfo:(NSDictionary *)info
```

```
{
    [picker dismissViewControllerAnimated:YES completion:nil];
    self.image = [info objectForKey:UIImagePickerControllerEditedImage];
}

- (void)imagePickerControllerDidCancel:(UIImagePickerController *)picker
{
    [picker dismissViewControllerAnimated:YES completion:nil];
}
```

Both methods dismiss the image picker, but imagePickerController:didFinishPicking
MediaWithInfo: also sets your image property to the picture you took (or chose).

Let's make sure everything is working. Run the application, take a picture, and tap Use.
Nothing should happen, but that's OK.

Picking the Message Sender

Figure 11-3 shows the activity view controller that gets exposed after you select a picture.
Let's set that up.

First, you'll define a method to show the activity view controller. Open ViewController.h and
add the following method declaration:

```
- (void)showActivityViewController;
```

Next, select ViewController.m and add the method implementation. We added ours after
selectAndMessageImage:.

```
- (void)showActivityViewController
{
    NSString *message = NSLocalizedString(@"I took a picture on my iPhone",
                                          @"I took a picture on my iPhone");
    NSArray *activityItems = @[ message, self.image ];
    UIActivityViewController *activityVC =
        [[UIActivityViewController alloc] initWithActivityItems:activityItems
                                         applicationActivities:nil];
    [self presentViewController:activityVC animated:YES completion:nil];
}
```

Now, you need to call the showActivityViewController method after you've picked your
picture. Add the following line to the end of imagePickerController:didFinishPickingMedia
WithInfo:. You need to delay the presentation of the activity view controller slightly to allow
UIImagePickerController time to be removed from the root view controller.

```
[self performSelector:@selector(showActivityViewController) withObject:nil afterDelay:0.5];
```

Check your work so far. Run the application and confirm the alert sheet appears. That's it. Wow, that was simple.

> **Note**   If you select a service and haven't configured your account information, iOS will pop up an alert telling you to set up an account.

Mailing It In...

In the course of this chapter, you saw how to send an e-mail, an SMS message, or a post to social media services. You should be able to add this functionality to any of your applications.

12

Media Library Access and Playback

Every iOS device, at its core, is a first-class media player. Out of the box, people can listen to music, podcasts, and audio books, as well as watch movies and videos.

iOS SDK applications have always been able to play sounds and music, but Apple has been extending the functionality with each iOS release. iOS 3 gave us the MediaPlayer framework, which, among other things, provided access to the user's audio library; iOS 5 extended this by giving us access to video stored in the user's library. iOS7 gave us speech synthesis and text-to-speech, which are used extensively to powering Siri.

iOS 4 extended the AVFoundation framework, which offers finer control of playing, recording, and editing of media. This control comes at a cost because most of the MediaPlayer framework's functionality is not directly implemented in AVFoundation. Rather, AVFoundation lets you implement custom controls for your specific needs.

In this chapter, you'll develop three applications: a simple audio player, a simple video player, and a combined audio/video player. The first two will use the MediaPlayer framework exclusively. The final application will use the MediaPlayer framework to access the user's media library but then use AVFoundation for playback.

The MediaPlayer Framework

The methods and objects used to access the media library are part of the MediaPlayer framework, which allows applications to play both audio and video. While the framework gives you access to all types of media from the user's library, there are some limitations that allow you to work only with audio files.

The collection of media on your iOS device was once referred as the *iPod library*, a term that we will use interchangeably with *media library*. The latter is probably more accurate because Apple has renamed the music player from iPod to Music and moved video media into an application called Videos. More recently, Apple has gone even further, creating a Podcasts application to handle your podcast collections.

From the perspective of the MediaPlayer framework, the entire media library is represented by the class MPMediaLibrary. You won't use this object often, however. It's primarily used only when you need to be notified of changes made to the library while your application is running. It was rare for changes to be made to the library while your application was running, since such changes usually happened as the result of synchronizing your device with your computer. Nowadays, you can synchronize your music collection directly with the iTunes Store, so you may need to monitor changes in the media library.

A media item is represented by the class MPMediaItem. If you want to play songs from one of your user's playlists, you will use the class MPMediaPlaylist, which represents the playlists that were created in iTunes and synchronized to your user's device. To search for either media items or playlists in the iPod library, you use a media query, which is represented by the class MPMediaQuery. Media queries will return all media items or playlists that match whatever criteria you specify. To specify criteria for a media query, you use a special media-centric form of predicate called a *media property predicate*, represented by the class MPMediaPropertyPredicate.

Another way to let your user select media items is to use the media picker controller, which is an instance of MPMediaPickerController. The media picker controller allows your users to use the same basic interface they are accustomed to using from the iPod or Music application.

You can play media items using a player controller. There are two kinds of player controllers: MPMusicPlayerController and MPMoviePlayerController. The MPMusicPlayerController is not a view controller. It is responsible for playing audio and managing a list of audio items to be played. Generally speaking, you are expected to provide any necessary user interface elements, such as buttons to play, pause, skip forward, or skip backward. The MediaPlayer framework provides a view controller class, MPMoviePlayerViewController, to allow for the simple management of a full-screen movie player within your applications.

If you want to specify a list of media items to be played by a player controller, you use a media item collection, represented by instances of the class MPMediaItemCollection. Media item collections are immutable collections of media items. A media item may appear in more than one spot in the collection, meaning you could conceivably create a collection that played "Happy Birthday to You" a thousand times, followed by a single playing of "Rock the Casbah." You could do that…if you really wanted.

Media Items

The class that represents media items, MPMediaItem, works a little differently than most Objective-C classes. You would probably expect MPMediaItem to include properties for things such as title, artist, album name, and the like. But that is not the case. Other than those inherited from NSObject and the two NSCoding methods used to allow archiving, MPMediaItem includes only a single instance method called valueForProperty.

valueForProperty works much like an instance of NSDictionary, only with a limited set of defined keys. So, for example, if you wanted to retrieve a media item's title, you would call valueForProperty and specify the key MPMediaItemPropertyTitle, and the method would return an NSString instance with the audio track's title. Media items are immutable on the iOS, so all MPMediaItem properties are read-only.

Some media item properties are said to be filterable. Filterable media item properties are those that can be searched on, a process you'll look at a little later in the chapter.

Media Item Persistent ID

Every media item has a persistent identifier (or *persistent ID*), which is a number associated with the item that won't ever change. If you need to store a reference to a particular media item, you should store the persistent ID, because it is generated by iTunes and you can count on it staying the same over time.

You can retrieve the persistent ID of a media track using the property key MPMediaItemPropertyPersistentID, like so:

```
NSNumber *persistentId = [mediaItem valueForProperty:MPMediaItemPropertyPersistentID];
```

The persistent ID is a filterable property, which means you can use a media query to find an item based on its persistent ID. Storing the media item's persistent ID is the surest way to guarantee you'll get the same object each time you search. We'll talk about media queries a bit later in the chapter.

Media Type

All media items have a type associated with them. Currently, media items are classified using three categories: audio, video, and generic. You can determine a particular media item's type by asking for the MPMediaItemPropertyMediaType property, like so:

```
NSNumber *type = [mediaItem valueForProperty:MPMediaItemPropertyMediaType];
```

Media items may consist of more than a single type. A podcast, for example, could be a reading of an audio book. As a result, the media type is implemented as a bit field (sometimes called *bit flags*).

Note   Bit fields are commonly used in C, and Apple employs them in many places throughout its frameworks. If you're not completely sure how bit fields are used, you can check out Chapter 11 of *Learn C on the Mac for OS X and iOS* by David Mark and James Bucanek (Apress, 2012). You can find a good summary of the concept on Wikipedia as well at http://en.wikipedia.org/wiki/Bitwise_operation.

With bit fields, a single integer datatype is used to represent multiple, nonexclusive Boolean values, rather than a single number. To convert type (an object) into an NSInteger, which is the documented integer type used to hold media types, use the integerValue method, like so:

```
NSInteger mediaType = [type integerValue];
```

At this point, each bit of mediaType represents a single type. To determine whether a media item is a particular type, you need to use the bitwise AND operator (&) to compare mediaType with system-defined constants that represent the available media types. Here is a list of the current constants:

- MPMediaTypeMusic: Used to check whether the media is music

- MPMediaTypePodcast: Used to check whether the media is an audio podcast

- MPMediaTypeAudioBook: Used to check whether the media is an audio book

- MPMediaTypeAudioAny: Used to check whether the media is any audio type

- MPMediaTypeMovie: Used to check whether the media is a movie

- MPMediaTypeTVShow: Used to check whether the media is a television show

- MPMediaTypeVideoPodcast: Used to check whether the media is a video podcast

- MPMediaTypeMusicVideo: Used to check whether the media is a music video

- MPMediaTypeITunesU: Used to check whether the media is an iTunes University video

- MPMediaTypeAnyVideo: Used to check whether the media is any video type

- MPMediaTypeAny: Used to check whether the media is any known type

To check whether a given item contains music, for example, you take the mediaType you retrieved and do this:

```
if (mediaType & MPMediaTypeMusic) {
    // It is music...
}
```

MPMediaTypeMusic's bits are all set to 0, except for the one bit that's used to represent that a track contains music, which is set to 1. When you do a bitwise AND (&) between that constant and the retrieved mediaType value, the resulting value will have 0 in all bits except the one that's being checked. That bit will have a 1 if mediaType has the music bit set or 0 if it doesn't. In Objective-C, an if statement that evaluates a logical AND or OR operation will fire on any nonzero result; the code that follows will run if mediaType's music bit is set; otherwise, it will be skipped.

The media type is a filterable property, so you can specify in your media queries (which we'll talk about shortly) that they should return media of only specific types.

BITWISE MACROS

Not every programmer is comfortable reading code with bitwise operators. If that describes you, don't despair. It's easy to create macros to turn these bitwise checks into C function macros, like so:

```
#define isMusic(x)      (x & MPMediaTypeMusic)
#define isPodcast(x)    (x & MPMediaTypePodcast)
#define isAudioBook(x)  (x & MPMediaTypeAudioBook)
```

Once these are defined, you can check the returned type using more accessible code, like this:

```
if (isMusic([type integerValue])) {
    // Do something
}
```

Filterable Properties

There are several properties that you might want to retrieve from a media item, including the track's title, its genre, the artist, and the album name. In addition to MPMediaItemPropertyPersistentID and MPMediaItemPropertyMediaType, here are the filterable property constants you can use:

- MPMediaItemPropertyAlbumPersistentID: Returns the item's album's persistent ID

- MPMediaItemPropertyArtistPersistentID: Returns the item's artist's persistent ID

- MPMediaItemPropertyAlbumArtistPersistentID: Returns the item's album's principal artist's persistent ID

- MPMediaItemPropertyGenrePersistentID: Returns the item's genre's persistent ID

- MPMediaItemPropertyComposerPersistentID: Returns the item's composer's persistent ID

- MPMediaItemPropertyPodcastPersistentID: Returns the item's podcast's persistent ID

- MPMediaItemPropertyTitle: Returns the item's title, which usually means the name of the song

- MPMediaItemPropertyAlbumTitle: Returns the name of the item's album

- MPMediaItemPropertyArtist: Returns the name of the artist who recorded the item

- MPMediaItemPropertyAlbumArtist: Returns the name of the principal artist behind the item's album

- MPMediaItemPropertyGenre: Returns the item's genre (such as classical, rock, or alternative)

- MPMediaItemPropertyComposer: Returns the name of the item's composer

- MPMediaItemPropertyIsCompilation: If the item is part of a compilation, returns true

- MPMediaItemPropertyPodcastTitle: If the track is a podcast, returns the podcast's name

Although the title and artist will almost always be known, none of these properties is guaranteed to return a value, so it's important to code defensively any time your program logic includes one of these values. Although unlikely, a media track can exist without a specified name or artist.

Here's an example that retrieves a string property from a media item:

```
NSString *title = [mediaItem valueForProperty:MPMediaItemPropertyTitle];
```

Nonfilterable Numerical Attributes

Nearly anything that you can determine about an audio or video item in iTunes can be retrieved from a media item. The values in the following list are not filterable—in other words, you can't use them in your media property predicates. You can't, for example, retrieve all the tracks that are longer than four minutes in length. But once you have a media item, there's a wealth of information available about that item.

- MPMediaItemPropertyPlaybackDuration: Returns the length of the track in seconds

- MPMediaItemPropertyAlbumTrackNumber: Returns the number of this track on its album

- MPMediaItemPropertyAlbumTrackCount: Returns the number of tracks on this track's album

- MPMediaItemPropertyDiscNumber: If the track is from a multiple-album collection, returns the track's disc number

- MPMediaItemPropertyDiscCount: If the track is from a multiple-album collection, returns the total number of discs in that collection

- MPMediaItemPropertyBeatsPerMinute: Returns the beats per minute of the item

- MPMediaItemPropertyReleaseDate: Returns the release date of the item

- MPMediaItemPropertyComments: Returns the item's comments entered in the Get Info tab

Numeric attributes are always returned as instances of NSNumber. The track duration is an NSTimeInterval, which can be retrieved from NSNumber by using the doubleValue method. The rest are unsigned integers that can be retrieved using the unsignedIntegerValue method.

Here are a few examples of retrieving numeric properties from a media item:

```
NSNumber *durationNum = [mediaItem valueForProperty:MPMediaItemPropertyPlaybackDuration];
NSTimeInterval duration = [durationNum doubleValue];

NSNumber *trackNum = [mediaItem valueForProperty:MPMediaItemPropertyAlbumTrackNumber];
NSUInteger trackNumber = [trackNum unsignedIntegerValue];
```

Retrieving Lyrics

If a media track has lyrics associated with it, you can retrieve those using the property key MPMediaItemPropertyLyrics. The lyrics will be returned in an instance of NSString, like so:

```
NSString *lyrics = [mediaItem valueForProperty:MPMediaItemPropertyLyrics];
```

Retrieving Album Artwork

Some media tracks have a piece of artwork associated with them. In most instances, this will be the track's album's cover picture, though it could be something else. You retrieve the album artwork using the property key MPMediaItemPropertyArtwork, which returns an instance of the class MPMediaItemArtwork. The MPMediaItemArtwork class has a method that returns an instance of UIImage to match a specified size. Here's some code to get the album artwork for a media item that would fit into a 100-by-100 pixel view:

```
MPMediaItemArtwork *art = [mediaItem valueForProperty:MPMediaItemPropertyArtwork];
CGSize imageSize = {100.0, 100.0};
UIImage *image = [art imageWithSize:imageSize];
```

User-Defined Properties

Another set of data that you can retrieve from a media item is termed *user-defined*. This data includes properties set on the media item based on the user's interaction. These are properties such as play counts and ratings.

- MPMediaItemPropertyPlayCount: Returns the total number of times that this track has been played

- MPMediaItemPropertySkipCount: Returns the total number of times this track has been skipped

- MPMediaItemPropertyRating: Returns the track's rating, or 0 if the track has not been rated

- MPMediaItemPropertyLastPlayedDate: Returns the date the track was last played

- MPMediaItemPropertyUserGrouping: Returns the information from the Grouping tab of the iTunes Get Info panel

AssetURL Property

There is one last property to mention that was added in iOS 4 for use in AVFoundation. We'll mention it here but discuss it later in the chapter:

MPMediaItemPropertyAssetURL: An NSURL pointing to a media item in the user's media library.

Media Item Collections

Media items can be grouped into collections, creatively called *media item collections*. In fact, this is how you specify a list of media items to be played by the player controllers. Media item collections, which are represented by the class MPMediaItemCollection, are immutable collections of media items. You can create new media item collections, but you can't change the contents of the collection once it has been created.

Creating a New Collection

The easiest way to create a media item collection is to put all the media items you want to be in the collection into an instance of NSArray, in the order you want them. You can then pass the instance of NSArray to the factory method collectionWithItems:, like so:

```
NSArray *items = @[mediaItem1, mediaItem2];
MPMediaItemCollection *collection = [MPMediaItemCollection collectionWithItems:items];
```

Retrieving Media Items

To retrieve a specific media item from a media item collection, you use the instance method items, which returns an NSArray instance containing all of the media items in the order they exist in the collection. If you want to retrieve the specific media item at a particular index, for example, you would do this:

```
MPMediaItem *item = [[mediaCollection items] objectAtIndex:5];
```

Creating Derived Collections

Because media item collections are immutable, you can't add items to a collection, nor can you append the contents of another media item collection onto another one. Since you can get to an array of media items contained in a collection using the instance method items, however, you can make a mutable copy of the items array, manipulate the mutable array's contents, and then create a new collection based on the modified array.

Here's some code that appends a single media item onto the end of an existing collection:

```
NSMutableArray *items = [[originalCollection items] mutableCopy];
[items addObject:mediaItem];
MPMediaItemCollection *newCollection = [MPMediaItemCollection collectionWithItems:items];
```

Similarly, to combine two different collections, you combine their items and create a new collection from the combined array.

```
NSMutableArray *items = [[firstCollection items] mutableCopy];
[items addObjectsFromArray:[secondCollection items]];
MPMediaItemCollection *newCollection = [MPMediaItemCollection collectionWithItems:items];
```

To delete an item or items from an existing collection, you can use the same basic technique. You can retrieve a mutable copy of the items contained in the collection, delete the ones you want to remove, and then create a new collection based on the modified copy of the items, like so:

```
NSMutableArray *items = [[originalCollection items] mutableCopy];
[items removeObject:mediaItemToDelete];
MPMediaItemCollection *newCollection = [MPMediaItemCollection collectionWithItems:items];
```

Media Queries and Media Property Predicates

To search for media items in the media library, you use *media queries*, which are instances of the class MPMediaQuery. A number of factory methods can be used to retrieve media items from the library sorted by a particular property. For example, if you want a list of all media items sorted by artist, you can use the artistsQuery class method to create an instance of MPMediaQuery configured, like this:

```
MPMediaQuery *artistsQuery = [MPMediaQuery artistsQuery];
```

Table 12-1 lists the factory methods on MPMediaQuery.

Table 12-1. MPMediaQuery Factory Methods

Factory Method	Included Media Types	Grouped/Sorted By
albumsQuery	Music	Album
artistsQuery	Music	Artist
audiobooksQuery	Audio books	Title
compilationsQuery	Any	Album*
composersQuery	Any	Composer
genresQuery	Any	Genre
playlistsQuery	Any	Playlist
podcastsQuery	Podcasts	Podcast title
songsQuery	Music	Title

* *Includes only albums with MPMediaItemPropertyIsCompilation set to YES.*

These factory methods are useful for displaying the entire contents of the user's library that meet preset conditions. That said, you will often want to restrict the query to an even smaller subset of items. You can do that using a media predicate. Media predicates can be created on any of the filterable properties of a media item, including the persistent ID, media type, or any of the string properties (such as title, artist, or genre).

To create a media predicate on a filterable property, use the class `MPMediaPropertyPredicate`. Create new instances using the factory method `predicateWith Value:forProperty:comparisonType:`. Here, for example, is how to create a media predicate that searches for all songs with the title "Happy Birthday":

```
MPMediaPropertyPredicate *titlePredicate =
    [MPMediaPropertyPredicate predicateWithValue:@"Happy Birthday"
                               forProperty:MPMediaItemPropertyTitle
                            comparisonType:MPMediaPredicateComparisonContains];
```

The first value you pass—in this case, `@"Happy Birthday"`—is the comparison value. The second value is the filterable property you want that comparison value compared to. By specifying `MPMediaItemPropertyTitle`, you're saying you want the song titles compared to the string `"Happy Birthday"`. The last item specifies the type of comparison to do. You can pass `MPMediaPredicateComparisonEqualTo` to look for an exact match to the specified string or `MPMediaPredicateComparisonContains` to look for any item that contains the passed value as a substring.

> **Note** Media queries are always case-insensitive, regardless of the comparison type used. Therefore, the preceding example would also return songs called "HAPPY BIRTHDAY" and "Happy BirthDAY."

Because you've passed `MPMediaPredicateComparisonContains`, this predicate would match "Happy Birthday, the Opera" and "Slash Sings Happy Birthday," in addition to plain old "Happy Birthday." Had you passed `MPMediaPredicateComparisonEqualTo`, then only the last one—the exact match—would be found.

You can create and pass multiple media property predicates to a single query. If you do, the query will use the AND logical operator and return only the media items that meet all of your predicates.

To create a media query based on media property predicates, you use the `init` method `initWithFilterPredicates:` and pass in an instance of `NSSet` containing all the predicates you want it to use, like so:

```
MPMediaQuery *query =
    [[MPMediaQuery alloc] initWithFilterPredicates:[NSSet setWithObject:titlePredicate]];
```

Once you have a query—whether it was created manually or retrieved using one of the factory methods—there are two ways you can execute the query and retrieve the items to be displayed.

- You can use the `items` property of the query, which returns an instance of `NSArray` containing all the media items that meet the criteria specified in your media property predicates, like so:

  ```
  NSArray *items = query.items;
  ```

- You can use the property collections to retrieve the objects grouped by one of the filterable properties. You can tell the query which property to group the items by via setting the `groupingType` property to the property key for the filterable attribute you want it grouped by. If you don't set `groupingType`, it will default to grouping by title.

When you access the collections property, the query will instead return an array of `MPMediaItemCollections`, with one collection for each distinct value in your grouping type. So, if you specified a `groupingType` of `MPMediaGroupingArtist`, for example, the query would return an array with one `MPMediaItemCollection` for each artist who has at least one song that matches your criteria. Each collection would contain all the songs by that artist that meet the specified criteria. Here's what that might look like in code:

```
query.groupingType = MPMediaGroupingArtist;
NSArray *collections = query.collections;
for (MPMediaItemCollection *oneCollection in collections) {
    // oneCollection has all songs by one artist that meet criteria
}
```

You need to be careful with media queries. They are synchronous and happen in the main thread, so if you specify a query that returns 100,000 media items, your user interface is going to hiccup while those items are found, retrieved, and stored in collections or an array. If you are using a media query that might return more than a dozen or so media items, you might want to consider moving that action off the main thread. You'll learn how to move operations off the main thread in Chapter 14.

The Media Picker Controller

If you want to let your users select specific media items from their library, you'll want to use the media picker controller. The media picker controller lets your users choose audio from their iPod library using an interface that's nearly identical to the one in the Music application they're already used to using. Your users will not be able to use Cover Flow, but they will be able to select from lists sorted by song title, artist, playlist, album, and genre, just as they can when selecting music in the Music application (Figure 12-1).

Figure 12-1. The media picker controller by artist, song, and album

The media picker controller is extremely easy to use. It works just like many of the other provided controller classes covered in the previous chapters, such as the image picker controller and the mail compose view controller that you used in Chapter 11. Create an instance of MPMediaPickerController, assign it a delegate, and then present it modally, like so:

```
MPMediaPickerController *picker = [[MPMediaPickerController alloc] initWithMediaTypes:MPMed
iaTypeMusic];
picker.delegate = self;
[picker setAllowsPickingMultipleItems:YES];
picker.prompt = NSLocalizedString(@"Select items to play", @"Select items to play");
[self presentViewController:picker animated:YES completion:nil];
```

When you create the media picker controller instance, you need to specify a media type. This can be one of the three audio types mentioned earlier—MPMediaTypeMusic, MPMediaTypePodcast, or MPMediaTypeAudioBook. You can also pass MPMediaTypeAnyAudio, which will currently return any audio item.

> **Note**   Passing nonaudio media types will not cause any errors in your code, but when the media picker appears, it will display only audio items.

You can also use the bitwise OR (|) operator to let your user select any combination of media types. For example, if you want to let your user select from podcasts and audio books but not music, you could create your picker like this:

```
MPMediaPickerController *picker =
    [[MPMediaPickerController alloc] initWithMediaTypes:MPMediaTypePodcast |
    MPMediaTypeAudioBook];
```

By using the bitwise OR operator with these constants, you end up passing an integer that has the bits representing both of these media types set to 1 and all the other bits set to 0.

Also notice that you need to tell the media picker controller to allow the user to select multiple items. The default behavior of the media picker is to let the user choose one, and only one, item. If that's the behavior you want, then you don't have to do anything, but if you want to let the user select multiple items, you must explicitly tell it so.

The media picker also has a property called prompt, which is a string that will be displayed above the navigation bar in the picker (see the top of Figure 12-1). This is optional but generally a good idea.

The media picker controller's delegate needs to conform to the protocol MPMediaPickerControllerDelegate. This defines two methods: one that is called if the user taps the Cancel button and another that is called if the user chooses one or more songs.

Handling Media Picker Cancels

If, after you present the media picker controller, the user hits the Cancel button, the delegate method mediaPickerDidCancel: will be called. You must implement this method on the media picker controller's delegate, even if you don't have any processing that needs to be done when the user cancels, since you must dismiss the modal view controller. Here is a minimal, but fairly standard, implementation of that method:

```
- (void)mediaPickerDidCancel:(MPMediaPickerController *)mediaPicker
{
    [self dismissViewControllerAnimated:YES completion:nil];
}
```

Handling Media Picker Selections

If the user selected one or more media items using the media picker controller, then the delegate method mediaPicker:didPickMediaItems: will be called. This method must be implemented, not only because it's the delegate's responsibility to dismiss the media picker controller but also because this method is the only way to know which tracks your user selected. The selected items are grouped in a media item collection.

Here's a simple example implementation of mediaPicker:didPickMediaItems: that assigns the returned collection to one of the delegate's properties:

```
- (void)mediaPicker:(MPMediaPickerController *)mediaPicker
        didPickMediaItems: (MPMediaItemCollection *)theCollection
{
    [self dismissModalViewControllerAnimated: YES];
    self.collection = theCollection;
}
```

The Music Player Controller

As we discussed earlier, there are two player controllers in the MediaPlayer framework: the music player controller and the movie player controller. We'll get to the movie player controller later. The music player controller allows you to play a queue of media items by specifying either a media item collection or a media query. As we stated earlier, the music player controller has no visual elements. It's an object that plays the audio. It allows you to manipulate the playback of that audio by skipping forward or backward, telling it which specific media item to play, adjusting the volume, or skipping to a specific playback time in the current item.

The MediaPlayer framework offers two completely different kinds of music player controllers: the iPod music player and the application music player. The way you use them is identical, but there's a key difference in how they work. The iPod music player is the one that's used by the Music app; as is the case with those apps, when you quit your app while music is playing, the music continues playing. In addition, when the user is listening to music and starts up an app that uses the iPod music player, the iPod music player will keep playing that music. In contrast, the application music player will kill the music when your app terminates.

There's a bit of a gotcha here in that both the iPod and the application music player controllers can be used at the same time. If you use the application music player controller to play audio and the user is currently listening to music, both will play simultaneously. This may or may not be what you want to happen, so you will usually want to check the iPod music player to see whether there is music currently playing, even if you actually plan to use the application music player controller for playback.

Creating the Music Player Controller

To get either of the music player controllers, use one of the factory methods on MPMusicPlayerController. To retrieve the iPod music player, use the method iPodMusicPlayer, like so:

```
MPMusicPlayerController *thePlayer = [MPMusicPlayerController iPodMusicPlayer];
```

Retrieving the application music player controller is done similarly, using the applicationMusicPlayer method instead, like this:

```
MPMusicPlayerController *thePlayer = [MPMusicPlayerController applicationMusicPlayer];
```

Determining Whether the Music Player Controller Is Playing

Once you create an application music player, you'll need to give it something to play. But if you grab the iPod music player controller, it could very well already be playing something. You can determine whether it is by looking at the playbackState property of the player. If it's currently playing, it will be set to MPMusicPlaybackStatePlaying.

```
if (player.playbackState == MPMusicPlaybackStatePlaying) {
    // playing
}
```

Specifying the Music Player Controller's Queue

There are two ways to specify the music player controller's queue of audio tracks: provide a media query or provide a media item collection. If you provide a media query, the music player controller's queue will be set to the media items returned by the items property. If you provide a media item collection, it will use the collection you pass as its queue. In either case, you will replace the existing queue with the items in the query or collection you pass in. Setting the queue will also reset the current track to the first item in the queue.

To set the music player's queue using a query, use the method setQueueWithQuery:. For example, here's how you would set the queue to all songs, sorted by artist:

```
MPMusicPlayerController *player = [MPMusicPlayerController iPodMusicPlayer];
MPMediaQuery *artistsQuery = [MPMediaQuery artistsQuery];
[player setQueueWithQuery:artistsQuery];
```

Setting the queue with a media item collection is accomplished with the method
setQueueWithItemCollection:, like so:

```
MPMusicPlayerController *player = [MPMusicPlayerController iPodMusicPlayer];
NSArray *items = [NSArray arrayWithObjects:mediaItem1, mediaItem2, nil];
MPMediaItemCollection *collection = [MPMediaItemCollection collectionWithItems:items];
[items setQueueWithItemCollection:collection];
```

Unfortunately, there's currently no way to retrieve the music player controller's queue using
public APIs. That means you will generally need to keep track of the queue independently of
the music player controller if you want to be able to manipulate the queue.

Getting or Setting the Currently Playing Media Item

You can get or set the current song using the nowPlayingItem property. This lets you
determine which track is already playing if you're using the iPod music player controller and
lets you specify a new song to play. Note that the media item you specify must already be in
the music player controller's queue. Here's how you retrieve the currently playing item:

```
MPMediaItem *currentTrack = player.nowPlayingItem;
To switch to a different track, do this:
player.nowPlayingItem = newTrackToPlay; // must be in queue already
```

Skipping Tracks

The music player controller allows you to skip forward one song using the method
skipToNextItem or to skip back to the previous song using skipToPreviousItem. If there is
no next or previous song to skip to, the music player controller stops playing. The music
player controller also allows you to move back to the beginning of the current song using
skipToBeginning.

Here is an example of all three methods:

```
[player skipToNextItem];
[player skipToPreviousItem];
[player skipToBeginning];
```

Seeking

When you're using your iPhone, iPod touch, or iTunes to listen to music, if you tap and
hold the forward or back button, the music will start seeking forward or backward, playing
the music at an ever-accelerating pace. This lets you, for example, stay in the same track
but skip over a part you don't want to listen to or skip back to something you missed.
This same functionality is available through the music player controller using the methods
beginSeekingForward and beginSeekingBackward. With both methods, you stop the process
with a call to endSeeking.

Here is a set of calls that demonstrate seeking forward and stopping and then seeking backward and stopping:

```
[player beginSeekingForward];
[player endSeeking];

[player beginSeekingBackward];
[player endSeeking];
```

Playback Time

Not to be confused with payback time (something we've dreamt of for years, ever since they replaced the excellent Dick York with the far blander Dick Sargent), playback time specifies how far into the current song you currently are. If the current song has been playing for five seconds, then the playback time will be 5.0.

You can retrieve and set the current playback time using the property currentPlaybackTime. You might use this, for example, when using an application music player controller, to resume a song at exactly the point where it was stopped when the application was last quit. Here's an example of using this property to skip forward ten seconds in the current song:

```
NSTimeInterval currentTime = player.currentPlaybackTime;
MPMediaItem *currentSong = player.nowPlayingItem;
NSNumber *duration = [currentSong valueForProperty:
MPMediaItemPropertyPlaybackDuration];
currentTime += 10.0;
if (currentTime > [duration doubleValue])
    currentTime = [duration doubleValue];
player.currentPlaybackTime = currentTime;
```

Notice that you check the duration of the currently playing song to make sure you don't pass in an invalid playback time.

Repeat and Shuffle Modes

Music player controllers have ordered queues of songs, and most of the time, they play those songs in the order they exist in the queue, playing from the beginning of the queue to the end and then stopping. Your user can change this behavior by setting the repeat and shuffle properties in the iPod or Music application. You can also change the behavior by setting the music player controller's repeat and shuffle modes, represented by the properties repeatMode and shuffleMode. There are four repeat modes.

- MPMusicRepeatModeDefault: Uses the repeat mode last used in the iPod or Music application.

- MPMusicRepeatModeNone: Don't repeat at all. When the queue is done, stop playing.

- MPMusicRepeatModeOne: Keep repeating the currently playing track until your user goes insane. Ideal for playing "It's a Small World."

- MPMusicRepeatModeAll: When the queue is done, start over with the first track.

There are also four shuffle modes.

- MPMusicShuffleModeDefault: Use the shuffle mode last used in the iPod or Music application.

- MPMusicShuffleModeOff: Don't shuffle at all—just play the songs in the queue order.

- MPMusicShuffleModeSongs: Play all the songs in the queue in random order.

- MPMusicShuffleModeAlbums: Play all the songs from the currently playing song's album in random order.

Here is an example of turning off both repeat and shuffle:

```
player.repeatMode = MPMusicRepeatNone;
player.shuffleMode = MPMusicShuffleModeOff;
```

Adjusting the Music Player Controller's Volume

As of iOS 7, the volume property of MediaPlayer is deprecated. You cannot simply use thePlayer.volume = 0.5 or a value between 0.0 and 1.0 to set the volume. Instead, you have to now use the MPVolumeView; this is a volume slider that allows you to adjust the volume of the device and also provides you with the functionality to play the audio via a connected AirPlay destination. This is a view object, so it needs to be created and added to a view hierarchy to be displayed and interacted with.

```
MPVolumeView *myVolumeView = [[MPVolumeView alloc]init];
[myVolumeView sizeToFit];

[self.view addSubview:myVolumeView];
```

Music Player Controller Notifications

Music player controllers are capable of sending out notifications when any of three things happen.

- When the playback state (playing, stopped, paused, seeking, and so on) changes, the music player controller can send out the MPMusicPlayerControllerPlaybackStateDidChangeNotification notification.

- When the volume changes, it can send out the MPMusicPlayerControllerVolumeDidChangeNotification notification.

- When a new track starts playing, it can send out the MPMusicPlayerControllerNowPlayingItemDidChangeNotification notification.

Note that music player controllers don't send any notifications by default. You must tell an instance of MPMusicPlayerController to start generating notifications by calling the method beginGeneratingPlaybackNotifications. To have the controller stop generating notifications, call the method endGeneratingPlaybackNotifications.

If you need to receive any of these notifications, you first implement a handler method that takes one argument, an NSNotification *, and then register with the Notification Center for the notification of interest. For example, if you want a method to fire whenever the currently playing item changed, you could implement a method called nowPlayingItemChanged:, like so:

```
- (void)nowPlayingItemChanged:(NSNotification *)notification {
    NSLog(@"A new track started");
}
```

To start listening for those notifications, you could register with the notification for the type of notification you're interested in and then have that music player controller start generating the notifications.

```
NSNotificationCenter *notificationCenter = [NSNotificationCenter defaultCenter];
[notificationCenter addObserver:self
                    selector:@selector(nowPlayingItemChanged:)
                        name:MPMusicPlayerControllerNowPlayingItemDidChangeNotification
                      object:player];
[player beginGeneratingPlaybackNotifications];
```

Once you do this, any time the track changes, your nowPlayingItemChanged: method will be called by the Notification Center.

When you're finished and no longer need the notifications, you unregister and tell the music player controller to stop generating notifications.

```
NSNotificationCenter *center = [NSNotificationCenter defaultCenter];
[center removeObserver:self
                  name:MPMusicPlayerControllerNowPlayingItemDidChangeNotification
                object:player];
[player endGeneratingPlaybackNotifications];
```

Now that you have all that theory out of the way, let's build something!

Simple Music Player

The first application you'll build is going to put to use what we've covered so far to build a simple music player. The application will allow users to create a queue of songs via the MPMediaPickerController and play them back via the MPMusicPlayerController.

> **Note** We'll use the term *queue* to describe the application's list of songs, rather than the term *playlist*. When working with the media library, the term *playlist* refers to actual playlists synchronized from iTunes. Those playlists can be read, but they can't be created using the SDK. To avoid confusion, we'll stick with the term *queue*.

When the application launches, it will check to see whether music is currently playing. If so, it will allow that music to keep playing and will append any requested music to the end of the list of songs to be played.

> **Tip**   If your application needs to play a certain sound or music, you may feel that it's appropriate to turn off the user's currently playing music, but you should do that with caution. If you're just providing a soundtrack, you really should consider letting the music that's playing continue playing, or at least giving the users the choice about whether to turn off their chosen music in favor of your application's music. It is, of course, your call, but tread lightly when it comes to stomping on your user's music.

The application you'll build isn't very practical because everything you're offering to your users (and more) is already available in the Music application on your iOS device. But writing it will allow you to explore almost all of the tasks your own application might ever need to perform with regard to the media library.

> **Caution**   This chapter's application must be run on an actual iOS. The iOS simulator does not have access to the iTunes library on your computer, and any of the calls related to the iTunes library access APIs will result in an error on the simulator.

Building the SimplePlayer Application

Your app will retrieve the iPod music player controller and allow you to add songs to the queue by using the media picker. You'll provide some rudimentary playback controls to play/pause the music, as well as to skip forward and backward in the queue.

> **Note**   As a reminder, the simulator does not yet support the media library functionality. To get the most out of the SimplePlayer application, you need to run it on your iOS device, which means signing up for one of Apple's paid iOS Developer Programs. If you have not already done that, you might want to take a short break and head over to `http://developer.apple.com/programs/register/` to check it out.

Let's start by creating a new project in Xcode. Since this is a simple application, you'll use the Single View Application project template and name the new project SimplePlayer. Since you have only one view, you don't need your project to use storyboards (though you can use them if you want).

Once your new project is created, you need to add the MediaPlayer framework to the project. Select the SimplePlayer project at the top of the Navigator Pane. In the Project Editor, select the SimplePlayer target and open the Build Phases pane. Find the Link Binary With Libraries (0 Items) section and expand it. Click the + button at the bottom of the section and add the MediaPlayer framework. If you've done this correctly, the MediaPlayer. framework should appear in the project in the Navigator pane. Let's keep things clean and create a group called Frameworks to move the MediaPlayer.framework to.

Building the User Interface

Single-click Main.storyboard to open Interface Builder. Take a look at Figure 12-2. There are three labels along the top, an image view in the middle, and a button bar on the bottom with four buttons. Let's start from the bottom and work our way up.

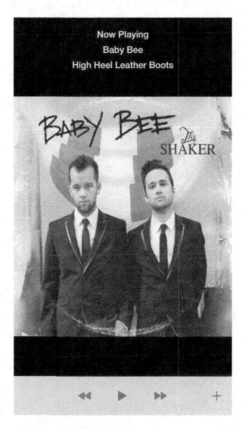

Figure 12-2. The SimplePlayer application playing a song

Drag a UIToolbar from the Object Library to the bottom of the UIView. By default, the UIToolbar gives you a UIBarButtonItem aligned to the left side of the toolbar. Since you need four buttons in your toolbar, you'll keep this button. Drag a flexible space bar button item (Figure 12-3) to the left of the UIBarButtonItem. Make sure you use the flexible space, not the fixed space. If you placed it in the correct spot, the UIBarButtonItem should now be aligned to the right side of the UIToolbar (Figure 12-4).

Figure 12-3. *The flexible space bar button item in the Object Library*

Figure 12-4. *The SimplePlayer toolbar with the flexible space*

Add three UIBarButtonItems to the left of the flexible space. These will be your playback control buttons. To center these buttons, you need to add one more flexible space bar button item to the left side of your UIToolbar (Figure 12-5). Select the leftmost button and open the Attributes Inspector. Change the identifier from Custom to Rewind (Figure 12-6). Select the button to the right of your new Rewind button and change the identifier to Play. Change the identifier to right of your Play button to Fast Forward. Select the rightmost button and change the identifier to Add. When you're done, it should look like Figure 12-7.

Figure 12-5. *Toolbar with all your buttons*

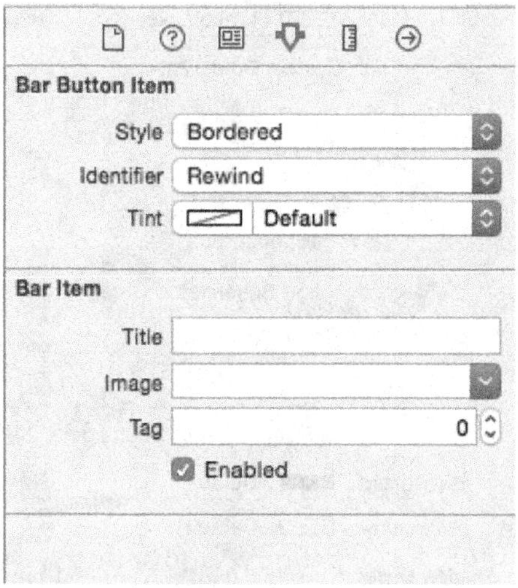

Figure 12-6. *Changing the bar button item identifier to Rewind*

Figure 12-7. *The completed toolbar*

Moving up the view, you need to add a UIImageView. Drag one onto your view, above the toolbar. Interface Builder will expand the UIImageView to fill the available area. Since you don't want that, open the Size Inspector in the Utility pane. The UIImageView should be selected, but if it isn't, select it to make sure you're adjusting the right component. The Size Inspector should show that your UIImageView width is 320. Change the height to match the width. Your image view should now be square. Center the image view in your view, using the guidelines to help.

Now you need to add the three labels across the top. Drag a label to the top of your application's view. Extend the area of the label to the width of your view. Open the Attributes Inspector and change the label text from Label to Now Playing. Change the label's color from black to white, and set the font to System Bold 17.0. Set the alignment to center. Finally, change the label's background color to black (Figure 12-8). Add another label below this label. Give it the same attributes as the first label, but set the text from Label to Artist. Add one more label, below the Artist label, with the same attribute settings, and set the text to Song.

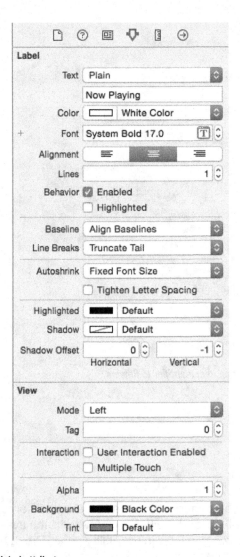

Figure 12-8. Your SimplePlayer label attributes

Finally, set the background of your view to black (because black is cool).

Declaring Outlets and Actions

In Interface Builder, switch from the Standard editor to the Assistant editor. The Editor pane should split to show Interface Builder on the left and ViewController.h on the right. Control-drag from the label with the text Now Playing to just below the @interface declaration. Create a UILabel outlet and name it status. Repeat for the Artist and Song labels, naming the outlets artist and song, respectively.

Control-drag from the image view to below the label outlets and create a UIImageView outlet named imageView. Do the same for the toolbar and the Play button. Now that you have your outlets set up, you need to add your actions.

Control-drag from the rewindButton and create an action named rewindPressed. Repeat for each button. Name the play action playPausePressed, the fast-forward action fastForwardPressed, and the add action addPressed.

Switch back to the Standard editor and select ViewController.h to open it in the editor.

First, you need to have your ViewController conform to the MPMediaPickerDelegate protocol, so you can use the MPMediaPicker controller. To do that, you need to import the MediaPlayer header file, right after the UIKit header import.

```
#import <MediaPlayer/MediaPlayer.h>
```

Then you'll add the protocol declaration to ViewController.

```
@interface ViewController : UIViewController <MPMediaPickerControllerDelegate>
```

You need to add another UIBarButtonItem property to hold the Pause button you'll display while music is playing. You also need to change the Play button property from weak to strong so you can toggle between the two.

```
@property (strong, nonatomic) IBOutlet UIBarButtonItem *play;
@property (strong, nonatomic)         UIBarButtonItem *pause;
```

You need two more properties: one to hold your MPMediaPlayerController instance and the other to hold the MPMediaItemCollection that the player is playing.

```
@property (strong, nonatomic) MPMusicPlayerController *player;
@property (strong, nonatomic) MPMediaItemCollection   *collection;
```

When the MPMusicPlayerController starts playing a new media item, it sends a notification of type MPMusicPlayerControllerNowPlayingItemDidChangeNotification. You'll set up an observer for that notification to update the labels in your view.

```
- (void)nowPlayingItemChanged:(NSNotification *)notification;
```

Select ViewController.m to open it in the Editor pane. First you need to set up things for when the view loads. Find the viewDidLoad method. After the call to super, you need to instantiate the Pause button.

```
self.pause = [[UIBarButtonItem alloc] initWithBarButtonSystemItem:UIBarButtonSystemItemPause
                                            target:self
                                            action:@selector(playPausePressed:)];
[self.pause setStyle:UIBarButtonItemStylePlain];
```

Next, create your MPMusicPlayerController instance.

```
self.player = [MPMusicPlayerController systemMusicPlayer];
```

Then register for the notification when the Now Playing item changes in the player.

```
NSNotificationCenter *notificationCenter = [NSNotificationCenter defaultCenter];
[notificationCenter addObserver:self
                    selector:@selector(nowPlayingItemChanged:)
                        name:MPMusicPlayerControllerNowPlayingItemDidChangeNotification
                      object:self.player];
[self.player beginGeneratingPlaybackNotifications];
```

Note that you must tell the player to begin generating playback notifications. Since you registered for notifications, you have to remove your observer when the view is released.

```
- (void)didReceiveMemoryWarning
{
    [super didReceiveMemoryWarning];
    // Dispose of any resources that can be recreated.
    [[NSNotificationCenter defaultCenter]
        removeObserver:self
                  name:MPMusicPlayerControllerNowPlayingItemDidChangeNotification
                object:self.player];
}
```

Let's work on the button actions next. When the user taps the Rewind button, you want the player to skip to the previous song in the queue. However, if it's at the first song in the queue, it'll just skip to the beginning of that song.

```
- (IBAction)rewindPressed:(id)sender
{
    if ([self.player indexOfNowPlayingItem] == 0) {
        [self.player skipToBeginning];
    }
    else {
        [self.player endSeeking];
        [self.player skipToPreviousItem];
    }
}
```

When the Play button is tapped, you want to start playing the music. You also want to the button to change to the Pause button. Then, if the player is already playing music, you want to player to pause (stop) and have the button change back to the Play button.

```objc
- (IBAction)playPausePressed:(id)sender
{
    MPMusicPlaybackState playbackState = [self.player playbackState];
    NSMutableArray *items = [NSMutableArray arrayWithArray:[self.toolbar items]];
    if (playbackState == MPMusicPlaybackStateStopped || playbackState ==
    MPMusicPlaybackStatePaused) {
        [self.player play];
        [items replaceObjectAtIndex:2 withObject:self.pause];
    }
    else if (playbackState == MPMusicPlaybackStatePlaying) {
        [self.player pause];
        [items replaceObjectAtIndex:2 withObject:self.play];
    }
    [self.toolbar setItems:items animated:NO];
}
```

You query the player for its playback state and then use it to determine whether you should start or stop the player. To toggle between the Play and Pause buttons, you need to get the array of items in the toolbar and replace the third item (index of 2) with the appropriate button. Then you replace the entire array of bar button items for the toolbar.

The Fast Forward button works similarly to the Rewind button. When it's tapped, the player moves forward in the queue and plays the next song. If it's at the last song in the queue, it stops the player and resets the Play button.

```objc
- (IBAction)fastForwardPressed:(id)sender
{
    NSUInteger nowPlayingIndex = [self.player indexOfNowPlayingItem];
    [self.player endSeeking];
    [self.player skipToNextItem];
    if ([self.player nowPlayingItem] == nil) {
        if ([self.collection count] > nowPlayingIndex+1) {
            // added more songs while playing
            [self.player setQueueWithItemCollection:self.collection];
            MPMediaItem *item = [[self.collection items] objectAtIndex:nowPlayingIndex+1];
            [self.player setNowPlayingItem:item];
            [self.player play];
        }
        else {
            // no more songs
            [self.player stop];
            NSMutableArray *items = [NSMutableArray arrayWithArray:[self.toolbar items]];
            [items replaceObjectAtIndex:2 withObject:self.play];
            [self.toolbar setItems:items];
        }
    }
}
```

When the Add button is tapped, you need to modally display the `MPMediaPickerController`. You set it to display only music media types and set its delegate to `ViewController`.

```
- (IBAction)addPressed:(id)sender
{
    MPMediaType mediaType = MPMediaTypeMusic;
    MPMediaPickerController *picker =
        [[MPMediaPickerController alloc] initWithMediaTypes:mediaType];
    picker.delegate = self;
    [picker setAllowsPickingMultipleItems:YES];
    picker.prompt = NSLocalizedString(@"Select items to play", @"Select items to play");
    [self presentViewController:picker animated:YES completion:nil];
}
```

This seems like a good point to add the `MPMediaPickerControllerDelegate` methods. There are only two methods that are defined in the protocol: `mediaPicker:didPickMediaItems:`, called when the user is done selecting, and `mediaPickerDidCancel:`, called when the user has canceled the media selection.

```
#pragma mark - Media Picker Delegate Methods

- (void)mediaPicker:(MPMediaPickerController *)mediaPicker
        didPickMediaItems:(MPMediaItemCollection *)theCollection
{
    [mediaPicker dismissViewControllerAnimated:YES completion:nil];

    if (self.collection == nil) {
        self.collection = theCollection;
        [self.player setQueueWithItemCollection:self.collection];
        MPMediaItem *item = [[self.collection items] objectAtIndex:0];
        [self.player setNowPlayingItem:item];
        [self playPausePressed:self];
    }
    else {
        NSArray *oldItems = [self.collection items];
        NSArray *newItems = [oldItems arrayByAddingObjectsFromArray:[theCollection items]];
        self.collection = [[MPMediaItemCollection alloc] initWithItems:newItems];
    }
}

- (void)mediaPickerDidCancel:(MPMediaPickerController *) mediaPicker
{
    [mediaPicker dismissViewControllerAnimated:YES completion:nil];
}
```

When the user is done selecting, you dismiss the media picker controller. Then you look at the media collection property. If your `ViewController` collection property is nil, then you simply assign it to the media collection sent in the delegate call. If a collection exists, then you need to append the new media items to the existing collection. The `mediaPickerDidCancel:` method simply dismissed the media picker controller.

Lastly, you need to implement the notification method for when the Now Playing item changes.

```
#pragma mark - Notification Methods

- (void)nowPlayingItemChanged:(NSNotification *)notification
{
        MPMediaItem *currentItem = [self.player nowPlayingItem];
    if (currentItem == nil) {
        [self.imageView setImage:nil];
        [self.imageView setHidden:YES];
        [self.status setText:NSLocalizedString (@"Tap + to Add More Music", @"Add More
        Music")];
        [self.artist setText:nil];
        [self.song setText:nil];
    }
    else {
        MPMediaItemArtwork *artwork = [currentItem valueForProperty:
        MPMediaItemPropertyArtwork];
        if (artwork) {
            UIImage *artworkImage = [artwork imageWithSize:CGSizeMake(320, 320)];
            [self.imageView setImage:artworkImage];
            [self.imageView setHidden:NO];
        }

        // Display the artist and song name for the now-playing media item
        [self.status setText:NSLocalizedString(@"Now Playing", @"Now Playing")];
        [self.artist setText:[currentItem valueForProperty:MPMediaItemPropertyArtist]];
        [self.song setText:[currentItem valueForProperty:MPMediaItemPropertyTitle]];
    }
}
```

The nowPlayingItemChanged: method first queries the player for the media item that it is playing. If it is not playing anything, it resets the view and sets the status label to tell the user to add more music. If something is playing, then it retrieves the artwork for the media item using the MPMediaItemPropertyArtwork property. It checks to make sure the media item has artwork, and if it does, it puts it in your image view. Then you update the labels to tell you the artist and song name.

Build and run the SimplePlayer application. You should be able to select music from your media library and play it. This is a pretty simple player (duh) and doesn't give you much in terms of functionality, but you can see how to use the MediaPlayer framework to play music. Next, you'll use the MediaPlayer framework to playback video as well.

MPMoviePlayerController

Playing back video with the MediaPlayer framework is simple. First, you need the URL of the media item you want to play back. The URL can point either to a video file in your media library or to a video resource on the Internet. If you want to play a video in your media library, you can retrieve the URL from an MPMediaItem via its MPMediaItemPropertyAssetURL.

```
// videoMediaItem is an instance of MPMediaItem that point to a video in our media library
NSURL *url = [videoMediaItem valueForProperty:MPMediaItemPropertyAssetURL];
```

Once you have your video URL, you use it to create an instance of MPMoviePlayerController. This view controller handles the playback of your video and the built-in playback controls. The MPMoviePlayerController has a UIView property where the playback is presented. This UIView can be integrated into your application's view (controller) hierarchy. It is much easier to use the MPMoviePlayerViewController class, which encapsulates the MPMoviePlayerController. Then you can push the MPMoviePlayerViewController into you view (controller) hierarchy modally, making it much easier to manage. The MPMoviePlayerViewController class gives you access to its underlying MPMoviePlayerController as a property.

To determine the state of your video media in the MPMoviePlayerController, a series of notifications are sent (Table 12-2).

Table 12-2. *MPMoviePlayerController Notifications*

Notification	Description
MPMovieDurationAvailableNotification	The movie (video) duration (length) has been determined.
MPMovieMediaTypesAvailableNotification	The movie (video) media types (formats) have been determined.
MPMovieNaturalSizeAvailableNotification	The movie (video) natural (preferred) frame size has been determined or changed.
MPMoviePlayerDidEnterFullscreenNotification	The player has entered full-screen mode.
MPMoviePlayerDidExitFullscreenNotification	The player has exited full-screen mode.
MPMoviePlayerIsAirPlayVideoActiveDidChange Notification	The player has started or finished playing the movie (video) via AirPlay.
MPMoviePlayerLoadStateDidChangeNotification	The player (network) buffering state has changed.
MPMoviePlayerNowPlayingMovieDidChange Notification	The current playing movie (video) has changed.

(continued)

Table 12-2. (*continued*)

Notification	Description
MPMoviePlayerPlaybackDidFinishNotification	The player is finished playing. The reason can be found via the MPMoviePlayerDidFinish ReasonUserInfoKey.
MPMoviePlayerPlaybackStateDidChangeNotification	The player playback state has changed.
MPMoviePlayerScalingModeDidChangeNotification	The player scaling mode has changed.
MPMoviePlayerThumbnailImageRequest DidFinishNotification	A request to capture a thumbnail image has completed. It may have succeeded or failed.
MPMoviePlayerWillEnterFullscreenNotification	The player is about to enter full-screen mode.
MPMoviePlayerWillExitFullscreenNotification	The player is about to exit full-screen mode.
MPMovieSourceTypeAvailableNotification	The movie (video) source type was unknown and is now known.

Generally, you only need to worry about these notifications if you use MPMoviePlayerController.

Enough talk. Let's build an app that plays both audio and video media from your media library.

MPMediaPlayer

You're going to build a new app using the MediaPlayer framework that will allow you to play both audio and video content from your media library. You'll start with a tab bar controller with a tab for your audio content and another tab for your video content (Figure 12-9). You won't be using a queue to order your media choices. You'll keep this simple: the user picks a media item, and the application will play it.

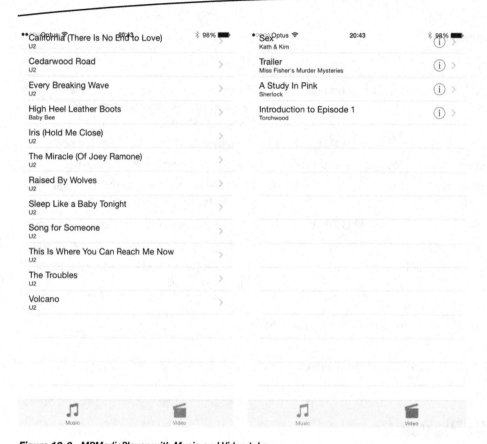

Figure 12-9. MPMediaPlayer with Music and Video tabs

Create a new project using the Tabbed Application template. Name the application MPMediaPlayer and have the project use storyboards and Automatic Reference Counting. Add the MediaPlayer framework to the MPMediaPlayer target. If you're not sure how to do that, review how you did it in the SimplePlayer application.

Xcode will create two view controllers, FirstViewController and SecondViewController, and provide the tab bar icons in universal format as PDF files. You're going to replace these controllers and images, so delete them. Select the controller files, FirstViewController.[hm] and SecondViewController.[hm], and the .pdf files in the Navigator pane. Delete the files. When Xcode asks, move the files to the Trash. Select MainStoryboard.storyboard to open it in the storyboard editor. Select the first view controller scene and delete it. Repeat for the second view controller. The storyboard editor should consist of the tab bar controller only (Figure 12-10).

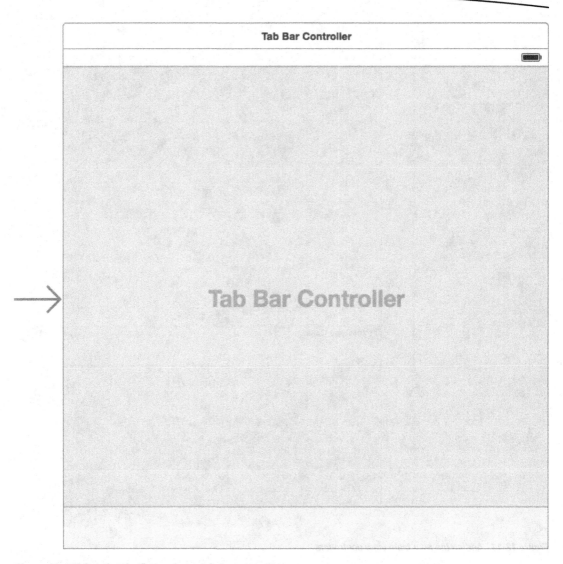

Figure 12-10. Deleting the first and second view controllers

Looking at Figure 12-10, you see that each tab controller is a table view controller. Drag a UITableViewController from the Object Library to the right of the tab bar controller in the storyboard editor. Control-drag from the tab bar view controller to the new table view controller. When the Segue pop-up menu appears, select the view controllers option under the Relationship Segue heading. Add a second UITableViewController and Control-drag from the tab bar controller to it, selecting the view controllers option again. Align the two table view controllers and try to make your storyboard look like Figure 12-11.

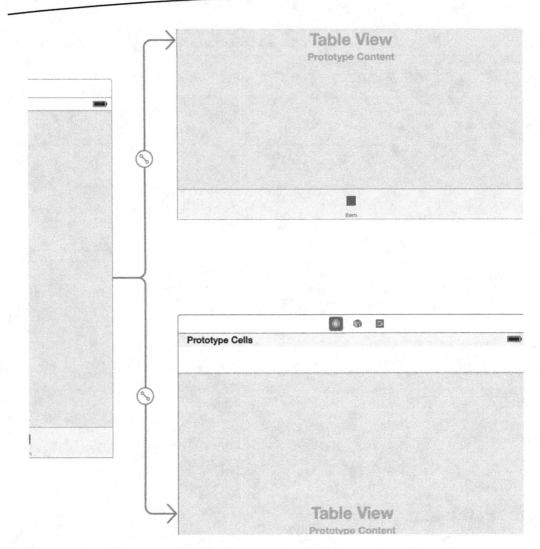

Figure 12-11. Adding the new table view controllers

Select the table view cell from the top table view controller. Open the Attributes Inspector and set the Style attribute to Subtitle. Give it an Identifier attribute a value of MediaCell. Set the Selection attribute to None and the Accessory attribute to Disclosure Indicator. Repeat the attribute settings for the table view cell for the bottom table view controller.

You'll use the top table view controller for your audio media and the bottom table view controller for your video media. So, you'll want an audio view controller and a video view controller. However, each view controller is really just a media view controller. Therefore, you'll begin by creating a MediaViewController class and then subclass it. Create a new file using the Cocoa Touch Class template. Name the class MediaViewController and make it subclass of UITableViewController.

You want the MediaViewController to be generic enough to handle both audio and video media. That means you need to store an array of media items and provide a method to load those items. Open MediaViewController.h. You'll need to import the MediaPlayer header to start. Add it after the UIKit header import.

```
#import <MediaPlayer/MediaPlayer.h>
```

We said you needed to store an array of media items. You'll declare that as a property of the MediaViewController class.

```
@property (strong, nonatomic) NSArray *mediaItems;
```

And you'll declare a method to populate the mediaItems depending on media type.

```
- (void)loadMediaItemsForMediaType:(MPMediaType)mediaType;
```

Select MediaViewController.m and adjust the implementation. First, you need to fix your table view data source methods to define the number of sections and rows per section in the table view.

```
- (NSInteger)numberOfSectionsInTableView:(UITableView *)tableView
{
    // Return the number of sections.
    return 1;
}

- (NSInteger)tableView:(UITableView *)tableView numberOfRowsInSection:(NSInteger)section
{
    // Return the number of rows in the section.
    return self.mediaItems.count;
}
```

Next, you want to adjust how the table view cell is populated.

```
- (UITableViewCell *)tableView:(UITableView *)tableView
         cellForRowAtIndexPath:(NSIndexPath *)indexPath
{
    static NSString *CellIdentifier = @"MediaCell";
    UITableViewCell *cell = [tableView dequeueReusableCellWithIdentifier:CellIdentifier
                                                           forIndexPath:indexPath];

    // Configure the cell...
    NSUInteger row = [indexPath row];
    MPMediaItem *item = [self.mediaItems objectAtIndex:row];
    cell.textLabel.text = [item valueForProperty:MPMediaItemPropertyTitle];
    cell.detailTextLabel.text = [item valueForProperty:MPMediaItemPropertyArtist];
    cell.tag = row;

    return cell;
}
```

Finally, you need to implement your loadMediaItemsForMediaType: method.

```
- (void)loadMediaItemsForMediaType:(MPMediaType)mediaType
{
    MPMediaQuery *query = [[MPMediaQuery alloc] init];
    NSNumber *mediaTypeNumber= [NSNumber numberWithInt:mediaType];
    MPMediaPropertyPredicate *predicate =
        [MPMediaPropertyPredicate predicateWithValue:mediaTypeNumber
                                        forProperty:MPMediaItemPropertyMediaType];
    [query addFilterPredicate:predicate];
    self.mediaItems = [query items];
}
```

You have defined your MediaViewController class. Let's create your audio and video subclasses. Create a new file using the Cocoa Touch Class template, named AudioViewController, which will be a subclass of MediaViewController. Repeat this process, this time naming the file VideoViewController. You only need to make two minor adjustments to each file. First, open AudioViewController.m and add the following line to the viewDidLoad method, after the call to super:

```
[self loadMediaItemsForMediaType:MPMediaTypeMusic];
```

Do the same for VideoViewController.m, except this time you want to load videos.

```
[self loadMediaItemsForMediaType:MPMediaTypeAnyVideo];
```

Let's get your app to use your new view controllers. Select MainStoryboard.storyboard to open the storyboard editor. Select the top table view controller. In the Identity Inspector, change Custom Class from UITableViewController to AudioViewController. Change the bottom table view controller class to VideoViewController.

Before moving on, let's update the tabs for each view controller. Select the tab bar in the audio view controller. In the Attributes Inspector, set Title to Music and set Image to music.png. You can find the image files, music.png and video.png, in this chapter's download folder. Select the tab bar in the video view controller and set its title to Video and its image to video.png.

Build and run your app. You should see all your media library's music when selecting the Music tab and all the media library's videos when selecting the Video tab. Great! Now you need to support playback. You'll be using MPMoviePlayerViewController to play back video, but like the SimplePlayer, you need to make an audio playback view controller. You're going to make an even simpler version of your audio playback controller. Create a new Objective-C file named PlayerViewController, which will be a subclass of UIViewController.

Select the MainStoryboard.storyboard so you can work on the PlayerViewController scene. Drag a UIViewController to the right of the audio view controller. Select the new view controller, and open the Identity Inspector. Change its class from UIViewController to PlayerViewController. Control-drag from the table view cell in the audio view controller to the UIViewController and select the modal Manual Segue. Select the segue between AudioViewController and PlayerViewController, and name it PlayerSegue in the Attributes Inspector.

Your audio playback view controller will look like Figure 12-12 when you're done. Starting at the top, add two UILabels. Stretch them to width of the view. Like you did with the SimplePlayer, extend the labels to the width of the view and adjust their attributes (System Bold 17.0 font, center alignment, white foreground color, black background color). Set the top label text to Artist and the bottom label text to Song.

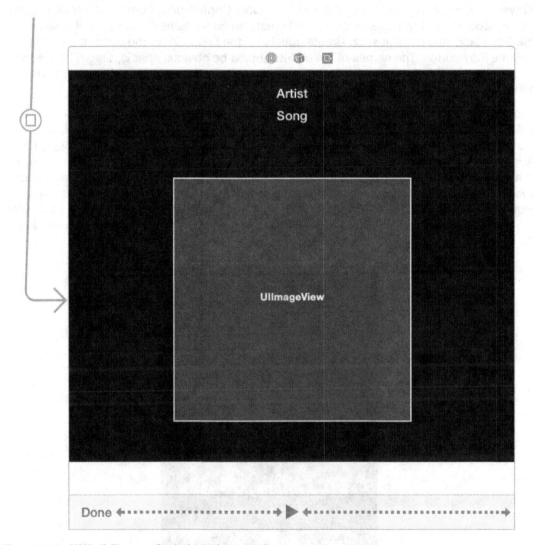

Figure 12-12. MPMediaPlayer audio playback view controller

Drag a UIImageView into the scene, just below the Song label. Use the blue guide lines to space it properly. Adjust the size of the image view to fit the width of the view, and make it square (320px by 320px). Just below the image view, drag a UIView. Adjust the width of the view, using the blue margin guidelines. Finally, drag a UIToolbar to the bottom of the PlayerViewController view. Select the UIBarButtonItem on the left side of the toolbar. Using the Attributes Inspector, change the identifier from Custom to Done. Drag a flexible space bar button Item to the right of the Done button. Next, add a `UIBarButtonItem` to the right of the flexible space item. Select the new bar button item and change its identifier to Play in the Attributes Inspector. Finally, to center your Play button, add another flexible space bar button item to the right of the Play button.

Just as you did with SimplePlayer, you need to create some outlets and actions for your `PlayerViewController`. Enter Assistant Editor mode. Control-drag from the Artist label to the `PlayerViewController` implementation and create an outlet named `artist`. Do the same for the Song label and name it `song`. Create outlets for the Image View, the slider, the toolbar, and the Play button. The names of the outlets should be obvious (that is, `imageView` for the image view), except for the slider. You'll name the outlet `volume` since you're going to use the slider to control the volume level.

You may think there is a glaring mistake here because you have dragged an `UIView` and are calling it `volume` while talking about dragging the slider to manage the volume. Well, you are partially correct. You are right because you need a slider and an `UIView` isn't one. Since iOS 7, Apple has made the `volume` property redundant, and you instantiate an `MPVolumeView`, which is a volume slider on steroids for audio playback. It is connected to the media player and can even allow you to play your audio over AirPlay or Bluetooth to other devices. You can see in Figure 12-13 that the `UIView` is a placeholder and the `MPVolumeView` sits in its place, and when the AirPlay icon is tapped, it offers to play the audio on the iPhone or the iMac (it is running Air Server).

Figure 12-13. MPVolumeView displaying the options for AirPlay

You need to define two actions. Control-drag from the Done button to create a donePressed: action. Control-drag from the Play button to create a playPausePressed: event. Put the editor back into Standard mode and select PlayerViewController.h.

First, you need to import the MediaPlayer header file. You add the import declaration after the UIKit header import.

```
#import <MediaPlayer/MediaPlayer.h>
```

As you did with the SimplePlayer, you need to redefine the play property outlet from weak to strong. You also declare your pause (button) property.

```
@property (strong, nonatomic) IBOutlet UIBarButtonItem *play;
@property (strong, nonatomic)         UIBarButtonItem *pause;
```

You need to add two more properties: one to hold the MPMusicPlayerController and one to hold the MPMediaItem that is being played.

```
@property (strong, nonatomic) MPMusicPlayerController *player;
@property (strong, nonatomic) MPMediaItem *mediaItem;
```

You need to know when the player state has changed and when the player media item has changed. Remember, these are handled via notifications. You'll declare some methods to register with the Notification Center.

```
- (void)playingItemChanged:(NSNotification *)notification;
- (void)playbackStateChanged:(NSNotification *)notification;
```

Let's move to PlayerViewController.m and work on the implementation. You need to create your Pause button since it's not part of your storyboard scene. Find the viewDidLoad method and create it after the call to super.

```
self.pause = [[UIBarButtonItem alloc] initWithBarButtonSystemItem:UIBarButtonSystemItemPause
target:self action:@selector(playPausePressed:)];
[self.pause setStyle:UIBarButtonItemStylePlain];
```

At the end of the viewDidLoad, add the following lines:

```
CGRect main_frame = [[UIScreen mainScreen] bounds];
CGRect frame = [self.volume bounds];
frame.size.width = main_frame.size.width;
MPVolumeView* newVolume = [[ MPVolumeView alloc ] initWithFrame: frame];
[self.volume addSubview:  newVolume];
newVolume.userInteractionEnabled = true;
```

You need a MPMusicPlayerController instance to play your music.

```
self.player = [MPMusicPlayerController applicationMusicPlayer];
```

You want to observe the player notifications, so you register for those and ask the player to start generating them.

```
NSNotificationCenter *notificationCenter = [NSNotificationCenter defaultCenter];
[notificationCenter addObserver:self
                        selector:@selector(playingItemChanged:)
                            name:MPMusicPlayerControllerNowPlayingItemDidChangeNotification
                          object:self.player];
[notificationCenter addObserver:self
                        selector:@selector(playbackStateChanged:)
                            name:MPMusicPlayerControllerPlaybackStateDidChangeNotification
                          object:self.player];
[self.player beginGeneratingPlaybackNotifications];
```

You need to pass your media item to the player. But the player takes MPMediaItemCollections, not an individual MPMediaItem. You'll do this assignment in the viewDidAppear: method where you'll create a collection and pass it to your player.

```
- (void)viewDidAppear:(BOOL)animated
{
    [super viewDidAppear:animated];
    MPMediaItemCollection *collection =
        [[MPMediaItemCollection alloc] initWithItems:@[self.mediaItem]];
    [self.player setQueueWithItemCollection:collection];
    [self.player play];
}
```

You need to stop generating notifications and unregister your observers when the PlayerViewController is released. Find the didGenerateMemoryWarning method and add the following calls:

```
[self.player endGeneratingPlaybackNotifications];
[[NSNotificationCenter defaultCenter]
    removeObserver:self
              name:MPMusicPlayerControllerPlaybackStateDidChangeNotification
            object:self.player];
[[NSNotificationCenter defaultCenter]
    removeObserver:self
              name:MPMusicPlayerControllerNowPlayingItemDidChangeNotification
            object:self.player];
```

The donePressed: method stops the player and dismisses the PlayerViewController.

```
- (IBAction)donePressed:(id)sender
{
    [self.player stop];
    [self dismissViewControllerAnimated:YES completion:nil];
}
```

Your playPausePressed: method is similar to the one in SimplePlayer. You don't update the Play/Pause button in the toolbar; you'll handle that in the playbackStateChanged: method.

```
- (IBAction)playPausePressed:(id)sender
{
    MPMusicPlaybackState playbackState = [self.player playbackState];
    if (playbackState == MPMusicPlaybackStateStopped || playbackState ==
    MPMusicPlaybackStatePaused) {
        [self.player play];
    }
    else if (playbackState == MPMusicPlaybackStatePlaying) {
        [self.player pause];
    }
}
```

Implementing your notification observer methods is pretty straightforward. You update the view when the player media item changes. Again, it's similar to the same method in SimplePlayer.

```
- (void)playingItemChanged:(NSNotification *)notification
{
        MPMediaItem *currentItem = [self.player nowPlayingItem];
        if (nil == currentItem) {
        [self.imageView setImage:nil];
        [self.imageView setHidden:YES];
        [self.artist setText:nil];
        [self.song setText:nil];
    }
    else {
        MPMediaItemArtwork *artwork = [currentItem valueForProperty:
        MPMediaItemPropertyArtwork];
        if (artwork) {
            UIImage *artworkImage = [artwork imageWithSize:CGSizeMake(320, 320)];
            [self.imageView setImage:artworkImage];
            [self.imageView setHidden:NO];
        }

        // Display the artist and song name for the now-playing media item
        [self.artist setText:[currentItem valueForProperty:MPMediaItemPropertyArtist]];
        [self.song setText:[currentItem valueForProperty:MPMediaItemPropertyTitle]];
    }
}
```

The playbackStateChanged: notification observer method is new to you. You added this notification so that when the player automatically starts playing music in viewDidAppear:, it'll update the Play/Pause button state.

```
- (void)playbackStateChanged:(NSNotification *)notification
{
    MPMusicPlaybackState playbackState = [self.player playbackState];
    NSMutableArray *items = [NSMutableArray arrayWithArray:[self.toolbar items]];
```

```
    if (playbackState == MPMusicPlaybackStateStopped || playbackState ==
    MPMusicPlaybackStatePaused) {
        [items replaceObjectAtIndex:2 withObject:self.play];
    }
    else if (playbackState == MPMusicPlaybackStatePlaying) {
        [items replaceObjectAtIndex:2 withObject:self.pause];
    }
    [self.toolbar setItems:items animated:NO];
}
```

You need to send the music media item from the AudioViewController when the table view cell is selected to the PlayerViewController. To do that, you need to modify your AudioViewController implementation. Select AudioViewController.m and add the following method:

```
- (void)prepareForSegue:(UIStoryboardSegue *)segue sender:(id)sender
{
    if ([segue.identifier isEqualToString:@"PlayerSegue"]) {
        UITableViewCell *cell = sender;
        NSUInteger index = [cell tag];
        PlayerViewController *pvc = segue.destinationViewController;
        pvc.mediaItem = [self.mediaItems objectAtIndex:index];
    }
}
```

One last thing—you need to import the PlayerViewController into the AudioViewController.m file. At the top of the file, just below the import of AudioViewController.h, add this import:

```
#import "PlayerViewController.h"
```

Build and run the app. Select a music file to play. The app should transition the PlayerViewController and start playing automatically. Slide the volume slider and see how you can adjust the playback volume now. Next, let's add video playback. It's trivially easy with the MediaPlayer framework. Open VideoViewController and implement the table view delegate method tableView:didSelectRowAtIndexPath:, like so:

```
- (void)tableView:(UITableView *)tableView didSelectRowAtIndexPath:(NSIndexPath *)indexPath
{
    MPMediaItem *mediaItem = [self.mediaItems objectAtIndex:[indexPath row]];
    NSURL *mediaURL = [mediaItem valueForProperty:MPMediaItemPropertyAssetURL];
    MPMoviePlayerViewController *player =
        [[MPMoviePlayerViewController alloc] initWithContentURL:mediaURL];
    [self presentMoviePlayerViewControllerAnimated:player];
}
```

That's it. Build and run your application. Select the Video tab and pick a video to play. Easy!

Note   While the list shows videos, there can be issues playing them. The various cases can be if the videos are part of your account but not downloaded on the device, and so on.

AVFoundation

The AVFoundation framework was originally introduced in iOS 3 with limited audio playback and recording functionality. iOS 4 expanded the framework to include video playback and recording, as well as the audio/video asset management.

At the core, AVFoundation represents an audio or video file as an AVAsset. It's important to understand that an AVAsset may have multiple tracks. For example, an audio AVAsset may have two tracks: one for the left channel and one for the right. A video AVAsset could have many more tracks; some for video, some for audio. Additionally, an AVAsset may encapsulate additional metadata about the media it represents. It's important to note that simply instantiating an AVAsset does not mean it will be ready for playback. It may take some time for the function to analyze the data that AVAsset represents.

To give you fine-grained control on how to play back an AVAsset, AVFoundation separates the presentation state of a media item from the AVAsset. This presentation state is represented by an AVPlayerItem. Each track within an AVPlayerItem is represented by an AVPlayerItemTrack. By using an AVPlayerItem and its AVPlayerItemTracks, you are allowed to determine how to present the item (that is, mix the audio tracks or crop the video) via an AVPlayer object. If you want to play back multiple AVPlayerItems, you use the AVPlayerQueue to schedule the playback of each AVPlayerItem.

Beyond giving finer control over media playback, AVFoundation gives you the ability to create media. You can leverage the device hardware to create your new media assets. The hardware is represented by an AVCaptureDevice. Where possible, you can configure the AVCaptureDevice to enable specific device functionality or settings. For example, you can set the flashMode of the AVCaptureDevice that represents your iPhone's camera to be on, off, or use autosensing.

To use the output from the AVCaptureDevice, you need to use an AVCaptureSession. AVCaptureSession coordinates the management data from an AVCaptureDevice to its output form. This output is represented by an AVCaptureOutput class.

It's a complicated process to create media data using AVFoundation. First, you need to create an AVCaptureSession to coordinate the capture and creation of your media. You define and configure your AVCaptureDevice, which represents the actual physical device (such as your iPhone camera or microphone). From the AVCaptureDevice, you create an AVCaptureInput. AVCaptureInput is an object that represents the data coming from the AVCaptureDevice. Each AVCaptureInput instance has a number of ports, where each port represents a data stream from the device. You can think of a port as a capture analog of an AVAsset track. Once you've created your AVCaptureInputs, you assign them to the AVCaptureSession. Each session can have multiple inputs.

You have your capture session, and you've assigned inputs to your session. Now you have to save the data. You use the AVCaptureOutput class and add it to your AVCaptureSession. You can use a concrete AVCaptureOutput subclass to write your data to a file, or you can save it to a buffer for further processing.

Your AVCaptureSession is now configured to receive data from a device and save it. All you need to do is tell your session to startRunning. Once you're done, you send the stopRunning message to your session. Interestingly, it is possible to change your session's input or output while it is running. To ensure a smooth transition, you would wrap these changes with a set of beginConfiguration/commitConfiguration messages.

Asset metadata is represented by the AVMetadataItem class. To add your own metadata to an asset, you use the mutable version, AVMutableMetadataItem, and assign it to your asset.

There are times where you may need to transform your media asset from one format to another. Similar to capturing media, you use an AVAssetExportSession class. You add your input asset to the export session object and then configure the export session to your new output format and export the data.

Next, let's delve into the specifics of playing media via AVFoundation.

TL;DR: AVKit

Creating apps is all about fun and enjoying it; it is not meant to be tedious. You used MediaPlayer earlier in the chapter. It is quite involved and long. Prior to iOS 8, playing videos using AVFoundation was equally tedious. Note the use of the word *was*. Apple now has AVKit, which sits on top of AVFoundation and provides you with a complete encapsulated player with controls, and other functionality, that interacts with the AVFoundation.

The AVKit framework has just one class, AVPlayerViewController. It is available to you even from Interface Builder, so you can build your UI using the player. It shaves off pages of code to present a controller onscreen.

> **Note**   If you use AVPlayerViewController in Interface Builder, then you have to link the framework manually; otherwise, it could crash your app.

Use the Single View Application template to create an application called AVKitMediaPlayer. First click Main.storyboard to open it. Drag a button to the center of this form and change the text to Play Video. If you are using Auto Layout, simply select the button and add the Horizontal Center in Container and Vertical Center in Container constraints. Next drag an AVPlayerViewController onto the storyboard. Place it to the right of the existing ViewController. Now Control-drag from the button to the AVPlayerViewController and select the Present Modally option from the pop-up. This will present the AVPlayerViewController when you click the button. One last thing: click the Project folder in the navigation and create a new Cocoa Touch Class file called PlayerViewController, which is a subclass of AVPlayerViewController. This should open the PlayerViewController.m file in the editor, and Xcode should be displaying some errors. Add these lines after the #import <UIKit/UIKit.h> statement:

```
#import <UIKit/UIKit.h>
@import AVKit;
@import AVFoundation;
```

Now click Main.storyboard again and select the AVPlayerViewController. In the Identity Inspector (Cmd+Opt+3), change the class to PlayerViewController. Now run the application and click the button. The player is presented as shown in Figure 12-14. When you tap the Done button, it is removed and takes you back to the screen with the Play Video button. You have hardly written any code at all. Rotate the interface in your simulator or the device or tap the screen to make it full-screen. You get all of this functionality for free. However, all you see is a black screen; there is no video to play.

Figure 12-14. The AVPlayerViewController and the UI

Playing Video

To play a video file, you need to set the AVPlayer property of the AVPlayerViewController. The AVPlayer requires a URL; this is a standard NSURL that can reference a remote or a local file. The player would load/buffer the file and start playing.

Open ViewController.m and add the method prepareForSegue; you will pass the video link to the player when this segue is invoked. As with most files referring to another class, you need to import them. Also add the #import "PlayerViewController.h".

```
-(void) prepareForSegue:(UIStoryboardSegue *)segue sender:(id)sender {
    PlayerViewController *videoPlayer = [segue destinationViewController];

    NSString *AppleWatch = @"http://images.apple.com/media/us/watch/2014/videos/e71af271_
    d18c_4d78_918d_d008fc4d702d/tour/reveal/watch-reveal-cc-us-20140909_r848-9dwc.mov";
    NSURL *theURL = [[NSURL alloc]initWithString:AppleWatch];
    videoPlayer.player = [[AVPlayer alloc]initWithURL:theURL];
}
```

The AppleWatch URL is taken from the Apple web site. When you tap the button, it creates a new AVPlayer object and sets the player on the player view controller as a URL. It then downloads the video and plays it, as shown in Figure 12-15.

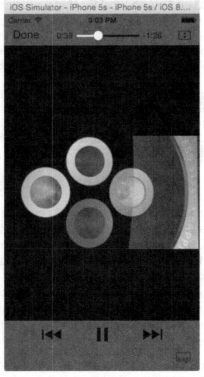
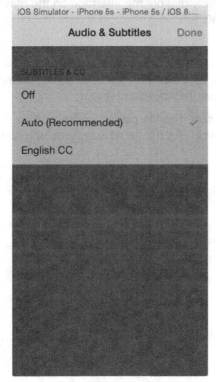

Figure 12-15. The player view controller with the UI and all the extras like fit to screen and subtitles

Now to load and play a local file that you might have included in the application, the method is the same; the only difference is that the URL is created from a local path to the file.

```
-(void) prepareForSegue:(UIStoryboardSegue *)segue sender:(id)sender {
    PlayerViewController *videoPlayer = [segue destinationViewController];

    NSString *filePath = [[NSBundle mainBundle]pathForResource:@"stackofCards"
    ofType:@"mp4"];
    if (filePath){
        NSURL *theURL = [NSURL fileURLWithPath:filePath];
        videoPlayer.player = [[AVPlayer alloc]initWithURL:theURL];
    }
}
```

Replace the existing function with this code to load a file from the project. You can drag your own videos into the project and pass them to the player view controller. There is only one little snag; the reason for the line if (filePath) { is that while you might have dragged a video onto the project, it does not mean it will be available to the application. Xcode copies .mov files automatically but not some other formats including .mp4. You can click the project to show the project properties. Under Build Phases, expand Copy Bundle Resources to see the files that are available as resources (that is, not compiled but copied). If your video is not in this list, it will not be available. Click the + sign, select your video, and click Add. Now when you run, it will be available. (You might have to clean and build again if it still does not play.)

If you were to use this player to play an intro video that you want to control and not allow the user to interact with its playback, you could simply disable the interface on the player view controller by setting showsPlaybackControl to NO.

```
[videoPlayer setShowsPlaybackControls:NO];
```

You can also play a series or videos like a video juke box with queued items; however, instead of using an AVPlayer item, you would use the AVQueuePlayer.

This creates a new AVPlayer with the URL and sets it to the player property of the AVPlayerViewController, which in this case is self. As the name suggests, you can queue video items to play.

If you select an AirPlay destination, the video is played onto the external source. In Figure 12-16 you can see the iOS interface when playing on an external source.

Figure 12-16. The player playing on an external source via AirPlay

AVMediaPlayer

Your AVMediaPlayer will look similar to the MPMediaPlayer, but there is a small difference; instead of the tabs, you will have a single TableView that displays all the available videos and then plays them just like the MPMediaPlayer did earlier.

You saw how easy it is to create a player view controller. You can also embed the view from this ViewController into your own view as a subview. You can create a AVPlayerViewController and then add it as the childViewController and add its view to the subview of the main view. Set the frame to the location and dimensions you want.

```
NSString *thePath = [[NSBundle mainBundle]pathForResource:@"stackofCards" ofType:@"mp4"];
AVPlayer *player = [[AVPlayer alloc]initWithURL:[NSURL fileURLWithPath:thePath]];
AVPlayerViewController *playerViewController = [[AVPlayerViewController alloc]init];
playerViewController.player = player;

[self addChildViewController:playerViewController];
[self.view addSubview:playerViewController.view];
playerViewController.view.frame = self.view.frame;
[player play];
```

The biggest issue is how to list the videos available on the device. You saw one way where you could list the same using `MediaPlayer`. Apple introduced a new framework called the `Photos` framework. This provides access to the photos on the device. This is another source of where you can find videos.

You can query the Camera Roll or the Photos application for videos as simply as this:

```
PHFetchResult *videoAssets = [PHAsset fetchAssetsWithMediaType:PHAssetMediaTypeVideo
options:nil];
```

The `fetchAssetsWithMediaType` method returns a `PHFetchResults` object that contains the video assets of type `PHAsset`. This `PHAsset` can be then be used to create a player and play the asset.

```
PHImageManager *imageManager = [PHImageManager defaultManager];
PHAsset *videoAsset = [videoAssets objectAtIndex: 0];
[imageManager requestPlayerItemForVideo:videoAsset options:nil resultHandler:^(AVPlayerItem
*playerItem, NSDictionary *info) {
    self.player = [AVPlayer playerWithPlayerItem:playerItem];
    // set the player and start playing
}];
```

Similarly, you can also request the poster frame or the image of the video in a similar fashion using the `requestImageForAsset` method.

```
[imageManager requestImageForAsset:videoAsset
                       targetSize:CGSizeMake(150, 150)
                      contentMode:PHImageContentModeAspectFill
                          options:nil
                    resultHandler:^(UIImage *result, NSDictionary *info) {
    // This is an UIImage, use it as you want
}];
```

AVMediaPlayer v2

Using Xcode, create a new application based on the Single View Application template and name it AVKitMediaPlayer2. Click `Main.storyboard` and delete the view controller. Now drag a `TableViewController` from the Object Library and select the menu option Editor ➤ Embed In ➤ Navigation Controller. Select the navigation controller and in the Attributes Inspector set is Initial View Controller to true. Click the table view controller and select the prototype cell. Change the Cell style to Basic and set Identifier to VideoCell. Next change the selection to None. Now add a new Cocoa Touch Class file, name it `MediaListViewController`, and make it a subclass of `UITableViewController`. Click `Main.Storyboard` and change the class for the `UITableViewController` to `MediaListViewController`; then click the `MediaListViewController.h` file to open it in the editor. First you need to import the libraries after the line #import <UIKit/UIKit.h>.

```
#import <UIKit/UIKit.h>
@import AVFoundation;
@import AVKit;
@import Photos;
```

After the class declaration, you need to declare two properties: one to hold the Image Manager of type PHImageManager and the other to hold the videos available in your Photos Library of type PHFetchResult (detailed in the next section).

```
@property (nonatomic, strong) PHImageManager *imageManager;
@property (nonatomic, strong) PHFetchResult *videos;
```

Apple takes access to the various functionality of the iOS quite seriously and has authorization dialogs that prompt the user the first time for authorization. The Photos Library is one such functionality, and the first time around it will ask users if they want to allow access. If the user denies access, then the code will fail to fetch results until the user explicitly allows access from the Settings ➤ Privacy ➤ Photos section. However, you need to know in your application whether the user authorized this. First you query all the video assets into the videos variable in ViewDidLoad.

```
- (void)viewDidLoad {
    [super viewDidLoad];

    [super setTitle:@"Video Browser"];
    self.imageManager = [PHImageManager defaultManager];
    [self setVideos:[PHAsset fetchAssetsWithMediaType:PHAssetMediaTypeVideo options:nil]];
}
```

If the user has denied access to the Photos Library, there would be nothing in videos, and hence the list view would populate nothing; you need to let the user know of this. You use the viewDidAppear method to check the status and display an alert.

```
-(void)viewDidAppear:(BOOL)animated{
    [super viewDidAppear:animated];

    if ([PHPhotoLibrary authorizationStatus] == PHAuthorizationStatusDenied) {
        UIAlertController *alert = [UIAlertController
                                    alertControllerWithTitle:@"Requires Access to Photos"
                                    message:@"Please allow this app to access your Photos
                                    Library from the Settings > Privacy > Photos setting"
                                    preferredStyle:UIAlertControllerStyleAlert];
        UIAlertAction *OKButton = [UIAlertAction
                                   actionWithTitle:@""
                                   style:UIAlertActionStyleDefault
                                   handler:nil];
        [alert addAction:OKButton];
        [[[[UIApplication sharedApplication] keyWindow] rootViewController]
        presentViewController:alert animated:YES completion:nil];
    }
}
```

Now in the numberOfSectionsInTableView method, change it to return 1.

```
- (NSInteger)numberOfSectionsInTableView:(UITableView *)tableView {
    return 1;
}
```

Change numberOfRowsInSection to return the video.count, and if that is nil, return 0 instead.

```
- (NSInteger)tableView:(UITableView *)tableView numberOfRowsInSection:(NSInteger)section {
    NSInteger count = [self.videos count] ;
    if (!count) {
        count = 0;
    }
    return count;
}
```

Finally, uncomment the cellForRowAtIndexPath method, and for the video asset at that row, you need to query the image and the details such as the size of the video, duration, creation date, and modification date.

Get the asset from the video results.

```
- (UITableViewCell *)tableView:(UITableView *)tableView cellForRowAtIndexPath:(NSIndexPath *)
indexPath {
    UITableViewCell *cell = [tableView dequeueReusableCellWithIdentifier:@"VideoCell"
    forIndexPath:indexPath];
    // Configure the cell...

    PHAsset *theAsset = [self.videos objectAtIndex:[indexPath row]];
    CGSize theSize = CGSizeMake(150, 150);

    [self.imageManager requestImageForAsset:theAsset
                            targetSize:theSize
                          contentMode:PHImageContentModeAspectFill
                              options:nil
                        resultHandler:^(UIImage *result, NSDictionary *info) {
    UIGraphicsBeginImageContextWithOptions(CGSizeMake(100, 100), false, 1);
    [result drawInRect:CGRectMake(0, 0, 100, 100)];
    UIImage *image = UIGraphicsGetImageFromCurrentImageContext();
    UIGraphicsEndImageContext();

    cell.imageView.image = image;
    NSString *duration = [NSString stringWithFormat:@"%0.1fs", theAsset.duration];
    NSString *details = [NSString stringWithFormat:@"(%ld) x (%ld) - (%@)",
                theAsset.pixelWidth,
                theAsset.pixelHeight,
                duration];
    cell.textLabel.text = details;
    }];
```

The videos can be in landscape or portrait orientation, and the previous code renders them in a square, which can cause the image to be squashed or stretched. You could alternatively use the original image passed by the function by simply assigning it directly to cell.imageview.image = result.

You can get the duration and the dimensions from the asset itself, so it is a matter of simply formatting it as a string and displaying it as the textLabel on the cell.

```
return cell;
}
```

If you run your app, you should be able to see the list of videos on your device in the table view, as shown in Figure 12-17.

Figure 12-17. The list of videos available on the device

Photo Library

Introduced with iOS 8, the Photos framework consists of PHImageManager and PHPhotoLibrary. You used portions of PHImageManager earlier. PHPhotoLibrary represents all of the images and videos stored on the device including stored on iCloud (if enabled).

Like MediaPlayer, the element that actually holds metadata information about the item is a PHAsset. It can be one of the three media types, namely, Image, Audio, or Video. It also has other properties such as pixelWidth and pixelHeight that indicate the size of the image or the video (as you used in the earlier sample). It also has creationDate and modificationDate.

To know the location where the image was taken, it has another property called location, which is of type CLLocation and holds the GPS coordinates of where the image or video was taken. The duration property holds the length of the video. In photos, you can also flag images or videos as favorites, and the favorite property indicates whether this item was flagged as favorite.

PHAsset objects are held in a PHAssetCollection. This is the collection item that represents the albums, smart albums, and moments. It is an ordered list and has properties that are estimates rather than actuals. The properties such as approximateLocation and estimatedAssetCount along with startDate and endDate define this PHAssetCollection class. The property assetCollectionType is the type of collection, that is, an Album, Smart Album, or Moment collection.

The other collection is PHCollectionList, which is what forms the folders and the years in moments. This has a similar set of properties as PHAssetCollections. These together allow you to access the architecture model of the Photo Library.

Every time you query any of the classes, you are actually returned asset metadata in PHFetchResults form. This is similar to an NSArray but is loaded lazily. To get the image or the video associated with that asset, you have to then query the PHImageManager like you did earlier to get all the videos. To get all the images, you can simply use the following:

```
self.videos = [PHAsset fetchAssetsWithMediaType:PHAssetMediaTypeImage options:nil];
```

While iterating through each of the asset contained in the results, you could request the image details like so:

```
PHAsset *theAsset = [self.videos objectAtIndex:[indexPath row]];
CGSize theSize = CGSizeMake(150, 150);

[self.imageManager requestImageForAsset:theAsset targetSize:theSize contentMode:
PHImageContentModeAspectFill options:nil resultHandler:^(UIImage *result,
NSDictionary *info) {
//
}
```

This is the same technique you used to get the video image earlier in the chapter.

Modifying the Photo Library

The Photos framework runs on threads to provide smoother UI and interaction. Because of this, the objects are immutable, which make them thread-safe but also difficult to use with the dot syntax. You cannot simply get an asset, alter the data, and persist it. The way to handle it is to create a new changeRequest object using the PHAssetChangeRequest and then perform the changes allowing the framework to apply the changes asynchronously via the performChanges block. There are four properties that you can change, namely, favorite, hidden, creationDate, and location.

```
[[PHPhotoLibrary sharedPhotoLibrary] performChanges:^{
    PHAssetChangeRequest *request = [PHAssetChangeRequest changeRequestForAsset:theAsset];
    request.favorite = !request.favorite;
} completionHandler:nil];
```

You can make a few modifications in the code to create an image viewer and to view it each time you tap the image.

First modify the `viewDidLoad` method to change the title of the app from Video Browser to Image Browser; next alter the query to fetch all images instead of videos.

```
- (void)viewDidLoad {
    [super viewDidLoad];

    self.imageManager = [PHImageManager defaultManager];

    //[super setTitle:@"Video Browser"];
    [super setTitle:@"Image Browser"];

    //self.videos = [PHAsset fetchAssetsWithMediaType:PHAssetMediaTypeVideo options:nil];
    self.videos = [PHAsset fetchAssetsWithMediaType:PHAssetMediaTypeImage options:nil];
}
```

You can run and see the list being populated with images from your device/simulator. Now, in the `cellForRowAtIndexPath`, you can use the `AccessoryType` to display whether the image is a favorite. Just before the line return cell, add this code:

```
cell.accessoryType = theAsset.favorite ? UITableViewCellAccessoryCheckmark :
UITableViewCellAccessoryNone;
```

This will display a check mark if the image is marked as a favorite. To test it, switch to the Photos app on your device or simulator, select a couple of images, and set them as favorites by tapping the heart, as shown in Figure 12-18.

Figure 12-18. Marking an image as a favorite in Photos and a check mark displaying next to it in the app

If you tap any of the images, the video player will display with nothing to play. That can be easily fixed. Modify the didSelectRowAtIndexPath as follows:

```
-(void)tableView:(UITableView *)tableView didSelectRowAtIndexPath:(NSIndexPath *)indexPath {
    PHAsset *theAsset = [self.videos objectAtIndex:[indexPath row]];
    if (theAsset.mediaType == PHAssetMediaTypeVideo) {
        [self.imageManager requestPlayerItemForVideo:theAsset options:nil
        resultHandler:^(AVPlayerItem *playerItem, NSDictionary *info) {
            AVPlayerViewController *playerVC = [[AVPlayerViewController alloc]init];
            AVPlayer *player = [AVPlayer playerWithPlayerItem:playerItem];
            playerVC.player = player;
            [player play];

            [self presentViewController:playerVC animated:YES completion:nil];
        }];
    }
}
```

If you run the app and tap any of the cells, it will do nothing because it displays only images, not videos. However, if you change the type of items in the viewDidLoad to PHAssetMediaTypeVideo and tap the cell, it will start playing.

Are You Talking To Me?

Technology is developing fast, but not as fast as we expected. The Jetsons were far more advanced than we are in 2015. That does not prevent our mobile devices from talking to us. Siri started it all, and now your apps can too. With iOS 7, Apple included text-to-speech synthesis as part of its SDK. So, you can have the alert boxes speak, which not only adds value to your app but also makes it more accessible. It can also work with applications for kids, where you can use recorded .wav or .mp3 files to ask "What is 2 + 2?" or any other questions.

The AVFoundation framework is quite a powerhouse; it also houses the Speech Synthesis APIs. The first step in text-to-speech is to create a synthesizer. The class AVSpeechSynthesizer returns a synthesizer object.

```
AVSpeechSynthesizer *synthesizer = [[AVSpeechSynthesizer alloc]init];
```

The next step is to create an utterance, which is the text that the synthesizer will convert from text to speech. The class AVUtterance creates an utterance from the specified string you pass to it.

```
NSString *thisSentence = @"This sentence";
AVSpeechUtterance *utterance = [AVSpeechUtterance speechUtteranceWithString:thisSentence];
```

Then give it a voice, literally. You need to specify the language and voice you want the synthesizer to use. The voice is set for the utterance. These are based on the BCP47 language tag; you can find more information at http://tools.ietf.org/rfc/bcp/bcp47.txt. Apple supports about 36 languages. Passing nil for the language uses the default language set on the system.

```
[AVSpeechSynthesisVoice voiceWithLanguage:@"en-US"];
```

Finally, you need to tell the synthesizer to synthesize this text as speech.

```
[synthesizer speakUtterance:utterance];
```

That is all there is to converting text to speech; however, the SDK offers a lot more. You can change the pitch and the volume. There are other methods to manipulate the speech playback such as stopSpeakingAtBoundary:, pauseSpeakingAtBoundary:, and continueSpeaking:. The boundaries for speech synthesis are either AVSpeechBoundary. Immediate or AVSpeechBoundary.Word.

You can also set the delegate to handle notifications of important speech utterance events such as didStartSpeechUtterance, didFinishSpeechUtterance, didPauseSpeechUtterance, didContinueSpeechUtterance, and didCancelSpeechUtterence.

The speech synthesizer has a delegate method that is called for every word spoken by the synthesizer. The method `speechSynthesizer:willSpeakRangeOfSpeechString:utterance:` gets a range from the original string that you pass to the synthesizer to play. This can be used for highlighting the words as the synthesizer is synthesizing them. You could even set the volume to 0 and simply highlight the words on the screen.

> **Tip** You can find all the supported languages using `[AVSpeechSynthesisVoice speechVoices]`. This returns an array of all the voices/languages.

Avast! Rough Waters Ahead!

In this chapter, you took a long but pleasant walk through the hills and valleys of using the iPod music library. You saw how to find media items using media queries and how to let your users select songs using the media picker controller. You learned how to use and manipulate collections of media items. We showed you how to use music player controllers to play media items and how to manipulate the currently playing item by seeking or skipping. You also learned how to find out about the currently playing track, regardless of whether it's one your code played or one that the user chose using the iPod or Music application. You further explored the AVFoundation, AVKit, and the Photos frameworks to access and display images and videos.

But now, shore leave is over, matey. It's time to set sail into using the Camera app on the iOS. Batten down the hatches, secure the ship, and look pretty!

Chapter 13

Lights, Camera, and Action

Every new mobile device has a camera; in fact, in many cases, a device has two of them and is used more as a camera than an actual camera is. It is important to note that cameras are an essential part of the iOS device family. In this chapter, you will explore the functionalities of light, camera, and action—in that order.

Lights

When a light-emitting diode (LED) flash was added to the iPhone, the first thing a lot of developers did was make flashlight and strobe applications. The store was full of them. At the time, Apple did not have APIs that provided access to the flash. However, now AVFoundation has integrated functionality for accessing the flash. To use the LED flash, the first thing you need to do is to find the devices that are available for capturing an image (and that can make use of the flash). You can do this via the class AVCaptureDevice; then you can query whether the device has the capabilities to support the flashlight, focus, and so on. The method hasTorch returns true if there is hardware that can support this functionality and returns false otherwise.

```
NSArray *devices = AVCaptureDevice.devices;
AVCaptureDevice *device;
for (device in devices) {
    if (device.hasTorch) {
        // Code to work with the Flash
    }
}
```

Just because the capture device has a "torch" does not mean that it is available for use, so you must check whether the torch is available using the isAvailable property. (It could be unavailable for a couple of reasons; one of them is if the LED overheats and needs to switch off for a while to cool off.)

```
if (device.torchAvailable){
        // Can use the torch
    }
```

Once you have ascertained that the capture device has the capabilities of an LED and that it is available, you can simply change torchMode to AVTorchModeOn, AVTorchModeOff, or AVTorchModeAuto. While the flash is on, you can also retrieve the flash brightness via torchLevel (read-only), which is a value between 0 and 1.

```
device.torchMode = AVCaptureTorchModeOn;
```

Put these lines together and you have a flashlight application. However, Apple might not approve of this on the App Store anymore. Plus, the torch is now part of the iPhone as you can see in Figure 13-1, and you can switch it on or off by simply swiping up from the bottom of the screen and tapping the torch.

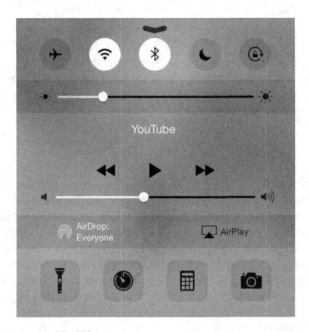

Figure 13-1. The torch is now part of the iOS

Camera

An important part of the iPhone is the camera. In fact, it has two—the front-facing one and the higher-resolution back camera with a flash. Pictures captured via the Camera app are stored in the Camera Roll (accessible via the Photos app). From the AVFoundation perspective, there is a lot more that you can do with the camera.

First let's explore the architecture to get an idea of how things sit in the framework. The framework allows you to capture images or sound, and the base is a capture device, designated by the AVCaptureDevice class. In the previous section, you enumerated all of the available capture devices to query whether it had hardware flash. The AVCaptureDevice class can represent a camera or a microphone. The next is the AVCaptureInput class that configures the ports from the input device. Then comes the AVCaptureOutput class that specifies the end point of the output of where the captured data (image, sound, or video) is to be stored. All of these are tied together in an AVCaptureSession class. You can configure multiple inputs and outputs that are coordinated by the AVCaptureSession class.

```
device = [AVCaptureDevice defaultDeviceWithMediaType:AVMediaTypeVideo];
AVCaptureDeviceInput *input = [AVCaptureDeviceInput deviceInputWithDevice:device error:nil];
AVCaptureSession *session = [[AVCaptureSession alloc]init];
[session addInput:input];
[session startRunning];
```

If you need to preview what the camera is recording, you can access that via the AVCaptureVideoPreviewLayer class, which is a subclass of CALayer.

```
AVCaptureVideoPreviewLayer *previewLayer = [AVCaptureVideoPreviewLayer layerWithSession:session];
[previewLayer setVideoGravity:AVLayerVideoGravityResizeAspectFill];
[previewLayer setFrame:theView.frame];
[theView.layer addSublayer:previewLayer];
```

This will add a layer that provides a live camera feed; if the view is the same size as the full size of the screen, you have a full-screen camera preview. Since it is a CALayer, you can add more layers and can transform, scale, rotate, and even transform in 3D.

> **Note** Apple's technical documents indicate that it is not possible to capture from both the front-facing and back-facing cameras simultaneously.

The session can be configured to specify the image quality and resolution via the available preset values. You might use a couple of settings in the following list:

Symbol	Resolution	Comments
AVCaptureSessionPresetHigh	High	Highest recording quality
AVCaptureSessionPresetMedium	Medium	Suitable for Wi-Fi sharing
AVCaptureSessionPresetLow	Low	Suitable for 3G sharing
AVCaptureSessionPreset640x480	VGA	Suitable for VGA capture
AVCaptureSessionPreset1280x720	1280×720	720p HD
AVCaptureSessionPreset1920x1080	1920×1080	Full HD
AVCaptureSessionPresetPhoto	Photo	Captures using the full resolution; not supported for video

You can also query the capture devices based on their characteristics to ensure that you are using the correct device and it has the capabilities that you might require. If you wanted to capture using the back camera at full HD resolution, you can use the following:

```
if ([device hasMediaType:AVMediaTypeVideo] &&
    [device supportsAVCaptureSessionPreset:AVCaptureSessionPreset1920x1080] &&
    [device position] == AVCaptureDevicePositionBack)  {
    // This device has the capabilites you require
}
```

Changing Settings

In most of the cases, changing settings is as easy as simply assigning new values to the object. However, to get exclusive access to the *hardware* to change the settings, you must set a lock prior to changing the settings. Once you are done, you must unlock it again. The methods to lock and unlock are lockForConfiguration and unlockForConfiguration.

```
[device lockForConfiguration:nil];
//Change the settings here
[device unlockForConfiguration];
```

The capture device offers properties to fine-tune settings such as the Exposure Mode, Focus Mode, Flash Mode, Torch Mode, Video Stabilization, and White Balance properties. For instance, you can lock the focus of the camera to be at a point onscreen.

```
if ([device isFocusModeSupported:AVCaptureFocusModeContinuousAutoFocus]) {
    CGPoint autoFocusPoint = CGPointMake(0.5, 0.5);
    [device lockForConfiguration:nil];
    [device setFocusPointOfInterest:autoFocusPoint];
    [device setFocusMode:AVCaptureFocusModeContinuousAutoFocus];
    [device unlockForConfiguration];
}
```

You can choose from one of these focusMode settings:

- AVCaptureFocusModeLocked locks the camera focus at a particular focal point. This can be used to offer the user a facility to lock the focus.

- AVCaptureFocusModeAutoFocus helps to focus and maintain the focus on an item that is not in the center of the screen by having a single-pass scan focus and then reverting to the locked focus.

- AVCaptureFocusModeContinuousAutoFocus continuously performs autofocus as required.

If, after changing some of the AVCaptureSession settings such as changing the input or the output, you need exclusive access, the functions are beginConfiguration and commitConfiguration.

Putting It All Together

Start a new Xcode single view project and name it Camera_1. Click ViewController.h and add the line @import AVFoundation; before the interface declaration; then you can create properties to hold the session, the camera, the input source, and the preview layer.

```
#import <UIKit/UIKit.h>
@import AVFoundation;

@interface ViewController : UIViewController

@end

AVCaptureSession *session;
AVCaptureDevice *theCamera;
AVCaptureDeviceInput *theInputSource;
AVCaptureVideoPreviewLayer *thePreview;
```

In the viewDidLoad method of ViewController.m, you can detect the available cameras and set theCamera to the camera that is on the back of the device. The function AVCaptureDevice.devicesWithMediaType returns the devices that can handle the particular media type.

```
NSArray *allCameras = [AVCaptureDevice devicesWithMediaType:AVMediaTypeVideo];
```

You can now iterate through each of these to identify the camera that is at the back via the position property.

```
for (AVCaptureDevice *camera in allCameras) {
    if ([camera position] == AVCaptureDevicePositionBack){
        self.theCamera = camera;
        break;
    }
}
```

Now that you have identified the back camera, you need to create a session and an input device from this device.

```
self.session = [[AVCaptureSession alloc]init];
self.theInputSource = [AVCaptureDeviceInput
                          deviceInputWithDevice:self.theCamera
                                        error:nil];
```

With the input source created, you need to add it to the session; it is best to check whether you can add this input source to the session first using the canAddInput function.

```
if ([self.session canAddInput:self.theInputSource]) {
    [self.session addInput:self.theInputSource];
}
```

Now that all of this is in place, you can create a preview layer that shows what the camera specified as the input source is seeing. The preview layer is a subclass of the CALayer class and needs to be added to the sublayers of the layer collection in the view.

```
    self.thePreview = [AVCaptureVideoPreviewLayer layerWithSession: self.session];
    [self.thePreview setFrame:self.view.bounds];
    [self.thePreview setVideoGravity:AVLayerVideoGravityResizeAspectFill];
    [self.view.layer addSublayer: self.thePreview];

    [self.session startRunning];
}
```

If you run the project at this point, you would see the camera view displayed full-screen.

> **Note**　In Figure 13-2, a text view has been added, and the background is the live camera view. So, you can type your text while you can also see through to the screen of the phone. This is not recommended for use in traffic or where accidents can occur. In addition, prolonged use of the camera can drain your device's battery.

Figure 13-2. *The camera preview with an overlaid text view*

Choosing a Camera

In most cases, the back camera is the default camera, which works great. But you might have a need to use the front camera. In the previous code, if instead of the AVCaptureDevicePosition.Back you use AVCaptureDevicePosition.Front, you can get the front camera. You can make that change and rerun the application to see the difference.

However, in your app, you might want to have a button that allows you to switch between the camera sources. It would be counterintuitive to change the camera source in the code, recompile the app, and run it. So, you need to store both the cameras and a variable that helps you determine which camera is used as the current source.

```
AVCaptureDevice *theFrontCamera;
AVCaptureDevice *theBackCamera;
NSInteger theSource = 0;
```

The `viewDidLoad` method will change slightly to now detect both cameras and assign them accordingly.

```
- (void)viewDidLoad {
    [super viewDidLoad];
    // Do any additional setup after loading the view, typically from a nib.

    NSArray *allCameras = [AVCaptureDevice devicesWithMediaType:AVMediaTypeVideo];

    for (AVCaptureDevice *camera in allCameras) {
        if ([camera position] == AVCaptureDevicePositionBack) {
            theBackCamera = camera;
        } else if ([camera position] == AVCaptureDevicePositionFront) {
            theFrontCamera = camera;
        }
    }

    self.theCamera = theBackCamera;
        ...
```

To switch between the two sources, you need a button, so add one in Main.storyboard. Set the layout constraints so that the button is visible when you run it on the device. In the Assistant editor, Control-drag and create an outlet called theButton. Control-drag again to create an action called switchCamera.

```
@property (weak, nonatomic) IBOutlet UIButton *theButton;
```

If you ran the code, you would still not see the button. It is not the constraints that would be the issue but that it is covered by the previewLayer. So, you need to bring the button layer on the top of the view hierarchy via the command bringSubviewToFront in the viewDidLoad function, just before the closing brace.

```
[self.view bringSubviewToFront: self.theButton];
```

Next in the function switchCamera, which is called every time the button is pressed, you first toggle the cameras based on the value of theSource. Then you start the configuration to change the session details, starting with first removing theInputSource, then creating a new InputSource based on the camera and adding it to the session, and finally committing the configuration.

```
- (IBAction)switchCamera:(id)sender {
    theSource = 1 - theSource;
    if (theSource == 1) {
        self.theCamera = theFrontCamera;
    } else {
        self.theCamera = theBackCamera;
    }

    [self.session beginConfiguration];
```

```
[self.session removeInput: self.theInputSource];

self.theInputSource = [AVCaptureDeviceInput
                              deviceInputWithDevice:self.theCamera
                                    error:nil];
[self.session addInput:self.theInputSource];

[self.session commitConfiguration];
}
```

Now every time you tap the button, the camera source will change.

Note   All devices that can run iOS 8 or Swift or are supported officially by Apple have dual cameras, one in the front and one at the back. The only devices that don't are first-generation iPads. If you want to ensure that your code is rock-solid, you could test whether theInputSource can be added to the session using the session.canAddInput function.

Choosing an Output

You have an input source, but if you want to record or take a picture, you need an output point. AVFoundation has an abstract class called AVCaptureOutput. You can choose from some of the output sources offered in the framework, as shown here:

Output Format	Description
AVCaptureVideoDataOutput	This is used to process the video data.
AVCaptureAudioDataOutput	This is used to process the audio data captured.
AVCaptureFileOutput	This starts writing the data to the file on the device.
AVCaptureMovieFileOutput	This writes the movie data from the capture device to QuickTime MOV format.
AVCaptureStillImageOutput	This writes the data as a single image to the file.
AVCaptureMetadataOutput	This reads the metadata such as barcodes or QR codes from the images.

If you want to take pictures, you might use AVCaptureStillImageOutput as the outputSource.

Then when you want to take a picture, you can trigger the captureStillImageAsynchrono uslyFromConnection:completionHandler: function on the outputSource. The completion handler is passed the CMSampleBuffer that contains the image. This can be converted into an UIImage and then saved to the Camera Roll or the app's sandbox.

Altering the code, first you create a new variable to reference the outputSource.

```
AVCaptureStillImageOutput *theOutputSource;
```

Then in viewDidLoad you add the output source to the session.

```
theOutputSource = [[AVCaptureStillImageOutput alloc]init];
[self.session addOutput:theOutputSource];
```

Go to Main.storyboard and add a new button, change the text to Take Picture, and add an image view. Open the Assistant editor, Control-drag from the button, and create an outlet called picButton. Control-drag from the button again, this time creating an action called takePicture. Create another outlet from the ImageView and call it theImage. Close the Assistant editor.

You can now write the implementation for the takePicture IBAction as follows:

```
- (IBAction)takePicture:(id)sender {
    AVCaptureConnection *theConnection = [theOutputSource connectionWithMediaType:AVMediaTy
peVideo];

    [theOutputSource captureStillImageAsynchronouslyFromConnection:theConnection completionH
andler:^(CMSampleBufferRef imageDataSampleBuffer, NSError *error) {
        NSData *imageData = [AVCaptureStillImageOutput jpegStillImageNSDataRepresentation:im
ageDataSampleBuffer];
        UIImage *theImage = [UIImage imageWithData:imageData];
        [_theImage setImage:theImage];
    }];
}
```

The first thing the function does is to create an AVCaptureConnection object; this is a connection link between the input and the output using the connectionWithMediaType function. The connection that links the video source to the output is retrieved. Next captureStillImageAsynchronouslyFromConnection is called, which calls the handler and passes it the buffer with the image as a CMSampleBuffer object. This is converted into an NSData representation using the jpegStillImageNSDataRepresentation function of the AVCaptureStillImageOutput class. A UIImage is created from the NSData using the UIImage imageWithData:imageData function, and this is then set to theImage.image and displayed on the screen. Since there is a previewLayer, the button would be covered. At the end of the viewDidLoad function, add the following line:

```
[self.view bringSubviewToFront:self.theButton];
```

```
[self.view bringSubviewToFront:self.picButton];
```

> **Note** You can add overlays and additional information prior to displaying this image or even saving it to the Photos Library.

Adding an overlay to an UIImage is also quite easy; this could be used to create a watermark or add data, a logo, or whatever you might fancy. To add a simple date and time to the image taken, you can alter the code as follows:

```
- (IBAction)takePicture:(id)sender {
    AVCaptureConnection *theConnection = [theOutputSource connectionWithMediaType:
                                    AVMediaTypeVideo];

    [theOutputSource captureStillImageAsynchronouslyFromConnection:theConnection
completionHandler:^(CMSampleBufferRef imageDataSampleBuffer, NSError *error) {
        NSData *imageData = [AVCaptureStillImageOutput jpegStillImageNSDataRepresentation:
                            imageDataSampleBuffer];
        UIImage *theImage = [UIImage imageWithData:imageData];

        UIGraphicsBeginImageContext([theImage size]);

        CGContextRef context = UIGraphicsGetCurrentContext();
        [theImage drawAtPoint:CGPointMake(0, 0)];
        UIColor *theColor = [[UIColor alloc]initWithWhite:0.5f alpha:0.5f];
        CGContextSetFillColorWithColor(context, [theColor CGColor]);
        CGContextFillRect(context, CGRectMake(0, 0, [theImage size].width, 20));

        UIFont *font = [UIFont systemFontOfSize:18];
        NSDictionary *attr = @{
                    NSForegroundColorAttributeName:[UIColor whiteColor],
                    NSFontAttributeName: font
                    };
        NSString *message = [NSString stringWithFormat:@"Taken on : %@",
                        [[NSDate date]description]];
        [message drawAtPoint:CGPointMake(0, 0) withAttributes:attr];

        UIImage *image = UIGraphicsGetImageFromCurrentImageContext();
        UIGraphicsEndImageContext();

    [_theImage setImage:image];
    }];
}
```

Now you will see an overlay on every picture taken that has the current date and time across it. This image is still not saved to the Photo Album, and saving to the Photos Album is also quite an easy task. The function UIImageWriteToSavedPhotosAlbum can save the image to the Photos Album. The first time this app is run, it will request for permissions to access the Photos Album. The parameters passed to this function are UIImageWriteToSavedPhotosAlbum (UIImage *image, id completionTarget, SEL completionSelector, void *contextInfo).

in this function the first parameter is the image itself that you want to save, and you can pass nil for the remaining parameters. To know whether the image was saved, you can set up the completionSelector. This has a specific signature.

```
UIImageWriteToSavedPhotosAlbum(image, self, @selector(image:didFinishSavingWithError:
contextInfo:), nil);
```

The completion handler function looks like this:

```
- (void)image:(UIImage *)image didFinishSavingWithError:(NSError *)error
                       contextInfo:(void *)contextInfo{
    if ([error code] != 0) {
        NSLog(@"Error : %@", [error localizedDescription]);
    } else {
        NSLog(@"Saved Image");
    }
}
```

The error could indicate why the image could not be saved to the Photos Album. There you have it—you capture an image an image, place a watermark like seen in Figure 13-3, and save it to the Photos Album.

Figure 13-3. Image with the custom overlay saved to the Photos Album

> **Note**   Figure 13-3 was not taken with the camera and is a low-resolution image. The text size
> would be smaller depending on the size and resolution of the image. The idea is to place the date/
> time text on the image; if you want this text to be larger, you might have to scale a font size up
> based on the width of the image.

Scanning Barcodes

Apple introduced scanning for barcodes as part of the AVFoundation framework in iOS 7.
AVFoundation supports a variety of different barcode formats, including QR Code, Code 128,
UPC, EAN, and Interleaved. It even has support for the newer formats such as Aztec and
DataMatrix.

With iOS devices becoming worthy replacements to a lot of industrial hardware equipment,
it makes sense to have the ability to scan barcodes built in. Scanning for barcodes is just
as simple as what you did in the previous topic with still images. The only difference is the
outputSource. If you recollect from the previous topic, you read about the various types of
output sources. For barcodes, the outputSource property is AVCaptureMetadataOutput.

Create a new single view project called Camera_2 (now you probably realize why we have the
numbers at the end). Click ViewController.h and add the following:

```
#import <UIKit/UIKit.h>
@import AVFoundation;

@interface ViewController : UIViewController

@end

AVCaptureSession *session;
AVCaptureDevice *theCamera;
AVCaptureDeviceInput *theInputSource;
AVCaptureMetadataOutput *theOutputSource;
AVCaptureVideoPreviewLayer *thePreview;
```

Next, click ViewController.m and add the code to initialize these properties in the
viewDidLoad as before:

```
- (void)viewDidLoad {
    [super viewDidLoad];
    // Do any additional setup after loading the view, typically from a nib.

    NSArray *cameras = [AVCaptureDevice devicesWithMediaType:AVMediaTypeVideo];
    for (AVCaptureDevice *camera in cameras) {
        if ([camera position] == AVCaptureDevicePositionBack){
            theCamera = camera;
            break;
        }
    }
}
```

```
    session = [[AVCaptureSession alloc]init];
    if (theCamera != nil){
        theInputSource = [AVCaptureDeviceInput deviceInputWithDevice:theCamera error:nil];
        if ([session canAddInput:theInputSource])
            [session addInput:theInputSource];

        thePreview = [AVCaptureVideoPreviewLayer layerWithSession:session];
        [[self.view layer] addSublayer:thePreview];
        [thePreview setFrame:[self.view bounds]];
        [thePreview setVideoGravity:AVLayerVideoGravityResizeAspectFill];
    }

    [session startRunning];
}
```

The only thing missing from this code block is the output source; for scanning barcodes, you need to create an output source of type AVCaptureMetadataOutput. You can place this code in between the InputSource and thePreview instantiation.

```
theOutputSource = [[AVCaptureMetadataOutput alloc]init];
if ([session canAddOutput:theOutputSource])
    [session addOutput:theOutputSource];
NSArray *options = [NSArray arrayWithObject:AVMetadataObjectTypeQRCode];
[theOutputSource setMetadataObjectsDelegate:self queue:dispatch_get_main_queue()];
[theOutputSource setMetadataObjectTypes:options];
```

AVCaptureMetadataOutput is slightly different in that you can set the metadataObjectTypes property to include the barcodes that you want recognized. If it is not added to the metadata types, it is not recognized. In the previous example, this will scan for and recognize only QR codes. The other thing that is different is the delegate method. It takes two parameters; one is the target that implements AVCaptureMetadataOutputObjectsDelegate, and the other is the dispatch queue on which the delegate methods are executed. You could create your own custom queue and use it for processing; however, in this case, the default priority queue is used. You can see the barcode detector in action in Figure 13-4.

Note   All UI updates are on the dispatch_main_queue, so if your code is run on any other queue, you will have to run the UI update code on the main_queue for the updates to work.

Figure 13-4. QR barcode recognized and displayed as an alert

Add AVCaptureMetadataOutputObjectsDelegate to the class definition in ViewController.h so that the class can be a delegate for metadataObjects.

```
@interface ViewController : UIViewController <AVCaptureMetadataOutputObjectsDelegate>
```

There is just one delegate method in AVCaptureMetadataOutputObjectsDelegate; it is captu reOutput:didOutputMetadataObjects:fromConnection. This function is called whenever the output captures any new objects.

```
#pragma mark AVCaptureMetadataObjectsDelegate Function

-(void) captureOutput:(AVCaptureOutput *)captureOutput didOutputMetadataObjects:(NSArray *)
metadataObjects fromConnection:(AVCaptureConnection *)connection{
    for (AVMetadataMachineReadableCodeObject *theItem in metadataObjects) {
        NSLog(@"We read %@ from a barcode of type %@", [theItem stringValue], [theItem type]);
    }

}
```

To display the QR codes as an AlertBox, you could add the following code:

```
[self showAlert:[NSString stringWithFormat:@"We got %@", [theItem stringValue]]
Message:[NSString stringWithFormat:@"Barcode type %@", [theItem type]] Button:@"OK"
handler:nil];
```

Add the showAlert as your custom code.

```
-(void)showAlert:(NSString *)theTitle
        Message:(NSString *)theMessage
         Button:(NSString *)theButton
        handler:(void (^)(UIAlertAction *action)) completionHandler {
    UIAlertController *alert = [UIAlertController
                    alertControllerWithTitle:theTitle
                                     message:theMessage
                              preferredStyle:UIAlertControllerStyleAlert];
    UIAlertAction *OKButton = [UIAlertAction
                        actionWithTitle:theButton
                                  style:UIAlertActionStyleDefault
                                handler:completionHandler];
    [alert addAction:OKButton];
    [self presentViewController:alert animated:YES completion:nil];
}
```

Generating Barcodes

You can use the previous code to scan and decode barcodes. Apple also has functionality to generate barcodes. The functionality is available in the CoreImage framework. It is perhaps one of the simplest ways to generate a barcode. Traditionally, a barcode holds the information encoded in it, and generating a visual representation is not the easiest of tasks (sans this API). The way to generate barcodes is to utilize the CIFilter functions. A CIFilter is so named because it is available as part of the CoreImage framework. A filter is just like a function; there is an input, and there is an output. The logic that processes the input to produce the output is not available to you. To generate a barcode, you need to initialize a CIFilter with the appropriate filter name.

```
NSString *theText = @"This is the Sample Text";
CIFilter *filter = [CIFilter filterWithName:@"CIQRCodeGenerator"];
[filter setDefaults];

NSData *data = [theText dataUsingEncoding:NSUTF8StringEncoding];
[filter setValue:data forKey:@"inputMessage"];
```

Abracadabra, you can now get an image via the outputImage property of the filter. Note that this output image is in CIImage format and needs to be converted into a UIImage, which can then be assigned to a UIImageView or saved to the Photos Album. The other thing is that this image is generally very small and would need a bit of scaling up to make it larger. Relying on the UIImageView to scale the image could result in blurry images.

```
CIImage *outputImage = filter.outputImage;
CIContext *ciContext = [CIContext contextWithOptions:nil];
CGImageRef cgImage = [ciContext createCGImage:outputImage fromRect:[outputImage extent]];
UIImage *image = [UIImage imageWithCGImage:cgImage scale:1
                               orientation:UIImageOrientationUp];
```

Figure 13-5 shows the results of this blurriness; however, surprisingly, it is still detectable and can be read even on an iPhone 4 camera.

Figure 13-5. The generated QR code, blurry but recognizable

To display a smooth scaled-up image, most algorithms use anti-aliasing, which is what causes the blurriness. For line art that needs to be crisp and does not need any anti-aliasing, the scaling options do not work well. This is because the algorithms try to interpolate (figure out the intermediate pixels) when scaling an image. To get crisp black-and-white line art like in Figure 13-6, you need to turn off the interpolation.

```
CGFloat scaleRef = [self.view bounds].size.width  / [image size].width;
CGFloat width = [image size].width * scaleRef;
CGFloat height = [image size].height * scaleRef;

UIGraphicsBeginImageContext(CGSizeMake(width, height));
CGContextRef context = UIGraphicsGetCurrentContext();
CGContextSetInterpolationQuality(context, kCGInterpolationNone);
```

```
[image drawInRect:CGRectMake(0, 0, width, height)];
    UIImage *temp = UIGraphicsGetImageFromCurrentImageContext();
    UIGraphicsEndImageContext();

    // Now assign this image in temp to the imageView instead
```

Figure 13-6. *Crisper and better-looking QR barcode achieved with a little scaling*

With interpolation set to none, the results shown in Figure 13-6 are crisp and better.

Make Some Noise

You saw how to play videos in the previous chapter, and in the last few sections you learned how to get the camera to work for taking still images or detecting barcodes. But in your application, you might simply want to play a sound for a bullet fired or even for congratulating the player or providing feedback. Text-to-speech can work in some cases, but you don't imagine hearing text-to-speech say "Bang" or "Kapow" instead of actual sound effects in a shooting or boxing game.

To play an audio file, you need an audio file and a player. A little understanding about audio files will help you understand the complexities involved in playing audio. All audio files are stored as binary data and are encoded and even compressed to save space. Similar to still image files, which could be stored in various formats such as JPEG, PNG, BMP, GIF, and so on, audio files are also stored in different formats. The data is specific to each type of file. To play an audio file, the player must identify, decode, and then convert the data into an audio signal and play it. Luckily, you do not have to bother with all of that low-level stuff, and you can focus on playing the audio and managing it from your UI. AVFoundation offers audio playback via AVAudioPlayer, but unlike AVPlayerViewController (from AVKit), you are presented with no UI presented to manage playback. You have to create your own UI like you did with MPMediaPlayer in the previous chapter. Another difference between AVAudioPlayer and the other classes you have used like AVPlayer is that AVAudioPlayer offers a delegate to manage the events, whereas with the others you have to set up notifications to monitor event changes.

```
NSString *file = [[NSBundle mainBundle]pathForResource:@"megamix" ofType:@"mp3"];
NSURL *theURL = [NSURL fileURLWithPath:file];
AVAudioPlayer *thePlayer = [[AVAudioPlayer alloc]initWithContentsOfURL:theURL error:nil];
[thePlayer play];
```

Now you can simply use [thePlayer play]; however, there is a small catch (there is always something, isn't there?). Since the loading of the file data is on an asynchronous queue, the player might not play any audio. If you put the play method in a button, the audio will play fine.

You can also change the playback rate to play the audio faster or slower than the normal playback rate. Simply setting rate = 0.5 would not set the playback rate to half-speed because you need to set enableRate = true before you call prepareToPlay or call play. That's all there is to playing an audio file; AVAudioPlayer does not play streaming audio but can play audio files located on a network. You can pause the audio playback using the pause method and query the state of the player via the isPlaying property, which returns true when playing and false when paused or stopped. The currentTime property provides information in seconds regarding the position of the playback in the audio file, and duration provides the total length of the file in seconds.

Recording Audio

Like AVAudioPlayer, if you want to record audio, you can use the AVAudioRecorder class. This is similar to AVAudioPlayer in the sense that it comes without a UI and you can create your own UI elements to work with the recorder class. The methods that you would use are as you might expect; you can start recording with the record method, pause the recording with pause, and stop the recording with stop.

Starting with iOS 8, access to most hardware features requires user permissions, and only if the user allows it can the app access that hardware functionality. The permissions are asked once the first time the app is run, and then those permissions are persisted (unless explicitly changed via the Settings app).

AVAudioSession needs to be set up for use prior to using AVAudioPlayer. This prepares the way sound is played from your application and the way the application behaves when the app goes to the background, such as when the screen locks. You have to be careful about this because it can even disable recording and playback in certain modes. For this application, since you want to record and then also be able to play back the recording, you require AVAudioSessionCategoryPlayAndRecord.

However, before you can start recording, you need to prepare the AVAudioRecorder object with the file you want to save the recording to. The file is a URL and passed to the class when initializing the same.

```
-(IBAction)record:(id)sender {
    AVAudioRecorder *recorder;
    NSURL *docsDir = [[[NSFileManager defaultManager]
                        URLsForDirectory:NSDocumentDirectory
                           inDomains:NSUserDomainMask] firstObject];
    NSURL *theFile = [NSURL URLWithString:@"recording.wav" relativeToURL:docsDir];
    recorder = [[AVAudioRecorder alloc] initWithURL:theFile settings:nil error:nil];
    [recorder recordForDuration:10.0];
}
```

The previous code first sets the docsDir variable with the URL path to the Documents directory on the device; next the filename recording.wav is appended to this URL. The resulting URL is then used to initialize the AVAudioRecorder object. If the file exists, the recording would overwrite the file. Next, to limit the recording to ten seconds, the recordForDuration method is used, passing it a value to 10. If you want longer recordings, you can simply change this to a larger value and, for custom length recordings, call the record method and then stop or pause when you are done.

When you call the pause method, the recording is paused, and the file is still open for more audio data to be added via the record method. However, when you call the stop method, all of the buffers are written to the device, and the file is closed. Any further record attempts would result in the file being overwritten with the new data. The file where the audio data is stored is specified when you create the AVAudioRecorder object. If you want to create another file as the destination for the recorded data, you need to create a new AVAudioRecorder object with the new file URL.

Playing back the recorded content is the same as you used earlier; the only difference is that this time around you are playing the file you have called recording.wav and stored in the Documents directory. Earlier everything was stored in this directory because Apple offered this as the writable directory in the sandboxed hierarchy of directories. Now, after the introduction of iCloud integration, Apple recommends *not storing* information in this directory because this directory gets synced.

> **Note**   If you run the code on the simulator, AVAudioPlayer and AVAudioRecorder both work fine; however, using a device to test is always best.

When creating an AVAudioRecorder class, you can also specify the settings for the recording. In the previous code, the settings have been passed a nil value, thereby using the default values. However, while creating the AVAudioRecorder, you could specify settings such as the audio format, the sample rate, the number of channels, and so on. Some of the settings that you would use are as follows:

- AVSampleRateKey: This is the sample rate in hertz and expressed in a floating-point value.

- AVNumberOfChannelsKey: This specifies the number of channels as an integer value.

- AVEncoderBitRateKey: This specifies the bit rate of the audio encoder.

- AVSampleRateConverterAudioQualityKey: This specifies the quality of the sample rate conversion.

The settings are passed as a key-value pair, and the sample settings look like the following:

```
NSDictionary *settings = @{
        AVSampleRateKey:@44100,
        AVNumberOfChannelsKey:@2,
        AVEncoderBitRateKey:@16,
        AVEncoderAudioQualityKey:[NSNumber numberWithLong: AVAudioQualityHigh]
                };
```

If you want to delete the recording, you can simply call the deleteRecording method.

```
[recorder deleteRecording];
```

> **Tip**   For more information about using and working with audio and video, the book *Beginning iOS Media App Development* from Apress is a good source.

The Show Must Go On

The functionalities offered in the iOS updates are not limited to the coverage in this chapter. In fact, it is so huge that there are books dedicated entirely to each of the functionalities. There are a couple of books from Apress that offer detailed information. Just search at Apress.com.

In the next chapter, you will read about the additions to Interface Builder and transitions between view controllers. So, get ready to enter a different section of the Willy Wonka Factory.

Interface Builder and Storyboards

As much as writing code is important in developing applications, getting a little help in the form of visual aids is nice. It is not difficult for a seasoned developer to whip up a user interface (UI) from code in a couple of minutes, but there could be other design considerations that might be an impeding factor when drawing UIs via code. For visual editing, Apple provides Interface Builder as an integral part of Xcode. It works quite well with the code editor too, whereby you can drag and drop to create outlets and actions.

A visual overview is critical to help you understand and manage a project. Storyboards are another tool that allow you to visually see the different view controllers and their connections. Developers in the past used various wireframe tools to create outlines and workflows and then had to convert them for use in Xcode. With storyboards, you not only can create these in Xcode but also can set up the flow between various view controllers and objects and have an interactive model ready at the click of a button. Following this, developers can take over and write the code to make your project work as expected.

You have used storyboards and connected them with segues in the preceding chapters, so by now you have a fair idea about the way storyboards work.

Storyboard View Controllers

A *storyboard* is a visual representation of several scenes. You can have multiple storyboards in your application. In the past, you had a xib file, which stored one scene per file. A single scene in a storyboard basically is made up of at least a view controller and a view. These views may in turn contain other objects, views, and controls that make up the UI of your application. This collection of views and subviews in the view controller makes up the content view hierarchy. A storyboard may have more than one scene, and these scenes can be connected by segues (pronounced as "seg-ways"). This represents the transition between view controllers. There are a couple of view controllers you can use in your projects, described here:

- *View controller*: This is the standard and most commonly used view controller in many applications. This is generally used with a custom class to provide the functionality.

- *Navigation controller*: This is a view controller that has a navigation controller and a root view controller. This is used in applications where you want the user to be able to easily navigate through scenes. The back button is displayed automatically and part of the functionality offered by this view controller.

- *Table view controller*: This is another one of the most commonly used view controllers; it manages and displays a UITableView as the view.

- *Tab bar controller*: This view controller acts like a container that connects to other view controllers and swaps displaying them based on the tab that has been selected. The tabs are displayed at the bottom of the window, allowing the user to select and switch.

- *Split view controller*: This view controller provides a master-detail interface, where the (primary) master view controller drives the information displayed in the (secondary) detail view controller. This view controller offers a split view, which is generally seen in iPad applications and in landscape mode of the new iPhone 6 Plus. On iPhones, it displays the same thing using a navigation bar.

- *Page view controller*: This view controller, like the tab bar controller, displays view controllers and allows the user to swipe between them and change the view controllers like pages with a page indicator at the bottom.

- *GLKit view controller*: This view controller houses a GLView that can be used to display OpenGL animation or objects.

- *Collection view controller*: Like the table view controller houses the table view, this displays and manages a collection view.

- *AVKit Player view controller*: This view controller is a fully featured AVPlayer, as shown in Chapter 12.

All storyboards have a single entry point that indicates that when this storyboard is instantiated, this is the view controller that is displayed first. Each view controller has a property called Is Initial View Controller, and only one view controller can be set as the initial view controller per storyboard. The storyboard that is the initial view controller is represented with an arrow to the left of the view controller, as shown in Figure 14-1.

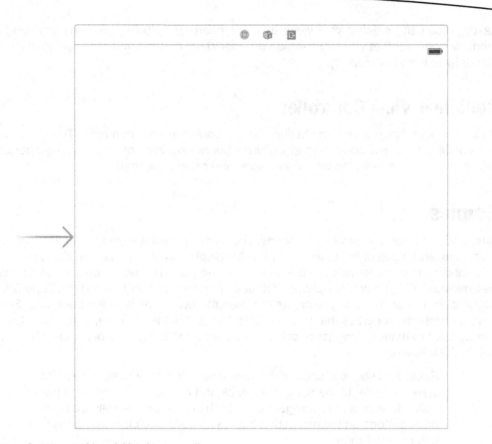

Figure 14-1. *Storyboard with an initial view controller*

> **Note**   You never instantiate an `UIViewController` object directly; you always use a subclass of
> `UIViewController`.

If a view is connected via a segue, then the view controller in which that view is
contained loads and allocates all of its objects and displays the view controller on
the device. You would never allocate or deallocate this view controller. If you need
to programmatically instantiate the view controller, you can do so by calling the
`instantiateViewControllerWithIdentifier` method on a storyboard object.

```
UIStoryboard *story = [UIStoryboard storyboardWithName:@"Main" bundle:nil];
frmCustomScene *tmpForm = [story instantiateViewControllerWithIdentifier:@"frmCustomScene"];
```

You can also use a view controller from a nib/xib file, but the relationships between
the subviews and other view controllers cannot be created or visualized like with
storyboards. If you were to create a view controller from a xib file, you would use the
`initWithNibName:bundle:` method.

Lastly, if you cannot define your views in a storyboard or a xib file, you can create and add them via code; for that you can override the loadView: method and then assign this view hierarchy to the view property.

Container View Controller

While it sounds fancy, a view controller is also a container view controller. The view controller can contain other view controllers as children. Some examples of container view controllers are split view controllers, tab view controllers, and page view controllers.

Segues

After you place some controls on a scene, you want to grant the user the ability to interact with them, and some of the tasks might involve displaying another scene. You can Control-drag from the element to the new scene, and upon releasing the mouse, you will be presented with a menu of options. You used this earlier while creating the SuperDB application. The connection you create between the two forms is called the *seque*. Seques have a couple of properties that you can alter. The first is the identifier, which is a string and can be used to manually trigger or call a segue. The next is the type of segue, which can be one of the following:

- *Push*: This segue is used with a navigation view controller. It adds the view controller to the navigation stack and provides the user with the ability to view and to navigate back to the previous controller using the back buttons on the navigation bar. If you have size classes enabled, this is called *show*.

- *Popover*: This segue works only on iPads and displays the view controller as a pop-up window. If you have size classes enabled, this is called *popover presentation*.

- *Replace*: This segue works with a master-detail split view controller. If you have size classes enabled, this is called *show detail*.

- *Modal*: This segue displays the new view controller on top of the existing view controller, and when this is dismissed, the previous view controller is visible. There is no provision for the back button, and you have to employ a way to dismiss the view controller. If you have size classes enabled, this is called *present modally*.

Note   The options listed here are if you are *not* using the size classes. When you use size classes, the options are named differently.

Start a new application based on the Single View Application template and call it Storyboarding_1. Click Main.Storyboard, and from the Object Library drag a button onto the view controller. Double-click it and change its text to Show. Then, drag another view controller to the right of the existing view controller. Control-drag from the button on the view controller on the left to the view controller on the right. Select the segue of type modal / present modally. Drag a label from the Object Library and drop it on the view controller on the right; change its text to This is a new Scene. Select the segue and change the animation from Default to Flip Horizontally. Run the project and tap the button. The view flips horizontally and displays the view controller with the text. The only issue is that you cannot go back to the first view controller.

Click the view controller on the left and from the menu select Editor ➤ Embed in ➤ Navigation View Controller. You will see that a new view controller, of type Navigation view controller, is added to the left of the first view controller. Click the segue you created between the view controllers with the button and the label. Change the type from Modal / Present Modally to Push / Show in the Attributes Inspector. Run the project again and click the button this time. You see a back button on the top, and the screen slides to show you the one with the label. If you click the back button, you are taken back to the first one with the button.

There is another type of segue that you can create, called a *manual segue*. The manual seque has pretty much the same options: Push, Modal, or Custom. However, these segues are set but not called automatically, and it is up to you to call these via code. You created and used manual segues in the SuperDB application.

Controls

The Object Library has a large collection of controls that help you create the UI for your application. You can drag objects onto the view controller, like you did with the label earlier, and you can change the location, the dimensions, and even some properties such as the text, the text color, or the background color. The changes are displayed immediately. This allows you to visually set up your interface quickly.

If you need a custom control, drag a view as a placeholder and imagine it as it would be rendered when the project is run. To add functionality to the control, you need to subclass it, add the properties, and set them when you run the app.

Drag a view onto the view controller with the button. Place it above the button and set the width and the height to 150 pixels each. Click Storyboarding_1, and create a new file of type Cocoa Touch Class as a subclass of UIView and name it BasicControl. The editor will open the newly created file. Add the two properties shown here to BasicControl.h:

```
#import <UIKit/UIKit.h>

@interface BasicControl : UIView
@property (nonatomic, strong) NSString *text;
@property (nonatomic) int secretID;
@end
```

Change to the storyboard and click the UIView you added. In the Identity Inspector, change Class to BasicControl. The control has two properties that are available to the control only when the project is run. It does not offer you the same parity as when using a label or a button, where you can change the property values in Interface Builder.

Inspectable

Since Xcode 6, you can mark properties as Inspectable, which means they will be available in Interface Builder. Click the BasicControl.m file and add the IBInspectable attribute to the properties.

```
@interface BasicControl : UIView
@property (nonatomic, strong) IBInspectable NSString *text;
@property (nonatomic) IBInspectable int secretID;
@end
```

Switch back to the storyboard and click the UIView. Then go to the Attributes Inspector, where you will see two new properties that you can modify, as shown in Figure 14-2.

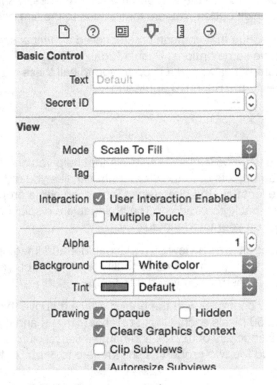

Figure 14-2. Attributes Inspector displaying the custom properties

Interface Builder cannot display and support all types of variables, but some supported ones are as follows:

- Int, Double, CGFloat
- String
- Bool
- CGPoint
- CGSize

- CGRect

- UIColor

- UIImage

The additional properties added to the BasicControl show up in the Attributes Inspector, as shown in Figure 14-3.

```
@property (nonatomic, strong) IBInspectable NSString *text;
@property (nonatomic) IBInspectable int secretID;
@property (nonatomic) IBInspectable UIImage *image;
@property (nonatomic) IBInspectable CGPoint position;
@property (nonatomic) IBInspectable CGRect rect;
@property (nonatomic) IBInspectable BOOL isVisible;
```

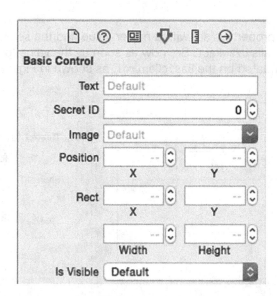

Figure 14-3. More custom properties displayed in the Attributes Inspector

Designable

Apple has added another attribute, IB_DESIGNABLE; this allows the control to be interactive and drawn in Interface Builder, not just at runtime. The IB_DESIGNABLE attribute is added before the class definition.

```
#import <UIKit/UIKit.h>

IB_DESIGNABLE
@interface BasicControl : UIView
```

You can simply add a drawRect function that draws your custom control. You can add the following code to the BasicControl:

```
-(void) drawRect:(CGRect)rect {
    [self.text drawAtPoint:CGPointMake(5, 5) withAttributes:nil];
}
```

This will draw the string in the text property. There is just one more change you need to make. When you change the value of the text property, the control does not know that it has to redraw itself and display the updated text. A simple change to the property text can fix that.

```
-(void) setText:(NSString *)text {
    _text = text;
    [self setNeedsDisplay];
}
```

This is called when the property is set with a newer value and the setNeedsDisplay function is called, which in turn calls drawRect. So, now as soon as the value for text is changed in Interface Builder, it is updated on the BasicControl, as shown in Figure 14-4.

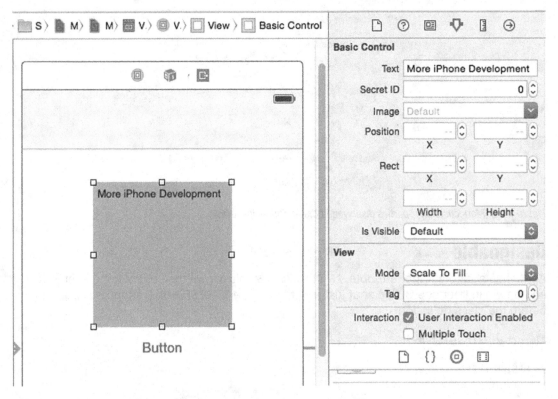

Figure 14-4. Basic control drawn with custom properties set in Interface Builder

When creating a custom control, you would create a custom class that subclasses an existing view object, mostly an UIView, but you could subclass a UITextField and add floating titles, add an UILabel, and so on. Xcode insists that you implement the initWithCoder function, which is the initializer that is called when the application is run; however, for the Interface Builder live preview, the initWithFrame initializer is called via Interface Builder.

```
-(instancetype)initWithCoder:(NSCoder *)aDecoder {
    self = [super initWithCoder:aDecoder];
    if (self) {
        [self initializeDefaults];
    }
    return self;
}

-(instancetype)initWithFrame:(CGRect)frame {
    self = [super initWithFrame:frame];
    if (self){
        [self initializeDefaults];
    }
    return self;
}

-(void) initializeDefaults {
    //Do the initialization here
}
```

Then you are also required to implement the layoutSubviews method, which is called when the view is instructed to reload its subviews. When the control is in Interface Builder, the layoutSubviews method is called to set up the IBDesignable view. Lastly, if you have any custom drawing, then you will also have to implement the drawRect method, which is called both at design time and at runtime.

A More Useful BasicControl

Let's get back to the BasicControl. You can make it slightly more useful than just displaying the text. The BasicControl will act as a progress bar inspired by Google material design. It fills up the view with a circle based on a progress value that is in the range of 0 to 1. The BasicControl will look like Figure 14-5.

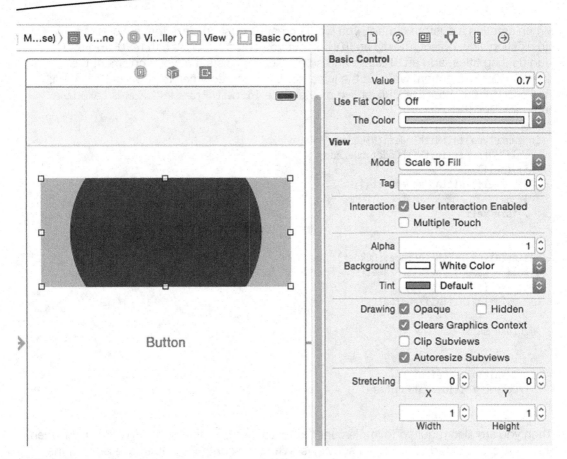

Figure 14-5. The BasicControl to act as a fancy progress bar

You need to first delete all of the code from the class implementation in BasicControl.m to before the @end. This control has a couple of properties, three of which are shown in Figure 14-5. These are value, which holds a number between 0.0 to 1.0; another Boolean called useFlatColor, which switches between a flat, colored fill and a gradient fill (the gradient fill is shown in Figure 14-5); and, lastly, theColor, which holds the flat color for the control. Apart from this, the control needs two private variables: one to reference the flat fill shape and the other for the gradient shape.

```
IB_DESIGNABLE
@interface BasicControl : UIView
@property (nonatomic) IBInspectable CGFloat value;
@property (nonatomic) IBInspectable BOOL useFlatColor;
@property (nonatomic, strong) IBInspectable UIColor *theColor;
@end
CAShapeLayer *shape;
CAGradientLayer *gradient;
```

For the three variables that are inspectable, you can use setXXX functions, which are observer functions that are called after the value of the variable is changed. The changes are applied to the custom control in those functions. If the value is changed, the control sends a message to redraw itself. When useFlatColor is changed, the gradient is hidden or displayed accordingly. The gradient layer simply overlays onto the flat, colored shape layer, so when the gradient layer is visible, the flat, colored layer is not visible. When the color is changed, it is applied directly to the shape as the fill color.

Next add the init functions for the control to be instantiated and created.

```
-(instancetype)initWithCoder:(NSCoder *)aDecoder {
    self = [super initWithCoder:aDecoder];
    if (self) {
        // Called when project run in Simulator or on Device if Control was in IB
    }
    return self;
}

-(instancetype)initWithFrame:(CGRect)frame {
    self = [super initWithFrame:frame];
    if (self){
        // Called when in Interface Builder or via Code created by passing a frame
    }
    return self;
}
```

The init function with the NSCoder is called when the control is placed on the view in Interface Builder. The init function with the frame is called when the control is placed in Interface Builder and also when you create an instance from code using this initializer.

There is an additional function that is available to set up your code only when rendering for Interface Builder at design time. You can call prepareForInterfaceBuilder; this is *not* called when the control is in runtime.

Now you need to implement the layoutSubviews function; this repositions and resizes the subviews. There are a number of triggers that will cause the layoutSubview to be called. This function is called when any of the following take place:

- When the view hierarchy is altered, like a subview is added or removed
- When the dimensions of the view are changed, like resizing the control in Interface Builder or via code (setting the frame)
- When the device is rotated

This is the best point to manage the control. First you can check whether the shape and gradient are initialized; if they are not, then instantiate them.

```
-(void)layoutSubviews {

    [super layoutSubviews];

    self.clipsToBounds = YES;

    if (!shape) {
        shape = [CAShapeLayer layer];
        [self.layer addSublayer:shape];
        [shape setBackgroundColor:_theColor.CGColor];
        [shape setMasksToBounds:YES];
    }

    UIColor *red = [UIColor redColor];
    UIColor *blue = [UIColor blueColor];
    NSArray *colors = [NSArray arrayWithObjects:(id)red.CGColor, (id)blue.CGColor, nil];

    if (!gradient) {
        gradient = [CAGradientLayer layer];
        [self.layer addSublayer:gradient];
        [gradient setColors:colors];
        [gradient setMasksToBounds:YES];
    }
```

Now, the radius is calculated, which is basically the hypotenuse with the height and width of the control container. This ensures that the corners are filled. The frame variable is set to the bounding rectangle of the container. The radius is scaled based on the _value assigned.

```
CGRect frame = self.bounds;
CGFloat x = MAX( midX(frame) , frame.size.width - midX(frame));
CGFloat y = MAX( midY(frame), frame.size.height - midY(frame));
CGFloat radius = sqrt(x*x + y*y) * _value;
```

The previous code uses two macros, namely, midX and midY. This is declared as follows:

```
#define midX(frame) (frame.size.width/2)
#define midY(frame) (frame.size.height/2)
```

You will need to import BasicControl.h in the ViewController.h file and create an IBOutlet property connected to your custom control; only then would you be able to access it in your application or from another view controller.

When you change the value of the control during runtime, it will jump a bit because the system will animate it. To make it not jumpy or nonanimated, you can stop the animation by first starting a transaction and then setting animationDuration to 0. This disables animation for the changes that follow and then calls the commit method. The code basically checks whether the value set is less than 0; if it is, the circle is hidden. The cornerRadius property is set to ensure the layers look circular. The same settings applied to the shape layer are applied to the gradient layer. The gradient layer sits on top of the shape layer, and when it is visible, it obstructs the flat single-colored shape layer, giving the impression that the layer is gradient filled.

```
frame = CGRectMake(midX(self.frame) - radius, midY(self.frame) - radius, radius * 2,
radius * 2);
CGRect bounds = frame;

[CATransaction begin];
[CATransaction setAnimationDuration:0];
[CATransaction setDisableActions:YES];

if (_value < 0){
    shape.hidden = YES;
    gradient.hidden = YES;
} else {
    shape.hidden = NO;
    gradient.hidden = (_useFlatColor == YES);
}

if (shape) {
    [shape setCornerRadius:radius];
    [shape setFrame:frame];
    [shape setBounds:bounds];
}

if(gradient) {
    gradient.cornerRadius = shape.cornerRadius;
    gradient.frame = shape.frame;
    gradient.bounds = shape.bounds;
}

[CATransaction commit];
}
```

If you switch between the code and the Interface Builder/storyboard, you will see the rendered circle in the view.

To ensure that the control is updated interactively, you can use the setters that take the format of setXXX, where XXX is the name of your property capitalized. You need to set these two functions to ensure that they update your control when you change their value.

```
-(void)setUseFlatColor:(BOOL)useFlatColor {
    _useFlatColor = useFlatColor;
    gradient.hidden = (useFlatColor == YES);
}

-(void) setValue:(CGFloat)value{
    _value = value;
    [self layoutSubviews];
}
```

Debugging these views is easy but confusing at first. If you set breakpoints in the BasicControl.m file, though, you see that Interface Builder runs that code to update the control every time you make changes to the control from the inspectors, but the breakpoints are never reached. So, it is difficult to debug, right? The NSLog statements do not work either, so you cannot display to the console what's happening. However, debugging is easy because to enable debugging on a custom control, all you need to do is select the Editor ➤ Debug Selected Views option with the Custom Control selected in the storyboard. The debugger breaks at the breakpoint set, and you can step through your code.

> **Note**   When debugging an IB_DESIGNABLE, you can step through code, but you cannot use the console to display the variable information using po and other commands.

View Controllers

In the previous section, you saw that there were transitions you could choose from when displaying a view controller. The transitions provided by Apple are good, but then with iOS development, developers are always getting more innovative. Those transitions might be good, but what if you wanted to have your own set of transitions? Apple has introduced a new class that allows developers to create their own transitions and apply them to the view controllers.

First let's take a closer look at view controllers to understand how they work and what makes them tick. View controllers, as the name suggests, control and manage the display of views on the screen. You could have one big view controller that manages each and every little view; however, by having multiple view controllers controlling different sections of your application, you can visualize and manage the relationships between the views better. This also separates the views into smaller, manageable chunks as they are instantiated, displayed, interacted with, and disposed of.

Each view controller manages a single view; this is generally referred to as the rootViewController, which is the root of the view hierarchy. A view controller loads and releases its views as required and is key in managing the resources in your application. Because it follows the Model-View-Controller (MVC) pattern, it has information about a subset of your application's data and knows how to access and display just that, as per what the model provides. The view controllers must communicate with each other to provide the seamless experience to the user because each is responsible for just a subset of the user experience. In the previous chapters, you used view controllers and probably recall that view controllers are commonly used to perform just one task. For example, in SuperDB, the first view controller was responsible for displaying the list of superheros, and when you clicked one, another view controller was loaded that displayed the details. Each of the view controllers also allowed you to edit/delete the data.

In the earlier example of view controllers, you had two view controllers, whereby clicking the button on the first displayed the second, and then you could navigate back using the back button. View controllers also offer a slightly advanced feature, where you can add the view of another view controller onto the first view controller. The view controller can also be displayed as a popover or simply be displayed from another view controller. It might make sense to you regarding the options that you are presented with when you try to change the segue type, as shown in Figure 14-6.

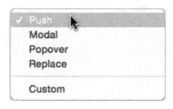

Figure 14-6. Segue options

When a segue is triggered, there are a couple of things that happen. It will load the view controller, and then, depending on the type of segue, the view controller is presented as discussed in the earlier paragraph. In your application, the view controller that triggers the segue will receive a callback to prepareForSegue, and the parameters passed to it are segue and sender. The segue object passed has three properties that you can access, namely, identifier, sourceViewController, and destinationViewController. The identifier property is the string that you can set to identify the segue so you can differentiate between different segues (if you have multiple segues). sourceViewController is the view controller from where this segue is being called, and destinationViewController is the new view controller that is going to be displayed. This can also be used to pass data between the two view controllers by assigning the properties to the destinationViewController from the current view controller.

Click the storyboard, and click the segue between the view controllers with the button and the label. Set the identifier to segueTour. Next click ViewController.m to open it in the editor and toward the end of the file add a function called prepareForSegue. This is the function that is called before a segue is invoked, which provides you with an opportunity to pass data to the destination (new) view controller.

```
-(void) prepareForSegue:(UIStoryboardSegue *)segue sender:(id)sender {
```

Create a new file using the Cocoa Touch Class template and call it DetailViewController; make it a subclass of UIViewController. The new file will open in the editor. Click the DetailViewController.h file and add these properties:

```
@property IBOutlet UILabel *theLabel;
@property (nonatomic, strong) NSString *theText;
```

Add the following line in the viewDidLoad method of DetailViewController.m file. This sets the text for theLabel to the value held in the property theText.

```
_theLabel.text = _theText;
```

Now switch to the storyboard and tap the view controller with the label. Click the yellow icon on the top of the form and in the Identity Inspector change the class to `DetailViewController`. Next Control-drag from the yellow icon to the label and select theLabel from the pop-up menu, as shown in Figure 14-7.

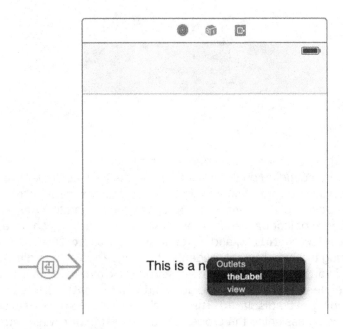

Figure 14-7. Connecting the label as an IBOutlet

Switch back to `ViewController.m`. First add at the top in the import section, `#import "DetailViewController.h"` and then add the code to the `prepareForSegue` function.

```
-(void) prepareForSegue:(UIStoryboardSegue *)segue sender:(id)sender {
    DetailViewController *dest = [segue destinationViewController];
    [dest setTheText:@"This is not sparta, Mate!"];
}
```

Now run the project, and when you tap the Show button, the text you have passed is displayed, not the text you had set via Interface Builder.

Transitions

You might have noticed that initially the scenes flipped to display the others, and then when the detail view controller was changed to be part of the navigation controller, it slides in or out. These animations used while presenting the view controllers are called *transitions*. UIKit has an object called `UIPresentationController` that it uses to present and manage advanced transitions for the presented view controllers. This is what animates the transitions of flipping, sliding, and so on. Your view controller can add its own animations on top of the already provided animation by the animator object. The method for managing the presentation process is `presentViewController:animated:completion:`.

Custom animation can be used for the view controllers that have the presentation style of UIModalPresentationCustom. You can also add decorations (*chrome*) to a view controller using the presentation controller.

The way a presentation controller works is that it adds its own views (if any) to the view hierarchy during the presentation or the dismissal phase and creates the appropriate animations for those views. All of these animations are managed by the animator object, which is an object that conforms to the UIViewControllerAnimatedTransitioning protocol. There are three distinct phases with the presentation process.

- *Presentation*: A new view controller is displayed onscreen, moving it into view with animation.

- *Management*: The animation that is required while the new view controller is onscreen, say responding to device rotation.

- *Dismissal*: The view controller is moved off-screen with animation.

You need to do two things: first implement the protocol and second implement the functions for presentation and dismissal and return a custom animation controller. Add these functions into ViewController.m:

```
-(id <UIViewControllerAnimatedTransitioning>) animationControllerForDismissedController:(UIV
iewController *)dismissed {
    MyAnimator *animator = [[MyAnimator alloc]init];
    return animator;
}

-(id <UIViewControllerAnimatedTransitioning>) animationControllerForPresentedController:(UIV
iewController *)presented presentingController:(UIViewController *)presenting sourceControll
er:(UIViewController *)source {
    MyAnimator *animator = [[MyAnimator alloc]init];
    animator.presenting = YES;
    return animator;
}
```

Click the ViewController.h file. First add the import statement to import MyAnimator.h and then add the protocol UIViewControllerTransitioningDelegate.

```
@interface ViewController : UIViewController <UIViewControllerTransitioningDelegate>
```

This way you can abstract the animations and have different effects that you could apply to your transitions. Create a new file using Cocoa Touch Class, make it a subclass of NSObject, and name it MyAnimator. Add a property in MyAnimator.h called presenting of type BOOL, which indicates whether the transition is presenting or dismissing the view controller. You need to also add #import <UIKit/UIKit.h>.

```
@interface MyAnimator : NSObject
@property (nonatomic) BOOL presenting;
@end
```

This class needs to conform to the UIViewControllerAnimatedTransitioning protocol. This protocol has two required functions that you will need to implement. One is transitionDuration, which returns the length of the transition, and the other is animateTransition, which actually performs the transition. Now click the MyAnimator.m file and add the functions to it.

```
-(NSTimeInterval) transitionDuration:(id<UIViewControllerContextTransitioning>)
transitionContext{
    return 0.5;
}


-(void)animateTransition:(id<UIViewControllerContextTransitioning>)transitionContext{
    UIViewController *fromView = [transitionContext viewControllerForKey:UITransitionContext
    FromViewControllerKey];
    UIViewController *toView = [transitionContext viewControllerForKey:UITransitionContextT
    oViewControllerKey];
    CGRect endFrame = [[UIScreen mainScreen] bounds];

    if (_presenting == YES){
        [fromView.view setUserInteractionEnabled:NO];

        [[transitionContext containerView] addSubview:fromView.view];
        [[transitionContext containerView] addSubview:toView.view];

        CGRect startFrame = endFrame;
        startFrame.origin.x += 320;

        [toView.view setFrame:startFrame];

        [UIView animateWithDuration:[self transitionDuration:transitionContext]
                        animations:^{
                            [fromView.view
                                setTintAdjustmentMode:UIViewTintAdjustmentModeDimmed];
                            [toView.view setFrame:endFrame];
                            [fromView.view setAlpha:0];
                        }
                        completion:^(BOOL finished) {

                        [transitionContext completeTransition:YES];
                        }];
    } else {
        [toView.view setUserInteractionEnabled:YES];

        [[transitionContext containerView] addSubview:toView.view];
        [[transitionContext containerView]addSubview:fromView.view];

        endFrame.origin.x += 320;

        [UIView animateWithDuration:[self transitionDuration:transitionContext]
                        animations:^{
                            [toView.view
                                setTintAdjustmentMode:UIViewTintAdjustmentModeAutomatic];
```

```
                        [fromView.view setFrame:endFrame];
                        [toView.view setAlpha:1];
                    }
                    completion:^(BOOL finished) {
                        [transitionContext completeTransition:YES];
                    }
            ];
        }
}
```

The only thing that remains is to prepare the view controller prior to displaying it. If you have a segue or you are creating and presenting it manually, you need to set the transitionDelegate to self (and you are conforming to the UIViewControllerTransitioningDelegate protocol) and set the view controller's modalPresentationStyle to Custom. Switch to Main.storyboard, click the DetailViewController, and set its storyboard ID to sparta. Click the view controller (the one with the buttons), add a new button, and change the text to No Segue. Add the following code in ViewController.m and then switch back to the storyboard:

```
-(IBAction)displayAnimated:(id)sender{
    UIStoryboard *story = [UIStoryboard storyboardWithName:@"Main" bundle:nil];
    UIViewController *newVC = [story instantiateViewControllerWithIdentifier:@"sparta"];

    newVC.transitioningDelegate = self;
    newVC.modalPresentationStyle = UIModalPresentationCustom;

    self.modalPresentationStyle = UIModalPresentationCurrentContext;
    newVC.modalPresentationStyle = UIModalPresentationCurrentContext;

    [self presentViewController:newVC animated:YES completion:nil];
}
```

Control-drag from the new button to the yellow icon on top of the view controller and connect to the displayAnimated method. (This is a way to connect an existing IBAction to a control.)

Switch to the storyboard, add a button to the DetailViewController, and change its text to Done. Create an IBOutlet called theButton of type UIButton and an IBAction called dismissButton for this button you just added. Click DetailViewController.h and create another property of type BOOL called hideButton. Then add these lines in ViewController.m in the prepareForSegue function, to look like this:

```
-(void) prepareForSegue:(UIStoryboardSegue *)segue sender:(id)sender {
    DetailViewController *dest = [segue destinationViewController];
    [dest setTheText:@"This is not sparta, Mate!"];
    [dest setHideButton:YES];
}
```

Add the line _theButton.hidden = _hideButton in the viewDidLoad function in
DetailViewController.m. Lastly, add the implementation for the dismissButton function as
follows:

```
-(IBAction)hideButton:(id)sender {
    [self dismissViewControllerAnimated:YES completion:nil];
}
```

The button will generally be hidden because hideButton is set as YES in the prepareForSegue
function when this DetailViewController is called via the segue. Now when you run the
program and tap the No Segue button, you will see the view controller transitioning from the
right and the original one fading to black. When it is dismissed (by clicking the Done button),
it appears from black, and the top view controller slides out toward the right.

You can have a different animator class and have an entirely different animation for
displaying and viewing view controllers. Since the effects are achieved on the views using
the UIView.animateWithDuration, all types of animations and transforms that can be applied
to the UIView can be applied for this transition.

The transitioningContext object passed to the function animateTransition has a couple of
references that are useful for creating and animating.

- ■ *containerView*: This is the container in which the transition takes place.
  In the case of a modal view, the view that is presenting the new view
  controller is the containerView. In the case of a navigation controller,
  this is the wrapper view that is the size of the rootViewController.

  ```
  UIView *theView = [transitionContext containerView];
  ```

- ■ *From view controller*: This is the view controller that is presenting the
  new view controller. This is the view controller that is currently visible on
  the stack.

  ```
  UIViewController *fromViewC = [transitionContext
                  viewControllerForKey:UITransitionContext
                  FromViewControllerKey];
  ```

- ■ *To view controller*: This is the view controller being presented, or in the
  case of a navigation controller transition, this is the view controller being
  pushed or popped.

  ```
  UIViewController *toViewC = [transitionContext
                  viewControllerForKey:UITransitionContext
                  ToViewControllerKey];
  ```

■ *Initial frame*: This is the frame where each of the view controller's views are when the transition animation begins.

```
CGRect toStartFrame = [transitionContext initialFrameForViewController:toView];
CGRect fromStartFrame = [transitionContext initialFrameForViewController:fromView];
```

■ *Final frame*: This is the frame where each of the view controller's views should be when the transition animation ends.

```
CGRect toEndFrame = [transitionContext finalFrameForViewController:toView];
CGRect fromEndFrame = [transitionContext finalFrameForViewController:fromView];
```

The frames might be a `CGRectZero` if the view controller is removed, like at the end of a dismiss transition.

Cue 'em Up

Apple has provided developers with a whole slew of functions and APIs to animate and work with. The idea of a magical device that transforms is taken a step further with effects that are limited only by your imagination. As we come toward the end of this book, there is still a lot more that needs to be covered so you know what is available in the iOS SDK. There are several resources listed in Chapter 16 that specifically deal with other topics in detail.

You have a fair idea of debugging by now; you've seen crashes, or maybe you missed a step and had to figure out where the error in the code was. In a live project, things are not much different. Put on your debugging hat and turn to the next chapter where you will learn a bit about debugging and Instruments.

15

Unit Testing, Debugging, and Instruments

One of the fundamental truths of computer programming (and life) is that not everything works perfectly. No matter how much you plan and no matter how long you've been programming, it's rare for an application you write to work perfectly the first time and then forever under all circumstances and possible uses. Knowing how to properly architect your application and write well-formed code is important. Knowing how to find out why things aren't working the way they're supposed to, and fixing them, is equally important.

There are three techniques you can leverage to help identify and solve these problems: *unit testing*, *debugging*, and *profiling*.

■ *Unit testing* is the idea of isolating the smallest piece of testable code and determining whether that code behaves as expected. Each unit of code is tested in isolation before testing the application, which can be seen as the integration of all the units of code. That's it. Apple has provided a unit-testing framework and integrated it into Xcode.

■ *Debugging*, as you're probably aware, is the task of eliminating errors, or *bugs*, from your application. While it may refer to any process you use to correct bugs, generally it means using a *debugger* to find and identify bugs in your code.

■ *Profiling* is the measurement and analysis of your application while running. You usually perform profiling with the goal of optimizing application performance. Profiling can be used to monitor CPU or memory usage to help determine where your application is expending resources. With iOS, Apple has provided a GUI tool called Instruments to make application profiling easier.

We'll cover each of these techniques briefly. Our goal here is not to be a comprehensive guide for these techniques. Rather, we introduce these techniques. If you want a more detailed explanation, you may want to read *Pro iOS Tools: Xcode Instruments and Build Tools*.

In this chapter, you're not going to build and debug a complex application. Instead, you're going to create a project from a template, and then we'll show you how to implement each technique, one at a time, by adding code to demonstrate specific problems.

Unit Tests

Let's start by creating a simple project. Open Xcode and create a new project. Select the Master-Detail Application template. Call it **DebugTest** and make sure you check Use Core Data (see Figure 15-1).

Figure 15-1. Creating the DebugTest project with unit tests

Let's take a quick look at the project. Select the project in the Navigator pane and look at the resulting Project Editor (Figure 15-2). Notice there are two targets: the application, DebugTest, and a bundle, DebugTestTests. This bundle is where the unit tests you'll be writing will reside. The DebugTestTests target depends on the DebugTest target (application). This means that when you build the unit testing bundle, it will build the application first.

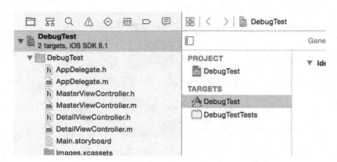

Figure 15-2. *Two project targets: the application and the unit testing bundle*

How do you run your tests? If you look at the Xcode scheme pop-up menu in the toolbar, there is no scheme for DebugTestTests, only one for DebugTest (Figure 15-3).

Figure 15-3. *Where is the DebugTestTests scheme?*

Xcode "automagically" manages this for you. When you select Product ➤ Test on the DebugTest scheme, Xcode knows to execute the DebugTestTests target.

Now run the unit test bundle and see what happens. Select Product ➤ Test.

Xcode should have notified you that the tests passed. If they had failed, the Issue Navigator would tell you where the error occurred. If you select the failure, the editor would go to the failed test in DebugTestTests.m (Figure 15-4).

Figure 15-4. The failed test in Xcode

This seems like a good time to discuss the format of the unit tests. In the Project Navigator, open the group named DebugTestTests and select DebugTestTests.m.

Let's look at DebugTestsTests.m.

```objc
#import <UIKit/UIKit.h>
#import <XCTest/XCTest.h>

@interface DebugMeTests : XCTestCase

@end

@implementation DebugMeTests

- (void)setUp {
    [super setUp];
    // Put setup code here. This method is called before the invocation of each test
    method in the class.

    self.debugMe = [[DebugMe alloc] init];
}

- (void)tearDown {
    self.debugMe = nil;

    // Put teardown code here. This method is called after the invocation of each test
    method in the class.
    [super tearDown];
}

- (void)testExample {
    // This is an example of a functional test case.
    XCTAssert(YES, @"Pass");
}
```

```
- (void)testPerformanceExample {
    // This is an example of a performance test case.
    [self measureBlock:^{
        // Put the code you want to measure the time of here.
    }];
}
@end
```

Each unit test follows a simple process: set up the test, execute the test, tear down the test. Since each test needs to run in isolation, each test method follows the set up/test/tear down cycle.

In the case of DebugTestsTests.m, you can see the one test method, testExample. The body of that method consists of one line, which invokes the function XCTAssert. XCTAssert is an *assertion* that tests the expression. If you explicitly want a test to fail, you can use XCTFail. Let's modify this to fail. Replace XCTAssert with this:

```
- (void)testExample
{
    XCTFail(@"Make this test fail");
}
```

Run the tests again (to shortcut this, hit Cmd-U). This time the tests should fail.

What have you done here? You made a test pass or fail without actually fixing or testing anything. This is an important point: unit testing is not a silver bullet. The tests are only as good as you write them. It's important to make sure you write meaningful tests. A generally accepted practice is called *test first*: you write your test, write your application code such that your test fails, and then you adjust the code to make the test pass. An interesting side effect is that your code tends to be shorter, clearer, and more concise.

Let's define an object with some simple methods that you can test. Create a new file, choosing the Objective-C class. Name the class DebugMe and make it a subclass of NSObject. When you save the file, make sure it is assigned only to the DebugTest target (Figure 15-5).

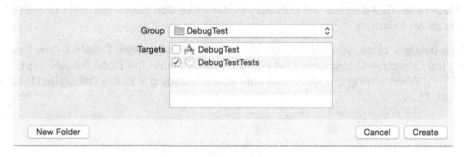

Figure 15-5. Save the DebugMe class to the DebugTest target only

Select DebugMe.h and edit it to appear as follows (add the code as required):

```
#import <Foundation/Foundation.h>

@interface DebugMe : NSObject

@property (nonatomic, strong) NSString *string;

- (BOOL)isTrue;
- (BOOL)isFalse;
- (NSString *)helloWorld;

@end
```

That's pretty simple. You can probably guess what DebugMe.m will look like.

```
#import "DebugMe.h"

@implementation DebugMe

-(BOOL)isTrue {
    return YES;
}

-(BOOL) isFalse {
    return NO;
}

-(NSString *)helloWorld {
    return @"Hello World!";

}

@end
```

Again, it's simple. Your classes will probably be far more complex than this, but we're just doing this as an example.

To test the DebugMe class, you need to create a DebugMeTests class. Create a new file, selecting the Objective-C test case class (Figure 15-6). Name the class DebugMeTests (Figure 15-7). When saving the file, make sure you are adding it to the DebugTestTests target only (Figure 15-8).

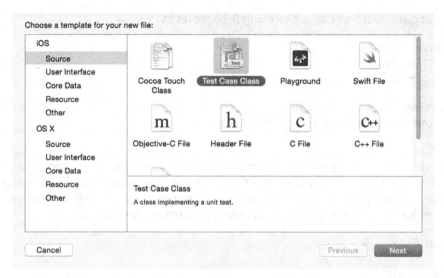

Figure 15-6. Select the Objective-C test case class template

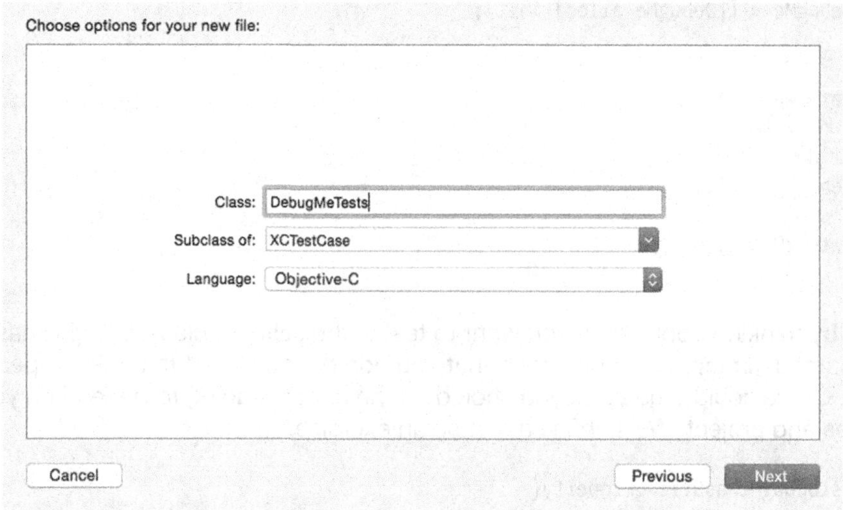

Figure 15-7. Name the test class DebugMeTests

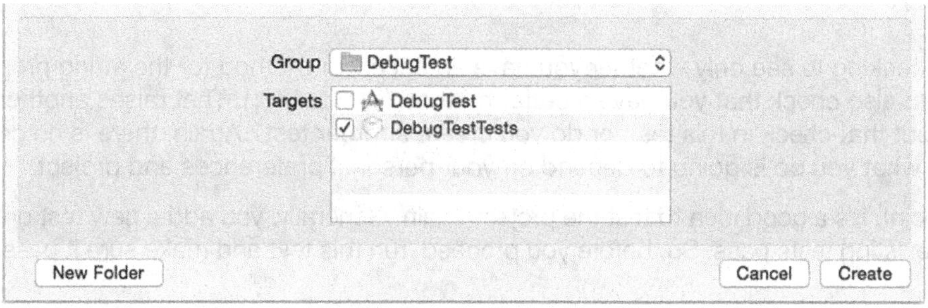

Figure 15-8. Add DebugMeTests to the DebugTestTests target only

Now, let's update your test class. Start with DebugMeTests.h.

```
#import <UIKit/UIKit.h>
#import <XCTest/XCTest.h>
#import "DebugMe.h"

@interface DebugMeTests : XCTestCase
@property (nonatomic, strong) DebugMe *debugMe;
@end
```

Select DebugMeTests.m to open the implementation file in the editor. You import the DebugMe header file and add the property debugMe. You'll be using this property in the implementation. Before you write any tests, you need to implement your setUp and tearDown methods. You'll use setUp to instantiate your debugMe property and tearDown to release it.

```
- (void)setUp
{
    [super setUp];

    // Set-up code here.
    self.debugMe = [[DebugMe alloc] init];
}

- (void)tearDown
{
    // Tear-down code here.
    self.debugMe = nil;

    [super tearDown];
}
```

Let's start by thinking about what you want to test in the DebugMe class. DebugMe has a property named string. We could argue that you don't need to test that this property is present. Or we could argue that you should. In the end, it's going to depend on your preferences and project. We'll define a test as an exercise.

```
-(void) testDebugMeHasStringProperty{
    XCTAssertTrue([self.debugMe
                    respondsToSelector:@selector(string)],
                    @"expected DebugMe to have 'string' selector");
}
```

You're checking to see only whether you have an accessor method for the string property. You could also check that you have a setter method (setString:). That raises another point: do you put that check in this test, or do you create another test? Again, there is no correct answer; what you do is going to depend on your personal preferences and project.

At this point, it's a good idea to test the project again. Generally, you add a new test only when all your existing tests pass. So, before you proceed, run this test and make sure it passes.

Your test should have passed, so let's move on to testing the isTrue method.

```
-(void) testDebugMeIsTrue {
    BOOL result = [self.debugMe isTrue];
    XCTAssertTrue(result, @"Expected DebugMe to be true, got %hhd", result);
}
```

Next, you write a test for the isFalse method.

```
-(void) testDebugMeIsFalse {
    BOOL result = [self.debugMe isFalse];
    XCTAssertFalse(result, @"Expected DebugMe to be false, got %hhd", result);
}
```

Finally, you write a test for the helloWorld method.

```
-(void)testDebugMeHelloWorld {
    NSString * result = [self.debugMe helloWorld];
    XCTAssertEqual(result, @"Hello World!",@"Expected debugMe hello world!, got %@", result);
    XCTAssertEqual(@"3", @"3", @"Equal??");
}
```

Success! You've written your first unit test cases.

As a general practice, you'll want to write a test class for each class in your application. There is a methodology called *test-driven development* (TDD) that suggests you should write your test cases first and then write your application code. A side effect of TDD is that you know how your application is supposed to behave before you start coding (isn't that a good idea?).

Note   You may want to read up on test-driven development (TDD). An excellent introduction can be found at the Agile Data web site (www.agiledata.org/essays/tdd.html). Kent Beck wrote an excellent book called *Test Driven Development* (Addison-Wesley, 2003) that we highly recommend.

There is an additional concept that is useful when writing tests: *mocking.* When the code you are testing is dependent on another object, you can define a *mock object* to emulate the dependent object. This helps maintain the *isolation* of each unit test. A good mocking framework is OCMock by Mulle Kyberkinetik (http://ocmock.org/).

Debugging

As you probably have noticed, when you create a project in Xcode, the project defaults into what's called the *debug configuration*. If you've ever compiled an application for the App Store or for ad hoc distribution, then you're aware that applications usually start with two configurations, one called *debug* and another called *release*.

So, how is the debug configuration different than the release or distribution configuration? There are actually a number of differences between them, but the key difference between them is that the *Debug* configuration builds *debug symbols* into your application. These debug symbols are like little bookmarks in your compiled application that make it possible to match up any command that fires in your application with a specific piece of source code in your project. Xcode includes a piece of software known as a *debugger*, which uses the debug symbols to go from bytes of machine code to the specific functions and methods in the source code that generated that machine code.

> **Caution**   If you try to use the debugger with the release or distribution configuration, you will get odd results since those configurations don't include debug symbols. The debugger will try its best but ultimately will become morose and limp quietly away.

One of the big changes since Xcode 4 was the integration of the debugger into the main window (Figure 15-9). Prior versions of Xcode had their own separate debugger console. Now Xcode changes a number of panes when debugging. We'll discuss the contents of each pane later.

Figure 15-9. Xcode in debugger mode

Breakpoints

Probably the most important debugging tool in your arsenal is the *breakpoint*. A breakpoint is an instruction to the debugger to pause execution of your application at a specific place in your code and wait for you. By pausing, but not stopping, the execution of your program, your application is still running, and you can do things like look at the value of variables and step through lines of code one at a time. A breakpoint can also be set up so that instead of pausing the program's execution, a command or script gets executed, and then the program resumes execution. You'll look at both types of breakpoints in this chapter, but you'll probably use the former a lot more than the latter.

The most common breakpoint type that you'll set in Xcode is the *line number breakpoint*. This type of breakpoint allows you to specify that the debugger should stop at a specific line of code in a specific file. To set a line number breakpoint in Xcode, you just click in the space to the left of the source code file in the editing pane. Let's do that now so you can see how it works.

Single-click `MasterViewController.m`. Look for the method called `viewDidLoad`. It should be one of the early methods in the file. On the left side of the Editing pane, you should see a column with numbers, as in Figure 15-10. This is called the *gutter*, and it's one way to set line number breakpoints.

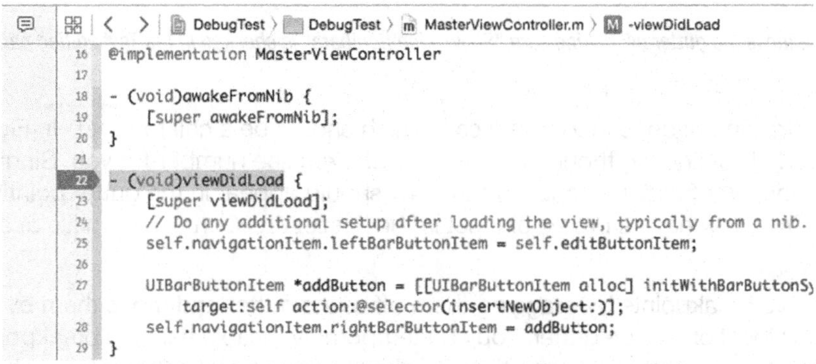

Figure 15-10. To the left of the editing pane is a column that usually shows line numbers. This is where you set breakpoints

---

Tip   If you don't see line numbers or the gutter, open Xcode's preferences, go to the Text Editing pane, and select the Editing tab (Figure 15-11). The first check box in that section is "Show: Line numbers." It's much easier to set breakpoints if you can see the line numbers.

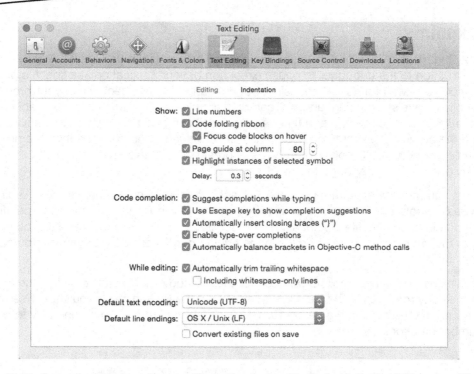

Figure 15-11. *Expose the gutter by making sure "Show: Line numbers" is checked in the Text Editing pane of Xcode Preferences*

Look for the first line of code in viewDidLoad, which should be a call to super. In Figure 15-10, this line of code is at line 22, though it may be a different line number for you. Single-click in the gutter to the left of that line, and a little arrow should appear in the gutter pointing at the line of code. You now have a breakpoint set in the MasterViewController.m file at a specific line number.

You can remove breakpoints by dragging them off of the gutter and move them by dragging them to a new location on the gutter. You can temporarily disable existing breakpoints by single-clicking them, which will cause them to change from a darker color to a lighter color. To reenable a disabled breakpoint, you just click it again to change it back to the darker color.

Before we talk about all the things you can do with breakpoints, let's try out the basic functionality. Select Product ➤ Run. The program will start to launch normally; then before the view gets fully shown, you'll be brought back to Xcode, and the project window will come forward, showing the line of code about to be executed and its associated breakpoint (Figure 15-10).

> **Note**   In the toolbar at the top of the debug and project windows is an icon labeled Breakpoints. As its name implies, clicking that icon toggles between breakpoints on or breakpoints off. This allows you to enable or disable all your breakpoints without losing them.

Remember we said we'd talk about the Xcode debugger layout? Let's do that now.

The Debug Navigator

When Xcode enters debugging mode, the Navigation pane (on the left) activates the Debug Navigator (Figure 15-12). This view shows you the stack trace of the application, the method and function calls that got you here. In this case, it highlights the call to viewDidLoad in the MasterViewController. The grayed-out rows indicate the classes and methods you don't have access to in the source code. You can see the next method is the view from UIViewController. Since UIViewController is part of the UIKit framework, it's not surprising you don't have the source code.

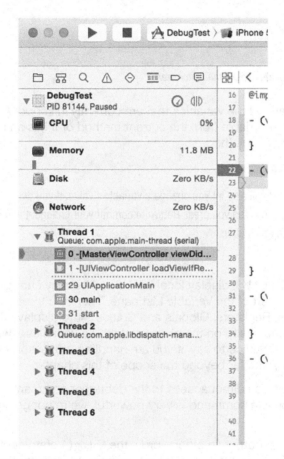

Figure 15-12. Debug Navigator, displaying the stack trace

If you click that line, the Editor pane will change to show the file, highlighting the line that was last called before reaching the breakpoint. This is a useful feature because it allows you to track the flow of method and function calls that lead up to a problem.

The Debug Area

The area underneath the Editor Area is called the Debug Area (Figure 15-13). It's composed of three components. Along the top is the Debug Bar. Below the Debug Bar, to the left, is the Variable List. To the right of the Variable List is the Console Pane. Let's discuss each one, starting with the Variable List.

Figure 15-13. Debug Area, located below the Editor Area

The Variable List displays all the variables that are currently *in scope*. A variable is in scope if it is an argument or local variable from the current method or if it is an instance variable from the object that contains the method.

> **Note**   The Variable List will also let you change a variable's value. If you double-click any value, it will become editable, and when you press Return to commit your change, the underlying variable will also change in the application.

By default, the Variable List will display local variables. You may change this by selecting the drop-down at the upper left of the Variable List pane. There are three options available: Auto; Local; and All Variables, Registers, Globals and Statics. Auto displays the variables Xcode thinks you'll be interested based on the given context. All Variables... will display all variables and processor registers. Suffice to say, if you are handling processor registers, you're doing some pretty advanced work, far beyond the scope of this chapter.

The Console Pane gives you direct access to the debugger command line and output. While using the debugger console command is very powerful, we're not going to discuss it in detail here.

It's important to note that output (in other words, the NSLog() statement) will direct you to the Console Pane. So, it's useful to look there and see what output is generated while debugging.

Finally, the Debug Bar contains a set of controls (Figure 15-14) and a stack trace jump bar. The jump bar displays the current location of the current thread in the application. This is just a distillation of the Debug Navigator view.

Figure 15-14. Debug Bar controls

The Debug Bar controls provide a series of buttons to help control your debugging session. From the left, the first button is a disclosure button to minimize the Debug Area. When minimized, only the Debug Bar is visible. Next is the Continue button. The Continue button resumes execution of your program. It will pick up right where it left off and continue executing as normal unless another breakpoint or an error condition is encountered. The Step Over and Step Into buttons allow you to execute a single line of code at a time. The difference between the two is that Step Over will fire any method or function call as a single line of code, skipping to the next line of code in the current method or function, while Step Into will go to the first line of code in the method or function that's called and stop there. The Step Out button finishes execution of the current method and returns to the method that called it. This effectively pops the current method off the stack trace's stack (you didn't think that name was accidental, did you?), and the method that called this method becomes the top of the stack trace.

The final button on the Debug Bar is the Location button. This allows you to simulate a location for an application that uses Core Location.

That might be a little clearer if you try it. Stop your program. Note that even though your program might be paused at a breakpoint, it is still executing. To stop it, click the stop sign in the Xcode or select Stop from the Product menu. You're going to add some code that might make the use of Step Over, Step Into, and Step Out a little clearer.

NESTED CALLS

Nested method calls like this combine two commands in the same line of code:

```
[[NSArray alloc] initWithObject:@"Hello"];
```

If you nest several methods together, you will skip over several actual commands with a single click of the Step Over button, making it impossible to set a breakpoint between the different nested statements. This is the primary reason to avoid excessive nesting of message calls. Other than the standard nesting of alloc and init methods, we generally prefer not to nest messages.

Dot notation has changed this somewhat. Remember, dot notation is just shorthand for calling a method, so this line of code is also two commands:

```
[self.tableView reloadData];
```

Before the call to reloadData, there is a call to the accessor method tableView. If it makes sense to use an accessor, we will often use dot notation right in the message call rather than using two separate lines of code, but be careful. It's easy to forget that dot notation results in a method call, so you can inadvertently create code that is hard to debug by nesting several method calls on one line of code.

Trying Out the Debug Controls

Select `MasterViewController.m`. Add the following two methods, right after the @implementation declaration:

```
@implementation MasterViewController

- (float)processBar:(float)inBar {

 float newBar = inBar * 2.0;
    return newBar;
}

- (NSInteger)processFoo:(NSInteger)inFoo {
    NSInteger newFoo = inFoo * 2;
    return newFoo;
}

- (id)initWithNibName:(NSString *)nibNameOrNil bundle:(NSBundle *)nibBundleOrNil
{
...
```

And insert the following (bold) lines of code into the existing `viewDidLoad` method:

```
- (void)viewDidLoad
{
    [super viewDidLoad];
    // Do any additional setup after loading the view, typically from a nib.
    NSInteger foo = 25;
    float bar = 374.3494;
    NSLog(@"foo: %d, bar: %f", foo, bar);

    foo = [self processFoo:foo];
    bar = [self processBar:bar];

    NSLog(@"foo: %d, bar: %f", foo, bar);

    self.navigationItem.leftBarButtonItem = self.editButtonItem;

    UIBarButtonItem *addButton =
        [[UIBarButtonItem alloc] initWithBarButtonSystemItem:UIBarButtonSystemItemAdd
                                          target:self
                                          action:@selector(insertNewObject:)]];
    self.navigationItem.rightBarButtonItem = addButton;
}
```

Your breakpoint should still be set at the first line of the method. Xcode does a pretty good job of moving breakpoints around when you insert or delete text from above or below it. Even though you just added two methods above your breakpoint and the method now starts at a new line number, the breakpoint is still set to the correct line of code, which is nice. If the breakpoint somehow got moved, no worries; you're going to move it anyway.

Click and drag the breakpoint down until it's lined up with the line of code that reads like this:

```
NSInteger foo = 25;
```

Now, choose Run from the Project menu to compile the changes and launch the program again. You should see the breakpoint at the first new line of code you added to viewDidLoad.

The first two lines of code are just declaring variables and assigning values to them. These lines don't call any methods or functions, so the Step Over and Step Into buttons will function identically here. To test that, click the Step Over button to cause the next line of code to execute and then click Step Into to cause the second new line of code to execute.

Before using any more of the debugger controls, check out the Variable List (Figure 15-15). The two variables you just declared are in the Variable List under the Local heading with their current values.

Figure 15-15. The variables in the Variable List

> **Note**   As you are probably aware, numbers are represented in memory as sums of powers of 2 or powers of ½ for fractional parts. This means that some numbers will end up stored in memory with values slightly different than the value specified in the source code. Though you set bar to a value of 374.3494, the closest representation was 374.349396. Close enough, right?

There's another way you can see the value of a variable. If you move your cursor so it's above the word *foo* anywhere it exists in the Editor pane, a little box will pop up similar to a tooltip that will tell you the variable's current value and type (Figure 15-16).

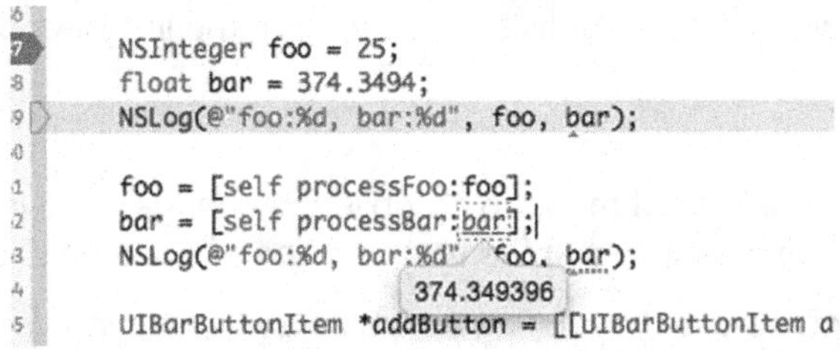

```
6
7     NSInteger foo = 25;
8     float bar = 374.3494;
9     NSLog(@"foo:%d, bar:%d", foo, bar);
0
1     foo = [self processFoo:foo];
2     bar = [self processBar:bar];
3     NSLog(@"foo:%d, bar:%d", foo, bar);
4                         374.349396
5     UIBarButtonItem *addButton = [[UIBarButtonItem a
```

Figure 15-16. Hovering your mouse over a variable in the editing pane will tell you the variable's current value

The next line of code is just a log statement, so click the Step Over button again to let it fire.

The next two lines of code each call a method. You're going to step into one and step over the other. Click the Step Into button now.

The green arrow and highlighted line of code should just have moved to the first line of the processFoo method. If you look at the stack trace now, you'll see that viewDidLoad is no longer the first row in the stack. It has been superseded by processFoo. Instead of one black row in the stack trace, there are now two because you wrote both processFoo and viewDidLoad. You can step through the lines of this method if you like. When you're ready to move back to viewDidLoad, click the Step Out button. That will return you to viewDidLoad. processFoo will get popped off of the stack trace's stack, and the green indicator and highlight will be at the line of code after the call to processFoo.

Next, for processBar, you're going to use Step Over. You'll never see processBar on the stack trace when you do that. The debugger is going to run the entire method and then stop execution after it returns. The green arrow and highlight will move forward one line (excluding empty lines and comments). You'll be able to see the results of processBar by looking at the value of bar, which should now be double what it was, but the method itself happened as if it was just a single line of code.

The Breakpoint Navigator and Symbolic Breakpoints

You've now seen the basics of working with breakpoints, but there's far more to breakpoints. In the Xcode Navigator pane, select the Breakpoints tab on the Navigation bar (Figure 15-17). This pane shows you all the breakpoints that are currently set in your project. You can delete breakpoints here by selecting them and pressing the Delete key. You can also add another kind of breakpoint here, which is called a *symbolic breakpoint*. Instead of breaking on a specific line in a specific source code file, you can tell the debugger to break whenever it reaches a certain one of those debug symbols built into the application when using the debug configuration. As a reminder, debug symbols are human-readable names derived from method and function names.

Figure 15-17. The breakpoint navigator allows you to see all the breakpoints in your project

Single-click the existing breakpoint (select the first line in the right-hand pane) and press the Delete key on your keyboard to delete it. Now, click the + button on the lower left of the Breakpoint Navigator and select Add Symbolic Breakpoint (Figure 15-18). In the pop-up dialog, enter **viewDidLoad** for the symbol. In the Module field, enter **DebugMe** and click the Done button. The Breakpoint Navigator will update with a line that reads viewDidLoad with a stylized sigma icon before it (Figure 15-19). The sigma icon is to remind you this is symbolic breakpoint.

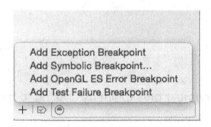

Figure 15-18. Adding a symbolic breakpoint

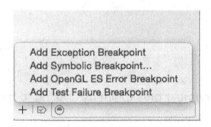

Figure 15-19. Breakpoint list updated with your symbolic breakpoint

Restart the application by clicking the Run button on the toolbar. If Xcode tells you the application is already running, then stop it. This time, your application should stop again, at the first line of code in `viewDidLoad`.

Conditional Breakpoints

Both the symbolic and line number breakpoints you've set so far have been *unconditional breakpoints*, meaning they always stop when the debugger gets to them. If the program reaches the breakpoint, it stops. But you can also create *conditional breakpoints*, which pause execution only in certain situations.

If your program is still running, stop it, and in the breakpoint window, delete the symbolic breakpoint you just created. In `MasterViewController.m`, add the following (bold) lines of code, right after the call to `super`, in `viewDidLoad`:

```
[super viewDidLoad];
// Do any additional setup after loading the view, typically from a nib.
for (int i=0; i < 25; i++) {
    NSLog(@"i = %d", i);
}

NSInteger foo = 25;
float bar = 374.3494;
...
```

Save the file. Now, set a line number breakpoint by clicking to the left of the line that reads as follows:

```
NSLog(@"i = %d", i);
```

Control-click the breakpoint and select Edit Breakpoint from the context menu (Figure 15-20). A dialog should appear, pointing to the breakpoint (Figure 15-21). Enter `i > 15` in the Condition field and click Done.

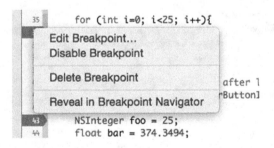

Figure 15-20. The context menu of a breakpoint

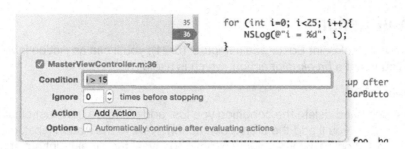

Figure 15-21. Editing the condition of a breakpoint

Build and debug your application again. This time it should stop at the breakpoint just like it has done in the past, but look in your debug console, and you should see this:

```
2014-11-28 13:29:41.801 DebugTest[84163:1718825] i = 0
2014-11-28 13:29:41.805 DebugTest[84163:1718825] i = 1
2014-11-28 13:29:41.808 DebugTest[84163:1718825] i = 2
2014-11-28 13:29:41.811 DebugTest[84163:1718825] i = 3
2014-11-28 13:29:41.815 DebugTest[84163:1718825] i = 4
2014-11-28 13:29:41.818 DebugTest[84163:1718825] i = 5
2014-11-28 13:29:41.821 DebugTest[84163:1718825] i = 6
2014-11-28 13:29:41.824 DebugTest[84163:1718825] i = 7
2014-11-28 13:29:41.827 DebugTest[84163:1718825] i = 8
2014-11-28 13:29:41.831 DebugTest[84163:1718825] i = 9
2014-11-28 13:29:41.835 DebugTest[84163:1718825] i = 10
2014-11-28 13:29:41.838 DebugTest[84163:1718825] i = 11
2014-11-28 13:29:41.841 DebugTest[84163:1718825] i = 12
2014-11-28 13:29:41.844 DebugTest[84163:1718825] i = 13
2014-11-28 13:29:41.847 DebugTest[84163:1718825] i = 14
2014-11-28 13:29:41.851 DebugTest[84163:1718825] i = 15
(lldb)
```

If you look in the Variable List, you should see *i* has a value of 16. So, the first 16 times through the loop, it didn't pause execution; instead, it just kept going because the condition you set wasn't met.

This can be an incredibly useful tool when you have an error that occurs in a long loop. Without conditional breakpoints, you'd be stuck stepping through the loop until the error happened, which is tedious. It's also useful in methods that are called a lot but are exhibiting problems only in certain situations. By setting a condition, you can tell the debugger to ignore situations that you know work properly.

> **Note** The Ignore field, just below the Condition field, is pretty cool too—it's a value decremented every time the breakpoint is hit. So, you might place the value 16 into the column to have your code stop on the 16th time through the breakpoint. You can even combine these approaches, using Ignore with a condition. Cool beans, eh?

Breakpoint Actions

If you look at the Breakpoint Editor again (Figure 15-21), you'll see an Action label. This allows you to set a *breakpoint action*, which is useful.

Stop your application.

Edit the breakpoint and delete the condition you just added. To do that, just clear the Condition field. Now you'll add the breakpoint action. Next to the Action label, click the text "Click to add an Action." The area should expand to reveal the breakpoint actions interface (Figure 15-22).

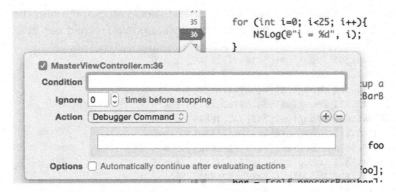

Figure 15-22. The breakpoint actions interface revealed

There are a number of different options to choose from (Figure 15-23). You can run a debugger command or add a statement to the console log. You can also play a sound or fire off a shell script or AppleScript. As you can see, there's a lot you can do while debugging your application without having to litter your code with debug-specific functionality.

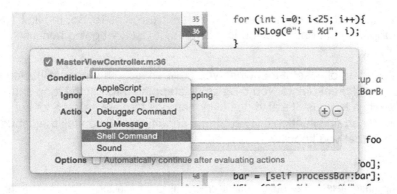

Figure 15-23. Breakpoint actions allow you to fire debugger commands, add statements to the log, play a sound, or fire a shell script or AppleScript

From the Debugger Command pop-up menu, select Log Message, which will allow you to add information to the debugger console without writing another `NSLog()` statement. When you compile this application for distribution, this breakpoint won't exist, so there's no chance of accidentally shipping this log command in your application. In the white text area below the pop-up menu, add the following log command:

```
Reached %B again. Hit this breakpoint %H times. Current value of i is @(int)i@
```

%B is a special substitution variable that will be replaced at runtime with the name of the breakpoint. %H is a substitution variable that will be replaced with the number of times this breakpoint has been reached. The text between the two @ characters is a debugger expression that tells it to print the value of i, which is an integer.

Any breakpoint can have one or more actions associated with it. Click the + button at the right side to add another action to this breakpoint.

Next, check the Options box that reads "Automatically continue after evaluating action" so that the breakpoint doesn't cause the program's execution to stop.

> **Note** You can read more about the various debug actions and the correct syntax to use for each one in the *Xcode 4 Users Guide* available at `http://developer.apple.com/library/mac/#documentation/ToolsLanguages/Conceptual/Xcode4UserGuide/000-About_Xcode/about.html`.

Build and debug your application again. This time, you should see additional information printed in the debug console log, between the values printed by your `NSLog()` statement (Figure 15-24). While statements logged using `NSLog()` are printed in bold, those done by breakpoint actions are printed in nonbold characters.

```
ead 1 > 0 -[MasterViewController viewDidLoad]
Reached -viewDidLoad again. Hit this breakpoint 1 times. Current value of i is 0
2014-11-28 13:35:45.441 DebugTest[84705:1723383] i = 0
Reached -viewDidLoad again. Hit this breakpoint 2 times. Current value of i is 1
2014-11-28 13:35:45.449 DebugTest[84705:1723383] i = 1
Reached -viewDidLoad again. Hit this breakpoint 3 times. Current value of i is 2
2014-11-28 13:35:45.456 DebugTest[84705:1723383] i = 2
Reached -viewDidLoad again. Hit this breakpoint 4 times. Current value of i is 3
2014-11-28 13:35:45.463 DebugTest[84705:1723383] i = 3
Reached -viewDidLoad again. Hit this breakpoint 5 times. Current value of i is 4
2014-11-28 13:35:45.470 DebugTest[84705:1723383] i = 4
Reached -viewDidLoad again. Hit this breakpoint 6 times. Current value of i is 5
2014-11-28 13:35:45.477 DebugTest[84705:1723383] i = 5
Reached -viewDidLoad again. Hit this breakpoint 7 times. Current value of i is 6
2014-11-28 13:35:45.485 DebugTest[84705:1723383] i = 6
Reached -viewDidLoad again. Hit this breakpoint 8 times. Current value of i is 7
Reached -viewDidLoad again. Hit this breakpoint 9 times. Current value of i is 8
Reached -viewDidLoad again. Hit this breakpoint 10 times. Current value of i is 9
Reached -viewDidLoad again. Hit this breakpoint 11 times. Current value of i is 10
2014-11-28 13:35:45.492 DebugTest[84705:1723383] i = 7
2014-11-28 13:35:45.499 DebugTest[84705:1723383] i = 8
2014-11-28 13:35:45.506 DebugTest[84705:1723383] i = 9
2014-11-28 13:35:45.514 DebugTest[84705:1723383] i = 10
Reached -viewDidLoad again. Hit this breakpoint 12 times. Current value of i is 11
2014-11-28 13:35:45.521 DebugTest[84705:1723383] i = 11
Reached -viewDidLoad again. Hit this breakpoint 13 times. Current value of i is 12
2014-11-28 13:35:45.528 DebugTest[84705:1723383] i = 12
Reached -viewDidLoad again. Hit this breakpoint 14 times. Current value of i is 13
2014-11-28 13:35:45.535 DebugTest[84705:1723383] i = 13
Reached -viewDidLoad again. Hit this breakpoint 15 times. Current value of i is 14
2014-11-28 13:35:45.542 DebugTest[84705:1723383] i = 14
Reached -viewDidLoad again. Hit this breakpoint 16 times. Current value of i is 15
2014-11-28 13:35:45.549 DebugTest[84705:1723383] i = 15
Reached -viewDidLoad again. Hit this breakpoint 17 times. Current value of i is 16
Reached -viewDidLoad again. Hit this breakpoint 18 times. Current value of i is 17
Reached -viewDidLoad again. Hit this breakpoint 19 times. Current value of i is 18
Reached -viewDidLoad again. Hit this breakpoint 20 times. Current value of i is 19
2014-11-28 13:35:45.556 DebugTest[84705:1723383] i = 16
2014-11-28 13:35:45.564 DebugTest[84705:1723383] i = 17
2014-11-28 13:35:45.572 DebugTest[84705:1723383] i = 18
2014-11-28 13:35:45.579 DebugTest[84705:1723383] i = 19
Reached -viewDidLoad again. Hit this breakpoint 21 times. Current value of i is 20
2014-11-28 13:35:45.586 DebugTest[84705:1723383] i = 20
Reached -viewDidLoad again. Hit this breakpoint 22 times. Current value of i is 21
2014-11-28 13:35:45.593 DebugTest[84705:1723383] i = 21
Reached -viewDidLoad again. Hit this breakpoint 23 times. Current value of i is 22
2014-11-28 13:35:45.600 DebugTest[84705:1723383] i = 22
Reached -viewDidLoad again. Hit this breakpoint 24 times. Current value of i is 23
2014-11-28 13:35:45.607 DebugTest[84705:1723383] i = 23
Reached -viewDidLoad again. Hit this breakpoint 25 times. Current value of i is 24
2014-11-28 13:35:45.615 DebugTest[84705:1723383] i = 24
(lldb)
```

Figure 15-24. ***Breakpoint log actions get printed to the debugger console but, unlike the results of NSLog() commands, are not printed in bold***

That's not all there is to breakpoints, but it's the fundamentals and should give you a good foundation for finding and fixing problems in your applications.

Static Analysis

Under the Product menu in Xcode, there is a menu item labeled Analyze. This option compiles your code and runs a *static analysis* on your code that is capable of detecting any number of common problems. Normally, when you build a project, you will see yellow icons in the build results window that represent build warnings and red icons that represent build errors. When you build and analyze, you may also see rows with blue icons that represent potential problems found by the static analyzer. Although static analysis is imperfect and can sometimes identify problems that aren't actually problems (referred to as *false positives*), it's good at finding certain types of bugs, most notably code that leaks memory. Let's introduce a leak into your code and then analyze it.

If your application is running, stop it.

In `MasterViewController.m`, in the `viewDidLoad` method, add the following code just after the call to `super`:

```
NSArray *myArray = [[NSArray alloc] initWithObjects:@"Hello", @"Goodbye", "So Long", nil];
```

Before you analyze, it's a good idea to select Clean from the Product menu. Only files that get compiled will be analyzed. Code that hasn't been changed since the last time it was compiled won't get compiled again and won't get analyzed. In this case, that wouldn't be an issue since you just changed the file where you introduced the bug, but it's good practice to analyze your entire project. Once the project is done cleaning, select Analyze from the Product menu.

You'll now get a warning about an unused variable, which is true. You declared and initialized `myArray` but never used it. If you look in the Issue Navigator (Figure 15-25), you'll also see two additional rows in the build results from the static analyzer, with one telling you that `myArray` is never read after initialization. This is essentially telling you the same thing as the unused variable warning from the compiler. The next one, however, is one the compiler doesn't catch. It says: "Argument to 'NSArray' method 'initWithObjects:' should be an Objective-C pointer type, not 'char *'." That's the static analyzer telling you that you passed the wrong kind of pointer to your array.

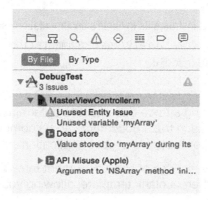

Figure 15-25. Issues Navigator after running the static analyzer

To find out more, click the disclosure triangle to the left of the message and then click lower message. Pretty informative, eh?

Before you begin testing any application, you should run Build and Analyze and look at every item it points out. It can save you a lot of aggravation and trouble.

One More Thing About Debugging

You now know the basic tools of debugging. We haven't discussed all the features of either Xcode or LLDB, but we've covered the essentials. It would take far more than a single chapter to cover this topic exhaustively, but you've now seen the tools that you'll use in 95 percent or more of your debugging efforts. Unfortunately, the best way to get better at debugging is to do a lot of it, and that can be frustrating early on. The first time you see a particular type of problem, you often aren't sure how to tackle it. So, to give you a bit of a kick-start, we're going to show you a couple of the most common problems that occur in Cocoa Touch programs and show you how to find and fix those problems when they happen to you.

Debugging can be one of the most difficult and frustrating tasks on this green Earth. It's also extremely important, and tracking down a problem that's been plaguing your code can be extremely gratifying. The reason the debugging process is so hard is that modern applications are complex, the libraries we use to build them are complex, and modern operating systems themselves are complex. At any given time, there's an awful lot of code loaded, running, and interacting.

Profiling With Instruments

We're not going to dive deep into Instruments. That's a topic for another book (like *Pro iOS Tools*). Let's take a look at how to start Instruments and what it offers. Select Product ➤ Profile in Xcode. Xcode will build the application (if necessary) and launch Instruments.

> **Tip** You can read more about Instruments in Apple's documentation as well. It's located at
> http://developer.apple.com/library/ios/documentation/DeveloperTools/
> Conceptual/InstrumentsUserGuide.

Instruments operates by creating a trace document to determine what it monitors during your application's execution. Each trace document can be composed of many *instruments*. Each instrument collects different aspects of your application's running state.

On startup, Instruments offers a series of trace document templates to help begin your Instruments session. It also offers a blank template, allowing you to define your own set of instruments to use (Figure 15-26).

Figure 15-26. Launching Instruments from Xcode

Let's review some of the templates Instruments offers:

- *Blank*: An empty template for you to customize

- *Allocations*: Template to track memory usage on an object basis

- *Leaks*: Another memory usage template, focused on finding memory leaks

- *Activity Monitor*: Monitor system resource usage of the application

- *Zombies*: Another memory usage template, focused on finding over-released memory

- *Time Profiler*: Sample processes running the CPU

- *System Trace*: Monitors application threads moving between system and user space

- *Automation*: Scripting tool to allow simulation of user interaction

- *File Activity*: Monitors file system usage by application

- *Core Data*: Monitors Core Data activity within the application

Let's just start with the Allocations template. Double-click it, and Instruments should open (Figure 15-27). The application should launch in simulator, and you will note that you are now tracking memory usage. You might need to press the red record button to start Instruments capturing the data.

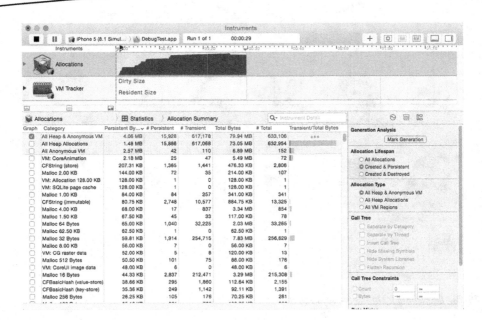

Figure 15-27. Main Instruments window

Add some items to your application and then delete them. You should see Instruments trace memory usage.

While running one trace instrument is useful, the real power behind Instruments is the ability to run many traces simultaneously and determine where your application may have performance issues.

Play around with Instruments and see whether it helps you optimize your applications.

End of the Road

As we stated at the beginning of the chapter, there's no teacher like experience when it comes to unit testing, debugging, and profiling, so you just need to get out there and start making your own mistakes and then fixing them. Don't hesitate to use search engines or to ask more experienced developers for help if you truly do get stuck, but don't let those resources become a crutch, either. Put in an effort to find and fix each bug you encounter before you start looking for help. Yes, it will be frustrating at times, but it's good for you. It builds character.

And with that, we're close to the end of our journey together. We do have one more chapter, though, a farewell bit of guidance as you move forward in your iOS development travels. So, when you're ready for it, turn the page.

Chapter **16**

The Road Goes Ever On...

You've survived another journey with us. Great! At this point, you know a lot more than when you first opened this book. We would love to tell you that you now know it all, but when it comes to technology, you never know it all. This is particularly true of iOS development technologies. The programming language and frameworks you've been working with in this book are the result of more than 25 years of evolution. Our engineering friends at Apple are always feverishly working on that Next Cool New Thing™. Despite being much more mature than it was when it first launched, the iOS platform has still just begun to blossom. There is so much more to come.

By making it through another book, you've built yourself an even sturdier foundation. You've acquired a solid knowledge of Objective-C, Cocoa Touch, and the tools that bring these technologies together to create incredible new iOS applications. You understand the iOS software architecture and the design patterns that make Cocoa Touch sing. In short, you are even more ready to chart your own course.

Getting Unstuck

At its core, programming is about problem solving and figuring things out. It is both fun and rewarding. But there will be times when you run up against a puzzle that seems insurmountable or a problem that does not appear to have a solution.

Sometimes, the answer just appears—a result of a bit of time away from the problem. A good night's sleep or a few hours of doing something different can often be all that you need to get through it. Believe us, sometimes you can stare at the same problem for hours, overanalyzing and getting yourself so worked up that you miss an obvious solution.

And then there are times when even a change of scenery doesn't help. In those situations, it's good to have friends in high places. Here are some resources you can turn to when you're in a bind.

Apple's Documentation

Become one with Xcode's documentation browser. The documentation browser is a front end to a wealth of incredibly valuable sample source code, concept guides, API references, video tutorials, and a whole lot more.

There are few areas of iOS that you won't be able to learn more about by making your way through Apple's documentation. And the more comfortable you get with Apple's documentation, the easier it will be for you to make your way through uncharted territories and new technologies as Apple rolls them out.

Mailing Lists

The following are some useful mailing lists that are maintained by Apple:

- `https://lists.apple.com/mailman/listinfo/cocoa-dev`: A moderately high-volume list, primarily focused on Cocoa for Mac OS X. Because of the common heritage shared by Cocoa and Cocoa Touch, many of the people on this list may be able to help you. Make sure to search the list archives before asking your question, though.

- `https://lists.apple.com/mailman/listinfo/xcode-users`: A mailing list specific to questions and problems related to Xcode.

- `https://lists.apple.com/mailman/listinfo/quartz-dev`: A mailing list for discussion of Quartz 2D and Core Graphics technologies.

Web Sites

Here are some web sites that you may want to visit:

- NSHipster: `http://nshipster.com/`

- WWDC Videos: `https://developer.apple.com/videos/wwdc/2014/`

- `http://www.cocoadevcentral.com/`: A portal that contains links to a great many Cocoa-related web sites and tutorials.

- `http://cocoaheads.org/`: The CocoaHeads site. CocoaHeads is a group dedicated to peer support and promotion of Cocoa. It focuses on local groups with regular meetings where Cocoa developers can get together and even socialize a bit. There's nothing better than knowing a real person who can help you out, so if there's a CocoaHeads group in your area, check it out. If there isn't one, why not start one up?

- `http://cocoablogs.com/`: A portal that contains links to a great many blogs related to Cocoa programming.

- `http://stackoverflow.com/questions/tagged/ios`: The iOS tagged question for the free programming Q&A web site. Overall, this is a great source for finding answers to questions. Many experienced and knowledgeable iPhone programmers, including some who work at Apple, contribute to this site by answering questions and posting sample code.

- `http://www.quora.com/iOS-Development`: Another excellent Q&A web site. Though not focused on programming, this tag is for iOS development questions.

Blogs

Check out these blogs:

- `http://theocacao.com`: Scott Stevenson, an experienced Cocoa programmer.

- `http://raywenderlich.com/`: Ray Wenderlich's blog and tutorial site. Ray runs an excellent site for supplemental tutorials and information.

- `http://www.objc.io/`: Targeted at Objective C and lots of "how to" do specialty stuff like photo, gpu, etc.

- `http://www.cocoawithlove.com/`: Mark Gallagher's iOS site. Lot's of cocoa and Objective-C discussion.

- `https://www.mikeash.com/pyblog/`: Mike Ash's site. Plenty of information on Swift, in addition to Objective-C and a popular Friday Q&A session.

- `http://www.cimgf.com/`: Matt Long's "Cocoa is my Girlfriend" blog. Ample shorter but insightful pieces.

- `http://iosdevweekly.com/`: Quasi blog that posts abstracts and links to articles on other sites on a timely basis.

Combination

For those who are purists, skip this section because it is going to mention Swift. Objective-C is like assembly, whereas Swift is more like a high-level language. Objective-C is faster in quite a few tasks as have been benchmarked by various developers and web sites/blogs. The fact remains that Swift is getting better and might be equally fast. A good developer knows that fast is not a criteria to measure performance alone. Swift can provide relief in the form of easy-to-read and manageable code in comparison to the complex Objective-C code. Swift 1.2 was released in beta while this book was being written, and it has a lot of promising features in comparison to the earlier versions of Swift. You can make use of it along with playgrounds for creating algorithms or testing functions and modules, and you can even integrate Swift source in your Objective-C programs and vice versa. Both are official Apple-supported languages and work well together. You can read more about it in the Swift version of this book: *More iOS Development with Swift*.

Farewell

We sure are glad you came along on this journey with us. We wish you the best of luck, and we hope that you enjoy iOS programming as much as we do.

Index

Get the eBook for only $5!

Why limit yourself?

Now you can take the weightless companion with you wherever you go and access your content on your PC, phone, tablet, or reader.

Since you've purchased this print book, we're happy to offer you the eBook in all 3 formats for just $5.

Convenient and fully searchable, the PDF version enables you to easily find and copy code—or perform examples by quickly toggling between instructions and applications. The MOBI format is ideal for your Kindle, while the ePUB can be utilized on a variety of mobile devices.

To learn more, go to www.apress.com/companion or contact support@apress.com.

Printed in the United States
By Bookmasters